Cinematic *Hamlet*

CINEMATIC
Hamlet

The Films of Olivier, Zeffirelli, Branagh, and Almereyda

PATRICK J. COOK

Ohio University Press
Athens

Ohio University Press, Athens, Ohio 45701

www.ohioswallow.com

© 2011 by Ohio University Press

All rights reserved

Printed in the United States of America

Ohio University Press books are printed on acid-free paper ∞ ™

18 17 16 15 14 13 12   5 4 3 2

Library of Congress Cataloging-in-Publication Data

Cook, Patrick J., 1951–
  Cinematic Hamlet : the films of Olivier, Zeffirelli, Branagh, and Almereyda / Patrick J. Cook.
      p. cm.
  Includes bibliographical references and index.
  Includes filmography.
  ISBN-13: 978-0-8214-1944-1 (alk. paper)
  ISBN-10: 0-8214-1944-7 (alk. paper)
  ISBN-13: 978-0-8214-4365-1 (electronic)
  1. Shakespeare, William, 1564–1616. Hamlet. 2. Shakespeare, William, 1564–1616.—Film adaptations. I. Title.
  PR2807.C58 2011
  791.43'6—dc22
                            2010045071

Contents

INTRODUCTION

Cinematic Hamlet arose from two convictions. The first was a belief, confirmed by the responses of hundreds of university students with whom I have studied the films, that the *Hamlet*s of Laurence Olivier, Franco Zeffirelli, Kenneth Branagh, and Michael Almereyda are remarkably successful films.[1] Numerous film *Hamlet*s have been made using Shakespeare's language, but only the four included in this book represent for me outstanding successes. One might admire the fine acting of Nicol Williamson in Tony Richardson's 1969 production, or the creative use of extreme close-ups of Ian McKellen in Peter Wood's Hallmark Hall of Fame television production of

1971, but only four English-language films have thoroughly transformed Shakespeare's theatrical text into truly effective moving pictures. All four succeed as popularizing treatments accessible to what Olivier's collaborator Alan Dent called "un-Shakespeare-minded audiences."[2] They succeed as highly intelligent and original interpretations of the play capable of delighting any audience. Most of all, they are innovative and eloquent translations from the Elizabethan dramatic to the modern cinematic medium. It is clear that these directors have approached adapting *Hamlet* much as actors have long approached playing the title role, as the ultimate challenge that allows, as Almereyda observes, one's "reflexes as a film-maker" to be "tested, battered and bettered."[3]

An essential factor in the success of the films after Olivier's is the challenge of tradition. The three films that followed the groundbreaking 1948 version are what a scholar of film remakes labels "true remakes": works that pay respectful tribute to their predecessors while laboring to surpass them.[4] As each has acknowledged explicitly and as my analyses demonstrate, the three later filmmakers self-consciously defined their places in a vigorously evolving tradition of *Hamlet* films. The creativity of each film's response to its predecessors has resulted in a series of remakes unprecedented not only in the history of Shakespearean film but also in the larger history of film. Paradoxically, it seems, the very originality of these remakes has been a significant factor in their decidedly mixed reception among scholars. Each of the films has received significant critical attention, but the fact that each film after Olivier's defines itself more through emphatic difference than through similarity has contributed to severe disagreements about their relative success. Many critics who admire one film's approach find the calculatedly different approach of another to be a source or symptom of failure. I argue, to the contrary, that each filmmaker creatively establishes differences with his predecessors and develops a new, highly distinctive, and remarkably effective fusion of the Shakespearean text and the film medium.

A second conviction motivating the current work concerns methodology. This book responds to what I consider to be a general reluctance in the scholarship on Shakespeare on film to focus closely on the complex ways in which film as a distinctive medium engages, controls, and provokes the viewer. Scholars working in the field have been much more inclined to praise and blame Shakespearean adaptations, and to point out their broader ideological implications, than to analyze the cinematic art and craft by which they create meaning. As a result, most existing criticism differs little from treatments of theatrical productions, focusing on acting performance, thematic interpretation, and cultural context and significance. This book is in part a response to my belief that the field today is out of balance, filled with informed and sometimes brilliant discussion on such important issues as ideology, gender, and psychoanalysis, for which all can be thankful. Existing criticism contains, however, few detailed and sustained analyses of the techniques of storytelling and signification that are distinctive to cinema. My analyses present ways in which closer attention to these techniques allows one to understand how writer-directors of very different backgrounds and sensibilities have each forged a unique synergy of Shakespeare's endlessly interpretable play-text and film's unprecedented expressive resources, creating a *Hamlet* that speaks powerfully to modern audiences.

Four Roads to Hamlet

A crucial reason why the four films succeed is the fact that Shakespeare's play exerted an early and a profound influence on the artistic development of all four directors. In return, each, by a fortuitous combination of chance and plan, found an especially opportune moment in his career to adapt the play to film. Stimulated by long personal investment in Shakespeare's character and story, each approached *Hamlet* at the height of his filmmaking powers, producing, I believe, his finest work.

Laurence Olivier's recorded experience with *Hamlet* began in 1925 at the age of eighteen, when he was greatly impressed by John Barrymore in the title role at London's Haymarket Theatre. Several features of the performance appear to have influenced Olivier's overall approach to Shakespeare. Foremost was Barrymore's "natural" style of acting, which brought him both acclaim and condemnation. Conservative critics complained of the lack of poetry, as they would later complain about Olivier in comparison with the more mellifluous John Gielgud. The pursuit of naturalness did not, however, keep Barrymore from indulging in expressive postures and bouts of athleticism. He knelt with his back to the audience to hear the ghost's narrative, as Olivier would do in the film, and was thought to "sprawl a little ludicrously" in the languid pose that Olivier too would adopt.[5] He pursued the final swordfight with Laertes with great vigor, stabbing Claudius after what was described as a ten-foot leap through the air.

Barrymore played up the sexual relation of Hamlet and Gertrude in the closet scene, inevitably eliciting references to Sigmund Freud and the Oedipus complex. It is generally assumed that the famous oedipal inflection of Olivier's Hamlet began when his 1937 producer, Tyrone Guthrie, introduced him to the work of Ernest Jones, Freud's disciple and biographer.[6] But if the articulated theory was lacking until that point, the underlying psychological appeal that it explained seems to have begun much earlier. Peter Donaldson argues for the influence of a sexual assault "on a staircase at All Saints School at age nine" on Olivier's use of staircases in his film as settings for violence, culminating in the fourteen-foot leap onto Claudius at the end.[7] The presence of a vast staircase at the center of the stage and a similarly dangerous leap by Barrymore's Hamlet may help to explain young Olivier's enthusiastic response to the production. Olivier found his first opportunity to imitate this influential performance in 1934. In *Theatre Royal,* he played a character who, as his most recent biographer, Terry Coleman, observes, was a "thinly disguised John Barrymore," fighting a duel and making "a Fairbanks-style leap from a balcony," the "first of many athletic and dangerous stunts for which he became notorious."[8]

Coleman's research reveals that in 1936 "Olivier decided to become a Shakespearean actor."[9] He had already had success on stage in *Romeo and Juliet* as both Romeo and Mercutio and had played Orlando in the hapless film *As You Like It* directed by Paul Czinner, released in 1936. But becoming a Shakespearean actor for Olivier meant starring in *Hamlet,* which he proceeded to do at London's Old Vic in 1937. As is well known, a visit to Jones by Olivier and Guthrie was instrumental in developing their Freudian approach. Too few details of the 1937 production were recorded to determine how closely it resembled the 1948 film, although the few available are suggestive. In the first soliloquy, Hamlet described his flesh as too "sullied," a reading that had become popular only in 1934. As he spoke it, Hamlet "wiped his mother's parting kiss from his face as though defiled by it."[10] The set for the duel scene resembles the film set in its raised platform reached by a stairway on the left. The rest, unfortunately, is silence.

The 1937–38 season at the Old Vic launched with *Hamlet* made Olivier the star Shakespearean actor he aspired to be. He returned to film for William Wyler's *Wuthering Heights,* in which he finally mastered the very different form of acting that the medium requires, and Alfred Hitchcock's *Rebecca,* the film that most influenced his *Hamlet* visually. These films not only established him as a movie star but also restored his faith in the expressive power of cinema that Czinner's *As You Like It* appears to have undermined. Observing such talented directors changed his mind as well on the more specific subject of filming Shakespeare. In 1933 he turned down the role of Romeo in George

Cukor's adaptation, claiming that Shakespeare would never succeed as film. In 1935 he was seduced by a generous salary to suppress his conviction for the Czinner film, to his ultimate disappointment, and the following year he would proclaim, "I don't really like Shakespeare on the screen at all."[11] While working with Wyler and his pioneering cinematographer Gregg Toland in 1938–39, Olivier finally came to understand the capacities of the medium. Wyler told him, "There's nothing you can't do on film. You tell me you can't do *Hamlet* on film. You can do *Hamlet* on it."[12] Olivier came to believe him, and when a film of *Henry V* was proposed in 1943, he insisted on total control, claiming, "I had the advantage of knowing more about the medium than anyone else."[13] In 1947 Olivier yielded to a request to make a second Shakespearean film. His confident mastery of the medium, the challenge implicit in his conversations with Wyler, and the meaning that the play had held for him since at least 1925 came together to make *Hamlet* the only possible choice. The sheer success of Olivier's *Hamlet*—artistic, critical, and popular—helps to explain why four decades intervened before the next major film adaptation of the play in English.[14]

For Franco Zeffirelli, theater, film, and Shakespeare were dominant and intertwined components of his imaginative life from childhood. He grew enamored of Shakespeare at around the age of twelve in the mid-1930s, when language lessons with a Scottish expatriate in Florence enabled him to study the plays and enact scenes with his tutor. His principal toys were miniature theaters that he constructed himself for this purpose. At the same time, he was viewing films almost daily and developing what he describes as a great vulnerability to the medium that he never outgrew. He wrote in 1986, "[E]ven today I laugh and cry openly and believe quite passionately in what is taking place on the screen."[15] Given his passions, it is not surprising that a 1945 screening of Olivier's *Henry V* determined his career path, providing "the clearest idea of my future, the road to follow: theater, cinema."[16] We do not know when he first saw Olivier's *Hamlet*, but it must have been soon after its release, for he writes that Olivier became "the Hamlet and Henry V of my youth."[17] In the years after the war, he studied the British theater from afar. He recalls that Olivier's 1937 director, Tyrone Guthrie, "was one of those avant-garde stars of the London theatre whom I knew about from the magazines my wartime British friends sent me."[18]

Zeffirelli mastered the art and craft of both theater and film as an assistant to Luchino Visconti during the postwar revival of Italian cinema. He began his career-long alternation among projects in theater, film, and opera at this time but declared that films were always his "ultimate goal," especially "filming a stage classic," by which he always seems to have meant Shakespeare.[19] On forming his own theater company in 1964, he staged an Italian-language version of *Hamlet* that toured European capitals during the Shakespeare quadricentennial. Discussing this production, he claims that "always I wanted to bring it to the cinema. Either the actor wasn't ready or I was not, or the money was not. . . . Every project has its own season."[20] All three elements were ready for his first major film, *The Taming of the Shrew* (1967), which exploited the popularity of its stars, the recently scandalous and then more recently married Richard Burton and Elizabeth Taylor. Its success enabled him to develop his previous biggest hit in the English theater, the 1960 *Romeo and Juliet* staged at the Old Vic, which he had been invited to direct, into one of the most popular and profitable Shakespeare films of all time. With such box office successes, all would have been ready for the long-awaited filmed *Hamlet*, but a nearly fatal automobile accident soon after the completion of *Romeo and Juliet* provoked something of a religious conversion, diverting the cinematic side of Zeffirelli's creativity into projects with Christian subject matter. This was followed by a decade of concentration in the 1980s on opera and operatic films, a genre in which Zeffirelli proved himself a considerable innovator. His attempted swing back to nonoperatic film with *Young Toscanini* was a debacle. Amidst charges that he uttered anti-Semitic remarks at the 1988 Venice Film Festival, where a rough cut was shown, the film was never completed. In his Italian autobiography, he describes the period as one of life crisis, using language resembling his description of the effect of Olivier's first film: "Now I found myself in a sort of void, in a desert land, and I no longer saw clearly in what direction I could go." At that moment he returned to Shakespeare, and at last to *Hamlet*. Believing that the work would allow an empowering return to his "deepest cultural roots," he felt that he "could offer a version probably superior to any other."[21]

Like Zeffirelli, Kenneth Branagh is an artist who was destined to add filmmaking to his notable theatrical accomplishments. In his autobiography, he recounts on adjacent pages his early fascination with movies watched on television, which seemed uncannily "real" to him, and his first experience of the "magic" of theater.[22] It would eventually become predictable that these two passions would converge in *Hamlet*. "Hamlet is a part that obsesses me," he confessed to a journalist in 1992.[23] If anything, that is an understatement. The stages of Branagh's road to a filmed *Hamlet* have been repeatedly told. His interest in Shakespeare and theater was profoundly influenced by his trip to Oxford at age fifteen to see Derek Jacobi in the role. Reflecting in the introduction to his screenplay, Branagh writes, "I believe that much of what has followed in my life was affected by that experience."[24] He auditioned at the Royal Academy of Dramatic Arts using a passage from the play. At the academy, he recited the "rogue and peasant slave" soliloquy to a visiting John Gielgud and subsequently starred in the play, winning the school's highest prize. He played Laertes for the Royal Shakespeare Company. Derek Jacobi directed him as Hamlet for the Renaissance Theatre Company in 1988. By 1987 he had begun planning for a project that had percolated in his mind for a long time, a film version of Shakespeare's greatest play.[25]

That was not yet to be. Negotiations were already under way to finance the Zeffirelli film, eliminating the possibility for another version of the same play. As a result, Branagh's dream project was delayed eight years. During that time, the *Hamlet* film being storyboarded in Branagh's imagination would significantly change. His full-text stage production with the Royal Shakespeare Company in 1992 convinced him that a full-text film was not only desirable but also possible. Given the slumping interest in Shakespeare films, the latter, at least, would not have been true in 1988. During that time as well, of course, Branagh with *Henry V* and *Much Ado About Nothing* helped restore Shakespearean film to commercial viability. Branagh in the interim continued mastering the process of filmmaking and collected around him a group of artists ever more capable of translating Shakespeare into film. One can see across his career the acquisition of techniques that would find their way into his *Hamlet*: the explanatory insets and long tracking shot of *Henry V;* the montage of clips that opens *Peter's Friends;* the long and complicated take that ends *Much Ado;* the circling camera of *Mary Shelley's Frankenstein.* No one could have been better prepared in 1996 to undertake what Samuel Crowl rightly calls "the most ambitious and audacious Shakespeare film ever made."[26]

Michael Almereyda did not pursue a career in theater, but filming *Hamlet* was an aspiration no less natural for him than for Olivier, Zeffirelli, and Branagh. Blessed with a talent for visual arts, his ambitions began turning toward film following his family's move from Kansas to southern California in 1972, when Almereyda was twelve. In the next few years, he became fascinated with European films, especially those of the New German Cinema and Jean-Luc Godard.[27] This new interest coincided with an interest in *Hamlet.* In the screenplay preface, he recalls, "I found myself thinking back to my first impressions of the play, remembering its adolescence-primed impact and meaning for me—the rampant parallels between the melancholy Dane and my many doomed and damaged heroes and imaginary friends: James Agee, Holden

Caulfield, James Dean, Egon Schiele, Robert Johnson, Vladimir Mayakovsky, Jean Vigo."[28] Rampant parallels include the trauma of parental loss, alienation, suicidal inclinations, early death, and, through the familiar yet mysterious alchemy, the creativity that can rise out of tragic events.[29]

Dean and Mayakovsky make their appearance in his *Hamlet*, but it is the last-named "hero" who suggests the depth of Almereyda's personal investment in his title character. He has not discussed his name in any of his numerous published interviews, but one might deduce that his decision to become a filmmaker coincided not only with a fascination with *Hamlet* but also with his assumption of a *nom de caméra*. The French anarchist Miguel Almereyda was murdered in prison in 1917, probably by an agent of the French state. The traumatized twelve-year-old son he left behind, Jean Vigo, would become, in the words of film historian David Thomson, "the first young martyr to 'cinema'" and a hero to subsequent cinematic avant-gardes.[30] His mythic status and potential as a *Hamlet* figure are encapsulated in the back-cover copy of the standard biography, which proclaims that Vigo was "haunted all his life by the injustice done to his father" and "spent most of his working life battling against authorities wary of his political background, against censors suspicious of the subversive nature of his films."[31] Although Almereyda's career as an independent filmmaker has included much battling with producers, it cannot be said that he is a politically subversive director in the manner of Vigo, and wringing speculative meaning from an artist's pseudonym is hazardous. What can be said is that Almereyda aspired to film a character associated since his adolescence with the son of the man after whom he named himself. In a gesture that I will not attempt to interpret, but which should not go unnoticed, his avant-garde filmmaker Hamlet will contemplate Jean Vigo's image before going to the scene of his death.

The three features written and directed by Almereyda before *Hamlet* concern dysfunctional families, youthful alienation, parental death, and suicide, themes that suggest how easily Shakespeare's play fits into his career. His experience in making these films determined his approach to *Hamlet*. He describes the making of his first feature, *Twister* (1989), about an extended Kansas family unable to break free from the patriarchal domicile, as "a travesty" in which he lost control over the editing and the soundtrack.[32] Making *The Eternal* (1998), a better-funded excursion into the horror genre, the frustrated director found himself confronting the "very confused worries and whims" of the producers.[33] Only with the low-budget, independently produced *Nadja* (1994), which reworks material from vampire film and André

Breton's surrealist novel to create a variation on the Shakespearean comic plot, were his artistic ambitions satisfied. His resolve to maintain similar control over *Hamlet* necessitated a similarly miniscule budget.

Produced for under two million dollars, the 2000 *Hamlet* is by far the least expensive of the four major treatments in English. At least in part for this reason it is also the shortest, presenting like all but Branagh's film a significantly cut version of Shakespeare's text. The final version became even shorter than the shooting script when several scripted scenes remained unshot and completed scenes proved unsatisfactory, due to the difficulties of filming in found settings with a schedule so "fast and furious" that his star, Ethan Hawke, claimed soon after to "remember very little of it."[34] Nevertheless, Almereyda's film merits the longest chapter in this book because it makes up for insufficient money and time with ceaseless and often astonishing creativity. Even though the film's editing tempo is leisurely, its 111 minutes are crammed with such a density of visual details, and these details are so cunningly organized, that it continually grabs and challenges the viewer's interpretive attention.

A New Approach to Shakespeare on Film

The four chapters that follow contain close readings of the films on a level of detail that is admittedly unusual. Their level of detail is not as high as the frame-by-frame descriptions of the prepsychoanalytic Christian Metz or his colleague Raymond Bellour, but it is much higher than that of most current film criticism, which typically selects only a few details to support an overarching thematic argument. The readings are less close than those of Metz and Bellour because my goal is not to support an all-inclusive theoretical model but, more practically, to explicate the adaptational procedures of four filmmakers. The readings are much closer than those of more thematically minded critics because understanding the filmmaker's craft requires a continual effort to resist that craft, which deploys a stalwart set of devices that efface themselves, that direct our attention through the screen to the object represented rather than to the means by which our attention is directed. It is a situation perhaps unique to the art of cinema that an increased familiarity with a work generally does not imply greater awareness of its methods. Unless one steps back from the seductive and effortless pleasure of immersion to look closely and systematically at technique, what discourse analysts call elements of "surface structure" are subject to a relentless "push down" into forgetfulness.[35] As Edward Branigan states the matter, "When we say we remember a film, we do not normally mean that we remember the angle from which it was viewed in the theater, or the exact angles assumed by a camera in a scene. Rather, when we speak of comprehending something, we mean that our knowledge of it may be stated in several equivalent ways; that is, our knowledge has achieved a certain independence from initial stimuli."[36] Branigan is claiming, rightly, that we remember the contents of the film setting as if they are objects in real space and time, not as they were presented from the camera's limited point of view and, moreover, that we recall the objects themselves rather than the formal means by which they were so presented.

The philosopher Colin McGinn has recently made a similar argument, observing that film's distinctiveness as an art results from its unique promotion of "looking into" rather than "looking at." The latter activity, in fact, is not the viewer's "typical stance and detracts from the power of the film."[37] As one result of this process of self-effacing devices, just as viewers naturally prefer the pleasures of immersive looking into the screen over the labors of analytic looking at the screen, criticism of films is much more often about what they contain than how they create this content. Stefan Sharff observes that in critical writing about film "there is a persistent lack of clarity about matters strictly cinematic."[38] Greater clarity can be achieved only through raising into our analytic awareness the teeming plenitude of devices whose job is to vigilantly point beyond themselves toward the desired object within.

The nature of these devices might be approached through considering how radical the transformation of Shakespeare's theatrical text must be to produce a successful film. An early review of Olivier's *Hamlet* by George Barbarow captures with naïve brilliance the difference between the two media. Likening viewing the film to looking at the play "through a telescope," Barbarow complains of the endless details that "unintentionally distract us from the action of the drama." To solve what he views as an essential incompatibility between theater and film, Barbarow concludes by proposing an alternative method of adaptation. His proposal so starkly rejects what would now be called the "cinematic" dimension of Olivier's film that it is worth quoting extensively:

> It would make the camera and microphone as much as possible the exact recorders of a stage performance. The camera should be fixed at one point, and remain in this position without moving, while each scene is played out before it. The machine would thus have a single but very important function: to be a non-participant observer of the play. It should be totally subservient to the scenic action and speech, while rigidly maintaining the physical

boundaries of the scene. Everything should be held within the fixed frame; it would then be up to Shakespeare (who has done quite well in this work) to provide the drama, and it would be up to the actors to do their acting in compliance with the play. The spectator would have "the best seat in the house," would not be burdened with constant readjustments to new views, and would quickly thank the camera for not interfering. It muddles a play (written from one viewpoint) if one hops about visually during a scene; this can easily be discovered by moving four or five times to different seats during a theatrical performance, getting new perspectives each time and then coming away from the theatre with jumbled memories.[39]

Barbarow's proposed method, which would negate at least four decades of film history, reverting to preclassical "primitive" cinema and reducing the filmic part of Shakespeare film to the most basic documentary function possible, provides a useful starting point for understanding how any successful adaptation must break radically with theatrical practice.[40] By analyzing why such a restriction on "the machine" would produce something totally unwatchable, would in fact place us not in the best but in the worst seat in the house, I hope to establish the base points from which the filmmaker must proceed.

The four *Hamlets* of this book are unequivocally examples—virtuosic examples, I argue—of "classical Hollywood cinema," a style of audiovisual storytelling that compels audience attention using devices that are at once grounded in fundamental mental processes and reinforced through the experience of watching motion pictures. As defined by such theorists as David Bordwell, Kristin Thompson, and Noël Carroll, classical style is fundamentally realistic but also strongly controlling of viewers' mental responses. Most of its devices were established as conventions in the early decades of the twentieth century, and because of the efficiency by which these devices make film narratives comprehensible and exciting for large audiences, the classical style became, and remains, the international norm for mass-marketed films. Some of its defining features might be realized by Barbarow's restricted machine, just as they might be realized on the stage: for example, a focus on individuals with recognizable psychologies who become the principal causal agents of the plot by pursuing identifiable goals; and the question-and-answer or "erotetic" rhetoric that Carroll proposes as fundamental to film narrative. But even in these cases, classical cinema has developed enormous additional resources over what is available on the stage. Psychologies can be rendered more recognizable than they are both in the theater and in real life through close-ups of emoting faces, interpretive music, expressive camera angles, even editing rhythm. Goals can be identified and approached visually, with their attractions made clear to see and defined as subjective or objective. Questions can be posed by the intriguing audiovisual detail and the selective release of information, techniques in which film excels.

More fundamentally, Barbarow's alternative cinema would be unwatchable, because it would not activate many of film's most potent means of engaging the viewer. To translate into modern film jargon, what Barbarow claims that the adaptor must eliminate is "variable framing." Of course, this is exactly what he cannot do if he aspires to popular comprehension and enjoyment, avowed goals of our four directors. Variable framing through editing and camera motion, which makes us continually focus on what is most significant and produces intense identification with characters by allowing us to share their optical point of view, is generally considered the most fundamental source of "the power of movies."[41] It allows, indeed conventionally relies on, the creation of a coherent three-dimensional space that is essential to classical storytelling. In addition, as Jean Mitry argues, both editing and camera motion establish a film's rhythm, which allows us to comprehend its temporal dimension and its structure, a structure that relentlessly unfolds in a present that we continuously strive to link up with the past and extrapolate into a future.[42] To follow the plot of a film, we must experience shots combining into spatially coherent scenes, scenes into larger storytelling segments, segments into the larger movements of the narrative. Storytelling in film is not a mere recording process but an art of multileveled segmentation, communicating in large measure through its elaborate structures, although in the classical aesthetic it labors to efface the construction process, making it something we look through rather than look at.

On a deeper psychological level, the coherent space and the rhythmic segmentation produced through variable framing allow film to underscore its narrative with powerful instinctive drives. Most viewers will stare with intense interest at a flat screen for hours only if an impression of movement through a realistic three-dimensional space is maintained. In part, this interest derives from highly conscious participation in the story. As recent research on moving picture media by cognitive psychologists has illuminated, movement within and into this represented space also triggers the brain's largely involuntary and subliminal "orienting response," which directs immediate attention to any new environmental stimulus to determine whether it is a threat. First described by Ivan Pavlov in 1927 (coinciding, interestingly, with silent cinema's apogee of motion effects), the orienting response, nicknamed by Pavlov the "what's this?" response, is now a well-studied component of our evolutionary heritage: it developed to allow our ancestors to survive on the African savanna by alerting them to potential predators. In film, changes in the visual field redirect our attention much more continually and variously than occurs in most other activities. As communications psychologist Annie Lang and others have recently demonstrated in laboratory experimentation, the most elementary formal features by which classical cinema constructs its narratives—camera movements and editing transitions—measurably activate the orienting response, gluing attention to the screen. What allowed our ancestors to survive several million years ago and become our ancestors began empowering an art of unprecedented mass appeal at the end of the nineteenth century.[43]

Acutely sensitive to what made movies pleasurable and therefore profitable, the pioneers of early film quickly settled into a standard practice that combined repeated camera movements with rhythmic editing transitions. As films lengthened to accommodate longer stories, groups of shots constituting a scene continuous in space and time were succeeded by additional such groups, producing a more complex rhythm in which the rapid sequence of same-scene transitions is punctuated by a slower sequence of transitions between scenes. Editing within the scene grew dependent on the "master shot discipline": an "establishing shot" depicts the overall setting and configures the characters in space, then closer shots direct attention to selections within the space of the scene via "analytic editing."[44] As editing within the scene grew more sophisticated and formalized, transitions between scenes became more elaborately highlighted. Such punctuation as the dissolve, wipe, and fade developed as devices to reinforce an already present difference between same-scene and different-scene transitions.

Lang's research into what she calls "the limited capacity model of mediated message processing" reveals that between-scene transitions produced heightened demands on the orienting response that momentarily overload our mental processing, interfering with our memory.[45] Cognitive studies using other methodologies demonstrate that crossing spatio-temporal "event boundaries" in both film and real life immediately shifts previous events from working (short-term) memory to long-term memory. The precise implications of such research are not yet clear for film studies.[46] At the very least, because transitions affect memory and because the orienting response is largely subliminal, it may eventually provide new cognitive explanations for film's effacement of its devices. Offering a new cognitive explanation for the development of punctuation devices, it also, at least, underlines the importance of complex rhythmic segmentation for film art.

A source of engagement perhaps as important as film's activation of the orienting response is its activation of the "mirror neuron" systems. Since their discovery in the early 1990s, mirror neurons, which simulate within ourselves the movements performed by others and the emotions we witness in others through facial expressions, have been offered as the clearest biological explanation for empathy and altruistic morality.[47] We might explain the tendency of all films to be "action" films, as Almereyda's Hamlet sadly observes in his "to be" soliloquy, from the fact that the fixed screen, on which we must remain focused, and other, more social aspects of the settings in which films are viewed discourage physical imitations of actors' nonfacial actions. The activation of mirror neurons in the experience of merely viewing an action is identical in nature to imitating that viewed action, but significantly lower in intensity.[48] As a result of this difference, we might infer, film developed as our primary means of experiencing motor actions that we do not, cannot, and would not perform; our mirror neurons allow us to experience the viewed action in vicarious safety, even if we squirm in our seats.

The situation is different for facial expressions. Among primates, humans are the greatest specialists in processing information through the face. We read emotions primarily through interpreting what Paul Ekman in a series of books calls the facial action system, in which the eyes work together with the eyebrows and mouth. Mirror neuron research reveals that actual motor mimicry by our own faces is crucial to our processing of this information. The fact that facial expressions are the one area of motor action not discouraged by the viewing context means that film art specializes not only in normally unacceptable action but also in facial observation. Another source of its variety and rhythm is the alternation between action-adventure and emotional engagement, which most commonly takes the form of an alternation between longer shots depicting movement and closer shots depicting reactions. In both areas, of course, classical film possesses great advantages over the stage. It is no accident that facial expression became the predominant use of the close-up at the very beginning of film. Nor is it an accident that Almereyda's Hamlet concludes his soliloquy among the action films at Blockbuster with the scene's closest shot of his face.

Barbarow's naïve model sees a successfully adapted Hamlet as deriving from the stripping away of devices that complicate and compromise our viewing of the profilmic dramatic performance. A more accurate view would consider how a filmmaker re-creates Shakespeare's greatest play while maximizing the advantages of the medium. Because a film contains something approaching an infinite amount of information recorded onto its audiovisual tracks, any analysis must be highly selective. Although the subsequent chapters do not ignore the occasional failures in the films covered, they concentrate on the most creative and effective uses of these advantages.

Variable framings achieved through camera movement and placement, present in every sequence of shots, cannot, of course, be analyzed exhaustively. Continually at work in directing the viewer's attention, their operation is more often than not of a relatively neutral, inexpressive, or conventional nature that does not require comment. But against this background there can be seen more creative uses. Variation deployed through editing together shots of different camera distance, for example, can become meaningful when it organizes a segment, as when Olivier's first soliloquy divides into a circular journey not only through the actor's motions to and from the thrones but also through the placement of close-ups at the beginning, middle, and end, a sequencing that controls and organizes the intensity of our responses. It enhances, in effect, the mirror-neuron activation of the close-ups through alternation with the lesser activation produced by his more distanced gestures. Camera movement that serves principally to "reframe," adjusting to a figure's change of position on screen, is not often noteworthy, but it can be. It may be used to neutrally follow a figure's motion, or to enhance it, as when the camera following Olivier's Ophelia as Hamlet throws her down onto stone steps in the nunnery scene disturbingly amplifies the action's violence and calls Hamlet's sanity into question.

Recognizing the importance of the orienting response and mirror neurons in motion pictures can lead to new ways of thinking about various conventional devices and illuminate their potential for specialized exploitation in a Shakespeare film. For example, in terms of camera movement, tracking toward an object stimulates the orienting response less than a camera tracking away, because the latter continually brings new objects into view that need to be identified and assessed. Slow camera movement is inherently less demanding than fast, for a similar reason. The relaxing of orienting stimulus through such devices allows the mind's limited capacity for processing information to be redirected away from instinctual, involuntary threat assessment toward something else: say, the emotional nuances of Branagh's "to be" soliloquy spoken during a slow camera track-in toward his mirror reflection. The most familiar image in the entire film, Hamlet's expressive face, is brought slowly nearer as the voice-over forces us to watch for the smallest facial gesture that will help us to interpret the emotional content of the words—indeed, to search ever more closely for visually expressed meaning. One critic finds that Branagh "plays the scene with seething, self-contained anger."[49] The very act of self-containment, the absence of gesture that becomes a gesture through its absence, combined with an intense, unblinking concentration that is mirrored in our own, represents a remarkable development in the film medium's use of the face, an instance of cinematic artistry worthy of Shakespeare's verbal artistry.

In addition to introducing such concepts not traditionally applied to film criticism, the following chapters make considerable use of several more traditional categories explored in Stefan Sharff's highly informative, if overconfidently titled, *The Elements of Cinema*. Sharff attempts to define cinema's "unique methods of providing aesthetic gratification," which he calls its "cinesthetic elements." Several of these elements, such as "parallel action" and "moving camera," are devices of variable framing that are familiar enough to require no definition. Two less familiar on which Sharff is especially persuasive, however, should be mentioned. He is illuminating on the power of "delayed disclosure," the creation of questions or incorrect assumptions through insufficient or misleading visual cues.[50] In the earliest uses of the master-shot discipline, the establishing shot came at the beginning of a scene, minimizing the new stimuli of the more closely framed "cut-in" shots that followed. Soon after this undemanding norm was established, filmmakers developed more demanding sequences that might begin, for example, with a close-up and then offer an establishing shot to place it within a context. This early form of delayed disclosure emerged as a simple reversal of the norm, to stimulate the viewer's interest but inevitably at the expense of other forms of attention. Delayed disclosure would therefore be used most effectively not at moments when the demands of Shakespearean poetry require our fullest concentration but when the erotetic narrative poses tantalizing questions: what is in the mind of Zeffirelli's Ophelia as we see her rise mysteriously from behind a rock after Hamlet's departure for England, or what is Almereyda's Hamlet planning when we see him in extreme close-up after killing Polonius? Delayed disclosure has also become important in Shakespeare films because it effortlessly produces desirable effects difficult to produce on the stage. The delayed revelation of Hamlet's presence in the first court scene (1.2) becomes such a conspicuous device in three of the films that Almereyda transposes it to a later scene to surprise the viewer familiar with the tradition.

Sharff is equally valuable for his emphasis on the power of what he calls a "separation" sequence. A two-party conversation may be constructed using

objective two-shots, with both characters fully visible; a shot/reverse-shot sequence of "semisubjective" over-the-shoulder shots; and a "separation" sequence,
subjective shots/reverse-shots that alternate presenting one interlocutor alone
on screen.[51] The semisubjective sequence is the most commonly employed,
to the point of signifying conversation even where conversation is not taking
place, as in Zeffirelli's mute encounter between Hamlet and Ophelia in the
weaving room. The semisubjective sequence also generally engages the viewer
more emphatically than the more stagy objective two-shot, because it includes
optical point of view, the opportunity for a closer camera, and the orienting
demands of editing. Most intense for the viewer is the separation sequence,
which includes not only undiluted focus on one interlocutor at a time and the
occasion for the closest camera, but also a form of engagement described by
Sharff as follows:

> The viewer is engaged in the dramatics not only as a mere observer of the
> plot, but as an actor playing the part, of A when B is on the screen, of B
> when A is on the screen. Once "playing" the part, the viewer tries to impose
> his interpretation, expecting or wanting the next shot to conform to it. . . .
> If this happens the viewer is gratified and encouraged to participate further.
> The pictured reaction of B in shot 2 is, in a sense, a replay of what the viewer
> has already acted out.[52]

The three types of conversational shots, separately or in combination, allow
filmmakers to calibrate the intensity of their conversations. The power of
Zeffirelli's ghost scene, for example, is heightened by his unusually extensive
separation after using the technique minimally before this privileged moment
of father-son communication.

Sharff is primarily concerned to assert film art's reliance on what he calls
"grammar" ("the relationships among shots in a sequence") and "syntax" ("the
system by which larger units are organized into structural elements").[53] Wary
of a potentially confusing linguistic analogy, I will avoid his vocabulary of
grammar and syntax but follow his recommendation in paying especially close
attention to each film's complex and multileveled segmentation and organization, which is a much less systematic and formulaic affair than linguistic
grammar and syntax. The stage director of a full, modern-text *Hamlet* mounts
nineteen discreet scenes punctuated by the emptying of the stage.[54] The filmmaker develops a shooting script consisting of hundreds of planned shots,
to which more are almost always added in filming, because filming produces

added opportunities and uncovers previously unrealized needs for images. After the act of filming, this enormous set of building blocks is assembled, and reassembled, to form coherent scenes and larger segments: Olivier's completed film, for example, which acquired additional shots to fulfill needs not foreseen in the shooting script, assembles 433 shots into scenes, which are then assembled into sequences, which are then assembled into still larger segments that I will be calling "movements."[55] Shots are varied using the devices of variable framing not only to tell the story but also to interpret, focus interest, facilitate the construction of meaningful structural units on various scales, and produce complex rhythms along these scales. Structural units can be constructed in myriad ways: through continuity of action and time (the standard definition of a film "scene"), of course, but also through sustained or recurring images, settings, or music, indeed, through the sustaining or recurrence of any device available to film. A major part of the difficulty of reading films closely is the sheer variety of segments and means for their construction, which are continually being invented. All films reveal extensive patterning, but few present global organizing patterns that can be precisely delineated. In that, they are like life itself, which they purport to represent. With so many building blocks and construction techniques at his disposal, the filmmaker can organize this virtual life by creating simple or elaborate symmetries, contrasts, and audiovisual echoes that enhance comprehension and enjoyment.

One partial exception to the lack of global organizing patterns is revealed in Kristin Thompson's recent work, which offers new insight into larger-scale structures of classical Hollywood feature films. Providing a thoroughly documented corrective to the three-act model advocated almost universally in screenwriting manuals, she demonstrates that such films more often than not "break perspicuously into *four* large-scale parts, with major turning points usually providing the transitions."[56] The narrative changes direction, dividing the film into four roughly equal movements, usually when there is a shift in the protagonist's goals. To fit within a commercially viable feature-film length, Shakespeare's longest play must be substantially shortened. Yielding to this necessity, all of the films except Branagh's full-text version delete, divide, and transpose Shakespeare's text to move, in varying degrees, in the direction of this "global Hollywood" paradigm, as well as to readjust emphases to suit modern values. Consequently, the chapters on all but Branagh's film are subdivided by movement to trace this process.

On the one hand, Shakespeare facilitates screenwriters' attempts to accommodate the movie audience's highly conditioned expectations of this kind of segmentation. The play divides nicely into four parts, shifting motivations with the ghost's revelation of the murder (end of 1.5); the confirmation (at, say, 3.2.287) in the aftermath of the Mousetrap; and Hamlet's return to Denmark after the death of Ophelia and the escape from Claudius's plan for his death (5.1), until the moment of his death (5.2.342). Most simply stated, *Hamlet*'s pattern of motivation moves from Hamlet's motiveless melancholy to his seeking to confirm the ghost's message to a more complicated third movement in which Hamlet's desire for revenge is thwarted by his mother's beckoning and Claudius's desire to ensure his own safety and, finally, to continuing or renewed desire and new opportunity for revenge. On the other hand, *Hamlet* presents formidable obstacles to realizing such a pattern. There is, of course, the ultimately unmovable obstacle of Shakespeare's endless psychological complexity. To ask merely one complicating question among the many that any reader might add: is the Mousetrap really motivated by the need to confirm, and does it renew Hamlet's desire to obey his father's ghost? (As Hamlet might say, that's two questions.) Nor is Shakespeare's plot as neatly balanced as a typical Hollywood plot, for it frames two much longer central segments within a shorter beginning and end. The filmmaker wishing both to popularize and to present a subtle interpretation of the play has many interesting problems to solve.[57]

Barbarow's primitive documentary model ignores not only the fundamental attractional and structural devices of film but also its unbreakable habit as a "realist" medium of documenting a represented world in detail. David Bordwell describes two closely related forms of "density" increasingly incorporated into modern film that should be of interest to the student of Shakespearean adaptation. The first he calls "worldmaking," the provision of "a rich, fully furnished ambience for the action."[58] Although even by the film standards of his time Olivier's Elsinore provides a minimally furnished ambience, Barbarow finds its level of visual detail distracting. The few crucial props and locations—the precarious battlement, Hamlet's distinctive chair, Ophelia's corridor leading to daylight, Gertrude's spacious bed—stand out in high relief against the castle's plain background, allowing the film's concentrated, evocative repetitions of a small number of visually characterized items to become one of its most memorable innovations. Later directors moved in the direction of ever more abundant, if not necessarily more evocative, visual detail. Zeffirelli's medieval setting is relatively austere among period films, but it contains a much more fully realized world than Olivier's.[59] Seamlessly uniting scenes from three historical castles with a soundstage and exterior sets, he uses an "archaeological" approach reminiscent of the Victorian stagings of Charles Kean. His Elsinore communicates its period materially, through stone and wood surfaces, forged metal, textiles, and geometrical ornamentation that visually connects the full range of human artifact, from jewelry to clothing to architecture. Inspired by the Bayeux Tapestry, panels of which are being prepared by the castle's women, Zeffirelli surrounds Hamlet with the everyday life of a medieval community. This economic activity culminates in the enormous banquet that fills the hall while Hamlet awaits the ghost, altering the nature of the prince's alienation, which, in Zeffirelli's film, is from an integrated community in which the populace has a stake in the travails of the royal family. Branagh's Elsinore retains such features of Olivier's as a reliance on fewer, more evocative locations and a schematic and symbolic architecture that sometimes sacrifices realism for meaning. But like Zeffirelli's, it also contains a large implied community and a wealth of interpretable visual details, especially in the décor and paraphernalia of characters' rooms, which the 70mm cinematography displays in sharp abundance. It expands the scope of the family story into the international arena with its visual elevation of Fortinbras to the status of a major character. Almereyda's film likewise implies an international scope through the iconography of multinational capitalism. Filmmaker Hamlet's obsession with images adds a rich virtual dimension to the worldmaking of Almereyda's film, extending his mental reach across the history of art and cinema. Indeed, the film generates the kind of information overload that Bordwell finds in such pioneer worldmaking films as Ridley Scott's *Blade Runner*.

Even as density is creating a compelling effect of reality, it can also be producing what Bordwell calls "maximal design" incorporating appeals to a wide variety of audiences. "With many films designed to appeal to a wide range of viewers," he writes, "there are pressures to sprinkle in details that might be caught by only a few."[60] As popularizing treatments and aesthetic creations in their own right, original-language Shakespeare films are almost inevitably aimed at an audience gamut that is broad even while it contains numerous subgroups of the "few"—as, of course, were Shakespeare's plays, with their mix of clowns and kings and their wide-ranging allusiveness. One goal of the following studies is to take this gamut much more into account than most recent criticism has done. The four *Hamlets* all embrace a viewership that ranges from those unfamiliar with the play to the *Hamlet* literate. The audience embraced also includes groups with competencies and interests that are more specific: Shakespeare scholars, cineastes and film scholars, fellow filmmakers, auteurists who follow the director's career, and numerous other groups that can follow allusions unremarked by others. Bernice Kliman recognizes the complexly allusive nature of Branagh's *Hamlet:*

> This is a film that stands back from itself and asks the audience in the know to recognize allusions—to Gielgud's famous pose holding the skull at arm's length; to the celebrities, and the relation of some of them to Branagh; to the Adrian Noble/Branagh RSC production of 1992. These presumably are meant to function like Shakespeare's metatheatrical references. The actor-friends passing through this film—reprising Branagh's career—and the many celebrity actors, some who stand in a parental role to him, make for multiple texts, multiple significations.[61]

Kliman is correct to assume that one specialized audience for Branagh's film is viewers who have studied the play's performance history, while another is viewers who have followed Branagh's career. Other targeted subgroups can be identified for this and the other films, including, of particular interest in a book on *Hamlets*, the audience who will note the allusions that develop within the evolving tradition. Having closely studied his predecessors, each film-maker acknowledges his debt with gestures large and small.

One result of the broad reach of Shakespeare films is that many more people, of course, have by now experienced the dramatist in performance through film than through stage productions, and the disproportion will continue to grow. I believe that it is important to study the complex procedures of adaptation because for most people today Shakespeare is experienced primarily, and for many even exclusively, through films. We need to understand what the films are doing to and with Shakespeare, and they are inevitably doing much more than any single viewing experience reveals; moreover, the films as "looked-through" artifacts are working hard not to advertise what they are doing. This book is intended to assist anyone viewing any of the four *Hamlets* to "look at" the remarkable panoply of devices deployed by four brilliant film-makers who are simultaneously popularizing and subtly interpreting the play. Because the book grew out of numerous university classes that ranged from using film as an aid in teaching Shakespeare to using Shakespeare as an aid in teaching the critical study of film, I especially hope that it will prove useful to the vast and growing number of instructors, at a variety of levels, who find any of the ways of combining Shakespeare and film a synergistic, miraculous means for engaging the minds of students.

LAURENCE OLIVIER'S
Hamlet

The Triumph of the Cinesthetic

Olivier's *Hamlet* has long been recognized as a formal hybrid. A common complaint among early reviewers was, in effect, that too much of the play was sacrificed in favor of the movie. Cutting the bard's sacred words, indispensable characters, and crucial scenes and speeches to create an "essay in *Hamlet*" considerably shorter and less polysemic than the original produced predictable laments.[1] Less predictable are complaints that what remained of Shakespeare's words was compromised by the processes of film. George Barbarow, as discussed earlier, wrote of the endless series of visual details that "distract us from the action of the drama" and of the endless "fresh perspectives that demand new visual adjustments almost constantly, always diverting attention away from the speech."[2] Later critics, in a contrast that measures the way Olivier's breakthrough film has altered perceptions over time, have frequently found virtue in hybridity. Sheryl Gross, for example, sees "a special mixture of poetry and realism, poetic realism if you will, which can find its truest expression only in films like *Hamlet*."[3] The most influential in this vein has been Bernice Kliman, who describes Olivier's production as "a hybrid form, not a filmed play, not precisely a film, but a film-infused play or a play-infused film." Kliman argues that Olivier viewed film as "a way to expand theater," freeing him from spatial and temporal limitations while allowing him to retain theater's "sense of flow."[4]

To understand the nature of Olivier's innovation, and the reasons why his film holds such a foundational position in the history of Shakespearean adaptations, we should revisit the distinction between its filmic and theatrical aspects. Olivier himself acknowledged that his first film, *Henry V*, was "not quite a film, not quite a play," but for *Hamlet* his "earliest and deepest resolutions were to find a cinematic interpretation of the play." Finding greater inspiration in directing and editing than in acting the role before the camera, and dissatisfied with the techniques of all previous Shakespearean films, he sought a more complete translation into the new medium. After the fact, he concluded that he had succeeded, that "the film of *Hamlet* was a rattling good story, inside and outside Hamlet's mind, told cinematically."[5] His success at such translation was remarkable and unprecedented but, not surprisingly, less thoroughgoing than that of later film adapters. Jack Jorgens points to "deliberate" use of theatricality "to underscore Shakespeare's use of the 'world as stage' metaphor."[6] But there are also, undeniably, stretches of the film that are simply uninspired cinema. Perhaps that was not entirely unfortunate. The co-presence of theatrical and cinematic techniques did not merely successfully mediate the sometimes conflicting expectations of a 1948 audience willing to experience the novelty of seeing both Shakespeare and a movie at the same time; it also provided an influential schooling for future filmmakers, who could see the residuals of the older art form juxtaposed with more truly cinematic transformations. Olivier taught later adapters through his failures to fully achieve what Stefan Sharff calls "cinesthetic impact" as much as through his successes.[7]

Olivier highlights the cinematic aspect of his "essay in *Hamlet*" by opening with both modes conspicuously present. In the paratexts that take up over three minutes of opening time, theatrical and cinematic modes elaborately interact. The orchestra warming up that for Kliman "suggests a play more than a film," presumably because one hears such tunings only at live musical performances, begins halfway through the title announcing "A Two Cities Film."[8] Lining the bottom of the screen are the logo for D&P Studios, the seal of approval from the Motion Picture Producers and Distributors Association, and "Western Electric Recording": familiar film brandings all and labels affixed to finished products, in counterpoint to any "live" significations of the yet-to-begin orchestra. Theater returns visually when this is followed by a frame of "Laurence Olivier presents" over an illustration of stage paraphernalia as the warming up continues on the soundtrack. A dissolve to the title for *Hamlet* accompanies a shift into fully realized orchestral music, which now becomes a conventional film title accompaniment, its turbulent energy echoed visually in the next shot as the credits form over a view of Elsinore surrounded by churning sea. Even the credits enter into the modal interplay, with those listing the more properly film participants scrolling up the screen, followed by groupings of "The Players" by category on nonscrolling displays, the latter a convention more common on playbills than on screen. For both the credits and the later printed screen of the "vicious mole of nature" speech, a black border moves into the sides and top of the screen, an innovation that manages to recall at once the masking effects popular in silent film and the theatrical proscenium.[9]

Intentional intimations of theater now drop away, for the shots remaining before the action proper begins are linked by established filmic methods. Indeed, Olivier emphatically uses the medium's variable framing to establish throughout the film an unusually elaborate spatial articulation that repeatedly alternates between the horizontal and the vertical dimensions, with the result that one remembers the action largely as a series of passages through Norman arches and up and down staircases.[10] A fade leads to replacement of the horizontal view of Elsinore with a nearly vertical view, while the continuing fog and surging sea suggest that these are simply alternative vantages of the same scene, an announcement of the power of variable framing. Now Olivier interweaves three sets into a near-seamless continuity: an elaborate three-dimensional model of Elsinore, a full-sized battlement platform on a soundstage, and a painted version of the model as seen from above. The camera cranes down slowly toward the model as denser fog obscures the view, forming a background to the printed text of the "vicious mole of nature" (1.4.24) speech. The speech is printed for our perusal but also voiced with more attention to meaning than musicality by Olivier, inspiring confidence in a portion of the audience that Shakespeare's language will be comprehensible;

Olivier observed that his success as a filmmaker "had much to do with the way [he] adapted the sound of the lines to the modern ear"[11]—and, one should add, to the modern ear hearing the lines spoken softly and intimately on a film soundtrack rather than declaimed in a theater. By the time the fog clears, the implied motion of the camera has brought us to precisely the appropriate location where now the body of young Hamlet is borne atop the soundstage tower, and the camera continues downward as if it had never stopped, despite the change in sets that is apparent to many viewers. As soon as Olivier has continued building confidence with his oft-criticized observation, "This is the tragedy of a man who could not make up his mind," a dissolve presents the soundstage tower optically superimposed on the painted scene. This view in effect moves the camera back out and to a new angle in time for a special effect to make the men vanish before our eyes.

The First Movement

Accompanied by a tolling bell that continues the funereal associations, additional dissolves continue the patterns of camera relocation, from the castle viewed from above to its walls and tower viewed from below to a closer shot of a stairway from yet another new angle. Elsinore has not been mapped coherently, but its principal external features have been viewed repeatedly and from a variety of vantages, with the effect that it is at once mysterious and familiar, a fully three-dimensional site that piques curiosity even as it serves believably as the location into which the first character enters. A guard soon to be revealed as Bernardo enters screen left, preceded by his shadow and then his spear point, two ominous visual forerunners that might remind us how important the orienting response can be even within a single shot. He climbs a steep stairway, and as the bell stops tolling he warily halts and looks behind him, as the violently panning camera will force us to do at the ghost's arrival. If we have been counting, and most viewers have been on some level of attention, the twelfth and final toll transforms the funereal bell into an ominous temporal signal. While Bernardo pauses, Francisco passes across the top of the stairway unperceived by his replacement. He is a two-dimensional, back-lit silhouette, more akin to Bernardo's shadow than to the fully modeled man bathed in light upon the stairway, who fools us into thinking him three-dimensional despite the flat screen. The midnight hour, the atmosphere of death and danger, and the chance failure of contact motivate the mutual alarm of the two sentries when they suddenly meet at the top of the stairs and open the play with their famous interchange: "Who's there? Nay, answer me." This is not merely fine cinematic storytelling but almost an allegory of cinema's power.

Offscreen space and unconventional camera placement are used masterfully to enhance our apprehension. Bernardo's ascent is recorded first by a low camera, which is then followed by three shots from a high camera that emphasize the laborious physicality required to climb to the heights of the battlement. Once Bernardo has arrived on high, and again after the same downward-tilted camera finds Marcellus and Horatio laboring upward, a horizontal camera that denies sight of the battlement floor suspends the characters in this vertiginous location, from which Horatio gazes downward toward a raging sea that our mind's eye recalls from the opening shots. When Horatio sits with Bernardo to hear his account of the ghost, the mind's eye is turned in two directions: first, to the right of the screen by Bernardo's gaze and finger pointing toward "yond same star that's westward from the pole" (1.1.35), followed by Horatio's turn to follow his eye-line; and second, to a point in front of the screen by Marcellus's gaze, which grows more fearful as the camera tracks toward him and an amplified heartbeat accompanies going in and out of focus. Significantly, the film's first close-up, which momentarily ratchets up our mirror-neuron stimulation, is of a man experiencing terror. Marcellus's close-up also implies that the other men's gaze is an indirection, and thus it comes as no surprise that the next cut brings us to a camera position following Marcellus's eye-line from behind the men. What is surprising is that the three men spin violently to look to their rear, while a flash pan to the right spins us along with them with equal violence to reveal the ghost in close-up. The men had entered from the left, expectations pointed right and forward, leaving only the space behind the screen unsurveyed. From this direction the ghost does not so much enter as pop frightfully into presence, then dissolve back into the proper distance.

Olivier's inspired handling of the ghost's first arrival gives way to an odd decline in intensity. The music disappears, the camera becomes static, and shots alternate conventionally between the ghost and the three men, whose array, geometrized by the lines of upraised spears, remains unchanged. The men's tone of voice is subdued. Their facial expressions scarcely register emotion. Horatio's "It harrows me with fear and wonder" (1.1.43), spoken with his back turned, is blandly expressionless, verging on unintended irony. Olivier may have been seeking a calm interval that would make his single ghost appearance resemble the two provided by Shakespeare in act 1, scene 1, which are divided by leisurely exposition of the Fortinbras material. Whatever the reason, the sudden decline turns the opening scene into one of the film's most uneven. When the ghost begins to approach after the cock's crow, close-ups and music reveal the men's renewed fright, but the emotion is shared by the audience only by being observed. Bernardo and Horatio each cries, "'Tis here" (140), looking upward in nearly opposite directions, but there is no shared audience disorientation and building suspense comparable to that which accompanies the ghost's arrival. A dissolve to a high shot and the men's upward gazes suggest the ghost's perspective, but the suggestion weakly deflates when the camera descends. The men discuss the event dispassionately until Marcellus imports from Shakespeare's second ghost scene, "Something is rotten in the state of Denmark" (1.4.90). The men all look toward the site of this rottenness. The camera turns to join their gaze, and Olivier's filmmaking recovers from its first serious flaw.

The renowned transition via moving camera and one usually unnoticed dissolve midway to the court scene performs for Elsinore's interior what earlier shots did for its exterior. We become familiar with details and are intrigued but cannot map the space or interpret confidently. Most critics and reviewers who comment upon the transition note that the camera pauses above the throne room and then approaches Hamlet's chair, Ophelia's archway, and finally the royal bed. But these same writers rarely note that the sights at which the camera pauses have different effects on different parts of the audience gamut. The Hamlet-literate may sense Hamlet's connection to the chair, which implies by its position both a place in and alienation from the court, and the ubiquity of oedipal readings may link the bed with Gertrude, but the archway has as yet no inherent linkage to Ophelia. The camera's approach to it, more tentative and incomplete than to the bed, produces a shift in musical theme and instrumentation, suggesting its owner's less central role in the plot. With the deeper penetration of the hallway leading to the bed, the music develops the new theme but returns to its original orchestration, adumbrating a complicated relationship between the owners of the second and third sites. The Hamlet-literate will make some of these identifications and begin to assess the film's interpretations, awaiting further developments of these ideas. The new public is probably no less engaged. The question-then-answer, or "erotetic," form of narrative that Noël Carroll believes is favored by cinema is being put to work with memorable images whose meanings will be supplied, some sooner and some later.

With a dissolve from the bed to a close-up of the king emptying his wine cup and the sound of a crowd loudly celebrating, the bed might be assumed the site of a recent or imminent sexual consummation. The impression is re-inforced when the royal couple leans toward each other in a visual echo of the bed's notable canopy, which has frequently invited the adjective *vaginal*. Claudius's gravitational pull upon his queen's posture, which will continue until late in the film, is but one visual indication among many of the new king's power. His triumphal arm gesture calls forth the row of trumpets, but only after a subliminally nondiegetic trumpet blast manifests his will almost as if by magic. The trumpets unleash the cannons, which are also heard before they are seen, keeping us aware of the space offscreen. After Claudius quaffs, his tossed empty cup is deftly caught by an elderly courtier, whose dignified mien does not disqualify him from this specialized role of demeaning service to his sovereign, which he will perform again for our pleasure in the duel scene. During the king's opening remarks, the camera pulls back across the long table to display the rapt courtiers, who form diagonal lines converging on the royal figure at the screen's center. Most telling of all, the king remains on-screen for all but thirty seconds of a six-and-one-half-minute scene. In close-ups, medium shots, and long shots that keep him in view through the film's first innovative use of deep focus, Claudius presides over the scene even when other characters speak. As the implied endpoint of the eye-line of the men on the battlement, extended across space and time by the moving camera, Claudius is that which is rotten in the state of Denmark, but he is also a formidable presence.

Not until the scene nears its midpoint does the camera move far enough back to reveal Hamlet, seated in the already familiar chair and staring sullenly into space. Film's effortless capacity for delayed disclosure has finally realized what has been attempted only with difficulty on stage: to bring the prince forth from among the courtiers as a discovery.[12] From this point, the action is organized around two parallel journeys from the thrones to the chair. Hamlet fails to answer Claudius's question, "How is it that the clouds still hang on you?" (1.2.66), prompting the queen to go to her son, an action that turns all eyes toward him. When Hamlet replies to his mother's ministrations with the "suits of woe" (86) speech, delivered while turned away from the king, Claudius surprisingly responds from the deep-focus distance. He follows Gertrude's path, though at his own deliberate pace, gathering all gazes to himself and removing Hamlet from sight for a full minute. En route he lectures Hamlet, the courtiers, and us, looking into the camera as he asks with a cynical chuckle, "Why should we in our peevish opposition / Take it to heart?" (100–101). The fawning courtiers reply with a nervous laugh.

The king's ambulatory speech, an assertion of royal power during which the nodding and bowing courtiers closely observe his movement down the table, climaxes in the dramatic proclamation that Hamlet is "the most immediate to our throne" (109), delivered with a Roman salute and greeted with applause from the rising court and trumpet fanfare. Having countered Hamlet's peevishness with this display of royal bravura, Claudius uses a brusque, scolding tone in his request that the prince not return to Wittenberg. The king's provocations reveal the depth of Hamlet's self-control, since he makes no response to anything Claudius says or does, with the single exception of removing his right hand from his face, a gesture whose very meaninglessness stores it in our memory for further consideration, which will soon be called upon at the end of the first soliloquy. At the same time, this stoicism highlights Hamlet's contrasting weakness toward his mother. She steps in between her husband and son to plead, "Go not to Wittenberg" (119). Hamlet agrees while glancing repeatedly into the maternal bosom carefully positioned right below his eyes. He is rewarded with a kiss on the mouth that lasts long enough to catch the king's attention. Perhaps noticing that his nephew is taking too literally his request, "Be as ourself in Denmark," he orders, "Madame, come" (122).

A high shot reveals the royal party exiting behind the thrones while numerous courtiers move laterally into the wings. The latter look back quizzically toward the enigmatic prince as they leave, making the queen's failure to look back upon the son she has just kissed passionately even more obvious. The careful observer will notice that Laertes watches Hamlet the longest among them, looking as if he wishes to speak to the prince. The image effortlessly plants a question about what he might wish to say. When the camera cranes in closer, and the brooding string music from the end of the ghost scene returns, Hamlet glances up suddenly toward the thrones, planting more questions: is he seeking the conspicuously missing maternal glance, and do the empty thrones evoke other emotions in the prince, as well? A close-up that begs comparison with the similarly right-facing close-up of quaffing Claudius (drinking versus somber sobriety, public celebration versus melancholy solitude . . .) shows him turning away, back to his meditational solitude. Close-ups have defined the film's emotional range, punctuating the action with Marcellus's terror, Claudius's lusty arrogance, and now Hamlet's more complex melancholy, which draws into itself the two earlier, more primitive emotions. Further uniting this sequence of three punctuating close-ups raising our mirror-neuron activity is parallel motion in the latter two: the king's turn toward the camera from full right profile became his command to trumpet and cannon, while the prince's similar turn launches his meditation on powerlessness.

Against the background of soliloquies in earlier films, Hamlet's first stands out for its impressive innovations.[13] Earlier Shakespearean films used simple camera placements and movements to follow characters who simply mouthed their words into the void. Olivier introduces careful choreography and the alternation of voice-over and mouthed speech. The camera follows Hamlet from his chair to a place between the two thrones and then back again, a circuitous journey that signifies his stasis and frustration. The pattern of procession and return is supported by camera distances: close shots are reserved for the beginning and end (while he is seated) and for the midpoint, where he looks with his mind's eye upon the father and mother who have sat upon the thrones. Beginning and ending in voice-over, he breaks into speech five times during his journey. In each instance, he is unable to "hold his tongue" when he reflects angrily on the speed of his mother's remarriage. He rises from his chair at the beginning into the frame from lower left and in right profile. The scene ends in a complex symmetry, with the camera tracking in a way that makes him, now in left profile, exit the frame at lower right. He has raised his right hand to his face, imitating our first sight of him in the previous scene and undoing the only effect on him of the king's address. The simple gesture is thus both a triumphant sign of rejecting the king and a sad return to his opening melancholy. Olivier has set a new standard for filming a soliloquy, one that does justice to his character's complexity.

The camera tracks to reveal the archway at which it paused in the transition following the ghost scene, and to the same music. The implication is that it follows Hamlet's thoughts, and a dissolve carries it farther down the hallway, promising further revelations about where his mind would turn following his melancholy meditation. To our surprise, as the camera continues tracking, Laertes rounds a corner to approach it. The shot metamorphoses into Laertes' point of view when Ophelia comes into sight over his shoulder, complicating our sense of the camera's function and establishing an associative link between the two young men: answering a question planted earlier, the camera suggests that Ophelia was what Laertes wished to discuss with Hamlet at the end of the court scene. The music halts suddenly and a scene of smiling farewell converts into something more serious when Laertes examines the letter that his sister has been reading so intently. When Polonius arrives for his famous speech of paternal advice, Ophelia restores frivolity by playing with Laertes' person while the dutiful son listens with full attention and respect.

She also unwittingly justifies her brother's too-explicit warning about opening her "chaste treasure" (1.3.30) to Hamlet's "unmastered importunity" (1.3.31) by fondling him too suggestively, grabbing his phallic dagger and reaching into the purse at his waist.

Kliman astutely notes that Olivier's insertion of the Ophelia material from act 1, scene 3 at the end of the soliloquy, which in the play ends when Horatio arrives to report on the ghost, "connects her with [Hamlet's] dejection over his mother's betrayal." To his mother's betrayal in the past is now added Ophelia's apparent betrayal in the present. Ophelia responds to her father's forbidding her "to give words or talk with the Lord Hamlet" (1.3.133) with what appears to be a moment of indecision. She begins to follow Polonius into her room but then turns and walks several steps toward Hamlet, with whom she exchanges a loving gaze. But in what Olivier famously called "the longest distance love scene on record," when Ophelia is ordered, "Come your ways" (134), as Kliman notes, Hamlet "does not see Polonius, only Ophelia's rejection of him."[14] Because the moving camera has represented Hamlet's outreaching thoughts, even if that implication is countered by the arrival of Laertes, for Hamlet Ophelia's appearance and approach are a kind of daydream come true, which makes her sudden reversal even more painful. Hamlet is now shown from the same camera position where we earlier saw him interact with his mother, a parallel reinforced by the identical positioning of his legs. The violence that Hamlet typically afflicts upon both Ophelia and Gertrude in film, a medium conducive to amplifying such action, is thus given added motivation.

The traumatic double betrayal also adds motivation to Hamlet's behavior in the subsequent scene, where he momentarily fails to notice that he is addressed by his "good friend" (1.2.163) Horatio. When, building the film's important series of intruding shadows, the shadows of the men cover the very spot on the floor where Gertrude accused him of seeking his "noble father in the dust" (1.2.71), he understandably flees company. But after such brilliant transitions to and from the interpolated Ophelia scene, the perfunctory filming of the ghost report is all the more apparent. Composed mostly of static tableaux of the four men, with Hamlet's reaction highlighted several times in closer shots, the scene blandly conveys information to Hamlet and to us. The closing soliloquy returns to the method of following voice-over with speech, but without the first soliloquy's implication of irrepressible emotion. Perhaps this very failure of imagination is what stimulated later filmmakers to incorporate into the ghost report some of their more surprising innovations.

In addition to creating a sense of double betrayal by women, Olivier's transposition of the Ophelia material allows the ghost scene to follow hard upon Hamlet's promise to meet "upon the platform 'twixt eleven and twelve" (1.2.250), creating a more concerted rush toward the goal reorientation that will end his film's first movement in classic Hollywood fashion. The filmgoer is eager to move toward this first climax, and this eagerness is echoed within the film: the men hurry up a stairway as chiming bells recall the first ghost scene; Hamlet leans out the doorway through which they exited and gazes up the stairway, his back turned to us, embodying his wish, "Would the night were come" (257); Hamlet becomes the first character to walk off the edge of the screen, purposively striding in the direction from which his visitors arrived. We await his reappearance as a fade to Elsinore towering over the raging sea, repeating the image under the film's opening credits, forms an appropriately anticipatory transition.

In Hamlet's encounter with the ghost, for many viewers the film's most memorable sequence, the horizontal interior space meaningfully traversed by characters and the camera is replaced by a strongly vertical space that recaptures some of the creative disorientation of the earlier ghost scene. In a low shot from below the battlement, Hamlet approaches its precarious edge and looks down. Cannon fire and a trumpet fanfare lead the men in another direction, where they look down upon the "heavy-headed revel" (1.4.17) in the courtyard far below, as we look down upon both the observed and the observers in a high shot complementing the opening low shot. Hamlet crosses back to his first location for the "vicious mole of nature" (24) speech. The procession-and-return motion recalls the first soliloquy, reminding us of the impasse from which Hamlet is hoping to be released, and the men's instinctive following sets up the difficulty he will have breaking away from them. During the heartbeat pulses announcing the ghost's presence, he looms above the camera until falling deliriously to the floor, justifying his companions' reluctance to have him follow the ghost.[15] Hamlet's ascent is slow and laborious. After three dissolves suggesting the passage of time reveal him entering higher stages of the battlements, the camera tilts and tracks to follow his feet on the final climb. The narrow steps force him almost to tiptoe. When he reaches the top, both Hamlet's right foot and the camera move backward for a fraction of a second in vertiginous recoil, an effect that is strongly felt without the viewer discerning how it was produced. The vertical emphasis is maintained throughout the interview, during which Hamlet kneels before the standing ghost and is filmed both from behind and in frontal reaction shots with a high camera.

The interview with the ghost is accompanied by steadily intensifying effects of subjectivity and complex identifications tied to Olivier's oedipal reading of the play. Following Hamlet's promise to "sweep to [his] revenge" (1.5.31), the vantage shifts from an angle that aligns the two parties diagonally on the screen to directly behind Hamlet, forming a nearly vertical alignment closer to his point of view. This alignment will be repeated in the scene's final interchange but in a closer shot and with greater precision. The shots of Hamlet's reactions move progressively closer, until the response to "won to his shameful lust / The will of my most seeming virtuous queen" (44–45) is portrayed in a very tight close-up that lasts until Hamlet closes his eyes and the camera in effect enters his head from behind. The visual portrayal of the murder, viewed within an iris of mist, brings on an impressive surge of ambiguities. It belongs to the ghost, in a sense, and might be called a flashback accompanying his narration, but the ghost speaks with the voice of Olivier, electronically modified but not entirely to the point of nonrecognition. It is primarily a subjective visualization seen through the mind's eye of Hamlet, as we are reminded by a shot showing the prince muttering "O horrible!" (80), with his eyes still closed. In addition, as the ghost imparts, "Upon my secure hour thy uncle stole" (61), the camera steals in slowly and hovers near the sleeping king, suggesting the murderer's point of view, visually amplifying the ghost's mere hint of accusation in the shift of possessives from "my" hour to "thy" uncle. A tree trunk at the head of the couch obscures barely glimpsed movement toward the king from the left edge of the frame. Only after the poison is poured, when Claudius strides from behind the tree as the camera pulls back, is a reading of the camera's vantage as the murderer's eliminated definitively—definitively, but of course not retroactively, for within the mind's depths, identifications can be denied or repressed but not erased. The suggestion has been made.

Although some early viewers complained that Olivier's visual details were distracting, in the foggy and isolated ghost scene one such detail, the rings worn by both Hamlets, focuses the viewer's interpretive questionings. When Hamlet raised his hand to his face at the climactic revelation of incest, his ring was conspicuously displayed and highlighted. The ringed hand of the sleeping king defined the track-in of the camera, which kept it on the screen's vertical center line and then watched it lifted to point accusingly at Claudius. When old Hamlet rolls off the couch, the camera comes forward again to linger on the writhing hand, again located on the center line. A reaction shot shows Hamlet reaching forth and leaning down slightly, identifying his as the subjectivity focusing obsessively on the hand. Following this, we return to Hamlet's point of view. He is reaching desperately into the space of the murder, in which we can now see only the empty couch.[16] When the ghost warns, "nor let thy soul contrive / Against thy mother aught" (85–86), Hamlet again raises his ringed hand to his face, now to cover his eyes. Although one might be hard-pressed to pull all of these details into a coherent interpretation, they appear designed to tease us into questions relevant to Olivier's oedipal subtext. Do Claudius and Hamlet share the desire to usurp old Hamlet's marital position? Is Hamlet reaching out for his lost father or his father's ring? Is Hamlet's covering his eyes a denial of what contriving against his mother might mean—that is, is the gesture a defense against the ghost's paternal prohibition of "damned incest" (83), a prohibition that in Freudian terms involves the threat of castration and its most common upwardly displaced form, blinding?

If the visit of the ghost imparts essential new information that ushers in a second movement in which Hamlet will begin his revenge, Olivier's strongly Freudian interpretation complicates matters. Although the mission of the prince has been clarified, his internal conflict has also been enormously heightened. In the reading that Olivier adopted from Ernest Jones, the ghost's message has stirred up in Hamlet's unconscious the twin desires to possess his mother sexually and to kill the rival father: "The call of duty, which automatically arouses to activity these unconscious processes, conflicts with the necessity of 'repressing' them still more strongly; for the more urgent is the need for external action the greater is the effort demanded of the 'repressing' forces."[17] Hamlet's disabling ambivalence is immediately apparent in the actions that accompany his swearing to obey the ghost's request for revenge. Upon rising from his swoon, he picks up his sword and raises it in support of his promise to record the ghost's commandment "unmixed with baser matter" (1.5.104). But as Peter Donaldson observes, "At the climax of his vow, 'Yes, by heaven,' he throws his rapier down upon the stones, a gesture that registers his anger but also, like similar actions later in the film, leaves him without a weapon at the very moment when the idea of using one is strongest."[18]

The remainder of act 1, scene 5 that follows the ghost's exit incorporates this conflict into the film's "spatial articulation," the vertical dimension of which has been well explicated by Anthony Davies.[19] Hamlet must somehow manage to incorporate the ghostly demands now associated with the vertical into the action amidst the "baser matter" associated with the horizontal. His internal conflict produces hesitations and reversals. After shouting, "Yes, by heaven!" (104) while on his knees, instead of rising immediately he again falls prostrate, cursing his mother and stepfather before standing to finish his vow with eyes upturned. His eagerness to act upon the new information is visible in the rapidity of his flight down the tower stairs to the friends who wait below. But after beginning to confide in his companions, he changes course after looking upward while declaring, "There's never a villain in Denmark / But he's an arrant knave" (122–23). The ghost's "call of duty" again has aroused both knavish desires and the need to repress them. As the men descend successive stages of the battlements, they interact alternately in vertical arrays on the stairways and horizontal arrays on the landings, with vertical and horizontal camera placements, and with Hamlet alternately leading them downward and halting their descent. Hamlet responds to the ghost's command, "Swear" (149), which traditionally comes from the ghost under the stage, by looking upward. He casts one final glance up toward the tower before exiting into the horizontal world. The tower lingers on-screen for several seconds before fading to black.

The Second Movement

Olivier jettisons Polonius's interview with Reynaldo, moving directly to Ophelia's narration in act 2, scene 1 of her encounter in her closet with an apparently mad Hamlet. Rather than occurring as a report to her father, her voice-over narration is accompanied by a visualized flashback that represents a personal memory, suggesting that Hamlet's purpose is not to begin fooling the court with an assumed "antic disposition" but to clear psychological impediments to moving forward with his new mission. This interpretation is supported by the fact that Hamlet reenters the horizontal world at precisely the point where his traveling thought, represented by the camera tracking down the archway, had been blocked following the first soliloquy. He appears in Ophelia's doorway where Laertes had lingered earlier before entering. The parallel with Laertes makes his action more emphatically a farewell, although also a farewell without the expectation of return, while the transformation of his desiring thought into renunciation signals the change in Hamlet's mind-set occasioned by the ghost's revelations.

Hamlet's weakness evident in his vacillations following the ghost's visit and in his silent interaction with Ophelia is now countered by a portrayal of his opponents' weakness. The film leaps over the introduction of Rosencrantz and Guildenstern, evidence of clever royal scheming against Hamlet, and the return of the ambassadors, evidence of successful royal action against one of Hamlet's doubles, in favor of allowing Polonius to report on Hamlet's madness. The scene opens not with action to counter threats but with a slightly voyeuristic view of Claudius and Gertrude from behind, sitting closely together in a dark room, looking as if they are about to kiss. Accompanying the old counselor's ludicrously patterned oratorical "art" is a no less patterned and comical filmic art. Polonius's voice addressing "My liege and madam" (2.2.86) unexpectedly intrudes, and the two absorbed lovers move apart, allowing the buffoonish speaker to appear between them. The camera will return to this compromising configuration two more times. On the third instance, the old man's manipulation takes the form of pacing to the left, then to the right, then back to the left, while the camera tracks each time in the opposite direction, maintaining the royal point of view and the Polonian intrusion for over forty seconds. Such forced swiveling of the crowned heads by addled Polonius, played with comic brio by Felix Aylmer, undercuts the impression of royal power created by the first court scene. One feels now, with some relief, that even a Hamlet straining under the burden of oedipal ambivalence might stand a chance.

When Claudius inquires how they might test Polonius's theory of love madness, a high shot reveals Hamlet listening to the conversation in secret. Critics have generally assumed that Olivier follows John Dover Wilson's addition of an entry to the inner stage at line 159, thus affording Hamlet knowledge of both Polonius's plan to "loose" (2.2.162) his daughter and his theory that the prince is "from his reason fallen thereon" (165).[20] But unlike the stage, film does not require a defined entrance. The cut to Hamlet reveals him not entering but already present, and because we have not previously been afforded any view that would expose Hamlet's presence or absence, the viewer is free retroactively to suppose that his eavesdropping began at any point. Like the "seeing unseen" (3.1.32) camera behind the royal couple, Hamlet may have observed them on the brink of lovemaking, his nightmare scenario. Hearing Polonius observe that Hamlet often walks "here in the lobby" (2.2.158) cues him to enter as an actor on stage for Polonius's first attempt to test his madness. He can thus manipulate Polonius in the rest of the scene as an actor speaking from the raised platform on which he walks, with the implication that Polonius confuses dramatic role and reality, a joke at his expense to which Hamlet will return before the Mousetrap. In the nunnery scene, the possibility of his having seen and heard much more, including hearing that Ophelia "in her duty and obedience" (2.2.106) gave her father Hamlet's love letter, helps to motivate his extreme rage.

In the play, over four hundred lines separate Polonius's leaving Hamlet after his triplet on "Except my life" (2.2.212) from the instruction to Ophelia,

"Read on this book" (3.1.43), that begins the next test of Hamlet's madness. In the film, the latter line immediately follows the former, although Ophelia's entrance by means of a dissolve allows for the passage of any amount of time. This compression adds clarity in several ways. Ophelia's movement from her archway into the throne room recalls the two shots of the archway from Hamlet's point of view that frame the Ophelia-Laertes-Polonius material of act 1, scene 3. Recalling these emotionally charged shots evokes both Hamlet's desire for Ophelia and his subsequent anguish at her apparent betrayal. These emotions help to explain Hamlet's wild oscillations in the upcoming nunnery scene. The temporal proximity of Hamlet's pantomime in Ophelia's closet, the space from which she now enters in the same clothing a mere seven minutes of screen time later, helps to explain her severe distraction: she is unaware of her father's presence until his arm thrusts in with a book from the right edge of the screen.[21] Once Polonius and Claudius have hidden themselves within a curtained alcove, Hamlet returns through the same double doorway through which he exited. Polonius's second test thus follows hard upon the first and radically ups the emotional ante. We cannot be surprised when the self-control maintained throughout the first test finally collapses.

Hamlet realizes immediately upon his return that the second test is beginning. He glances about, checks the archway and adjoining room, even brushes his book across the curtain, causing Ophelia to react with visible guilt. He knows of the men's presence, and he can unquestionably discern from Ophelia's repeated awkward glances that she knows as well. Reducing the play's multiple possibilities for both characters' motives, the film implies that Hamlet has two deliberate intentions for the scene: primarily, to use the occasion to continue his guise of madness established in the first test and, secondarily, to continue the break with Ophelia that he had initiated in the closet scene. The clarity introduced through the unreported closet scene and Hamlet's overhearing Polonius's proposal in turn clarifies Hamlet's failure to sustain his plans. In the play, the eavesdropping scheme tests Polonius's love theory after Rosencrantz and Guildenstern were employed to test what Jan Blits calls Claudius's "ambition theory."[22] Hamlet passes this test well enough that the two "friends" can report no evidence that Hamlet's strange behavior is caused by disappointed ambition. The film omits the ambition test, but Hamlet manages nevertheless to fail it. He remains true to his intentions until asserting, "I could accuse myself of such things that it were better my mother had not borne me" (3.1.122–23). As the woman who gave him birth merges with the potential "breeder of sinners" (121) standing before him, Hamlet's discourse becomes not only cruel but also self-destructive. Against his own clear interest, he labels himself "revengeful, ambitious" (124), speaking the latter term with a raised voice directly at the hidden men. It is true, as in most productions of the play, that Hamlet's show of anger rises when Ophelia openly lies about her father's whereabouts, but the triggers for his two overt acts of violence are Ophelia's attempts to embrace him, as his mother did in the first court scene, before the ghost radically elevated what Jones calls "the effort demanded of the 'repressing' forces."

The film medium assists Olivier in intensifying Hamlet's violence. When he thrusts Ophelia down upon the stone prie-dieu, we hear two painful thuds timed to the fall of her arm and her head. The second time he pushes her down, the camera swings rapidly to follow her as her face lands upon the stone steps. As one early reviewer commented on the latter action, "[I]t is an act of physical violence that is more immediate and striking than it could be on a stage. It almost seems to be her main motive for going mad."[23] It is certainly one motive for her, but more important is that it reveals Hamlet's lapse into unfeigned madness. "It hath made me mad" (145–46) is announced convincingly while Hamlet stands pressed against the stone wall, rolling his head back and forth. Perhaps he redeems himself somewhat by tenderly kissing her hair before departing. Claudius and Polonius on reentering also deflect some viewer outrage away from Hamlet, for they all but ignore the weeping figure lying prostrate upon the stairs.

Olivier's oft-noted relocation of the "to be" speech to follow the nunnery scene sensibly allows the soliloquy's despair to follow what Kliman calls Hamlet's "lowest point, after Ophelia's betrayal of him," although one should add, following Jones, that "Hamlet is really expressing his bitter resentment against his mother."[24] The relocation also allows us to witness an astonishing emotional transformation. The energy driving Hamlet's disturbing outburst of violence is released in the famous climb of the camera up to the battlements. Leaving behind Ophelia on the lowest stairway, but after the second spiral providing a longer-distance view of her that contrasts her stasis with the rapid, one might say desperate, movement of Hamlet's mind, five ascents of spiral stairways are edited together in an accelerating rhythm echoed by William Walton's frenetic music. Each successive stairway is less dark than the previous, presenting an onrush upward into both light and freedom as the camera tilts above a final straight stairway toward the sky. The rise decelerates and is replaced by a tilt downward toward the sea, creating a realistic arc of emotional depletion that is well interpreted by Donaldson: "[T]he moment at which the camera movement reverses its ascent marks a transition from rage to depression."[25] Vertical movement ends with a special-effects insertion of Hamlet's head, seen from behind, from the bottom of the screen. The camera then enters into Hamlet's head and consciousness, as it did in the ghost scene.

The famous first line of the soliloquy is recited over a montage of unfocused and focused waves and an extreme close-up of Hamlet's eyes.[26] The latter images "to be," whereas a return of the former images its negation. From here, the speech divides into distinct segments. The first segment is speech mouthed as Hamlet sits on a stone merlon, isolated against the sky. The second begins at "to die: to sleep" (3.1.59), the point of his greatest temptation to seek oblivion. Having drawn his dagger, he closes his eyes and proceeds in voice-over. The appeal of ending "the heartache and the thousand natural shocks that flesh is heir to" (61–62) is conveyed through the arrival of slow music and a moving camera, which pushes in slowly to an extreme close-up of Hamlet's face. But now the "rub" intrudes suddenly. A harsh musical trill is followed by a return at "perchance to dream" (64) to the film style of the earlier segment: speech, no music, Hamlet isolated against the sky, an unmoving camera. Olivier delivers the soliloquy in its entirety but places special emphasis on ideas central to his overall interpretation: the heartache and fleshly shocks of the musical segment and, in the next segment, "the pangs of despised love" (72), a phrase highlighted by his looking directly into the camera. He eventually drops his dagger, perhaps signifying abandonment of the suicidal option. A cutaway to the weapon falling toward the sea occasions a cut back to a higher vantage affording our first view of the tower floor, a clearer foundation in reality. But then he walks first to its perilous edge at screen left, then to its back edge. Despite the speech's apparent resolution in inaction, Olivier maintains suspense to the end by showing Hamlet looking down as Walton's brooding strings reenter. The melancholy prince steps off the edge! But no, he is only descending a stairway that cannot be seen.

After a fade to black, we next see Hamlet as the very image of inaction and depression. Flickering light soon shown to be from the torch of approaching Polonius reveals that Hamlet is sitting in darkness in the familiar chair with his head down. Despite the ghost's visit, the repeated image implies, he has made no progress since first seen in the throne room. But his situation now changes quickly, for Polonius announces the arrival of the players, and Hamlet's response, "He that plays the King shall be welcome" (2.2.285), reveals that he has found a new course of action. Before three minutes of screen time pass, he has welcomed the players, arranged for the performance, and exultantly announced, "The play's the thing / Wherein I'll catch the conscience of the King" (2.2.539–40), reducing the long "rogue and peasant slave" soliloquy to its final one and one-half lines, which encapsulates the plan that will carry the film toward its central turning point. The lines are delivered as he twirls on a stage set up for the upcoming performance while Walton's horns perform a kind of fanfare. Following a fade, the performance is almost ready to begin. With the relocated nunnery scene and "to be" soliloquy behind him, Olivier can move the film briskly and directly toward the Mousetrap.

All that remains is to instruct the players. Given the extent of Olivier's deletions throughout the screenplay, and given the relocations that allow his second movement to end with such focus, the near-complete nature of Hamlet's wordy instructions is surprising. As in the play, it contributes little to Hamlet's real project of exposing Claudius. The only incident from the scene that remains memorable for most is an added visual business. Hamlet places a blond wig with braids upon the boy who will play the queen. Taken aback by the resemblance to Ophelia, he reveals once again that the two women in his life cannot be separated. This incident plays to Olivier's Freudian reading, but so may the larger insistence of Hamlet's theatrical obsession. Olivier has removed the two passages in which Hamlet expressed doubt about the ghost's veracity (beginning at 2.2.533 and 3.2.76), leaving his exact purpose in arranging the Mousetrap unclear. His source for this may be Jones, who argues, "That his pretext for arranging the play—to satisfy himself about Claudius's guilt and the ghost's honesty—is specious is plain from the fact that *before* it he had been convinced of both and was reproaching himself for his neglect." Jones borrows from Otto Rank the idea that for Hamlet as "a creature of highly charged imagination," the fictional killing on stage "is an equivalent for fulfilling his task."[27] Hamlet's obsession with dramatic naturalism might assist Olivier in making this suggestion. The crucial importance of the upcoming portrayal is again emphasized when Olivier pauses in meditation, his arms behind his back, at the center of the empty stage set up in the throne room, where he had danced his intention to catch the conscience of the king. He then moves forward to pause with identical posture before the thrones: he is an actor anticipating a performance, and the great enactment that he seems to be envisioning will somehow be acted by himself, in the theater and in the throne room.

With its fanfare, choreographed torchbearers, and stately procession down the curving stairway into the throne room, the play-within scene is the most elaborate show of royal power yet, best viewed as at once a statement and a defense by Claudius in response to the threat Hamlet now more clearly poses. The high stakes put both men on their best behavior at the start. Hamlet runs to his mother to escort her down, both broadly smiling, to her throne. Claudius courteously inquires how his "cousin" (3.2.88) fares, avoiding the offense of "son," to which Hamlet replies with a cryptic witticism that conveys an "antic disposition" rather than insults, if one judges by the visible reactions rather than by Shakespeare's words. Only with the visual juxtaposition of Gertrude and Ophelia's "metal more attractive" (106) does Hamlet's self-composure crack. His leading Ophelia off to sit in his familiar chair and his bawdy innuendos reasonably help him support the love theory of Polonius, but his pushing her down into the chair does not. A second time, looking from one woman to the other breaks his self-composure. Turning from Ophelia to Gertrude, with the bawdy thought of the "nothing" (114) between a maid's legs fresh in his thought, he points boldly and observes with raised voice, "how merrily my mother looks" (119–20, with "cheerfully" replaced by "merrily"). No one pays him heed, however, for the court's eyes are upon the center of power.

The Mousetrap, now reduced to its dumb-show component only, consists of eight shots dividable into three segments. The first segment consists of two long takes, the first including a crane-in to the player king and queen pantomiming their mutual love. With a cut to behind Horatio, who stands to the right of the stage, the first of a series of four semicircular tracking movements begins. The camera sweeps left behind Claudius and Gertrude, seated directly in front of the action, to behind Hamlet and Ophelia, who are seated to the left of the stage. It will soon return within the same shot in the other direction. Attention during these sweeps concentrates on (1) the action on stage, which is always kept in focus in the background; (2) the reactions of Claudius and to a lesser extent Gertrude, which shift from inattention on the first sweep, while Claudius kisses her hand, to rapt interest in the second, after Lucianus pours poison in the sleeping king's ear; and (3) the gazes of those observing Claudius, which in the first segment includes only Horatio and Hamlet, both of whom alternate between watching the action and the king. Textual cuts prevent an unfamiliar audience from hearing exactly what Hamlet's intention is in staging the play, but their close attention to the king's behavior throughout helps to indicate Hamlet's desire to "unkennel" his "occulted guilt" (3.2.76–77).

When the second sweep of the camera arrives behind the royal couple, who have both raised their hands, the second segment begins. This consists of five much shorter takes beginning with a cut from a view of the poisoning from behind Claudius, where the tracking camera has paused, to a frontal close-up of him. A closer shot of the stage represents his intensified interest and displays the poisoned king pointing accusingly at his murderer in near-exact imitation of the scene visualized by Hamlet during the ghost's narration. Three shots follow that show the spreading attention to Claudius through individual reactions. Two of these show Hamlet and Ophelia. Hamlet looks to the stage and then to Claudius, while Ophelia looks from the stage to Hamlet. Two shots later, she will allow Hamlet's redirected attention to redirect her own to Claudius. In between these shots, we see Horatio looking at the royals, followed by a courtier who then follows Horatio's gaze. The film's most elaborate use of the "deictic gaze," in which a look directs another's look, will culminate in all, characters and audience, sharing Claudius's second and final close-up.[28]

The third segment moves from individual to group perceptions. In a single take over a minute and a half long, the film's most complex and elegant camera movement brings the scene to a climax. Polonius comes forth to see what is wrong with the king. His movement attracts the gaze of the increasingly agitated crowd on Horatio's side, which is scanned in a pan to the left to Hamlet and the renewed action on stage as the queen reenters and finds her husband dead. A new semicircular track to the right continues past the royal couple as Lucianus comforts the stricken queen and attendants remove the body. Horatio's movement toward Claudius leads the camera in reverse until Hamlet and Horatio exchange glances. The camera turns toward the stage where the queen is succumbing to Lucianus's seduction and tracks back to watch the two exit arm in arm from between Claudius and Gertrude, who are seeing the very image of their overhasty marriage. The camera finally comes to rest upon Claudius and, significantly, Gertrude, who looks twice toward her son, with her hand raised in a gesture of apparent puzzlement. Is she seeking to understand his insult to her husband or the meaning of the romantic success of the nephew in the play, a potential declaration of her son's desire? Perhaps both. The effect on Claudius is less ambiguous. In close-up, we see a rich combination of earlier close shots: the terror of Bernardo, the defensively covered eyes that contrast with our earlier gazes deep into Hamlet's, even a repeat of the denial, so unnatural for facial close-ups, of our look into the ghost's hidden eyes. After the stricken king halts the play, Hamlet continues his provocation by waving a torch in his face with a mad laugh. Claudius's striking the torch, rather than his cry, "Give me some light" (261) is the real climax of the scene, accompanied by a tremendous orchestral "crash chord."[29]

This is masterful filmmaking, packing its four wordless minutes with evidence to ponder: Claudius kissing Gertrude on the hand as he did in his first court scene, suggesting that his confidence has been restored; the repeated intrusion between, and the repeated espial upon, the amorous royal couple seen from behind; Horatio's exchange of glances with Hamlet before the entry of Lucianus, suggesting the degree of Horatio's knowledge despite textual cuts removing this information; Polonius's inevitably counterproductive intervention to assist the stricken king; the powerful contagion of the gaze, first in close companions then spreading to the public; Gertrude thinking of Hamlet's role in the production when the widow is seduced. The repeated camera movements produce meaning through parallel and progression, but they are also gracefully varied: the second semicircular sweep is aborted halfway through by Claudius's terror; the fourth is begun by Horatio's motion and pirouettes toward the stage before continuing. Walton's music plays throughout, turning camera movement and the interactions among the courtiers into artful choreography, reinforcing parallels between characters (for example, first Ophelia behind Hamlet and then the courtier behind Horatio imitate their respective companion's gaze to the same notes), shifting at dramatic moments between implied stage music (despite the addition of an absent harpsichord) from the instrumentalists seated above the stage and the full symphony orchestra, and highlighting with sudden silence Claudius's moment of panic.

Into the film's longest take, with its stately and continuous camera movement, crashes a sequence of fifteen shots tumbled out within fifty seconds, the most rapid cutting of the entire film. Pandemonium ensues as the king flees up the stairway, courtiers escape in every direction, screaming women fall into one another's arms, all to a crescendo of Walton's frenetic music. This is overkill, and one might indeed wonder how the events just seen could produce such universal tumult, but the effect is to overturn thoroughly the elaborate impression of royal order and power with which the scene began. The music fades to reveal Hamlet singing madly. As the room clears, a craning camera rises from a position down within the panicked evacuees, who streak past it left and right, to reveal Hamlet perched atop a chair. It is not the king's throne, a commonly used sign of Hamlet's "repossession of the realm by its rightful owner,"[30] but the queen's chair, next to which lies the upturned chair of the king. Hamlet is clearly seeking a different object to repossess.

Hamlet and Horatio quickly agree on the ghost's veracity. Their conference is cut short when Polonius bustles in to combine his lines as a messenger with those of the deleted Rosencrantz and Guildenstern, announcing the king's choler and the queen's wish to speak to her son presently. Hamlet seems to use the conversation with the old counselor to catch his breath before confronting his next large task. He bids Horatio leave and stares strangely into the darkness with his back to the camera. Horatio remains standing silently for over ten seconds, an extraordinarily long time, perhaps wondering what his clearly unstable friend will do now or contemplating the need to intervene, before turning to go. Suspense has built again.

The Third Movement

Olivier's Freudian interpretation may have diluted the purpose of the Mousetrap and therefore obscured as well the breakthrough to new motivation for the third movement. But there is no question that Hamlet is newly motivated, having accomplished something with his success, even if it is not a matter, or solely a matter, of removing doubt about the ghost. His "witching time" soliloquy, delivered with much of Olivier's face in darkness, proclaims him newly ready to "drink hot blood, / And do such bitter business as the day / Would quake to look on" (3.2.380–82, modified). As Blits notices, after the Mousetrap in the play, "Claudius appears entirely absent from Hamlet's thought. Hamlet is thinking of Nero the matricide. He is thinking of revenging his mother's shame, not his father's murder."[31] Claudius's absence is even stronger in the film. In the play, although Rosencrantz and Guildenstern deliver the message from the queen, they are more clearly agents of Claudius and in act 3, scene 2 again seek to test his ambition theory. This shameless manipulation provokes Hamlet to the fury of his speech on plucking out the heart of his mystery. The sycophants' absence from the film, and the resulting absence as well of the king's plotting with them to send Hamlet to England in act 3, scene 3 immediately after the soliloquy, strengthens the focus on Hamlet and his mother.

Shakespeare, of course, places Claudius's soliloquy in no particular room. Olivier locates the "prayer scene" in the chapel of stage tradition, identifiable by a statue of Jesus upon an altar. The implication that the king's response to the Mousetrap is not murderous action but attempted prayer elevates him morally. In contrast, the treatment of Hamlet in the scene brings out the moral horror of his hellish sentiments. The instability in Hamlet that we saw rising in the Mousetrap scene, where he could maintain composure only briefly, continues to rise in the third movement. Olivier solves the problem of providing Hamlet with a weapon after the weaponless Mousetrap scene by having him pull a thin dagger from a hiding place at his back. The effect is sinister and adds menace to his vow to "speak daggers" to his mother "but use none" (3.2.386), which now appears more a desperate attempt to persuade himself than a clear statement of his intention. As he raises the dagger over the kneeling king, the camera moves forward to remove Claudius from view and place Jesus in the conventional over-the-shoulder position of filmed dialogue. The camera setup implies an exchange of views, but something very different occurs. Hamlet looks up to the face of Jesus, and in a remarkable discordance between what is seen and the message of his voice-over soliloquy, his reconsideration looks like the Christian forgiveness that his choice of a "more dark intent" (3.3.87, modified) of sending the king's soul to hell utterly contradicts. His calm tone adds to the discordance. As Dale Silviria comments, "the absolute sanity of Olivier's voice may even heighten by contrast Hamlet's warped reasoning."[32] The unexpected dagger and the enhanced shock of the meditation, which even without such enhancement has been frequently expunged from productions that cannot accept such a vicious Hamlet, continues building suspense for the closet scene.

Having ignored the missing but implied counsel of a charitable Christ, Hamlet proceeds upward on a spiral stairway, preceded ominously by his shadow. Appropriately for his oedipal approach, Olivier turns the Folio's "Mother, mother, mother" (3.4.5) into his most nuanced triplet. From within the queen's closet, which has now become a luxurious bedroom, with Polonius and Gertrude we first hear a naturalistic, interrogatory address offscreen. Hamlet's second "mother" is a strangely automatic, almost hypnotic repetition that we watch him speak. For the third, Olivier drops the interrogatory inflection and speaks with lower volume as if to himself, implying reflection upon an intensely charged term and relationship.

The first part of the closet scene emphasizes the suddenness of Hamlet's impulsive violence. Hamlet enters as a large silhouetted shape poised in the doorway and dwarfing the deep-focus figure of vulnerable Gertrude in the background. His face is not seen until he throws her violently onto the bed, replacing the menace of graphic composition with the more real threat of action and an angry visage. The dagger, which he carried almost invisibly on his forearm up the stairway, appears suddenly in his hand. Its blade then hovers menacingly above her white throat from Hamlet's point of view, in a high shot that makes it appear closer than it is, adding realism to her question, "Thou wilt not murder me" (3.4.20). With the cry of Polonius from behind the arras, Hamlet's demeanor becomes demonic. Slight jump cuts speed the violent action. In the first, the dagger shifts from left to right hand with dazzling speed before he thrusts it almost into the camera lens. He turns his head very slowly back toward Gertrude, but at "Is it the King?" (24), a cut to Gertrude's point of view reveals Hamlet's face raised higher than before the cut, heightening his sense of wild exaltation as he stands before the arras. His blade has pierced the chest of a king woven into the arras, the image of Hamlet's mad hope. He stands holding the dagger in the king's chest for over half a minute, obviously relishing the long-awaited moment of revenge. When he removes it and Polonius tumbles toward the floor, in a movement almost too rapid to be recognized Hamlet reaches his right arm forward and then pulls it back again. The blade visually sweeps across the neck of Polonius, suggesting a beheading, either intended but then aborted or a more symbolic image of Hamlet's urges.[33] But of course this is the wrong victim for such an image of oedipal castration, and perhaps for this reason Hamlet tosses down his dagger.

The action shifts to the enormous bed, with Hamlet and Gertrude framed by the suggestive drapery first seen some eighty minutes earlier. Hamlet forces her to compare the images of the two brothers on his and her lockets. When he waxes enthusiastic about "what a grace was seated on this brow" (53), Gertrude's eyes turn in desire from the image of her former husband to the graceful brow of her son. As his rage moves him to envision the gross act of sex, "honeying and making love / Over the nasty sty" (91–92), Gertrude resorts to physically embracing him. The eroetic narrative that has increasingly posed questions about Gertrude does so again: is this a desperate act of defense, a yielding to desire, or both? The soundtrack heartbeat that has twice before signaled the ghost's arrival now accompanies Hamlet's lapse into silence—and Gertrude's most unmistakable look of desire. The effect is highly ambiguous. Does the throbbing beat, which is not accompanied as before with oscillating focus, indicate the ghost's arrival or Hamlet's arousal? Is Gertrude's desire stimulated by Hamlet's arousal or the presence of her former husband, whose image she earlier projected onto her son? He pushes her away and leaves the bed. Is it out of disgust with her desire, or with his, or is it the presence of the ghost?

Definitive answers are never provided, for Olivier has found highly innovative ways to blur the line between an objective and a subjective ghost. Hamlet's fall to the floor, recalling the earlier effect of the ghost on him, and additional sound effects from the ghost scenes tell us that the ghost is present, but in what sense, since now we cannot see it? The ghost's apparent point of view is present, coinciding with the camera, as it and we look from Hamlet to Gertrude and back again. But the gaze is exchanged only with Hamlet, as if only he can look upon himself with the ghost's eyes, for even when Hamlet points and demands, "Look you how pale he glares" (121), Gertrude does not look into the camera. When we return to Hamlet's point of view, a very pale shape is discernible in a doorway, but in a remarkable pan to Gertrude followed by a track to her point of view, when the doorway becomes visible again—after Hamlet has looked to her but before she looks up to the doorway—the shape is not there. Conventionally, one would expect a cut to separate the points of view. By keeping the shot continuous and making Hamlet's look away correspond to the ghost's visual but not aural disappearance, Olivier maintains as much confusion as possible.

The remainder of the interview illustrates a new alliance of mother and son but clears up nothing about the ghost's status. Suddenly and unexpectedly, after the emotional traumas of the killing, the torture of Gertrude, and the ghost's visit, Hamlet exudes sanity. Speaking calmly and persuasively, he immediately convinces Gertrude that not his madness but her "trespass" (144) speaks. She walks away in repentance, but for what: her relationship with Claudius or with Hamlet? The answer is both. From this point on, she appears to accept his request, "go not to my uncle's bed" (161), but she also makes efforts to avoid the trespass of desiring her son too sexually. Her behavior becomes more appropriately maternal, at least until Hamlet for the first time initiates a lingering kiss, while the camera begins but soon abandons a conventional lovers' circling movement.[34] As Mills notices, after the ghost departs, "all the embracing and kissing is not only passionless but stylized, rather like the love-making of characters in a classical ballet. Hamlet's desire for his mother remains securely locked in his unconscious mind."[35] A similar statement must be made about Gertrude.

Hamlet's return to sanity continues as Olivier jumps over act 4, scenes 1 and 2. Olivier opts to avoid any indication of wildness at this point, precisely to make its effect more powerful when madness returns. After calmly bidding his mother goodnight, Hamlet next appears with Claudius, who is seeking the location of the body. His witty discourse on "how a king may go a progress through the guts of a beggar" (4.3.29–30) is highly controlled, the most clearly feigned effort at putting on an antic disposition since his conversation with Polonius in act 2, scene 2. At a key moment, however, this "calculated blandness" ends and "the grieved insane face from the earlier, interpolated scene in Ophelia's chamber returns."[36] Hamlet says "Farewell, dear mother" provocatively to the king's face, but with his rejoinder, "Thy loving father, Hamlet" (4.3.48), dangerous instability replaces witty discourse. Hamlet shakes his head, the bell tolls the time as it had at the recent disappearance of the ghost, and the camera tracks in for a close-up of the sweating face of the prince.[37] The combination of chimes, track to close-up, and radical shift in demeanor also conspicuously echoes the pattern of interchange with his companions after Hamlet's original interview with the ghost. Such powerful connections explain, to the extent that cinematic elements can, why he completes his riddle, "Father and mother is man and wife. Man and wife is one flesh—so my mother" (49–50), while performing a choking motion with his hands. Hamlet departs for England and will not be seen again in Denmark for fifteen long minutes of screen time. The viewer's curiosity about how this unstable hero will act on his return has been piqued.

In the play, the king's initial reactions to the murder of his counselor include puzzlement over Gertrude's sighs, fear that the bloody deed "will be laid to us" (4.1.17), and a soul "full of discord and dismay" (45). Eliminating all of this weakness, Olivier shows a more formidable crisis manager who patiently bears Hamlet's insults and efficiently dispatches him to England. His soliloquy ordering "the present death of Hamlet" (4.3.63) from afar is delivered with calm determination, leaving us with a picture of murderous resolve that includes none of Hamlet's instability or indecision. The camera flies out his window then rises to the black wall above him. A fade-in transitions from self-assured evil to fragile innocence as the script jumps over Hamlet's view of the army of Fortinbras in act 4, scene 4 and goes straight to Ophelia's madness.

A flower floats in a "glassy stream" (4.7.165). Ophelia, revealed by her reflection, bends down to pick it up. Her image disappears as she rises, a scream pierces the serenity, and a cut reveals Ophelia writhing in anguish until a slight smile crosses her face and she dashes off, running across a log bridging the stream. The images are somewhat cryptic, but one might infer that Ophelia is terrified by the sudden disappearance of her reflected image. A dissolve to the familiar interior of her room reveals her rushing down a rustic path toward it. After running through the room, she turns down the familiar archway and halts in the large hall beyond. What is she seeking that might fill the terrifying void? Gertrude and Horatio may well ask the same question, as they look to where Ophelia is looking. It must be Hamlet, because she is completing the trajectory of desire blocked by her father after Laertes' departure and reversing the blocked, then finally completed, trajectory of Hamlet when he appeared, mad, as she was sewing in her closet.

Hamlet, however, is not there. Seeing that his chair stands empty through the next archway (returned to the position from act 1 after its altered position

at the Mousetrap, as symbolism trumps naturalism), she halts before entering the throne room. Shakespeare's first mad scene's equivocating on the twin
causes of Ophelia's grief, both her father's death and absent Hamlet's "death,"
is maintained. Polonius as cause is stressed through the deletion of the erotic
Saint Valentine song and the postponement of the no less erotic "By Gis and
by Saint Charity" (4.5.58), but the balance is tipped in Hamlet's favor by the
film's use of a setting to which have accrued powerful associations.

These associations, of course, are not possessed by Gertrude, but they add
nevertheless to our sense that Hamlet is on her mind as well. After Ophelia
and Horatio depart, Claudius attempts to embrace his wife, but she declines
and walks toward the stairway on the left. He seeks sympathy with the litany
of sorrows that "come not single spies, / But in battalions" (4.5.78–79) and
tries once more to embrace her, but she remains unresponsive. Her reaction
allows Olivier to improve on a problematic Shakespearean reference. "O my
dear Gertrude," he moans, "this, / Like to a murdering-piece in many places /
Gives me superfluous death" (94–96). "This" can now refer to the queen's cold
shoulder rather than the return of Laertes, the climactic "sorrow" of Shakespeare's list but less central to the film, with its emphasis on oedipal rivalry
and familial stories at the expense of politics and the larger social context.
The king receives another blow when Osric arrives with letters from Hamlet,
layering his presence once again onto the scene. A long shot graphically divides the frame using two diverging stairways as the queen and king read their
respective letters, which in the play arrive two scenes later and may or may
not be seen by the queen. In a more decisive split, Gertrude proceeds up her
stairway alone. Claudius turns in sorrow to proceed up his.

The story turns back to Ophelia, gathering flowers outside her room
while being watched by Horatio, who stands in her doorway in imitation of
both Laertes and Hamlet, perhaps to help us keep both young men and their
parallels in mind. The sailors who have just brought the divisive letters to the
royal couple have one for him also. Hamlet's story of rescue by the pirates
is another irised tableau scene, read silently by Horatio, spoken by Hamlet,
with the events portrayed visually. In the film's series of four such tableaux,
Ophelia's is subjective, allowing Hamlet's mad actions to be presented without disclosure to Polonius; Hamlet's vision of his father's death is originally
presented as subjective as well, but Claudius's response to its close re-presentation
in the Mousetrap also renders it objective; Hamlet's letter to Horatio is unambiguously objective, preparing the way for an equivalent depiction of Ophelia's
death, the play's strangest, most unaccountable narration. It is too poetic not

to be spoken, but it has also invited a wealth of visual depictions. Olivier will allow it to be both seen and told without confusingly implying that it is Gertrude's private vision.

As soon as Horatio finishes perusing the letter, the faint sound of Ophelia singing "By Gis and by Saint Charity" echoes in the hallway. As Horatio and the pirates—identifiable from within the tableau—depart, Ophelia makes her final trip down the corridor of desire toward Hamlet's chair. Now, however, additional voices precede our sight of their sources. Returned Laertes, shorn of his Shakespearean mob of supporters but not of his anger, is demanding answers about his father's death from Claudius. Ophelia's trajectory toward Hamlet's chair is diverted by their presence until she enters the throne room to caress her absent lover's face and lay rosemary "for remembrance" (4.5.169) on the arm of his chair. Diverting the gift of rosemary from its more conventional recipient, Laertes (though the play does not actually specify who receives which flowers), Ophelia is allowed to tell absent Hamlet, "Pray you, love, remember" (170), in an uncanny recall of the ghost's parting words. Her rue then is received by the queen, reminding us of the rueful bond between them as the film's relentlessly doubled object of Hamlet's desire. "You must wear your rue with a difference" (175–76) brings Gertrude to tears, because she knows that is all too true.

Ophelia collapses at her archway entrance, telling herself, "Go to thy death-bed," and bemoaning that "He never will come again" (186). After repeated journeys in the opposite direction, both desired and achieved, she for the only time walks outward through her corridor. The camera follows, offering a purely cinematic kind of closure by repeating precisely its motion carrying Hamlet's thought in act 1, scene 2. The movement of Hamlet's desire is ironically completed as Ophelia goes to her death. Along with a richly orchestrated variation of Ophelia's theme, the camera carries us to a final, poignant view of the room.

By transposing the long plotting between Claudius and Laertes in act 4, scene 7 to after the graveyard scene, Olivier can complete his third movement with continuous attention to poor Ophelia's fate. The empty room dissolves into the glassy stream as Gertrude's voice narrates. At "When down her weedy trophies and herself / Fell in the weeping brook" (4.7.172–73), the camera tracks slowly right to look for her. When it finds her, floating toward the left, she is singing, "How should I your true love know" (4.5.23), her first song in the play. The camera tracks in but halts as she looks into it before floating offscreen. The last we see of her is her hand making a slight grasping motion, another instance of the film's "motif of the extended hand" used to link scenes of loss.[38] Her garlands follow downstream, drawing the camera into a leftward movement that ends where the scene began, but Ophelia is nowhere in sight. The disappearance foreshadowed in her reflection scene and again in the camera's sad final look into her empty room has been fulfilled.

The Fourth Movement

The "weeping brook" (4.7.173) of Ophelia's drowning dissolves appropriately into a tall cross in a cemetery. The tone of the first part of the film's grave-yard scene, however, is anything but funereal. Olivier jettisons all of the first 110 lines of act 5 except the songs, eliminating both the clowns' debate over Ophelia's death and Hamlet's bitter lament on the vanity of life, which makes his own bones "ache to think on't" (5.1.87–88). Placed in immediate proximity to Ophelia's final song, the gravedigger's gaily sung lyric about youthful love becomes a comic counterpoint to it. Accompanying the gravedigger's playfulness is playful camera work: delayed disclosure of the song's origin until the camera descends into the grave; dirt tossed from the grave over the camera, which recoils upward in response; the intrusion of Hamlet's shadow, its head darkening the skull on the ground. The shadow might be seen as importing the morbid mood of his arrival in the play's final act, but lightly indeed.

Hamlet's last appearance before being shipped off to England primes the viewer to watch for signs of his mental instability. They are only slight and teasing here. Hamlet's badinage over the ownership of the grave is not a continuation of his morbidity, as it can easily be read in the play. It reveals, rather, a previously unwitnessed capacity to employ his formidable wit without malicious subtext. Even benevolent and sensible Horatio joins in the fun, taking over two of Hamlet's punning lines (5.1.117–19) and uncharacteristically initiating action by sitting at the grave's edge to extend the enjoyable conversation, after which Hamlet joins him. When the gravedigger mentions Hamlet's madness, the prince's voice develops a slight edge and rises in volume. At this point Horatio begins watching his reactions almost continuously, seconding our intensified scrutiny, but Hamlet changes the subject and is soon contemplating Yorick's skull. He delivers the famous "Alas, poor Yorick" (beginning at line 174) speech in its entirety in a single unmoving take, his slight smile indicating more amusement at recalling Yorick's infinite jest than sadness over mortality. Upon recalling "He hath bore me on his back a thousand times," Hamlet turns the skull around, as if entering into the moment from long ago.

Dirt falls from within the skull, occasioning "and now how abhorred in my imagination it is. My gorge rises at it," but a slight laugh and his continuing cheerful demeanor belie his words. At "Now get you to my lady's chamber," Hamlet waxes yet more playful, holding the skull to his cheek and turning his eyes mischievously to an unseen listener. Because a listener in Hamlet's eyeline has not been accounted for by the mise-en-scène, one might well wonder what effect the reference to "my lady" is having on a man for whom women often trigger psychic disruptions. But a cut reveals that Hamlet has been looking at the gravedigger, who has climbed offscreen from the grave. This is Hamlet at his most stable in the entire film.

At the peal of a bell, the men quickly conceal themselves to observe an approaching procession. Hamlet's desire not to be seen suggests that his revenge plot remains intact. This suggestion is supported by his monkish attire, a disguise that works, for the gravedigger will appear shocked when Hamlet identifies himself. It is also supported by his apparent concealment of his return from all but Horatio; the content of his letter to the king, which announces his imminent return in the play (4.7.43–46), is left undisclosed in the film. Horatio borrows more lines from Hamlet, concluding from the meager rites that a suicide is being buried. This realization causes Horatio to grasp Hamlet urgently with both hands. Even when Hamlet says "Mark" and points toward the gravesite, the eyes of spellbound Horatio remains fixed on Hamlet. Having witnessed Ophelia's madness and now deduced that the corpse is hers, his intense concern is the effect this will have on his unstable friend. Hamlet learns of Ophelia's death only when angry Laertes declares to the churlish priest, "A ministering angel shall my sister be / When thou liest howling" (5.1.230–31). He remains hidden, with the assistance of Horatio's physical restraint, until Laertes throws himself into the grave.

Once the corpse has been lowered into the ground, the central competition of the play and film begins anew. Gertrude's declaration, "I hoped thou shouldst have been my Hamlet's wife" (233), provokes Laertes' angry outburst against "that cursed head" (236), as the competition is taken up by surrogates. Viewed from a high shot that takes in the whole funeral party encircling the gravesite, Laertes' leap into the grave produces a remarkably strong reaction. As if shocked by sacrilege, the women turn away and attempt to depart, while the priest backs away from the grave in horror and makes the sign of the cross. Even the irreverent gravedigger beats a hasty retreat, covering his eyes! Impressively, Claudius reverses the motion of the entire party with a commanding hand gesture. Hamlet counters with his own impressive entrance.

"What is he whose grief / Bears such an emphasis?" (244–45) is shouted from offscreen. He enters with arms spread across nearly the entire frame and declares, "This is I Hamlet the Dane" (246–47). If the question is directed at Laertes, the declaration, with its implied claim to the throne, is a response to the visual demonstration of power by Claudius. Is it as well a suicidal gesture of sacrifice, inspired by the gravestone crucifixion scene placed conspicuously between Hamlet and the burial?

Laertes immediately attacks the man he holds responsible for his family's destruction, affording Claudius another opportunity to display his power. Ordering "Pluck them asunder" (253), he raises his right hand commandingly, repeating the gesture with which he declared Hamlet "most immediate to our throne" (1.2.109) so long ago. With the gesture, he not only responds to Hamlet's impetuous entrance but also takes on the roles of both a royal and a film "director" of the motion of everyone present, including the camera, which pans toward the struggling men and simultaneously tracks backward to watch the conflict from the king's point of view. The snarling contempt Hamlet displays for the man he knows he has wronged, and his claim to "rant as well" (273) as Laertes, amply justifies Gertrude's evaluation that "this is mere madness." He finally comes to his senses sufficiently to direct his parting threat, "and dog will have his day" (281), to Claudius. Literally unmoved, the king quickly asks Horatio to wait upon the prince. More imperiously, with a carefully chosen modifier, he does not ask but orders Gertrude, "set some watch over *your* son" (285).

As the gravesite clears, Claudius remains standing backed by the tall cross that opened the scene. Directly between him and the camera kneels Laertes, weeping into the grave. Donaldson comments that "Laertes's submission to his grief becomes, through this placement an implicit submission to the king, to whom he also seems to kneel."[39] The configuration also precisely echoes that of the ghost and kneeling Hamlet on the battlement, implying that the submission by the orphaned young man might become filial as well. Claudius indeed quickly moves to define his role as paternal. Placing his hand on the grieving man's shoulder, he leads Laertes toward the castle while explaining that two "special reasons" (4.7.10), Gertrude's love and the affection of the people, have prevented his proceeding against Hamlet. With the transposing of this explanation from the fourth act, from right after Ophelia's madness to after her death, it is received by a Laertes even more desperate for revenge. Unsure perhaps whether the king's explanation means that he will have to act on his own, he halts outside the castle door and converts his speech beginning "And so have I a noble father lost; / A sister driven to a desperate end" (4.7.26–27, modified), into a soliloquy delivered while overlooking the cemetery. As he enters the castle vowing to himself, "But my revenge will come" (30), he is startled to hear his new noble father-figure reply, "Break not your sleeps for that" (31).

The cunning manipulation of Laertes signaled by this unconventional overhearing of a soliloquy continues unabated. Servants are waiting in the throne room with two chalices in hand, as if the interview was prearranged rather than the spontaneous result of unexpected events at the burial. Claudius directs the young man to Polonius's chair. He thus at once adopts Laertes as his son and appoints the younger man chief counselor. The king's unusually casual sitting posture, leaning forward with his feet up, establishes a disarming intimacy while he confides his bold plan to murder Hamlet with "no wind of blame" (4.7.64), overcoming both "special reasons" for delay. When Laertes requests to be the instrument, they drink as if toasting their collusion, with the king's movement instantly followed by Laertes.

The atmosphere grows so friendly and personal that Claudius rises from his throne for the only time without his audience feeling obliged to rise with him. He flatters by reporting praise of Laertes' swordsmanship and Hamlet's envy, then walks to Hamlet's familiar chair at the end of the table, where he presents his boldest challenge: "Laertes, was your father dear to you? / Or are you like the painting of a sorrow, / A face without a heart?" (106–08). The visually reinforced comparison of the man sitting in his murdered father's chair with Hamlet, who has demonstrated with deadly force how dear his father was to him, is a master stroke. One might even recall the first court scene, where Laertes paused before Hamlet sitting in this precise spot after hearing Claudius lecture him on "filial obligation." As Blits describes the king's tactics, he "challenges Laertes as the Ghost challenged Hamlet (1.5.23). He makes revenge for his father a test of his filial love."[40] Both young men will rise to the challenge, to their mutual destruction, but in imitating the brother he murdered, Claudius will, ironically, also suffer his brother's fate. A more complex irony arises when Claudius appears to notice the rosemary branch left by Ophelia just before moving away from the chair. Neither Claudius nor Laertes observed her leave it, and neither knows that while doing so she imitated the ghost's request to "remember." Claudius is unwittingly imitating her imitation, while Laertes is unwittingly substituting himself for Hamlet in obeying the command to remember by avenging Ophelia's death. With perhaps surprising deftness, Olivier explores the paradoxical nature of revenge, revealing his plotters positioning themselves to self-destruct as they destroy their enemy.[41]

Olivier's handling of the spatio-temporal aspects of the narrative is no less deft than his handling of the dark psychology of revenge. The fourth, climactic movement of a film will often accelerate the action. Olivier allows necessary time to pass but creates a strong sense of onrushing events. The details of the plot against Hamlet are hatched in a series of three bold crane-out shots that recall the crane-in over the same space before the first throne scene—the film is bringing its beginning into its end. Each crane-out is of nearly the same duration, but each moves the camera considerably higher and farther than the previous, producing an accelerating triplet. Davies offers an enlightening interpretation: "While Hamlet is not visually present in this complex shot, there is a suggestion at this advanced point in the action that the camera-narrator is showing us a conspiracy and giving us the point of view in height and distance which would be closest to Hamlet's own. We are shown what we would like Hamlet to know, and from the elevated and distanced position from which we believe Hamlet would view it."[42] The sequence creates not only a wish that Hamlet know of the conspiracy but also an expectation that he will overhear the plot as he earlier, from an angle and height identical to that of the first crane shot's ending, overheard the plot to "loose" Ophelia to him. The first crane-out thus disappoints, the camera's second attempt to satisfy our wish for Hamlet to know disappoints again, and the third renews hope when it transforms into a tracking shot along an upper corridor, leaving the plotters below. The continuous tracking that soon reveals Hamlet entering from an outdoor stairway implies continuity in space and time, feeding our hopes, but as Hamlet and Horatio begin a desultory conversation on Fortune at a window, we are again disappointed. We have been kept off balance by the illusion of continuous camera motion, which suppressed perception of cues that space and time have not remained continuous: an apparent shadow on the wall that turns the screen momentarily black to hide a cut, Hamlet's change of costume from the monkish robe of the graveyard scene. The residual impression that Hamlet has just missed discovering the deadly conspiracy being hatched by Claudius and Laertes—an impression unerasable even if gradually dawning details allow our better understanding to reject it—lends irony to his tender concern that he "forgot" (5.2.75, in Folio) himself in being insensitive to Laertes' grief.

Hamlet's conversation with Horatio takes place, it turns out, much higher than the deceptive tracking camera implied. Osric's arrival begins the descent phase of the film's final "inverted parabola."[43] As the three men enter a stairway, the camera's new position reveals the sky above the walls; Hamlet and Horatio entered this exterior space from a higher exterior. Where were they? On High Tor? Now they descend four more flights of stairs, pausing repeatedly to allow Osric to complete his wordy message that the king has proposed a contest with Laertes. The multiple stairways recall the "to be" soliloquy, while the conversation conducted at repeated stops of the descent recalls the aftermath of the second ghost scene. Both associations foreshadow another momentous event at odds with Osric's buffoonery. Osric's business comes to an end at the top of a stairway leading to the great hall, down which he tumbles at once painfully and comically. A trumpet fanfare reveals that a scene surprisingly revealed to be not continuous with the conspiracy is now surprisingly continuous with the "immediate trial" (5.2.149).

The royal arrival down the great curving staircase is shot from a nearly identical camera location as the arrival in the Mousetrap scene. The procession moves in step with the same Walton march music, a semidiegetic performance that could be played by Elsinore's musicians had Olivier chosen to place a royal consort on screen. The emphatic audiovisual echo underscores both the similarities between the two scenes and their differences. If the courtly splendor of the Mousetrap scene was an assertion of royal power in the face of Hamlet's threat, Claudius now has, of course, much more reason for such an assertion. There is also the added pleasure of talion, eye-for-an-eye revenge. The king's original plan, "an exploit, now ripe in my device" (4.7.63), was that Laertes symmetrically "requite" (4.7.137) Hamlet with the unbated sword. Only after Laertes added the idea of poisoning the tip did Claudius pile on with still another application of his own favored method of homicide. Claudius may relish the prospect of requiting Hamlet with a performance in the great hall, and indeed both he and Laertes will play their hypocritical roles to perfection, nearly hoisting the prince on his own petard. Only Gertrude will see through her husband's marvelously feigned courtesy. That she does results from another crucial difference underscored by similarity. Gertrude's continuing estrangement is signaled immediately: Claudius leads the procession with Laertes in hand; Gertrude follows in the place of Ophelia, whose madness contributed to her estrangement; Hamlet escorts his mother to a throne set farther apart from the king's. It is not surprising that Gertrude, who early in the film looked lovingly into her husband's eyes, now avoids eye contact with him, until a crucial moment.

Hamlet's apology to Laertes is delivered with the utmost possible sincerity.[44] More than most Hamlets, Olivier's unstable prince can avoid the charge of cynicism in declaring that his madness rather than Hamlet himself was to blame. He stands in the same relation to Laertes and the camera that he stood at the gravesite when he contemptuously declared, "I'll rant as well as thou" (5.1.273), in a speech preceded by the king's and followed by the queen's pronouncing him mad. His current speech contrasts so markedly with the previous one, however, that sincerity is less at issue than how one might respond to an apologist who could make such a reversal. Perhaps understandably, Laertes deviates from the play and makes no reply. Fascinated, Claudius does not take his eyes off Hamlet while he speaks. Nor, of course, do we. The rapt court erupts in applause. Gertrude rewards her son by allowing two kisses upon her cheeks and momentarily teasing us with the possibility of a kiss on the mouth. Claudius now locks his gaze on his wife for a long eighteen seconds. His two fixed gazes suggest that he understands that he now confronts a son and a mother united against him.

It is now Claudius's turn to display his formidable acting skills. His promise to reward Hamlet's success in the early bouts and his ceremonious drinking meet with the evident approval of all, including Hamlet and Horatio, who appears to beam proudly at his royal friend at the idea of his receiving a pearl "Richer than that which four successive kings / In Denmark's crown have worn" (5.2.250–51). The unusually attentive viewer, or more likely the repeat viewer, might notice that Gertrude looks down briefly at the mention of the cup, but the unambiguous clues that she discerns her husband's intent remain to be shown.

When the two men face off in the preliminary ritual, a close-up of the opposed sword-points confirms that Laertes possesses the unbated sword. The close-up serves two purposes: it explains *unbated* for those unfamiliar with the term, while the rare and momentary removal of deep focus confirms as well that the camera's view is privileged, its perception of the points unavailable to all other spectators, who are relegated to the blurry background. The sword is quickly revealed to be Laertes' only advantage, for the first bout—shot in a long take with a high camera that keeps both men in constant view for comparison—establishes that Hamlet is the more skilled swordsman, despite Laertes' reputation.

In the play, it is probable that Laertes, the superior fencer, strategically toys with Hamlet in the first two bouts, provoking Hamlet's charges, "you do but dally" (280) and "you make a wanton of me" (282).[45] Laertes then probably wounds him in the third, after a suspenseful event of some kind—locked weapons, perhaps—that occasions Osric's adjudication, "Nothing neither way" (284). By allowing himself to fully display the expertise developed during his already long theatrical career, equalizing the opponents, Olivier creates additional opportunities for masterful cinematic storytelling. On Hamlet's winning the first bout, Claudius moves forward what he called his "back or second" plan (4.7.151). Hamlet's skillful performance explains why. In the play, he orders a servant to give Hamlet the poisoned cup. In the film, he first walks to the opposite side of the playing floor, where the wine is stationed. This movement places him in full view of Gertrude, who remains seated on her throne. He drops the pearl into the cup only after drinking from it, and in a highly dramatic manner that elicits the film's loudest cheers from the court. A track-in toward him makes visible a quick eye movement to his right, away from Hamlet toward Gertrude. A cut to Gertrude looking in his direction suggests that he is seeking the queen's reaction, which he would hope to be favorable. She, however, immediately looks down, at once continuing her refusal of eye contact and repeating more emphatically her first, fleeting thoughtful glance. Hamlet prefers not to drink before the bout. He directs the servant bearing the cup toward the side where his mother sits. Osric, an active conspirator with the king, unwittingly undermines his master by placing the cup-bearer next to the queen.

Only a few seconds of the much longer second bout are shown. The camera tracks through the fencers toward Gertrude to watch the real drama unfold. She turns slowly to contemplate the chalice and then turns back. After another glimpse of the fight, the only such shot from her point of view and one that places us deeper within her subjectivity at this crucial moment, she repeats the motion in a closer shot as the bout ends. It is enough. She knows and proceeds to create a new place for herself in the performance tradition. To allow Hamlet to wipe his brow, she places her napkin on the old servant's arm and relieves him of the chalice. By the time the servant ends his obscuring pass between the queen and our gaze, she is drinking the fatal liquid. She replies to the king's desperate command not to drink by saying that she will, but in fact she already has.

Rather than momentarily interrupting the third bout with the judgment of a nonhit, Olivier interprets the judgment as the bout's official end. Applause and the semidiegetic march that marked the pause between the second and third bouts now mark another hiatus between combats. The three conspirators exchange glances, appearing unsure how to proceed, until the king turns his head toward Hamlet. Laertes turns slowly to look at grim-faced Osric, who offers no assistance. His turn recalls the queen's toward the cup, indicating another fatal choice.[46] Obeying the king's implicit order, he lunges while

Hamlet stands conversing with Horatio, who holds the defenseless prince's rapier and dagger, and slices his arm. The music peters out, as if the invisible musicians share the universal shock.

A series of dazzling visual effects follows. In the action conveyed in the stage direction "in scuffling they change rapiers" (5.2.285), Hamlet knocks the rapier upward from his opponent's hand, an action made plausible by Olivier's earlier demonstration of superior swordsmanship. It is seen from directly above the two men, flying up and then landing on the floor. Hamlet's foot clamps it to the ground as Laertes' hand reaches into the frame, a new variation on the hand motif. The bated sword is offered and taken by Laertes before the camera draws back to include the two men. What becomes in effect the fourth bout now begins. New features of this bout include quickened editing and repeated shifts of camera position that allow us to experience this more desperate struggle from the alternating points of view of the antagonists.

The intense action and exclusive attention to the antagonists create a kind of void that is filled immediately upon Hamlet's wounding Laertes in the wrist. After being featured so prominently throughout the scene, Gertrude is withdrawn from view, first relegated to the distant background at the beginning of the third bout, then disappearing entirely for the ninety seconds between the two woundings. Her drinking the poisoned wine becomes in this time a "dangling cause" conspicuously awaiting its effect.[47] Laertes' hand seen in close-up is succeeded by a cut matching the action from a distance. From between the thrones, we see the wine cup tumbling from Gertrude's hand in the foreground as Laertes observes his fatal wound in the background. Nondiegetic music enters suddenly to accompany the cup's fall, and as the queen tumbles into the frame, Hamlet finally turns to look upon his mother. His paralyzed confusion registers through the momentary removal of deep focus, which makes his expression unclear, and through a delaying cut back to wounded Laertes before the view returns to the queen.

Kneeling over the dead queen, Hamlet cries "O villainy" then glances up at the king's empty throne. He rushes up the stairs, screaming, "Treachery! Seek it out" (296–97), but clearly he has already found it, as his high view over all three conspirators, but most directly over Claudius, confirms. Laertes' revelation that the point is envenomed and that Hamlet has left "not half an hour's life" (300) makes Hamlet's death-defying leap down upon Claudius a less mad option than it would otherwise appear. His revelations that Gertrude has been poisoned and the king is to blame, while superfluous for Hamlet, seem to turn the palace guard against their murderous ruler. Hamlet plunges his rapier into the supine king's chest three times without any sign of opposition, and when Claudius recovers his crown and rises, the guards surround him with their pointed spears. "The image," Silviria notes, "is of a trap closing in on the man."[48] The overhead shot of this striking configuration, from the vantage where before the duel Hamlet declared, "There's a divinity that shapes our ends" (5.2.10), becomes the very emblem of poetic justice. The crown is seen falling to the floor, followed by the dying king. He stretches out his hand toward both the crown and the queen, which he earlier declared "those effects for which I did the murder" (3.3.54).

After reconciling with Laertes, Hamlet goes to the throne for his final moments, perhaps following the example of Johnston Forbes-Robertson's silent film *Hamlet*. The entrapping circle of spears is replaced by a circle of courtiers, who gather round the throne to honor their new king for the brief time he has left. After Horatio borrows the command of Fortinbras, "Bear Hamlet like a soldier to the stage" (5.2.380), he kisses Hamlet on the brow, drawing the camera forward toward the back of dead Hamlet's head. Because this view of Hamlet's head through the approaching camera has twice been identified as an entry into Hamlet's subjectivity (in the "to be" soliloquy and the ghost interview), the long track that ends the film will inevitably carry this association as well.[49] Passing through the film's longest black screen, the subjectivity that we share with Hamlet's parting spirit first pauses at the doorway through which Ophelia's gravesite can be seen. We must notice that it remains unmarked by a gravestone, a reminder of the tragic heroine's "maimed rites" (5.1.208). As the soldiers bear the body through the hall, the camera next lingers over the view of Ophelia's corridor. It not only pauses over Hamlet's chair but does so first from the left vantage that ended the first soliloquy and then from the right vantage that began it. As the soldiers bear the body up the stairway that evokes the "to be" soliloquy, an inverted close-up of Hamlet's face recalls a very similar shot that accompanied Hamlet's swoon in the ghost scene.

Less expected is a stop to contemplate the statue of Jesus in Claudius's chapel, but the firing cannon, which marked the other stops, and a slight pan left after following the motion of Horatio to the right, place it unambiguously within the series of subjective pauses. Its meaning is less clear. Are we meant to recall Hamlet at his moment of greatest ethical disgrace? Is the dead prince's spirit uneasily revisiting this moment before proceeding to another questionable memory? At the very least, one can say that Hamlet's soliloquy in the chapel bespoke a crisis of unparalleled emotional intensity. Gertrude's bed follows, inevitably, the scene of the contemplated killing of the oedipal father, and the camera cannot resist approaching more closely before continuing up the stairway. For reasons "more sympathetic to the imagination than to logic," as set designer Roger Furse concedes, the body is carried to the topmost tower.[50] The film ends where it began.

There are many explanations for the success of Olivier's second film. As an "essay in *Hamlet*," its extensive textual deletions sacrificed poetry and reduced Shakespeare's wondrous polysemy, replacing these with a narrower focus that a feature-length film requires. Despite the narrowed focus, Olivier preserved considerable ambiguity, creating a relentless erotetic rhetoric that poses many questions, answers some, and leaves others tantalizingly unanswered, much in the manner of Shakespeare. The film more often than not succeeds in employing the wide range of the medium's devices to immerse the viewer in the compelling story. Olivier's directorial debut, *Henry V,* is a brilliantly creative film. It dazzles the viewer by repeatedly foregrounding its devices, making one notice, for example, its beautifully painted backdrop as much as its unfolding story and the words spoken in its setting of exquisite artifice. In contrast, Olivier's *Hamlet* is designed more for "looking through" than for "looking at," to borrow Colin McGinn's distinction. *Hamlet's* deep-focus cinematography, enabled by the lower lighting requirements of black and white, brought out details that distracted some early viewers, but for most of its original audience these details were so effectively subordinated to an exciting ongoing narrative that the film achieved unprecedented popular and critical success, effectively establishing the genre of filmed Shakespeare with mass appeal.

To explain a film's success or failure, Stefan Sharff falls back on an admittedly imprecise and metaphoric term, *orchestration*, which he describes as follows: "In cinema, all shots affect one another and whole scenes depend on and influence scenes around them. The interdependence is not merely progressive: it often operates in a zigzag fashion, a shot or scene touching upon both a preceding and a succeeding shot or scene, forming a bridge between two units of meaning in both a forward and [a] backward direction. . . . The aim, ideally, is to achieve an organic continuity which springs from the inner resources of the medium. Orchestration is the guardian of the overall harmonies in a cinematic continuum."[51] This chapter is an attempt to step back from the seductions of immersion that any good film offers, to "look at" Olivier's deployment of a variety of "inner resources" of the medium. It at least glances at various components that make their indispensable contributions: screen-play, acting, sets, music, graphic composition, and so forth. But it concentrates for the most part on film's unique, and uniquely powerful, most "inner" re-sources—variable framing and multilevel segmentation—because Olivier's surprisingly masterful orchestration of these resources is what allowed him, for the first time, I believe, to develop a Shakespearean play-text into a fully realized classical film. No future adapter could ignore his example.

FRANCO ZEFFIRELLI'S
Hamlet
Modernizing Medievalism

Franco Zeffirelli began his sixth feature film, which was also his third Shakespeare adaptation, confident that he knew how to reshape *Hamlet* into a powerful and popular film. In *The Taming of the Shrew*, he demonstrated an ability to adjust the play's emphases to the abilities and personalities of his stars, Richard Burton and Elizabeth Taylor. In his starless *Romeo and Juliet*, he demonstrated an ability to apply Olivier's essayistic method of streamlining the play's significations and replacing lost text-generated interest with cinematic interest. Both abilities are evident in his star-studded and streamlined *Hamlet*, although his casting of action star Mel Gibson and his textual adjustments provoked predictable complaints. The complaints about Gibson seem to have faded, but chagrin over the cutting and transposition of Shakespeare's text persists. James Welsh and Richard Vela, for example, find that "Gibson's acting deserves to be taken seriously," but they lament that Zeffirelli "restructured the play without regard to the consequences" and deleted so much that "the film might be incoherent to those who have not read and studied Shakespeare."[1] In my view, Zeffirelli carries Olivier's essayistic approach to a new level of accomplishment, very effectively coordinating the shortened text necessary in a film just over two hours long with cinema's distinctive storytelling resources and the requirements of mass-marketed film. Like Olivier, Zeffirelli sacrifices a considerable amount of Shakespearean poetry and polysemy, but he compensates for this necessary sacrifice with his characteristic combination of engaging visual artistry and creative segmentation.

The First Movement

Beginning a plot that focuses more closely and quickly on the central character, Zeffirelli begins distinguishing his *Hamlet* from Olivier's by eliminating, already in the shooting script (cowritten with Christopher DeVore), the first appearance of the ghost.[2] This deletion begins the process of shortening the film to a more standard feature length and segmentation. Like Olivier, he eliminates the Fortinbras material entirely. Unlike Olivier, he also shortens every long speech and every section of dialogue in act 1. Cutting more than half of Shakespeare's words reduces the first movement to thirty-four minutes, very much in line with feature films of the late twentieth century. The reduction also makes room for several wordless stretches of remarkable visual communication that immediately focus the first movement on the oedipal triangle.

The first such stretch, occurring during the credits, is an exemplary piece of question-and-answer filmmaking. As orchestral music covering an establishing shot of Elsinore castle gives way to the tones of an organ, mysteriously hinting at something liturgical, the camera tilts downward to reveal darkly clad women clustered on the castle steps, then a line of mounted soldiers in full armor, with pikes raised. The camera tracks slowly down the vast courtyard to reveal additional ranks of men: infantrymen, courtiers, and clergy. The dark dress and solemn demeanor of this varied medieval community lends gravity to this large public event, whatever its nature might be. We seem to be witnessing a large procession that has come to an expectant halt, an impressive effect without a known cause.

The nature of the event is revealed following a dissolve to the dark interior of a crypt when we hear a woman sobbing and see an armored body lying in an open coffin. Like Olivier's film, this *Hamlet* opens with a royal funeral. Before a word is spoken, we learn a great deal. A new, younger king has replaced the deceased old man. The widowed queen's consuming grief reveals that the former king was much beloved. She displays at this point no interest in the new king, eliminating Shakespeare's ambiguity about the nature of Gertrude's relationship with Claudius before old Hamlet's death. Claudius, however, takes great interest in her, as three cutaway shots to his watchful visage reveal, the first accompanied by the introduction of violins into a masterful Ennio Morricone score that has played continuously from the opening credits. In a subtle musical "usurpation," a cut back to the queen hovering tearfully over the body as the strings continue links Claudius's romantic interest in her with her love for the dead king.

A hand in close-up ritually sprinkles soil on the corpse. The previous cutaway shot implies that the king is performing this ritual, but that implication is revised when the camera, in a delayed disclosure, moves up the arm to reveal the hooded figure of Hamlet. As we gaze into Mel Gibson's pensive face, Hamlet is told by an echoing voice to "think of us / As of a father; for let the world take note / You are the most immediate to our throne" (1.2.107–9). For the viewer unfamiliar with *Hamlet*, the speech is most easily identified as a memory, until, in another revision, a cut to the usurper's face at the point in his speech when he adds, "And with no less nobility" (110) (a statement that would definitively preclude this identification), reveals its source. Music, camera work, and editing have produced their own subtly usurping substitutions, allowing us to share with Hamlet a dawning revelation that all is not as it seems.

Hamlet's response to Claudius's declaration of fatherly love is to comfort his mother, as if asserting a true familial bond in the face of one falsely and offensively claimed. Once the coffin is covered and Claudius has moved to its head for a sword-laying ritual, an ironic gesture for those who know his role as the murderer, Gertrude breaks from her son's embrace and desperately grasps the coffin. Now, for the first time, she returns the king's gaze. Despite her tears, we cannot fail to read into the exchange of impassioned looks the beginning of a relationship, an impression reinforced by the return of the violin melody that by now has established itself as a love theme. Nor is this beginning unread by Hamlet, even though his position behind Gertrude allows him to see the face of Claudius but not that of his mother. His quick glance at the king is followed by eye movements signifying the rapidity of his understanding: Claudius's words to Hamlet have been directed, we and Hamlet now understand, at Hamlet's mother, and very effectively indeed. The new king is revealed to be a formidable, manipulative competitor against both young Hamlet and the memory of old Hamlet for the affection of the queen, who would naturally appreciate the comfort offered simultaneously both to herself and to her son. Hamlet is revealed to be perceptive but not inclined to take action against a sea of troubles, for his reaction to Claudius's rivalry is to leave the crypt. The camera tracks right, precisely reversing the leftward movement that brought us into the crypt, but now it is following Hamlet. His exit suggests both voluntary exclusion from the newly emerging family group and power over the camera, the eye of the audience.

A long fade to black followed by a fade-in to the battlements graced by morning light indicates the passage of time into some kind of new beginning. Claudius delivers his first lines in the play in a scene that uses visual echoes to signify difference, providing details that fill in the narrative gap. Inside the enormous throne room, the camera tilts down to place the king in the center of the screen and then cranes upward to reveal Gertrude enthroned to his left. The central position on screen that Claudius assumed in the sword-laying ritual has now become his permanent royal possession, through the transformation of Gertrude into his queen. Polonius again mans the screen-left rear corner, while the two guards who framed Claudius in the crypt, individuated by their distinctive shields, now frame the royal couple. The silent mourners have been replaced by attentive courtiers who comment among themselves as Claudius speaks. These are not the stiff nodding figures of Olivier but an alert and clearly important audience whose approval Gertrude nervously awaits. Her visible panting, recalling her belabored moans in the crypt, ends only when the marriage announcement prompts the courtiers' applause. If we are familiar with the film tradition or even the play, the queen's delayed disclosure invites us to anticipate a similar disclosure of Hamlet, but he remains, surprisingly, absent.[3] Dividing up act 1 with repeated scene changes allows Zeffirelli to define evolving power relations visually. The new king's domination of the throne room, where only he speaks, as in the crypt, confirms his power in the public realm. The long dissolve on a radiant Gertrude that ends the scene, a revisionary allusion to Olivier's dissolve to Claudius that begins the scene, suggests another dynamic in their private relationship. Welsh and Vela find the court scene "severely and stupidly abridged."[4] I find that Zeffirelli has masterfully retold Shakespeare's story with visual means, retaining enough of Shakespeare's language to allow it to work in coordination with the film's other devices.

Visual characterization continues apace as act 1, scene 2 divides into four separate film scenes. Laertes' request for permission to return to France takes place in the castle scriptorium, where both the bureaucratic foundations of the king's public power and the considerable charm that he wields in private are manifest. Laertes cannot stop smiling at the man he ironically calls his "dread Lord" (50). Claudius knowingly returns a grin at Polonius's pomposities and kisses the beaming young man farewell on both cheeks. We are already being prepared to understand Laertes' conversion to the king's cause later in the film. But at this point, after we have been repeatedly impressed with the film's strong and likeable Claudius, we are also shown his weakness. After he kisses Laertes, a cut to the castle hall reveals Claudius preparing for the hunt. Gertrude bounds to him and kisses him passionately. She glows in the brilliant sunlight, introducing one of the film's major motifs.[5] Claudius's moment of ecstasy in the arms of his queen, however, proves fleeting. His face quickly registers disappointment and hurt once this radiant display of affection is followed by an inaudible whispered request and a glance upward toward the closed door of what will soon be revealed as Hamlet's room. Claudius won the battle in the crypt for primacy in Gertrude's affection, but he has not yet won the war.

Still wearing her smile, Gertrude leads Claudius, still wearing his frown but comforted by the large wine cup that has suddenly appeared in his hand, into Hamlet's upstairs room. As if she owns the room and its inhabitant, she enters without knocking and quickly flings open the window covering, bringing the bright sunshine that she had brought to her husband to her son, who was sitting sullenly in the darkness. On cue, Claudius shifts into his hale and hearty mode, initiating a family intervention in the private space that has replaced Shakespeare's original throne room. He seeks momentary encouragement with a glance to his wife following Hamlet's insulting "A little more than kin, and less than kind" (1.2.65) but proceeds undaunted into his paternal lecture on unmanly grief. The king's eloquence, however, is less effective on this young man. On his declaring Hamlet's return to Wittenberg "most retrograde to our desire" (114), in a line that introduces a string of four "ours" implying Gertrude's concurrence, Hamlet resumes packing his satchel with books. At the sound of a hunting horn, Gertrude signals with her eyes for the king to exit.

The scene's highly crafted organization supports the contrast between the powers of the king and queen over Hamlet. Shakespeare allows Claudius forty lines of persuasion, the queen a mere fourteen, and interweaves their speeches until the king at last acknowledges that Hamlet's "gentle and unforced accord / Sits smiling to my heart" (123–24). The film much more neatly divides the task of persuasion for the purpose of contrast, assigning Claudius fourteen lines for his opening salvo and then ushering him off to allow Gertrude's fourteen lines, including lines 123–24 reassigned from Claudius, to work on Hamlet in private. Her private segment is given almost twice as much screen time as the king's, much of which she uses for nonverbal persuasion. With a near-comic hesitation to touch the prince, Claudius accompanied his words with a quick pat on Hamlet's left shoulder, an attempt at bonhomie undercut by the large ring his raised left hand displays. Gertrude's initial touching of this same shoulder establishes similarity against which we better perceive difference. Her segment breaks down into three parts of nearly identical length. In the first and third, she and Hamlet are in intimate physical contact, accompanied by a seductive cello variation of the film's love music, the first instance of nondiegetic music since the crypt scene, and equally suggestive of a romantic turn. In the second, accompanied by almost inaudible music, Hamlet puts distance between them and continues packing. The third, in the sunlight near the window and with a resumed love theme on the soundtrack, begins with subtle anticipation of Hamlet's mad pantomime with Ophelia in act 2, scene 1, as Hamlet searches over his mother's face and hair and inhales her fragrance. It ends with the device that ended Claudius's less successful "hunt." As the sound of the hunting horn wafts in the window, Gertrude ends a descending series of kisses from forehead to eye to mouth and exits hurriedly, her mission accomplished.

The intense physicality of this encounter resonates with the first soliloquy. As in Olivier's version, Hamlet's first instance of talking to himself registers his isolation from the community, upon which he looks down from his high window. But even more than Olivier's, it registers his separation from his mother. Hamlet speaks his lines with unrelieved bitterness that contrasts with cheers for the royal couple by the crowd as they ride off into the freedom of the beautiful Dover countryside. In the play and Olivier's film, Horatio and his companions enter immediately after the first soliloquy, allowing its closing phrase, "for I must hold my tongue" (2.1.159), to indicate silence forced by the end of Hamlet's solitude but also relieving that solitude after the visitors are recognized. This film's more decisive and sexually jealous hero chooses to move deeper into solitude. Angrily spitting out, "Frailty, thy name is woman" (146), he roughly shuts his leaded window. Restructuring the play with careful regard to the consequences, Zeffirelli holds his Hamlet in sullen isolation.

A brief cut to a long aerial shot of the hunting party bridges across to a match cut to the interview of Laertes and Ophelia, which in displacing the ghost report juxtaposes two private familial interventions. After Hamlet removes his hand from the window ledge and shuts himself in, Laertes' hand precedes his opening the door and entering the castle's weaving room. Both Hamlet's bitterly misogynistic speech at the window and the image of Gertrude galloping freely with Claudius across the field resonate against the following scene. As the sound of the closing window matches the sound of the opening door, the masculine hunting horn modulates imperceptibly into the voices of the women, who are singing Ophelia's mad Saint Valentine song ("And I a maid at your window, / To be your Valentine" [4.5.50–51]) while they embroider the Bayeux Tapestry's propagandistic tale of masculine aggression in their crowded workroom. Laertes' warning against yielding to the trifling of Hamlet's favor rings truer and more ominous when it follows hard upon Hamlet's bitterly misogynistic speech. Ophelia's womanly "frailty" is painfully evident in the way she distractedly picks at a phallic plant form on a tapestry frame and plays with an imaginary ring on her left hand while her brother cautions her against sexual indulgence.

Polonius's famous speech of fatherly advice creates sympathy for his children. His response to his son's handshakes with politely deferential citizens paying their respects is "Be thou familiar, but by no means vulgar" (1.3.60), accompanied by disdainful looks. Advocacy of "rich, not gaudy" (70) apparel is accompanied by gestured condemnation of the large clasp on Laertes' cloak. After Laertes' departure, Polonius's approach to Ophelia is no less offensive. Following his order to "tender yourself more dearly" (106), delivered with startling gruffness, Ophelia must twice chase after her father to defend Hamlet's sincerity. The viewer does not know how much is heard by Hamlet, who has been repeatedly shown watching from above from early in the speech to Laertes, but reverberating sound during a point-of-view shot informs us that he does hear Polonius angrily order Ophelia not to "so slander any moment leisure / As to give words or talk with the Lord Hamlet" (132–33). Because Hamlet has ducked out of view to avoid detection by Polonius, we also know that he did *not* hear Ophelia reply, "I shall obey, my lord" (135). Her visibly aggressive argument with her father and Hamlet's not overhearing her acquiescence remove any justification for Hamlet's assuming that she wishes to cut off contact.

The report to Hamlet of the ghost's visit is often a tedious affair on stage and certainly one of Olivier's least engaging scenes. Perhaps in response, Zeffirelli packs it with visual interest. The group bringing the report displays an intriguing social dynamic. Once Barnardo has confirmed Hamlet's presence on the battlements, he orchestrates the group's presentation, allowing Horatio to move ahead while he remains behind next to Francisco, whom Zeffirelli has imported from act 1, scene 1. Hamlet is first seen from behind leaning out through a crenellation. After eight shots of him spying from above in the previous scene, one can only assume that he is continuing this activity and therefore that the scenes are continuous; the match cut from Ophelia entering a doorway to the men exiting an archway supports this sly misdirection. When Hamlet turns in response to Horatio's address, he sees a group that puzzles him, men who knowingly exchange glances and frustrate Hamlet's effort to isolate his friend for a more private conversation on the upper battlement. Hamlet repeatedly pauses to observe them, confused by their insistent presence and their unseen and unexplainable movement to the upper battlement and then down again to the lower.

If the un-Shakespearean presence of Francisco surprises *Hamlet*-literate viewers, Marcellus, who is no longer the gruff, middle-aged officer of stage tradition and Olivier's film, probably catches the attention for all. He contributes to a subtle homoerotic dimension created through such devices as the "sodomizing camera" that William Van Watson finds at work in the presentation of the visiting acrobats and Rosencrantz and Guildenstern "from behind" but strangely does not notice here, where Hamlet is introduced in the same way.[6] The eyes of both Hamlet and Horatio repeatedly rove downward as they address each other, most noticeably after Hamlet looks over Marcellus on the upper battlement, as if surprised by his friend's new companion. The two friends' extended handclasp, held for six seconds, demands comparison with Laertes' heteronormative handshakes in the previous scene. In several scenes that did not survive from script to film, Horatio, a "man of thirty," is accompanied by Marcellus, "a thin blond youth of twenty," whom Horatio introduces as "my young friend."[7] Played by eighteen-year-old Christien Anhalt, with his hair color changed from natural brown to blond, Marcellus stands out visually from his companions as sexually ambiguous, blond young men do in other Zeffirelli films. The screenplay's attention to his eyes and smile indicates an original intention to use close-ups of the beautiful male, "a signature of Zeffirelli's filmography."[8] In the finished *Hamlet*, homoeroticism has been toned down, remaining an unmistakable but relatively minor undercurrent.

Hamlet's claim to see his father as he stares out to sea corrects our initial impression of the battlement's location and that he began the scene trying to spy on Ophelia. A patriarchal image, not the image of a female beloved, dominates his internal vision. A homosocial group tinged with eroticism has arrived to assist him in viewing this image and obeying its desire. Surprisingly to viewers who know the play, Zeffirelli will allow the men to remain Hamlet's companions to the end.

The air of mystery accompanies the group into an interior scene. From within an unidentified room, we see Hamlet open an exterior door, enter, and suspiciously scan the room below. Horatio moves forward to lead the group across a high walkway before stopping to tell his tale. He soon leads Hamlet by the arm down a narrow stairway, but this action becomes confusing when we see the familiar window recess of Hamlet's room below: the men have implicitly laid claim to Hamlet's private space almost as boldly as did Gertrude. Hamlet puts distance between himself and the others by moving behind his vast, instrument-laden table, as if reluctant to accept things not dreamt of in our philosophy. When Horatio adds showing to telling, enacting the ghost's gesture of lifting up its head "as it would speak," and describes how "it shrunk in haste away / And vanished from our sight" (1.2.216–19), the combination of visualized presence followed by narrated absence induces Hamlet to rejoin the group and promise to join them again later that night.

Moving the first Ophelia scene to follow Hamlet's soliloquy, which ends with no goal but to "not think" (1.2.146) about his mother's hasty marriage, allows Zeffirelli to end his first movement with a more concerted rush toward the goal-orientation that Hollywood favors for its main characters. Hamlet now has the preliminary goal of meeting the ghost, hope that from this meeting "foul deeds will rise" (255), and a wish to hasten time: "Would the night were come" (254). His wish is fulfilled with a cut to an elaborate banquet scene that continues the triumphal rise of Claudius, who is again sitting enthroned with his queen before his court. Appropriately for a scene that echoes act 1, scene 2, and with irony at Hamlet's expense, the king regales the lively crowd with lines that originally celebrated Hamlet's agreeing to remain at Elsinore: "No jocund health that Denmark drinks today / But the great cannon to the clouds shall tell" (1.2.125–26). Hamlet's isolation is heightened by his second absence from the court. His homosocial group's additional isolation is heightened by the presence in the hall of many women, who are no longer separated off from the men as in the opening courtyard shot and the throne room scene but are actively engaged in socializing. An attractive couple converses with

Gertrude. Ophelia and the queen exchange toasts. In an overhead shot, we see Claudius circling the room and then embracing another woman. Interestingly, because the shot of the embrace is repeated, it combines with the circular motion to suggest a nonprogressive repetition that runs counter to the larger progress suggested by the scenic echoes.

The overhead shots of the banquet are indebted to Olivier, but Zeffirelli integrates them even more thoroughly into his cinematic articulation of three-dimensional space. The importance of the single ghost scene, and perhaps Zeffirelli's desire to outdo Olivier at his own game, is highlighted by the overabundance of spatial cues, which force us continually to reorient in the semidarkness. The scene begins within the hall, which is filled with detail in both foreground and background. The camera's long track rightward at eye level across the festivities matches the direction of Hamlet's gaze at the end of the previous scene. Space is strongly horizontal until Hamlet and his friends enter from the left on an elevated walkway that recalls the walkway above Hamlet's living quarters in the previous scene. This entrance establishes the overhead shots from the men's point of view, creating two vertical levels that will soon be joined by more. From here, Hamlet can literally look down upon the "heavy-headed revel" (1.4.17) and lament that it soils the reputation of Denmark to Marcellus, who as a newcomer to Elsinore more logically asks about the "custom" (12) than does the play's Horatio.

The men file up an Olivier-inspired winding staircase and enter a third, exterior level, which the camera again establishes through a rightward track, following Hamlet to an opening from which he can again look down, meditating now on the "vicious mole of nature" (24). This movement and speech are accompanied sonically by a sustained, low synthesized note that increases tension and helps define the third level against the distant voices and diegetic period music below. The speech is newly cast as a soliloquy, which allows it to effectively suggest a growing suspicion about Claudius, who has so far been much less the object of this Hamlet's anger than Gertrude has been. The ghost appears first in close-up, rising from the bottom of the screen to continue the pattern of ascent. It leads the men up the battlements to a fourth level, where Horatio attempts to dissuade Hamlet from proceeding. Now a whistling wind is layered into the soundtrack; it will disappear and then return at the highest level. On a fifth level, Hamlet with drawn sword decisively separates himself from his dissuaders. Another winding stairway brings Hamlet to the sight of the ghost continuing his ascent at the end of a long hallway. Finally, he rushes up another stairway to a seventh level. One must wonder whether Zeffirelli counted the six levels of Olivier's famous ascent to the "to be" soliloquy and added one for good measure!

The screenplay called for the ghost to be fully armed and intimidating upon his arrival: he stretches up "commandingly to brush the sky" and "raises a sword as if to hack the world in two." In the better wisdom of the finished film, Paul Scofield's unarmed ghost, in contrast, is wearing something resembling a monk's habit and from the start is the "dry, human, almost pitiable old man" that he was originally to become only after he was alone with his son.[9] As a result of this change, only the son raises his sword, and the oedipal anger conveyed by Hamlet's aggressive chase becomes more shocking. This anger grows even more evident when he pauses at the top to look at his raised sword and then rushes into the turret with a loud gasp, followed by the camera in a classic film setup for a violent confrontation. The violent star of *Lethal Weapon* performs a thorough, coplike "sweep" with his sword, spinning and darting frenziedly about the space before returning in confusion to its entrance. Now his father seems to appear in his mind's eye, and the longing returns that was evident in his gaze out to sea when he earlier claimed to see his dead father. Hamlet slowly turns around and drops his sword, somehow knowing where to look. A cut reveals the ghost sitting before a stone merlon that the camera has not viewed but that Hamlet cannot have missed in his "sweep." The carefully calibrated disclosure, for which I cannot recall a precedent in film treatments of the supernatural, leaves us as puzzled as Hamlet about this unexplainable presence. Does the ghost make himself visible only after Hamlet has dropped his hostility? Does Hamlet's ambivalence reverse polarity from hateful rivalry to loving identification with the prospect that the ghost may be gone? The scene provokes without explaining and through its enhanced oedipal scenario sets up a powerful linkage with the later scene in Gertrude's closet.

Distinct camera styles were employed in Hamlet's two previous intimate conversations. With Gertrude, he was seen in repeated two-shots of bodies touching. The conversation with Horatio kept the two friends together in middle shots, then ended with three over-the-shoulder exchanges standard in two-party conversations. Zeffirelli reserves the potency of an extended "separation" sequence of one-shots for the all-important ghostly visitation, where he can exploit the visual eloquence of Paul Scofield's face to the full. During his ascent, Hamlet is in the same frame as the ghost only once, when they are at opposite ends of the sixth level's long hallway. The ghost's appearances have been brief and nearly invisible in the dark, creating in the viewer a desire to see that parallels Hamlet's. Father and son now confront each other across thirty-six shots in just over three minutes, and in only one of these do they unambiguously appear together. To the power of separation is added another noteworthy technique. Olivier's motif of the reaching hand linked scenes across the film. Zeffirelli takes a different approach, reserving the motif largely for this scene to enhance its emotional impact.

The scene at the top of Elsinore is meticulously punctuated by body movements to divide the ghost's long speech into meaningful units of nearly identical length. A segment in which the ghost reveals his purgatorial plight ends when Hamlet walks toward him, imitating the camera, which had just tracked from medium to close shot. A cut to the sole nonseparation shot here, a medium shot of the ghost reaching forth with Hamlet's right hand and leg in the foreground, promises further intimacy, but the revelation of murder seems to shock the sequence back to separation, initiating twenty alternating one-shots.[10] These fall into two symmetrical segments of ten when the ghost rises and gazes out to sea, scenting the morning air and shifting to the narrative of his poisoning.

A fourth, closing segment begins when the ghost again rises to tell Hamlet, "Taint not thy mind" (1.5.85). He moves toward his son for the first time in his visit but then backs off and says, "Fare thee well at once" (88). At this point, the violins of desire rise and the ghost approaches again, with arms raised. At his third "adieu" (91), a cut to Hamlet seems to show the ghost's hands entering over his son's face, but whether we are seeing shadows or black silhouettes against Hamlet's lighted features is carefully made unclear. Stefan Sharff demonstrates that, normally, "at the close of a series of pure separation shots comes a resolution" returning the characters to the same frame. Zeffirelli invites us to see such a resolution, but its ambiguity adds frustration on the level of cinematic form to the poignancy of the father and son missing contact.[11] After a close-up of the ghost tearfully pleading, "Remember me" (91), we again see these dark shapes hovering over Hamlet. His hands rise eagerly to meet them, but they withdraw above the frame and are replaced by the unambiguous shadows of Hamlet's own hands as he closes his eyes. When he opens them, he sees the empty battlement against the sky. Zeffirelli then masterfully splices in the battlement shot from the "sweep," where it was sword-wielding Hamlet's point of view revealing the turret to be empty.[12] The resulting subliminal punctuation contributes to the scene's mystery, and perhaps to its irony, supporting any temptation to add in a contradictory reading of Hamlet's hand gesture and closed eyes as self-defensive as well as yearning, an economical expression of his ambivalence.

The ghost's status as an ascending figure, and thus implicitly an "honest ghost" (137), is reinforced by Hamlet's offscreen sitting down, which occurs soon after the ghost's rising begins the second segment of the interview. The ghost can thus approach Hamlet from a parental height at the end. The first part of Hamlet's subsequent promise to remember is directed, prayerlike, toward the sky. Like the descent of Olivier's Hamlet, his descent that follows is dazzlingly rapid, but even more so, as befits an action hero acquiring new motivation as the film's first movement approaches its end. One cut brings him leaping down onto the third level, from which he quickly gazes down onto the first through the familiar skylight. When a cut reveals Claudius and Gertrude kissing in close-up, the remainder of his promissory speech is directed downward toward the "baser matter" (1.5.104) upon which he now must act. With "So be it" (114), his body and weapon, lit against a black background, drop with symbolic near-abstraction through the bottom of the screen.

He is next seen descending a stairway to his companions, who have moved to a room adjoining the battlements where they first encountered the prince. The ghost's presence above is maintained when an overhead shot shows all turning upward upon its command to "Swear" (149) and when Hamlet's "Rest, perturbed spirit" (180) is directed skyward. But the schematic vertical geometry that governs the movements of the whole ghost scene has been replaced by the men's unmappable trajectory. When the group exits to the battlements, Hamlet's "Here as before" (167) shifts from requesting a second oath—the first oath having been omitted—to reminding them and us of the repeated setting, to which the men have surprisingly arrived. The recurring location thus pulls the ghost report from act 1, scene 2 and the ghost visit of act 1, scenes 4–5 together into one large segment of promise and fulfillment. After nearly twenty minutes of screen time, the band of five men brought together uneasily on the battlements now unites physically in the same locale by placing their hands on Hamlet's sword.

The Second Movement

Hamlet's newly motivated action takes the form of putting "an antic disposition on" (1.5.170), although neither the play nor the film reveals at this point what the assumed madness is meant to accomplish. The film's deletion of Polonius's interview with Reynaldo launches Hamlet immediately into his plan. For the action that Ophelia recounts to her father in the play as having occurred as she "was sewing in [her] closet" (2.1.74), Zeffirelli avoids Olivier's redundancy of telling while showing by creating a wordless scene in which Hamlet pantomimes the action. His disheveled appearance and enigmatic actions coupled with Ophelia's visible confusion allow us to see how convincingly Hamlet can put his antic disposition on. Ophelia's cueless noticing of Hamlet across the weaving room, much as Hamlet had cuelessly perceived the ghost's presence in the turret, adds a sense of uncanniness. Ophelia progresses from a welcoming half-smile through visible fear and compassion until she raises her hand to her mouth in astonishment, a gesture repeated by Polonius, who is spying from an archway above. Such redundancy of reaction effectively eliminates the possibility that other characters will doubt that Hamlet is mad. For the viewer, the effectiveness of Gibson's performance is enhanced by Zeffirelli's innovative use of cinematic conventions. Hamlet's wordlessness is incongruous not only with his open and sometimes moving mouth, but also with the repeated over-the-shoulder shots and reverse shots: the camera eerily portrays a "conversation" consisting of four such wordless exchanges, the last an eloquent sigh visible in the cold air, to which Ophelia replies with her hand gesture.

While viewers are interpreting Hamlet's pantomimed conversation, they are also making visual links with previous scenes. As in Olivier's film, Hamlet's farewell to Ophelia takes place in the same room as her brother's farewell; indeed, Hamlet is first seen in the alcove into which Laertes drew Ophelia to lecture her on the dangers of his love. Ophelia enters carrying the famous Halley's comet panel of the Bayeux Tapestry.[13] The phallic comet and her threading a needle over it, like her earlier plucking of vegetation from the banquet panel, point to her repressed sexuality, visually supporting her singing of the Valentine song. Polonius's spying from above on Hamlet and Ophelia recalls the reverse situation of spying on Polonius and Ophelia by Hamlet, who repeatedly placed his hand on the railing as Polonius does here. Even as it creates the impression of madness, Hamlet's pantomime also indicates how creatively he can counter his opponents. Is the silent conversation not a creative and satisfying response to overhearing Polonius forbidding his daughter "to give words or talk with the Lord Hamlet" (1.3.133) at the very doorway to this room?

Jettisoning the introduction of Rosencrantz and Guildenstern and the return of the ambassadors allows the focus to remain on Hamlet's madness. But at the same time, the focus on Hamlet allows Zeffirelli to place greater emphasis on his mother, whose visibly signaled power has risen steadily since the opening scene. Polonius's report is addressed to both king and queen, but now it is Gertrude who shows her dominance in the throne room, as she did earlier in Hamlet's room, taking over another Claudian line: "O, speak on that, that I do long to hear" (2.2.50, modified). Whereas in the play Polonius feels confident to delay obeying Claudius until after the ambassadors' report, he now immediately begins his explanation, directing it primarily to Gertrude. She takes the initiative in checking for eavesdroppers, after which Claudius imitates her by looking into an archway. Unlike Claudius, Gertrude declines to move from her chair when Polonius rather insolently asks them to "gather and surmise" (107), defining "gather" as physical rather than mental activity through a characteristic hand gesture. In contrast to her commanding presence, evident as well in the fact that close-up reaction shots are given only to her, Claudius appears to be growing ever more dependent on his cup, which does not leave his hand. An odd back-and-forth pan shows the cup being filled as Polonius enters, hides the completion of this act from the camera, and then returns to reveal a servant who attentively stands holding a pitcher. The servant then dutifully watches the king crossing the room, looking as if he expects to be needed again soon.

The "sweep" of the battlement in the ghost scene revealed this Hamlet to be unusually violent, and this impression was reinforced by his surprisingly rough grabbing of Ophelia in the weaving room. Both actions were not in the shooting script, suggesting that Mel Gibson's casting or input during shooting moved the character in this direction.[14] The same holds true for the fishmonger scene. Zeffirelli borrows the idea of two vertical levels from Olivier, whose Hamlet remains physically and symbolically above Polonius, descending from his high platform only for the brief advice about his daughter, followed by "friend—look to't" (182–83). Without the provocation that Olivier adds by having Hamlet overhear Polonius's plan to "loose" his daughter on him, an addition that contributes to the sense of his polite Hamlet's self-control, Gibson takes advantage of the castle library's elevated nooks to abuse Polonius cruelly. When Polonius responds to Hamlet's hand gesture to approach, a gesture that parodies his own in the previous scene, and mounts the library ladder, Hamlet confirms his comment on old men's "plentiful lack of wit" (196) by placing his one booted foot upon the top of the ladder. As the camera's steep angles and slight movements from both below and above amplify Polonius's vertiginous position, Hamlet forces him to fall to the stone floor. So rattled that he stumbles over a chair on exiting the room, Polonius maintains a respectful demeanor toward his persecutor, reversing the effect of Olivier's scene.

Hamlet's enhanced violence continues into the nunnery scene, from which all "nunnery" references are withheld for later use in the Mousetrap scene. Although he has not overheard the eavesdropping plan in the manner of Olivier's Hamlet, he sees Polonius and Claudius positioning Ophelia in the great hall to await his arrival, allowing expectations to form, much as in Olivier's version. Hamlet walks brusquely past Ophelia to avoid a confrontation, forcing her to chase after him. Ironically, in again crying "my lord" and hastening toward screen right, she is imitating her earlier chasing after her father to protest the honorableness of Hamlet's tenders of affection while Hamlet spied from above. Hamlet's suspicions are so evident in his repeated glances about the hall that a cutaway to the moving shadow of Claudius's head appears intended to confirm the king's presence to the viewer more than to the hero. As the scene approaches its climax, the repeated linear movements of both characters and cameras give way to a dizzy circling that presents Hamlet's exploding rage from Ophelia's point of view. After he throws her against the stone wall, bounds up a stairway, and hurls the "remembrances" (3.1.92) down to Ophelia's feet, a cut takes us to the elevated point of view that Hamlet has just occupied. This high view of Ophelia picking up the jewelry while her musical theme in romantic strings replaces Hamlet's shouted curses has a mixed effect. It enhances the violent impact of Hamlet's treatment of the small, vulnerable figure pressed against the stone wall of the enormous room. It also communicates the loss experienced both by Ophelia, whose marriage prospects Hamlet has declared ended, and by Hamlet, whose view from this site contrasts sadly with the camera's loving and pitying gaze.

As in the Second Quarto and First Folio, in the screenplay the nunnery scene follows the "to be" soliloquy, but Zeffirelli eventually opted to follow Olivier's much-noted reversal of Shakespeare's order. The new order allows Ophelia's betrayal to become an important inducement to Hamlet's meditation on death—but only one of several and certainly not the kind of violent triggering event that sends Olivier's Hamlet spiraling upward toward release. As described in the previous chapter, Olivier made the betrayal primary by returning twice to the image of Ophelia sobbing on the stairway after Claudius's decision to send Hamlet to England and by Hamlet's looking into the camera while lamenting "the pangs of despised love" (3.1.71) in the soliloquy itself. Zeffirelli carefully avoids assigning primacy to the love story by following the pitiful image of Ophelia with Hamlet's overhearing Claudius's decision from the doorway of his private room, and by holding the king's image on screen during the long dissolve that brings Hamlet to the familiar stairway to the crypt. As Hamlet returns to the site of his first competition with Claudius, "His father's death and our o'er-hasty marriage" (2.2.57), offered earlier by

Gertrude as explanations for Hamlet's "distemper" (55), implicitly return as crucial motivations for his most famous speech. To these are added not only Ophelia's betrayal but also the impending exile, to which Hamlet responded with a sorrowful grimace and which promises to sever all relationships and the mission of revenge. No less important are the sufferings of the ghost, which this film portrays more movingly than most performances.

In a systematic response to Olivier, Zeffirelli substitutes Elsinore's depth for its height, slow descent into a dungeon-like interior for racing ascent onto the liberating exterior of the battlement, straight speech for the mixed soliloquy of voice-over and speech, total absence of music for Walton's elaborate score, and a Hamlet who takes inspiration from the crypt's details for a hero who projects his internal turbulence onto a stormy sea. To the multiplicity of motivations flowing into his overwhelming "sea of troubles" (3.1.58) is added a variety of sights within it that inflect his meditation, assisting Zeffirelli in preventing Hamlet's "question" from becoming, as it so often has in performance and in critical opinion, a specific debate over any particular course of action. As Harold Jenkins insists in his Arden note, "the dramatic force of the speech comes rather from its enabling us to see Hamlet's situation in its most universal aspect," and "the question of 'To be or not to be' concerns the advantages and disadvantages of human existence." Clearly, Zeffirelli agrees.

A slow pan of the entire crypt from Hamlet's point of view ends with the brightly lit marble effigy of his father atop a tomb lying in opposition to an equally bright window to the exterior, posing the basic alternative of his first line. When after pondering his sea of troubles he considers "opposing" to "end them" (59), a cut to a fragmentary skeleton in a wall niche, to which Hamlet's view will return twice more, defines the unappealing result. A cut back to Hamlet with an effigy in the background, its hands raised in prayer, offers an alternative image of wholeness and repose, corresponding to Hamlet's new characterization of death as "to sleep, / No more" (59–60). He proceeds into the crypt, meditating death's relief over another effigy, but with "perchance to dream: ay, there's the rub," he turns and approaches his father's tomb. With "there's the respect / That makes calamity of so long life," he points his finger at his father, as if continuing the ghostly conversation that now prompts his rejection of death as relief. On concluding his litany of life's trials with the most general offense, "the spurns / That patient merit of th'unworthy takes" (73–74), he slaps his hand down emphatically. The plural of "spurns" thus emphasized might remind us of this film's multiplicity of motivations for Hamlet and signify as well his identification with his father, who has communicated his own multiple spurns so feelingly.

Hamlet's presence at his father's tomb helps him to define his dilemma. His identification with his father spurs him to action on his father's command for revenge, but it also reminds him of the deadly consequences of this action. Rather than posing a potential contradiction, as is sometimes suggested, Hamlet's evocation of "the undiscovered country from whose bourn / No traveler returns" (78–79) expresses his conviction that his father cannot return, despite the ghost's brief visitations. The third and final cut to the skeleton from the paternal effigy occurs during these lines and now equates rather than contrasts two visions of death. As he then moves to where he can stare upward into the flooding sunlight to complete the soliloquy, implying his choice of "to be" in the bright window to the exterior, we know that for this emotionally volatile and highly motivated Hamlet, the choice represents only a brief postponement of "not to be." His slow walk back to the stairway and pause at its base, in contrast to his unhesitant climbing of these same stairs in exiting the film's opening scene, reflects how difficult it is to "fly to other [ills that] we know not of" (81).

After Hamlet explores his dilemma verbally, the film develops it with a series of visual incongruities. A dissolve reveals Elsinore in the distance and a rider galloping on the rocky shore. When a closer shot reveals this to be Hamlet, we infer that he has indeed opted to "fly to other" ills, to take action, but he is soon revealed reclined on a grassy bank while his horse grazes, continuing the upward gaze of the soliloquy. He has hastened only to find solitude and repose in which to continue his meditation. Not seriously suicidal and therefore weaponless during the soliloquy, unlike Olivier's Hamlet, Gibson holds his sword upright, again suggesting renewed action, but its inverted position might also recall Olivier's self-directed bodkin. While Hamlet is in this ambiguous state, Rosencrantz and Guildenstern arrive on horseback, surprisingly accompanied by Horatio and Marcellus, to add to his sea of troubles.

Placing the encounter with Rosencrantz and Guildenstern after the soliloquy allows their belabored bonhomie to grate more harshly against Hamlet's disturbed state of mind. He greets them politely, but he hesitates in naming them, indicating that their status as "excellent good friends" (2.2.219) is dubious, and his expression during their absurd synchronized bow evinces misgiving. The oceanside setting, filled with sunlight and seagulls, offers the greatest contrast possible with the dark crypt and makes Hamlet's declaration that "Denmark's a prison" (240), delivered as his eyes glance about the spectacular scenery, a more deliberately aggressive provocation. Their repeated, simple-minded recourse to his ambition to explain his melancholy resonates insultingly against his recent agonizing over "enterprises of great pitch and moment" (3.1.85). Because the "bad dreams" (2.2.251) that Hamlet claims have produced his sense of imprisonment are now identifiable as the soliloquy's disturbing "dreams" (3.1.65) of the unknowable afterlife, Guildenstern's silly chop-logic, "for the very substance of the ambitious is merely the shadow of a dream" (2.2.253–54), does not endear him to the melancholy prince. Hamlet's response is to propose a change of scene as he walks away, rolling his eyes.

Ironically, in engaging the two young men as spies, Claudius prompts Hamlet to action. Kathy Howlett argues that "Zeffirelli concentrates on those aspects of the revenge drama that are shared by the film Western." If this perhaps overstates the case for the film as a whole, such generic interaction is certainly at work in the subsequent scene, when the five men ride to a "lonely, rustic structure looking every bit like exuberant cowboys galloping into a desolate Mexican outpost." Howlett also notices that the rustic outpost "suggests a stage and proscenium setting," forming "a stage for Hamlet to act out his conflicts."[15] In this western setting conducive to Hamlet's impulse toward violence, the frustrations already evident in the previous scene suddenly erupt into violence when Hamlet kicks the stool out from under Rosencrantz and confronts Guildenstern with a raised skewer. The action looks backward to his violence against Polonius in the library and looks forward metaphorically to his goal of pushing Claudius off the throne. Such action in a proscenium setting might also be viewed as the germ of Hamlet's plan to use a play to catch the conscience of the king.

Hamlet follows his violence with the poetic prose speech on losing his mirth. The first part proceeds conventionally, addressed to Rosencrantz and Guildenstern and containing at least a hint of deception and scorn. But as the speech develops, Gibson's demeanor grows more sincere and the reaction shots shift from the spies to an attentive Horatio, who has been standing in the background with blond Marcellus, who domesticates the scene by cooking meat for all. Hamlet moves off the porch to Horatio, looks affectionately at his friend, and addresses "What a piece of work is a man" (2.2.269, in Folio) to him in private, as if the thought is inspired by Horatio's physical presence. The close-up shot recalls the battlement scene of the ghost report, when Hamlet looked at his friend with a similarly roving eye and declared of his father, "He was a man" (1.2.186). The parallel is reinforced when Hamlet holds up both his hands, as Horatio had done to Hamlet in the indoor continuation of the ghost report ("These hands are not more like" [1.2.211]). Horatio moves offscreen as Hamlet continues (in a close-up tracking shot that has attracted the attention of several critics), still addressing Horatio and glancing toward him at his right at "the beauty of the world" (2.2.307).[16] The film's homoerotic element is thus linked here to a sharing of Hamlet's deepest feelings in a shot that spatially isolates him. Zeffirelli's "homosexual gaze" sheds its physicality as we and the camera in effect take over Horatio's point of view, moving into an intimacy with our on-screen friend that is more intense here than at any other point in the film. At "Man delights not me" (274–75), Hamlet turns surprisingly to his left. He addresses "nor woman neither, though by your smiling you seem to say so" (275–76) to Rosencrantz, whose grinning face intrudes joltingly into this intimate moment.

Hamlet's single moment of unalloyed joy occurs with the arrival of the players. He greets them with a laugh and then leads them into Elsinore as if in triumph over the monumental Constable's Gate of Dover Castle until the procession halts in the great courtyard. The upward-craning camera stops for an overview at precisely the vantage point it occupied once before: at the film's opening, when we viewed a halted procession (facing the opposite direction) following the royal funeral. The visual echo suggests that as the instruments of the second movement's culmination arrive, Hamlet's fortunes appear to be reversing.

The elation of the moment evaporates as Hamlet watches Rosencrantz and Guildenstern report to Claudius and then honor him with synchronized bows, just as they introduced themselves to Hamlet. The sight of Claudius standing with self-satisfied mien at the castle door, surrounded by attentive courtiers and receiving reports from his obsequious spies, launches Hamlet into his third soliloquy, much of which he spits out angrily, accompanied by furious gestures. In the play, Hamlet, who has already commissioned *The Murder of Gonzago* and planned to add "a speech of some dozen or sixteen lines" (2.2.476), angrily berates himself as a "coward" (506) and "ass" (517) after comparing his ineffectual actions to the emotions feigned by an actor. While Gibson's Hamlet has no such point of comparison and as yet has no plans beyond hearing "a play tomorrow" (472–73), his history of violence makes his rage more predictable than in the play.

Against this background of consistent characterization, the thought of using the play to "catch the conscience of the king" (540) enters with effective suddenness. "I'll have these players / Play something like the murder of my father" (529–30) no longer explains facts learned earlier but dramatizes a moment of insight. Hamlet's thoughts crystallize across a sequence punctuated by three point-of-view shots of the players unloading their wagon, as seen through a barred window. Their calm but purposeful activity in the courtyard below helps to move him from explosive rage to his calmer and more purposeful plans. If Hamlet's rage causes delay, his plotting moves the action forward with remarkable briskness. As the speech ends, Hamlet's head in close-up moves abruptly offscreen. The exit recalls, with a difference, his vertical exit from the ghost scene. And like that exit, it launches us briskly into the realization of his plan, without the 290 lines that intervene in the play. Hamlet, clapping his hands with eager anticipation, enters the hallway where the players are preparing. He declares, in a non-Shakespearean line, "'Tis almost the time, haste you," checks and nods approval of the play script, and quickly moves Horatio into position to observe the king.

Polonius unwittingly supports Hamlet's sense of urgency. He rushes toward the camera clapping, as Hamlet has just done, strikes up the band, and introduces "the best actors in the world" (2.2.392) with comic gusto. But from this point, the film's tempo slows, as the preliminary entertainments allow Hamlet repeated occasions to indulge his mocking humor. Because looking at the king triggered the soliloquy and because the king's conscience has been so recently mentioned, Hamlet's focus of this humor on the women, especially on Gertrude, is all the more noticeable. Zeffirelli is both preparing us for the upcoming violent confrontation with the queen in her closet and making the queen an outlet for Hamlet's rage to disarm the king of any suspicions that he is the target. His comment about "how cheerfully" (3.2.119) his mother looks is spoken loudly enough for his mother to hear and carefully ignore. The long speech beginning "Get thee to a nunnery" is then imported from act 3, scene 1, allowing its misogyny to be applied to his mother even if spoken to Ophelia. Consistent with this transposition, Gertrude is given a version of Ophelia's line, "'Tis brief, my son," allowing Hamlet's reply, "As woman's love" (3.2.145–46), to be redirected to his mother. Even the rhymed interchange between the Player King and Queen, which we conclude to be Hamlet's work from his checking the play script and mouthing some of the words, is altered to place more emphasis on the Queen's repeated denials that she would remarry.

Moving the dumb show to follow the Player King and Queen's performance allows Hamlet to concentrate his provocation of Claudius more realistically and more forcefully at the end of the scene. The provocation begins when Hamlet mentions "poison in jest" (228) before any poison has been seen, prompting a look of guilty recollection. "You shall see anon how the murderer gets the love of Gonzago's wife" (256–57) is then addressed to Claudius rather than to Ophelia, as in the play, building the offense to the king, who has already displayed insecurity about his competition with Hamlet for Gertrude's affection. At the sight of the king's nephew, dressed in black as Hamlet has been until now, pouring poison into the sleeping king's ear, Claudius rises in shock. But it takes one more offense to make him lose control completely. The hooded Lucianus picks up the crown and appears to kiss it, confusing the ideas of crown and queen as the rewards of his crime. This reinforcement of the oedipal challenge proves decisive. Claudius drops his cup and staggers forward, clutching his right ear, identifying with the poisoned as much as the poisoner. He points accusingly at the hooded figure attempting to stalk offstage, as if he has caught the oedipal Hamlet in the act, but we now are shown the actor unhooded in a closer shot staring back at Claudius, reflecting the king's understanding that he has confused fiction with reality and given himself away. He makes a desperate attempt to turn his action into a jest, but his laughter ends when he confronts the real Hamlet, whose serious and knowing look tells the king that he interpreted the fiction correctly. He looks back at the actor, seeking further clarity before demanding, "Give me some light" (261). In the dimly lit hall, Claudius has been convincingly provoked into a momentary hallucinatory madness.

Like Olivier, Zeffirelli stages the Mousetrap aftermath as a rapidly cut scene of crowd madness; the panicked king exits hurriedly as the men and women of the court scream and scurry wildly about. But Zeffirelli packs the aftermath with added meaning appropriate to the end of his film's second movement. A four-shot sequence near the scene's beginning portrays an exchange of glances among the three major players. The Player King, Queen, and Lucianus register astonishment at the effect of their playlet on the court. At the same time, a quick exchange of tense glances between the King and Lucianus prefigures the drama to come when the battle of wits between Claudius and Hamlet intensifies in the third segment.

A sequence of five over-the-shoulder reverse shots at the scene's end enacts the termination of Hamlet's relationship with Ophelia. Like the weaving room encounter, this is a deformed "conversation," visually bidirectional but including only Hamlet's speech. Hamlet recommends the nunnery once more and bids her a cold "farewell," while her response is limited to a passionate moan during the relationship's only kiss, which is poignantly enclosed within Hamlet's cruel lines. The echo of the weaving room scene helps to frame the movement and clarify Hamlet's concentration on the imperative to revenge. Samuel Crowl observes that Zeffirelli's Mousetrap is "less about Hamlet's power struggle with Claudius than about the conclusion of his relationship with Ophelia and the preparation for his confrontation with Gertrude that follows."[17] But, of course, concluding his relationship with Ophelia is needed so that he can concentrate on revenge.

Most important among the scene's closural gestures is an eight-shot sequence forming a middle panel within the scene's twenty-four shots. In place of the single puzzled glance from Gertrude in Olivier, Zeffirelli includes three reaction shots of an increasingly alarmed Gertrude watching her son express his hostility to Claudius openly for the first time with his shout of "false fire" (3.2.258, in Folio) and his mad singing and dancing with the players. When Hamlet swings a drumstick wildly in the air, Gertrude's eyes widen with amazement. She makes a rapid exit. The sequence visually predicts that their next encounter will include powerful emotions and even violence.

The Third Movement

Although the Mousetrap's confirmation of Claudius's guilt focuses Hamlet more securely on his revenge, Gertrude's prominence during the play and its aftermath suggests that his next confrontation will be with his outraged mother. Rosencrantz and Guildenstern, who exited with the queen, now return to find Hamlet leading the players in a mad procession. Already in the screenplay, the lines of the two "friends" are reassigned to direct Hamlet's violence against the more offensive Rosencrantz, who was also the victim of his violence at the ranch house. Perhaps this is an example of what Welsh and Vela describe as "transposing lines capriciously," but the changes are carefully coordinated with visual images to clarify Hamlet's motivation.[18] This redirection predicts and prepares us for Hamlet's violence against his mother, perhaps subliminally, for Rosencrantz has been linked emphatically to her. Seated closely to her left at the Mousetrap, Rosencrantz was included in thirteen of the fourteen shots of Gertrude from Hamlet's vantage point, and in six of these the two appear without the presence of the king—in only one does Gertrude appear alone. As Blits notes, Rosencrantz now overboldly "addresses Hamlet in the imperative."[19] Lamenting that Hamlet would "deny [his] griefs to [his] friend" (3.2.330), he draws out the last word with barely disguised hypocrisy. Unsurprisingly, Hamlet explodes once more in violence, pinning him to the wall with the recorder pressed to his throat during the speech on plucking out the heart of his mystery. The Player Queen, first in costume and then after removing it, sits behind Hamlet during Rosencrantz's provocation, further incorporating the image of the mother into the scene.

Without Shakespeare's second request that Hamlet visit his mother in her closet, delivered by Polonius, Hamlet can now proceed more directly from one explosion toward another that we await expectantly. Two delays heighten the tension. His brief soliloquy on "the very witching time of night" (3.2.378) comes as he catches his breath after the encounter with Rosencrantz. Cut is the second half of the speech containing the resolution not to use violence against his mother. The speech is delivered at the bottom of a dark stairway, adding a visual echo to the temporal link with the ghost scene. Such associations should further spur Hamlet to his revenge, and the occasion soon arrives. After Hamlet's exit to the left leaves the screen black, an Olivier-inspired transition returns us to Claudius. The king enters as a shadow whose edge moving to the right in a false wipe reveals a new setting. The opposing motions of Hamlet and Claudius suggest a momentous collision as Hamlet's vengeful impetuosity moves toward the enormous shadow that conveys the weight of the king's guilt, the "wretched state" of his "bosom black as death" (3.3.67). Although only four of the original thirty-nine lines in Claudius's soliloquy are spoken, he is visually portrayed at his nadir and about to be confronted by Hamlet at the peak of his fury.

Striding purposefully toward his mother's room, Hamlet glimpses Claudius at prayer, halts in a low shot that magnifies his power, and draws his sword for the kill before speaking. Now Hamlet's surging violent energy justifies his change of mind from simple revenge to the deeper revenge of eternal damnation. Zeffirelli has left no room for interpreting Hamlet's deferral as an excuse for continuing to delay. Deleted lines allow Hamlet's occasions for a more appropriate murder to end with "th'incestuous pleasure of his bed" (90). With this thought and with an inserted repetition of "now to my mother" (3.2.282) from the end of the "witching time" soliloquy, Hamlet proceeds on his way. The repression of violence against Claudius only strengthens expectations that violence will return.

After Hamlet declines to kill Claudius at the king's low point, he enters the most discussed moment of the film at his own high point of determination and rage and confronts a Gertrude who is no less determined and angry. The recent glimpse of the Player Queen in and out of costume might recall the actor's earlier preparations before the mirror. Gertrude's preening and combing before a nearly identical mirror at her bedside imply her resolve to assume a queenly role. Indeed, her initial demeanor toward Hamlet is stern and dignified, explaining why Hamlet's first response to "Have you forgot me?" is "You are the queen" (3.4.14). Yet even without the film's earlier eroticization of her relation with her son, her erotic intentions would be plain here. Zeffirelli indicates that she intends to encounter her son alone, as she had in her seductive persuasion of act 1, scene 2 after dismissing Claudius, where she wore the peculiar headdress that now tops her mirror stand, by importing from the play's previous scene with Claudius Polonius's urging that "more audience than a mother . . . should overhear" (3.3.31–32). Gertrude's resistance to the presence of Polonius at a meeting that the film makes her idea rather than his (compare the play's 3.1.183) is evident in the counselor's urgent tone and hand gestures and in the dismissive hand gestures that accompany her curt order to "withdraw" (3.4.6). Polonius hides behind the arras only because Hamlet's imminent arrival blocks his exit from the room. Not only is Gertrude's hair, as Samuel Crowl observes, now "down and fully displayed for the first time in the film," but her bosom is more fully displayed as well.[20] Since retreating to her bedroom, she has changed into a more revealing dress, which will amplify the effect of placing her hand on her breast when she asks, "Have you forgot me?"

The bedroom scene becomes "the climax of Zeffirelli's film" through its cinematic intensification of violence, both "lethal and sexual."[21] The distinction between the two forms of violence repeatedly breaks down. Gertrude's provocative question and gesture provoke the first eruption. Hamlet approaches his mother with rising anger evident in his voice and face, pointing his sword threateningly toward her for the first time. He moves toward her and the camera from the large stylized lion tapestry as he denies forgetting her: "You are the Queen, your husband's brother's wife, / And would it were not so, you are my mother" (3.4.14–15). During his approach, the camera slowly tilts upward until he looms above us ominously in a snarling close-up. This intense visual effrontery is further enhanced by the background's sliding out of focus. His assertiveness is met by hers with equal visual effect. After a cut to over Hamlet's shoulder, a point-of-view shot that leaves Hamlet facing for a split second only Gertrude's glass, her face and hand rise abruptly into the screen from below, and her powerful slap literally spins him full circle in close-up, while short pans left then right amplify the momentum of her blow. Mel Gibson's trademark roar is of sufficient ferocity to stop her in her tracks as she tries to exit, appropriately under the gaze of the tapestry's open-mouthed lion. Before she can recover, Hamlet forces her back into the room with pointed sword. His threat to "set you up a glass where you may see the inmost part of you" (18–19) is his sexual counter to the literal glass that represents Gertrude's weapon. The camera's position allows this threat to accompany the illusion of piercing this inmost part, as the sword's point appears momentarily to pass through her breast and emerge from her back.

When Hamlet forces his mother at sword-point to her bed, an inconspicuous step beneath a bearskin rug at the bed's edge transforms his approach into a sexual "mounting" as he towers over her. Her "Thou wilt not murder me—" (20) is followed by his raising the sword and uttering something indiscernible but that may reasonably be interpreted as "yes," and one may reasonably infer that only Polonius's cry for help saves the queen from her son's mad violence.[22] The cry causes Hamlet to redirect his sword away from Gertrude and into the arras, between the legs of the lion, a vast enlargement of the symbol of John the Evangelist in the illuminated *Book of Durrow*; students of the Middle Ages in the audience will appreciate the irony of having Gertrude's incest overseen by evangelical eyes.[23] The sword is allowed to bounce up and down repeatedly, in a grotesque fusion of violence and sexuality. Hamlet withdraws it with an exultant shout of "Dead!" (22), his arms raised in triumph as he activates one of Shakespeare's most notorious puns. Sex now moves from the metaphoric to the physical.

If the bedroom scene is the film's climax, Hamlet's wringing of his mother's "penetrable stuff" (34) becomes a climax within the climax. Zeffirelli's camera and editing form this barely disguised rape into a scene-within-the-scene, beginning with one of the longest takes of the film, which at nearly one minute contrasts with the preceding rhythm, a normative four seconds per shot. This long take becomes an "establishing shot" that tracks in as mother and son move onto the bed and Hamlet confronts her with the images of her two husbands. This symmetrically composed face-off ends when her twisting attempt to escape is met with more violence. The music fades and a second, somewhat shorter take in tighter close-up further isolates the couple—together—in the private world of their intensely emotional confrontation, which now occurs with no surrounding background visible and Hamlet above and behind her in a sexually suggestive position. Only their heads and upper bodies are visible, leaving the mind free to speculate on what might be happening elsewhere. When Gertrude responds with "O speak no more" (88, modified), he slips off the bed and can be seen sobbing behind her. Prurient eyes of the mind often glimpse more disturbing actions performed by Hamlet outside the frame.

Continuing a conventional scenic construction, the scene-within intensifies the "conversation" by shifting from the lengthy two-shots into two segments of more quickly edited shots/reverse-shots in close-up, approximating the over-the-shoulder convention although the now-supine Gertrude bounces in and out of the frame after, in a blur of motion, Hamlet flips Gertrude over onto her back, mounts, growls, and paws at her with animal ferocity. The first segment culminates as Hamlet's pelvic thrusts follow the rhythm of his cruelest tongue-lashing, "honeying and making love / Over the nasty sty!" (93–94).

The second segment ends when Gertrude, either shrewdly or passionately, replaces her verbal protestations with a kiss. The final shot of Hamlet in extreme close-up, kissing with his eyes closed, assumes a new camera angle that suggests that Gertrude is now above him, in part through the reversal of their heads' position on screen despite the continuation of intense lighting from the left. The scene thus traces its action through three sexual positions, the last supporting a reading of her kiss as passionately motivated.

The ghost enters as a figure first barely glimpsed by Hamlet, then fully perceived with startling suddenness. The effect begins sonically. A low, eerie sound is heard at the moment that the kiss silences Hamlet's ravings. In the tight close-up, his eye opens very slightly but closes again as a cut reveals the ghost entering through an arched doorway and the rising sound reveals itself to be the wind heard in the ghost's earlier visitation. Now Hamlet's eyes open wide with wonder, and Gertrude falls out of the frame softly sobbing, suggesting a postcoital swoon. The son caught in the act of oedipal usurpation leaps from the bed and prays to "heavenly guards" (101) for protection as vehemently as he earlier prayed, "Angels and ministers of grace defend us" (1.4.39), when he did not know what the creature was or whether its intent was hostile or benign.

The emotions evoked by the ghost's appearance are suitably complex. Initially terrified, Hamlet huddles defensively beside a post at the head of the bed and then moves forward, only to the protection of another post at the foot. The posts' distinctly phallic form keeps visible the nature of his transgression. Apparently contrite, he then seeks eagerly to please the chastising parent, glancing back at the ghost for approval when he steps between his mother "and her fighting soul" (3.4.109). As the ghost directs Hamlet to address Gertrude, his outstretched hands, which recall the poignant ending of the first ghost scene, encourage us to interpret Hamlet's subsequent move in the direction of the ghost as motivated by love and the fear of losing him again. But with the ghost's departure, he quickly turns his emotional attention back toward his mother. Gertrude is stricken by Hamlet's apparent madness, but despite her protest that "all that is I see" (129) and confirming cuts to the empty doorway, she continues to look toward it. Unlike Oliver's Gertrude, she seems to sense the truth of Hamlet's claims.

Following the long and relatively complete treatment of the bedroom encounter, act 4, scene 1 is filmed with brisk efficiency, using a mere eight of its forty-five lines. The emphasis is on Gertrude's radical shift of allegiance and the recovery of Claudius from his breakdown at the Mousetrap. As Hamlet lugs the corpse into the neighboring room, Gertrude raises the locket portraying old Hamlet for contemplation. Her renewed allegiance to her dead husband merges with allegiance to her son when she stares eerily at the camera, after which a cut reveals her looking toward the doorway from which Hamlet exited the room, much as she had continued to look at the ghost's empty doorway. The strength of her reverie is conveyed by her nonresponse to the voice of Claudius calling her name from offscreen, followed by her startled gasp and quick hiding of the locket when Claudius calls once more. A comparison is implicitly made between her delayed response to Claudius and her quick response to Hamlet's offscreen call of "Mother" at the beginning of the previous scene. To provide an additional sign of the competition in which Hamlet now prevails, the camera takes in the same view for the entrance of Claudius that it took for Gertrude awaiting Hamlet, including the mirror and the distinctive headpiece worn by Gertrude before Hamlet's first soliloquy, when her seductive approach to her son quickly gave way to her stronger relationship with her husband. Set up in this way, Gertrude's claim that Hamlet is mad is unambiguously meant to deceive.

Shakespeare's Claudius enters the scene confused, asking the meaning of Gertrude's sighs and inquiring about Hamlet perhaps because he suspects that the answer will involve the apparently mad prince. He fears that the killing will be "laid to us" (4.1.17) and proposes calling their "wisest friends" (38) to counter "envious slander" (40), ending with a couplet that proclaims, "My soul is full of discord and dismay" (45). Zeffirelli's more decisive and focused Claudius enters, immediately asking, "Where is your son?" (3), indicating that his new and improved reaction to the Mousetrap's threat is under way before he suspects additional bad news. After seeing the pools of blood and concluding, "It had been so with us had we been there" (13), a cut to another room translates this conclusion instantly into efficient crisis management. Claudius strides in resolutely, calling for guards and friends to "go join you with some further aid" (33). His henchmen instantly fan out to search the castle.

Claudius's visually enhanced control, of himself and of the court, continues into his next confrontation with Hamlet. Hamlet is not apprehended and brought before the king by guards but enters as if on cue at the king's question, "But where is he?" (4.3.13). He jumps up onto a table, scatters its load of scrolls with a kick, and proceeds through his provocative banter about "the worm that hath eat of a king" (26–27) with the grinning self-assurance of a madman. The power-signifying array of men surrounding the king, some with swords drawn, makes Hamlet's antic disposition all the more convincing. In a game of one-upmanship, persuasive madness permits Hamlet to vent his hostility with impunity. His successful performance, however, also has the paradoxical effect of improving Claudius's position, for it makes his plan to send Hamlet to England appear more reasonable, adding an extenuating circumstance to the killing of Polonius and making a therapeutic approach rather than "the strong law" (4.3.3) more evidently needed. Hamlet jauntily assumes control, exiting on his own accord with the command, "Come, for England" (51). But Claudius reveals that, as he says only in the play, "everything is sealed and done" (54) by placing his hands on the sealed letters portending "The present death of Hamlet" (63). The editing has left little implied time for their preparation, and it would not be unreasonable for the viewer to assume that the rapidly rebounding king began his scheme for Hamlet's death even before hearing of the murder.

Hamlet prepares to depart in the great courtyard, in darkness implying that events from now back through the Mousetrap occurred during one very eventful night in which the initiative radically reversed from Hamlet to Claudius. Gertrude hurries down the stairway before the castle entrance as she did once before, when leaving her son for the hunt with Claudius prior to the first soliloquy. In contrast, she is now running to Hamlet. But if Hamlet has prevailed in Gertrude's affections, both are shown to be at the mercy of Claudius. Gertrude's presence here, with dialogue borrowed from the bedroom scene, makes her absence in the previous scenes more conspicuous, and Hamlet's explanation, "I must to England—you know that" (3.4.198), implies that she has been cut off from contact with her son. When he gestures with his head toward his two schoolfellows, noting their plan to "marshal me to knavery" (3.4.207), Gertrude gasps. She is last seen raising her hand to her mouth in sorrow or despair, as Ophelia did in the weaving room on perceiving Hamlet's madness.

A slow triple dissolve indicating the passage of considerable time conveys us into the next scene: Gertrude with her hand over her mouth dissolves to a caravel sailing the glittering sea; which dissolves to a forlorn, rainy view of peninsular Elsinore; which in turn gives way to a shiny black slab of rock. There follows one of Zeffirelli's virtuosic delayed disclosures. As first a pair of hands and then Ophelia rise from behind the slab, the dissolves connect Gertrude's sorrowful thoughts of her departing son with what Ophelia might be seeing as she peers out into space. Is she scanning the sea, awaiting her lover's return?[24] Her rise from a passage in the middle of the familiar battlements, out of sight of the sea, reveals that, if so, the sea that bears Hamlet is visible only in her mad mind's eye. Or is the daughter of Polonius on an imaginary spy mission? we might ask, recalling her father's hands on the weaving room railing and watching her glance sneakily left then right. The dual cause of Ophelia's madness, Hamlet's rejection and her father's death, has been combined visually in the same shot.

Another puzzle presents itself. Gertrude is opening the window of Hamlet's room that we earlier saw Hamlet close angrily as he said, "Frailty, thy name is woman" (1.2.146). Horatio is glimpsed behind her. Why is Gertrude in Hamlet's room, and why is she with Horatio, who was last seen riding out the castle gate with Hamlet behind Rosencrantz and Guildenstern? She watches in horror as Ophelia lewdly amuses herself with an uncomfortable armed soldier, stroking and yanking his phallic belt. The queen shakes her head in disbelief and clasps the pendant cross that has replaced the locket of Claudius on her breast. Choking back a sob, she reaches for comforting support to Horatio and then steps behind Hamlet's table and places her hand on a hefty volume precisely as Hamlet had done during Horatio's report about the ghost. It is clear that her shift of allegiance to Hamlet has continued over the interim. It is equally clear that she has not rebounded in the manner of her husband from the long night of the Mousetrap. With a quavering voice, she confesses the "guilt" of her "sick soul" (4.5.17–20), in what was originally a soliloquy, to Hamlet's best friend. When Ophelia's "Where is the beauteous majesty of Denmark?" (21) wafts in through the window, she gasps and shrinks backward in fright. The idea of frailty connects the madwoman to the woman disturbed by the sight of madness.

Zeffirelli declines to specify a cause for Gertrude's decline from mastery over both of her men to a figure of frailty, depicting her as simply overwhelmed by her sea of troubles. One is invited to read into her state sorrow over the death of Polonius and the madness of Ophelia, fear for Hamlet's safety, guilt over her sexual conduct with her son, a new realization that her marriage was overhasty and is now untenable, and most interestingly, anxiety over her vulnerability to Ophelia's affliction. Ophelia's mad scenes play to all of these causes. Olivier's Gertrude took the lead in comforting Ophelia, taking a maternal approach to a young women who was still a potential daughter-in-law. Zeffirelli's responds initially in a composed manner to Ophelia's question and descends partway from Hamlet's room toward her, but she cannot for long bear the pressure of Ophelia's eye contact. Gertrude runs down the stairs to escape but is cut off much as Hamlet cut her off around the bed, and Ophelia begins playing distractedly with the queen's necklace. Despite her clearly signaled shift of allegiance to Hamlet,

Gertrude runs to Claudius in relief when he appears. She tries to remain uninvolved in the background while Claudius does what he can, calmly listening to the mad words that Ophelia confides to him.

Gertrude's attempted disengagement is undercut by visual details and Ophelia's repeated attentions. Although "we know what we are but not what we may be" (43–44, modified) is spoken privately to Claudius, Ophelia's gaze and nod indicate that she is referring to Gertrude. A cut to Gertrude shows her fingering her necklace as Ophelia had earlier. Ophelia recovers from the thought of her father in the "cold ground" (70) after a glance that causes her to raise her hand to her mouth. A cut to Gertrude with her hand to her mouth reveals the inspiration for Ophelia's imitative gesture. Ophelia then goes to Gertrude to kiss her hand and thank her for her "good counsel" (71), after which she offers her queenly hand to Claudius for a kiss. Waving regally to the grieving female attendants, as we have seen Gertrude wave to the adoring crowd, Ophelia bids them good night and exits. Nor does it escape attention that Ophelia's ragged purple garment is a lighter-hued version of Gertrude's royal robe. The admiration for Gertrude that Ophelia has displayed throughout the film has transformed into delusional identification with her. Within this context, one of the film's most striking images, a low shot of Ophelia beneath the radial walkways and central tower of the great hall, might be read as a gigantic oppressive crowning, a visualization of both her escape into the delusion of royalty and the overhanging weight of grief that this escape cannot actually relieve.

After over six dolorous minutes devoted to Ophelia's madness, Zeffirelli provides a change of pace and tone before returning to the long sequence that finishes Ophelia's story. He imports Hamlet's escape from act 5, scene 2, again showing rather than telling, as in Hamlet's meeting with Ophelia in the weaving room. Below deck on the ship, as Ophelia's music gives way to a reprise of the suspenseful, rising melody of the film's opening scene in the crypt, Hamlet reads the king's letter and slips two of his own into sleeping Rosencrantz's gear. As Hamlet reads, Claudius redelivers the "Do it, England" speech in voice-over (4.3.63). Because Hamlet has already prepared his substitute letters (rather than, as in the play, returning to his room to read the letter and then writing his own), one concludes that he at least suspects the content of the king's and has ruthlessly countered it before confirming. His preemptive preparation recalls the king's apparently similar preparation, before learning of Polonius's death, of the letter that Hamlet now removes. Rosencrantz and Guildenstern are shown being caught "between the pass and fell incensed points / Of mighty opposites" (5.2.61–62). Welsh and Vela note that Zeffirelli "completely ignores Hamlet's fourth soliloquy, in which he states his resolution, finally, to take action against his uncle."[25] Maintaining his status as a violent and mighty opposite throughout, Gibson's violent Hamlet does not need to declare, "O, from this time forth / My thoughts be bloody or be nothing worth" (4.4.65–66).

To emphasize his hero's relentlessly bloody thoughts, Zeffirelli ends the sequence with a startlingly brutal execution, by far the most cinematically magnified violence of the film. A loud percussive beat beginning below deck carries across a cut to Hamlet's schoolfellows being hustled forward in a dark hallway. The camera tracks back rapidly, stopping suddenly when an executioner poised above an ax and a block comes into view. As the percussion is joined by rising musical notes, the ax rises and the growling head of Rosencrantz is thrust upon the block. He lifts his head from the block to look with angry hostility at the camera. Carl Plantinga describes "the scene of empathy" often included in films, a gratuitous gaze upon a character's face "not warranted by the simple communication of information about character emotion" but simply designed "to elicit empathetic emotions in the spectator."[26] Our final sight of Rosencrantz is a brutal inversion of the norm, designed to elicit our hostility. A cut reveals the gleaming ax starting downward, and at the final percussive beat, overlaid by the crash of a cymbal, we know without seeing that Hamlet's odious companion is no more. The total effect is highly kinesthetic, an eruption of violent action that jolts the audience into anticipating more.

More violent action quickly ensues, but now it is Claudius's turn to display his formidability as an opponent, as the might of the opposites continues to build. The cymbal signaling the beheading of Rosencrantz resonates as a sound bridge into the next shot until replaced by a diegetic horn alerting the sentries posed atop Elsinore. A heedless galloping rider drives walkers from the road below the castle and disrupts the peaceful commerce in the great courtyard. Removal of his hood reveals Laertes, who with sword drawn charges into the castle demanding to see the king. Laertes fully evinces the play's "impetuous haste" (4.5.100), but he arrives without the usual mob of supporters, and rather than breaking down the doors he is quickly stopped by royal guards. The change allows the scene to focus on Claudius's courage: consistently with Zeffirelli's early shift of allegiance, Gertrude does not intervene heroically and therefore does not need to be told twice to let Laertes go, nor does Laertes bravely dismiss his followers. Claudius is not forced into confrontation but gratuitously invites Laertes to pose a mortal threat, calmly facing the sword pointed at his throat and gently tapping it aside with his ringed finger. He then immediately establishes an intimacy, protesting his innocence. A cut to Laertes' intense reaction reveals that the king has placed his hands affectionately on the young man's shoulders. He knows how to recruit the desperate to his cause.

At the sound of women wailing, Laertes rushes into the throne room, where he finds Ophelia sitting on the queen's throne playing with pieces of straw. In her final scene, Ophelia is the visual and verbal focus, as in Olivier's film. She retains almost all of the lines except for the three snatches of song, and she is in the most shots and the most close-ups. All of the characters, including minor bystanders, continually watch her with sad fascination. The scene, however, belongs as much to Laertes, despite the cutting of his lines from seventeen to two. His major role in the fourth movement would benefit from preparation, and he is accordingly endowed with a heightened subjectivity. As he walks toward his sister with a puzzled look, the film cuts to its most elaborately subjective shot: a tracking point-of-view camera that approaches Ophelia while Laertes' invisible but audible (like our own) footsteps continue, slow, then come to a stop with a cut to a close-up. An innovative series of six close-ups in "separation" alternate Ophelia offering her brother two bones, which he examines and then takes from her hand. For both characters' shots, the bone extends into the frame realistically out of focus while each looks at the other's face, but for the shots portraying Ophelia, the camera is almost aligned with the two siblings' eye-line: we see what he sees more than what she sees.

In addition to assisting our identification with Laertes, Zeffirelli continues developing the relations of the major characters. Previously, Gertrude was seen watching Laertes threatening Claudius but not intervening. Now she enters from a different direction from the men and is visually grouped with her attendant women. She looks only at Ophelia and reacts wordlessly but emotionally in four shots. If Ophelia's madness continues to encourage Gertrude's alienation from Claudius, it has the opposite effect on Laertes. On first seeing Ophelia on the throne, Laertes glanced to the king for guidance or explanation. Claudius returns the favor by glancing at Laertes after receiving both his "rue" (a piece of straw) and his "daisy" (a nail). Her royal duties completed, Ophelia walks from between the two men to the door through which they entered, glancing back contentedly at her loyal subjects.

In the drowning scene, Zeffirelli reciprocates Ophelia's extended identification with Gertrude through small filmic gestures. Like Olivier, he dissolves directly from Ophelia's exit to an exterior scene. She runs gaily down a valley or moat below the castle walls and onto a small footbridge over a stream, while female voices join the plangent melody earlier associated with her madness instrumentally. A cut to the running water below implies her point of view, but as Gertrude's narration begins in voice-over, replacing the music, the camera pans upward to reveal her sitting on the bridge. The subliminal effect is to connect this view with the narrating voice. As we zoom slowly in for our final look upon poor Ophelia, Gertrude's voice lowers almost to a whisper, as if she speaks from the camera's position. The queen's figure, dressed appropriately in black, dissolves into Ophelia's distracted visage, and her voice rises as she walks into the throne room through the doorway of Ophelia's exit, addressing Claudius and Laertes. Until the narration nears its end, Gertrude speaks through the hint of a smile. Anthony Guneratine reads the smile as indicating that she is "secretly delighted by Ophelia's fate."[27] Gertrude's alignment with the women in the previous scene and the filmic gestures sympathetically linking Gertrude and Ophelia here support a different reading, I propose, implying that she understands the release that is evident in the second mad scene and Ophelia's final gambol through beautiful sunlit nature. Returning to the scene of drowning, the camera zooms from the stream to the calm ocean framed by V-shaped cliffs, concluding the scene with the favored symbol of Riane Eisler's *The Chalice and The Blade*, a work of utopian feminism topping international best-seller charts at the time of filming.[28]

The Fourth Movement

Zeffirelli punctuates the transition to a new movement with attention-grabbing camera work and editing. Into the V-gap displaying the ocean that receives Ophelia's soul dissolves the image of two men on horseback. The centrifugal upward tilt and zoom-in of Ophelia's spiritual departure is countered by a centripetal shot that pans right then left, tilts down, and zooms out to bring us to the gravesite before the riders. We have been hustled kinesthetically through the portal from one scene to the next.

Hamlet's interaction with the gravedigger is handled with no less visual flair. His question-and-answer session with this wittily evasive character divides neatly into two segments around the idea of the dead woman. Both segments progressively move the shots closer to the speakers. The first occurs with Hamlet on horseback. On learning that the grave is being prepared for "one that was a woman" (5.1.128), Hamlet dismounts to begin a new and longer segment culminating in his contemplation of Yorick's skull. Pascale Aebischer observes that "Hamlet's own reflections over Yorick's skull never explicitly evoke the possibility of his own death but displace his mortality onto 'my lady' . . . in an uncanny flashback (or is it flash-forward?) to the death of Ophelia."[29] Hamlet does not know of Ophelia's death, but Zeffirelli's division of the gravedigger scene into two segments of parallel structure allows Ophelia's uncanny presence to be felt twice before her body's arrival.

Like the "to be" soliloquy, and as in most stage productions, for which Shakespeare's most anticipated words are rarely sacrificed, Hamlet's Yorick speech is given in its entirety. Gibson places the skull firmly on a grassy mound in front of him and begins in a medium shot that slightly displaces the point of view of Horatio, who crouches nearby to listen. With the shift to second-person address, the camera shifts to a close-up of Hamlet over the grassy "shoulder" of the skull. When his question "Where be your jibes now . . ." (179) goes un- answered, the failure of conversation is underscored visually by a failure to cut to a standard answering shot over Hamlet's shoulder. For "Now get you to my lady's chamber" (182–83), Gibson rises and hugs the skull, replacing his gaze into Yorick's empty eyes with a momentary gaze of his mind's eye. At the end of the speech, rather than following the play's diversion of attention for twenty lines to Alexander and Caesar, the film, following Olivier's precedent, uses the sound of an approaching funeral procession to reintroduce "my lady" herself.

Hamlet quickly conceals himself, indicating that his avenging mission remains intact and that he will be following a new course of outwitting his opponents, as he has done with Rosencrantz and Guildenstern, rather than playing the futile games of one-upmanship of the third movement. But with the uncovering of Ophelia's corpse, he seems to waver momentarily in his purpose. Olivier's prince triumphantly announced himself, declaring, "This is I, Hamlet the Dane" (246–47), which might well be taken as a provocative claim to the throne. Gibson approaches listlessly without any announcement and without reproaching Laertes for his grief that "bears such an emphasis" (244), allowing Laertes to become the aggressive party. The two young men struggle, but if the ostensible conflict now is between Laertes and Hamlet, the film keeps us mindful of the primary conflict with Claudius through a series of five reaction shots in close-up distributed through the scene. The king is the one who first notices Hamlet, spinning around quickly with the kind of uncanny, unseeing recognition that made Ophelia glance aside in the weaving room and Hamlet turn back to the ghost in the turret. When Laertes moves toward Hamlet, Claudius eyes him intently, perhaps seeing a new opportunity to recruit an angry ally. He also watches, no doubt assessing her allegiance, as Gertrude calms her son. Hamlet finally regains his balance at the end in a delayed disclosure that is effective because the king's surprise is shared by the audience. Hamlet's final lines, "Let Hercules himself do what he may, / The cat will mew and dog will have his day" (280–81), which is conventionally spoken to Laertes, is now delivered toward an unseen recipient, until a cut to Claudius defines the eye-line of Hamlet. The scene ends with a silent exchange of glances between the king and queen. Their relationship has evidently been altered by the events, but how remains unknown.

Zeffirelli follows Olivier in delaying the plotting of Claudius and Laertes for Hamlet's death until after the graveyard scene, but he uses this delay for greater effect, altering the impression of Claudius and intercutting smaller scenes for suspense and irony. Because letters alerted Olivier's king to Hamlet's survival and imminent return, the failure of Claudius to respond immediately to the threat is compromising. Zeffirelli's Claudius, in contrast, responds to this sudden and unexpected setback with admirable efficiency. He brings Laertes immediately to the walkway below Hamlet's room where he and Polonius earlier discussed sending Hamlet to England, treating Laertes as a trusted counselor while continuing the parental physical contact of the rebellion scene: in effect, both allowing Laertes to assume his father's role and offering himself as a substitute. From this vantage, the two men can signify their common cause through glances up to the familiar door. Zeffirelli brings in much of the same dialog from act 4, scene 7 as Olivier but breaks off the scene after Claudius ventures the general idea of a death that will be called an accident (4.7.67), leaving the details hanging. Three scenes follow that establish an effective four-part, intercut series.

In a scene identical in length to the previous one, Osric arrives to announce the wager and duel. The upward glances at Hamlet's closed door by the plotters are countered by a downward view of Hamlet's door from inside the room. This view will soon come to represent the vantage of Hamlet and Horatio, who have just entered on the familiar high walkway that connects the room to the battlements and will proceed to the stairway. The visual echo of the ghost report scene suggests the imminent completion of a story set in motion long ago; Horatio and Hamlet conversed on this identically shot walkway at almost precisely the same distance from the film's opening as they do now from its close. Striving for pathos in depicting Hamlet's choice to proceed, Zeffirelli cuts the portion of act 5, scene 2 containing the redundant messages of Osric and the unnamed "lord" to a mere fifth of its original length,

eliminating all satire. Osric becomes a dignified (indeed, conspicuously patient) messenger who smiles appreciatively at the remnant of antic disposition contained in the prince's closing reply: "If his fitness speaks, mine is ready.
/ Now or whensoever, provided I be so able as now" (180–81). Because the
detail that the duel will take place "tomorrow" has been added, the remark
waxes nonsensical. Played by John McEnery, whose portrayal of an antic and
homosexual Mercutio in Zeffirelli's *Romeo and Juliet* was widely praised, Osric
takes the remark as an invitation to recall that performance, rolling his eyes
downward for an appraising glance at the obviously "able" Mel Gibson. The
film's sympathetic homoerotic aspect remains intact.

This glimpse of Osric's traditional homosexuality introduces only brief
comic relief before the scene resumes its solemnity. Haunting high-toned woodwind music begins here and continues through the intercuts. When it is joined
at Osric's ceremonious bow of farewell by low and descending piano notes, the
music lends a combination of sublimity and ominousness to Hamlet's thought
of "how ill all's here about my heart" (5.2.190–91). Hamlet walks toward the sun-
filled window. A cut to Laertes conspiring with Claudius to poison both the
sword and the chalice supports his sense of unease. It also creates irony through
the juxtaposition of the murderous plotting with the claim by Hamlet to "defy
augury" (197), which precedes the plotting, and with the lines beginning "There
is special providence in the fall of a sparrow" (197–98), which then follows the
plotting. An expressive match cut further emphasizes the young men's colliding
trajectories. As Laertes moves a step down a stairway to the left while anticipating the joy of telling Hamlet, "Thus diest thou" (4.7.55, modified), Hamlet steps
up into the raised window well to the right. The meditations that culminate in
"The readiness is all" (5.2.200) occur during Hamlet's last view from his familiar window, as the sun setting over the ocean prefigures his fate.[30]

The cunningly intercut scenes of angry plotting and resigned "readiness"
build suspense for Shakespeare's greatest duel scene, which Zeffirelli significantly enhances through worldmaking and visual characterization. Hamlet
strides resolutely through the multiple openings—sliding doors, Norman archway, crossed spears—of the familiar entrance to the throne room, entering a
world elaborately furnished with rituals and assumed rules of conduct. He
is welcomed and wordlessly directed to his assigned place by Osric, who will
guide the competitors through a progression of three contests fought with
different weapons, armor, and opening ceremonies.

Because the role of Hamlet's principal antagonist has been reassigned
for the moment to Laertes, the young men's relationship is configured first.

Sympathy for Laertes has been undercut by the contrast between his thirst for revenge and the sublimity of Hamlet's meditations. This undercutting continues in the duel scene nearly until the end. The throne room setting is arranged with more emphatic symmetry than Olivier's, with Hamlet and his band of brothers aligned along the right side, overseen from her throne by Gertrude, who gazes almost ceaselessly upon her son. Hamlet and Horatio greet the forward-looking lineup of Marcellus, Francisco, and Barnardo affectionately upon entering, recalling their long-standing collective enterprise. Laertes and unfamiliar attendants cluster with a more conspiratorial air on the opposite side of the raised wooden platform in front of Claudius. Camera sitings reinforce our identifications, supporting moral bias with visual bias. Despite the rigid symmetry, and repeated shots to Laertes' side from the royal point of view, no shots provide the point of view from this side toward the thrones, in contrast to numerous such shots from the side of Hamlet. In addition, the only diagonal shots across the platform observe the action from a vantage between that of Hamlet and Gertrude.

Hamlet's apology to Laertes omits the false and therefore compromising excuse of madness, while Laertes' response retains his refusal of "reconcilement" (5.2.224) while omitting only his cautious explanation that he awaits advice on the matter from "some elder masters of known honour" (225). In the first combat, begun with sufficient ceremonial motion of swords, hands, and bodies to imply strict rules of engagement, Laertes surprisingly knocks Hamlet from the platform with an elbow blow to the head. This move produces a visible reaction of consternation by Gertrude and redoubles Hamlet's fury, quickly leading to his first hit, which is vehemently denied by Laertes despite its "very palpable" (5.2.262) nature. Laertes' subsequent remark, "Well, again" (263), announces an impulsive attack on startled Hamlet that prompts Claudius to quickly order, "Stay" (264). Laertes is hustled from the platform by his attendants.

After Laertes eagerly watches Claudius poison the chalice, it becomes still harder to sympathize with the young man. His impatience when Hamlet repeatedly clowns in the second combat—feigning inability to wield the heavier broadsword, running comically about, and sneezing in the face of Osric—is countered by the evident amusement of Gertrude, which we and the observing crowd share. In the third combat, after Laertes picks the poisoned sword, another elbow blow and his kneeing of Hamlet's stomach appear highly unsportsmanlike. Following this series of compromising actions, Hamlet's reaction to Laertes' wounding him in the arm during a break in the combat is all the more understandable. Only now does the prince's familiar violence explode. With a bestial growl and a grimace, he punches Laertes in the face, dislodging the offending sword. After backing up his terrified opponent, he presses the poisoned point onto Laertes' chest, in perhaps Hamlet's first violence for which we assess him sufficiently provoked. Indeed, after the prince's long series of outbursts, an audience now might admire his relative restraint.

Attention is divided during the third combat between the adversaries and Gertrude, who after drinking the poisoned wine displays its effects through nine inset shots. In Olivier's film, Gertrude's realignment leads to her knowing self-sacrifice. She slowly deduces the king's plan to poison Hamlet, then heroically drinks the wine herself. Zeffirelli's more complex Gertrude confirms her realignment no less emphatically through her repeated smiles and doting gazes on Hamlet and her reluctance to look at her husband. More confident in her well-proven power over men, and lacking the evidence that Olivier's queen seems to have acquired through the letter she received from Hamlet before his return, she beams with happiness when Claudius drops the poisoned pearl into the chalice to honor her son. Now she must experience the unmistakable effect of the poison before understanding dawns. Morricone's sudden harp chords accompany this sudden realization. She stares openmouthed at the cup and pitcher, then at her husband, and finally turns back toward Hamlet, maintaining her gaze through two more inset close-ups and even as she stumbles down from the throne in the direction of her approaching son.

As Gertrude lies dying, Claudius comes down from the throne to intervene in the duel. By this point, his authority and self-control, very evident earlier in the scene, have evaporated, and his demeanor and behavior recall his panicked reaction to the Mousetrap, setting up a series of satisfying ironies. His explanation of the queen's collapse, "She swoons to see them bleed" (293), is delivered with the dismissive laugh and hand gesture with which he hoped to alter public impressions of his reaction to Gonzago's murder, and with equal ineffectiveness. The wine cup, which Claudius prominently dropped as he approached the players, returns to view when Hamlet pours the poisoned wine down Claudius's throat. The king's crown lies on the step above where he rolls in death. One might well expect Hamlet to pick it up, as Lucianus picked his uncle's fallen crown up from the floor.

That he does not helps to define this Hamlet against Olivier's, whose final effort is to mount the throne. Zeffirelli's film has more fully replaced the play's Renaissance mystique of kingship and power with the more accessible values of oedipal attraction and homosocial bonding. If Olivier's prince might be said to succeed by attaining for a brief moment the position of the king, bowed to submissively by the courtiers, Zeffirelli's succeeds by moving from the throne dais to the center of the platform, where he collapses. While he is comforted by Horatio, repeated low shots of the courtiers gathered about him incorporate the fallen hero's point of view. When Horatio, also from a low angle, closes the film's dialogue with "And flights of angels sing thee to thy rest" (344), an overhead camera offers a counterpoint to such shots. It rises slowly, bringing into view first Marcellus and then Barnardo and Francisco. Hamlet's body lies at the center between his friends (who now flank him on both sides of the platform) and the bodies of the slain (which likewise configure around him geometrically). Accompanied by the ascending notes of Morricone's solemn music, the ascending view suggests, in the words of Kathy Howlett, "that Hamlet's death is a release, like Ophelia's own, to an infinite space beyond the confines of this earthly frame."[31]

Fortinbras does not enter at this point to reintroduce the world of politics, but the rising camera embraces the community that Zeffirelli's focus on family dynamics never excluded to the extent that Olivier's similar focus did.[32] It does so through the magic of variable framing, allowing our perspective to widen slowly from an erotically tinged relationship to the small band of brothers (who have surprisingly remained with Hamlet to the end as a kind of substitute family) to the larger crowd of Danes, who have never been out of our sight for very long. To the last shot, Zeffirelli has sought to improve upon the essayistic method of Olivier, the oedipal "hero" of his youth against whom he defined his filmmaking accomplishments, finding ever new means to compensate for his screenplay's necessary cuts to the play-text.[33]

KENNETH BRANAGH'S
Hamlet
The Challenges of the Full-Text Screenplay

The filmed *Hamlet* that Kenneth Branagh would
have made in 1988–89, if Zeffirelli's plans had not
materialized more quickly than his own, would
no doubt have been a shortened, essayistic version in the manner of Olivier and most subsequent Shakespeare films. Branagh's comments on
the film that took its place, *Henry V,* indicate that
at the time he recognized a need for commercial
length: "My own experience of cinema-going convinced me that two hours was the maximum span
of concentration that could be expected from an
audience for a film of this kind." This span dic-
tated extensive textual deletions to streamline the

plot for film's more rapid pace and clearer story line. To make "a truly popular film," he observed, "the pace and excitement of the plot would be presented with the greatest possible clarity." Character psychology would need stricter focus. For Henry, Branagh concentrated on "elements of the king's personality" that included not the exalted heroism of Olivier's filmed Henry but "the qualities of introspection, fear, doubt and anger" defining "an especially young Henry with more than a little of the Hamlet in him."[1] By the time Branagh resumed efforts to film *Hamlet,* he had completely changed his mind. Having performed in full-text versions on radio and on stage, by 1995 his success as a filmmaker had emboldened him to try a full-text film. He recognized the highly experimental nature of his project, noting that "aside from feeling that it would be fascinating to see all of that text played out in a film, I also wanted to see how much an audience might be encouraged to take it or to sit through it—what reaction there would be to that amount of dialogue."[2]

Samuel Crowl deftly summarizes the challenge that Branagh set himself with this radical change in approach: "To release all that language and allow its energy to propel rather than paralyze his film was the ultimate challenge for the filmmaker. Branagh met it by combining in the film five crucial ingredients: landscape, cast, camera, editing, and music."[3] One must begin analyzing Branagh's orchestration of these ingredients with the camera, for his *Hamlet* is not only much longer than previous films but also much wider. His unusual choice to employ a 70mm high-resolution film gauge means that every shot includes more space from left to right than in the earlier films. The wider screen of 70mm entails disadvantages and advantages. Vertical movement and perspective become less dramatic than in standard format, while possibilities (and challenges) open for horizontal movement and composition. One cannot expect the dazzling ascents and descents of the earlier films. More subtly, what part of the screen we look at will be more carefully controlled. In an influential essay, Charles Barr explains that the primary advantage of the ultra-wide-screen format is that "it gives a greater range for gradation of emphasis." By varying depth of field, for example, the cinematographer can exploit a greater variety of levels of attention directed to objects in the background and on the enlarged periphery. With deep focus, wide-screen can produce a greater demand on the spectator "to make a positive act of interpreting, of 'reading' the shot" to find meaning in its abundance of details seeking attention across the wide range of our vision.[4] In addition, the higher resolution of 70mm allows closer reading of faces in the middle distance, reducing the need for the conventional cutting in for a close-up to support the spoken word with visually communicated emotion. Such closer reading of faces allows for longer takes, which in turn allow for increased closely followed motion of characters and continuous camera movement. The format thus makes it easier for Branagh to film long stretches of dialogue in a single take without sacrificing the appeal of the orienting response, which camera movements can provide in calibrated fashion. With shallower focus, objects can be left unattended and demand for "reading the shot" can be reduced, allowing attention to be concentrated, although unfocused objects can also maintain a meaningful presence, hovering on some level of our awareness. Most often in this *Hamlet*, shallow focus will encourage scrutiny of a speaking or reacting face, scrutiny that is further encouraged by the format's high resolution. Even with fewer close-ups than in smaller format films, Branagh's well-chosen cast members have abundant opportunity to activate our facially responsive mirror neurons.

The new resources made available through the choice of camera add new possibilities for the visual variety that can sustain attention in the four-hour film. As for "landscape," it is often said that the wide screen lends an "epic" quality to the exterior shots at Blenheim Palace. The format also allows dramatic long shots of distant prospects to form one end of an enlarged spectrum of shot types, at the other end of which lies the immense and immensely detailed extreme close-up, for which, as Crowl notes, the 70mm format can be equally effective. Such variety in turn allows editing to create a greater variety of segments and rhythms. Filmmaker Sidney Lumet observes that, contrary to what is sometimes claimed, it is not rapid editing but tempo shifts that make a film feel faster: "If a film is edited in the same tempo for its entire length, it will *feel* much longer. It doesn't matter if five cuts per minute or five cuts every ten minutes are being used. If the same pace is maintained throughout, it will start to feel slower and slower. In other words, it's the *change* in tempo that we feel, not the tempo itself."[5] With a greater variety of shot types available, Branagh can shift tempos with ease, within shots and between them. On a larger scale, he can replace the four movements of classical film that he sacrifices to maintain Shakespeare's text and order with alternative structures, including segmentation punctuated by virtuosic long takes. Hamlet's five soliloquies are shot in this way, forming their own sequence of interestingly varied setting and choreography. So are other long takes designed to be compared to them and to join them in the work of punctuation, such as the ultimate un-soliloquy that begins act 2, scene 2, in which Claudius happily begins his royal day fussed over by an efficient entourage.

Act 1, Scene 1

Like Olivier's opening ghost scene, Branagh's has its inspired moments and its failures. It succeeds masterfully in creating a sense of "out of joint" uneasiness that will begin the tonal alternations needed to carry us through "all that text." As in Olivier's *Hamlet*, twelve tolls of a bell serve the dual purpose of signaling midnight and casting a funereal pall over the film's opening. This borrowed device throws into relief the thoroughness of Branagh's efforts to distinguish his film from those of his predecessors. The funereal pall hangs not over young Hamlet but over his father, whose monument we soon see. Instead of the stirring introductory music of Walton and Morricone, there is the eerie silence of a night interrupted by unidentifiable cries in the distance—from an animal, perhaps, or from something more sinister. Elaborate opening credits, calling attention in Olivier's *Hamlet* to the film/theater distinction and in Zeffirelli's film to the star power of the actors and director, have been replaced by a nondiegetic "WILLIAM SHAKESPEARE'S" that quickly gives way to a diegetic "HAMLET," the latter chiseled into a stone plinth. When the tracking camera passes beyond the plinth, Elsinore comes into view. It is not the traditional medieval castle towering over the sea but England's Blenheim Palace, a baroque monument that extends the horizontal reach of its Great Court beyond both edges of the film frame, conveying an aura of imperial power and civilized grandeur.[6] The focus racks in, blurring the foreground plinth to display the palace's monumental details in the background. A complementary rack-out focus several shots later will reveal what sits atop the plinth. These attention-grabbing camera actions announce that Olivier's renowned deep-focus cinematography has been replaced, at least for now, by dramatic shallow focus.

The unease of shallow focus limiting clarity to one plane at a time is but one component of Branagh's treatment of the calculated disorder that opens the play. The ghost is an eruption of what Branagh calls "the numinous, the otherworldly," which can be felt through repeated occasions of surprise and disorientation.[7] No one of these occasions is overwhelming in itself, but collectively they set the ghost scene off from the geometric rationality of the court scene that follows. A close-up of Francisco pacing before an iron gateway adds the crunch of his footsteps to the tolling bell and mysterious wailings. Both of the sounds heard earlier remain constant in volume on the soundtrack despite the change of location, creating a slightly confusing auditory space. Mystified by the wail, Francisco glances to his right. An eye-line match toward the

snowy distance reveals a barely visible landscape feature that will later be identified as the monument to old Hamlet, but this subjective shot pans strangely
to the left, contradicting Francisco's rightward glance. Elsinore reappears
in the distance as the camera reverses its earlier leftward track, now taking
in what continuity conventions stipulate should be the plinth from which it
departed but is instead the head of a statue facing with a stern expression
outward from the palace. We might locate this statue on the plinth, and thus
identify it with old Hamlet, but the film declines to specify the two objects'
relationship definitively for now, sustaining unease.

The statue is armored, Francisco in more modern uniform. He moves
his weapon from his shoulder, presumably readying to fire upon any intruder.
When the statue suddenly pulls its sword from the scabbard with a sharp
metallic sound, the guard falls abruptly out of the screen. What is the connection between these two startling events? There is no direct connection,
perhaps, for the next shot reveals a second soldier falling on top of prone
Francisco. Which guard speaks the opening line "Who's there?" is not evident
until the logical sequence of interchange is sorted out retrospectively. When
the two guards rise, their weapons are revealed to be not rifles but long spears,
confusing a temporal distinction earlier implied between them and the statue.
Our impression of their nervousness is enhanced by the contradiction between the loud sound of the drawn sword and their interchange: "Have you
had quiet guard? / Not a mouse stirring" (8). Understandably nervous in
this environment out of joint, they stay together while moving to where
Horatio and Marcellus approach. The latter two emerge from below like
Olivier's counterparts, but they are, oddly enough, climbing up from a depression in the ground.

After Francisco's departure, the three remaining men sit with their backs
against a pillar, clearly expecting that the ghost will approach along the line
demarcated by the gate and the monument. The palace behind them eliminates the possibility of a spatial trick in the manner of Olivier. Branagh adds
surprise in a different way. The ghost's arrival is anticipated by the men's gazes
and then made surprising by their reactions. In a ring structure of four frontal
and angular three-shots centered on an eye-line match shot on the glowing
night sky, Barnardo tells of the previous apparitions while gazing continually
upward, Horatio looks up twice, and Marcellus maintains his gaze on Barnardo. Horatio thus creates an expectation of the ghost's arrival that belies
his declared skepticism, until suddenly all three men are looking up together
at Marcellus's interjection, "Peace, break thee off" (39), which his gaze upon

Barnardo makes all the more unexpected. The ghost is then seen in silhouette against the sky, its frightening approach enhanced through a zoom up toward it. A cut to the ghost's elevated point of view reveals the men already having fled an undeterminable distance to the wrought-iron gate, which they push open in panic. The combination of "fear and wonder" (43) proclaimed by Horatio is embodied in frantic backpedaling into the Great Court.

The men's reactions are convincing and the atmosphere of disorientation helps the viewer to share them, but Branagh's ghost, especially in this scene, generally disappoints audiences. Inadequate special effects fail to communicate its intended monumentality, and its form as a rigid armed statue come to life eliminates the kinds of pathos achieved by other filmmakers. What impact it has comes from the characters' responses, and here Branagh must rely on the very capable Nicholas Farrell as Horatio. His declaration of belief in the ghost is delivered with a convincing display of jerky nervousness and cracking voice.

Farrell's challenge to carry the scene continues between the ghostly visits, although Branagh now offers him more assistance. Olivier, Zeffirelli, and Almereyda eliminate entirely the fifty-five-line discussion of warlike preparations disrupting Denmark that is initiated by Marcellus's request, "Good now, sit down, and tell me, he that knows" (69). In a rare textual revision, Branagh changes "sit down" to "look here," eliminating Shakespeare's parallel of two seatings before the ghost arrives but setting up visual additions helpful for a recitation of the full text.[8] Bewildered Horatio is hoisted up between the two guards and marched down a pathway. Accompanied by ominous percussive music, Marcellus's series of five questions registers almost as an angry interrogation, an effect enhanced when the pale and trembling scholar is directed to look through the barred window of a door into the "sweaty haste" (76) of weapons being assembled. Horatio now leads the guards in a lengthy tracking shot past a series of doors that rhythmically punctuate his detailed account of old Hamlet's slaying of old Fortinbras, a characteristic Branagh device traceable back to the throne room of *Henry V*. The rhythmic background helps to break up the long speech, the potential tedium of which was anticipated in the screenplay by a stage direction midway: "Horatio fully into his stride now is getting carried away with detail. MARCELLUS and BARNARDO exchange looks."[9] These looks are not needed in the final film.

As he shifts from ancient to modern history, Branagh introduces another method for visually segmenting the torrent of words. An apparent flashback visualizes Fortinbras in military council, beginning a series of insets of the young man that will form a crosscutting Norwegian plot to parallel the Danish plot. His "strong hand" (101) sweeps military-gaming markers from a map of the Baltic and rips down a map of Denmark. His intentions are unmistakably ominous, but what should really increase our unease is the discrepancy between Horatio's description of "lawless resolutes" (97) and the well-dressed, professional soldiers to whom Fortinbras speaks. Introducing us to Branagh's technique of ambiguous insets, the discrepancy opens several possibilities, among them that it is not a flashback to the past but depicts a later phase in which Fortinbras is no longer of "unimproved mettle" (95), and that Horatio is not appropriately addressed as "he that knows" (69).

Such complications and the fascination of watching the impulsive Fortinbras, played with glowering intensity by Rufus Sewell, make the speech go quickly, but Horatio must now get through another long speech, on the prodigies preceding Caesar's death, without such assistance. He does this standing still in medium close-up, looking off into space while picturing, as we have just been taught to do, with "the mind's eye" (111), but only after a diagonal three-shot centered on him recalls the repeated similar shots that introduced the first ghostly visit, subliminally prompting us to expect another visit as we listen in suspense. When the ghost appears, the men now possess the courage to approach, but the ghost, despite having his visor up and reaching out with his hand, is no more accessible than before. Surprisingly, Marcellus and Barnardo cast their spears as the ghost retreats rather than, as in Olivier's more logical treatment, as it moves threateningly toward them. The screenplay comments that at this moment "All is chaos," offering a possible, if inadequate, explanation for the guards' irrational behavior.[10]

As the guards cast their spears to the repeated cries of "'Tis here" (140), which have traditionally accompanied the mysterious appearance of the ghost in two places—one of the rare devices more effective on stage than on film—spatial disorientation is highlighted through a rapid-fire series of one-shots of the three men, six shots in a mere two seconds. But the ghost is gone, replaced by their now-shared view of the single-starred night sky that preceded the first visit, indicating closure for this night's visitation. During Marcellus's speech beginning "We do it wrong" (142), a cutaway to the statue only partially obscures the fact that a return to the speaker finds him in another location. Marcellus stands now before the iron gate, with its prominent royal insignia of two crowns within a golden wreath, a sight featured twice before: when Francisco and Barnardo rose from the ground before the gate and when the three men were seen pressed against it from the ghost's elevated point of view. The gate's presence here signals the completion of an action. As the men continue their conversation in the postvisitation calm, three more cutaway shots interrupt our view of them: a distant view of the monument, a low shot of the statue with the inscription of "Hamlet" finally attached, and the rising sun of Horatio's "morn in russet mantle clad" (165). The cutaways to the statue are difficult to justify, apparent lapses into variety for variety's sake, although lapses of various sorts have been effectively conveying the ghost's disruptive influence. The scene closes with the camera moving in to the crown insignia on the gate, indicating where the men will report to the "young Hamlet" (169), whose name implies that he should be wearing the crown.

Act 1, Scene 2

A slow dissolve to the State Hall both formally acknowledges Olivier's brilliant dissolve to his drinking Claudius and continues the delineation of difference between films. The crown is visually matched by the image replacing it, a similarly shaped balustrade crowded with onlookers that forms the upper tier of a large audience awaiting the arrival announced by Patrick Doyle's exultant, horn-filled overture. Claudius and Gertrude enter a scene whose every detail denies that anything is rotten in the state of Denmark. The vast hall's symmetries, beginning with the balustrade, deploy the absolutist vocabulary of space ordered around the king's presence. After the symbol of royal power has been visually associated with the balustrade, the latter provides our first glimpse of power in action, as the bourgeois civilians standing on the balustrade, dressed for the joyous occasion in their Sunday best, collectively move to the other side to keep the glamorous king and queen in view as they pass beneath on the geometrically tiled floor. Below, seated ranks of military courtiers and uniformly dressed court ladies bend their eyes more decorously but no less universally toward the processing couple; this shift of gaze begins with Ophelia, whose glance initiates a systematic cascade of turning heads from her position at the end of one of the courtiers' front rows. Derek Jacobi, presenting the most benign and competent Claudius possible, delivers his opening speech with pitch-perfect sensitivity to the recent death and foreign threat. His beautiful queen stands proudly at his side, dressed as if she has just come from the wedding. A double inset, flash-forwarding to decrepit old Norway receiving Claudius's letter and repeating part of Horatio's visualizing of wild Fortinbras, offers two strong visual contrasts to the wise and gentle king. The audience responds with smiles and enthusiastic applause not only to the royal "for all, our thanks" (1.2.16), the tearing of Fortinbras's pestering letter, and

the permission for Laertes' departure but even to the farewell to the ambassadors. The conspicuously multiracial crowd suggests the universality of this
mythical Danish empire, while the uniformity of its happy responses creates
a utopian vision beyond the wildest dreams of the late nineteenth-century
Hapsburg court that is the film's principal visual model.[11]

Halfway through the pre-soliloquy portion of act 1, scene 2, the camera
glides to the right wall to introduce the only discordant element. The inky-
cloaked prince stands stiffly in the corner. Notice of his presence seems to
end the applause. After responding to the king's address with "A little more
than kin and less than kind" (65) as a voice-over aside, he comes closer to the
thrones in an attention-grabbing shot that moves upward from his boots. He
sits down and, in his only fully public line in the scene, declares himself too
much "i'th'Sun" (67, in Folio). The crowd for the first time shows displeasure,
and Gertrude quickly intervenes. For the film audience, Hamlet's arrival also
subverts the scene's meticulous orientation, though probably not on a conscious level. During the first round of applause, the spot where Hamlet would
soon appear was visible—and empty. The corridor down which the camera
tracks to view this newly occupied space does not exist in the other shots that
take in its location. The chair in which he then sits is not visible before he arrives at it, or after he leaves it, until the soliloquy, confusing our understanding
of the prince's place in relation to the king and queen. The disorientation of
the ghost scene has entered Elsinore's "clean, well-spoken place" before Hamlet
learns of his father's return.[12]

Hamlet's entry is disruptive in that it also inserts an awkward private
sphere within this most public of events. The first character to be seen alone,
he initiates a sequence of twenty-five shots over two and one-half minutes in
which the family trio converse with lowered voices, as the focus reduces from
long to short, isolating the private foreground from the public background.
The persistence of unmoving figures out of focus in the background elevates
the awkwardness that Hamlet's private matter inserts into the State Hall. All
but six of these shots are "separation" close-ups that draw the viewer into the
suspense of shifting reactions communicated largely through the characters'
eyes. The eyes of Hamlet, who is given nine close-ups to five each for the king
and queen, are the most active, making and breaking contact with both his
mother and uncle, scanning the audience, nearly rolling once in exasperation,
and finally closing at Claudius's "think of us / As of a father" (107–8). With
this apparent surrender, Claudius reinstalls public discourse by raising his
voice, drawing Hamlet to the throne, and letting "the world take note" (108)

that Hamlet is "most immediate to [the] throne" (109). Along with the return of public discourse comes the return of its corresponding camera style. Prior to the disruption, the scene was dominated by repeated frontal shots of the royal couple followed by shots from behind the throne. Such axial views in deep focus emphasize the throne room's symmetries and express the king's power through the order that he visually configures, as does another group of shots taken from on high at a forty-five-degree angle to the axis, an angle that aligns with the edges of the floor's diamond tiles.

After this familial adjustment brings Hamlet into the public center, another adjustment in relationships begins more subtly. Applause greets the announcement of the royal succession, but Laertes ends his clapping suddenly. Ophelia notices this, and her applause slows. As the king and queen depart the hall in a cloud of confetti, Ophelia approaches Hamlet and takes his hand. Alert Laertes hurries forth to pull her away, covering the action by shaking hands with the prince. But even before Laertes' action, Hamlet turns his head back from Ophelia toward his departing mother and "father." Perhaps inspired by the First Folio's generally ignored stage direction that brings into act 1, scene 2 "Laertes, and his Sister Ophelia," Branagh takes advantage of cinema's ability to convey large meanings with small details. He has already redefined Hamlet's fateful relationship with two families.

When the doors slam shut, leaving Hamlet alone in the hall, he is standing between the thrones, the apogee of his circular journey in Olivier's film. The allusion conveys irony: in contrast to Olivier's stern Claudius, Branagh's Jacobi has generously brought him to his rightful position, but he is king only of an empty throne room and now must move away. The camera now introduces us to the room's mirrored doors, doubling Hamlet's leaning down in emotional exhaustion in both original and reflection, then moves in front of him to track his journey from a middle distance during the first soliloquy. The court scene's repetitive editing not only emphasized royal spatiality but also brought the pace of cutting up to the conventions of feature films at around five seconds per shot. Against this background, the soliloquy's enormously long take produces a powerful effect of concentration. For two and one-half minutes, Hamlet moves away from the throne, following in the direction of the public but delaying. He turns back from his forward trajectory eight times during the course of his anguished reflections. Although Branagh does not use voice-over now, these turns serve much the same purpose as Olivier's shifts into voiced speech, visualizing the pressures that delay his following the joyful crowd and royal couple. Deep focus, which contrasts with the previous private moments, and Hamlet's scanning of the vast room as he speaks lend a felt incongruity to this private discourse delivered in so public a room.

Near the exit doors when he halts, Hamlet vows to hold his tongue, but the sudden entry of Horatio and the sentries gives him an alternative to rejoining the public and turns Hamlet's reluctantly linear trajectory into an imitation of Olivier's circular movement, although his return is toward the throne rather than away from it. The sense of directional reversal is amplified by a 360-degree camera tracking that takes into view the exit doors and the thrones at the hall's opposite end and then follows the men back from the same side of the hall (the king's side) from which it followed Hamlet out. They stop midway, however, beneath the central balustrade, when Hamlet declares, "My father, methinks I see my father" (183). A configuration now forms that places Horatio and Hamlet on either side with Marcellus and Barnardo between them and behind. Horatio's revelation about the ghost makes the men more wary. They speak in low tones, glance about, and then move quickly from the hall. Hamlet does not return in resigned futility to where he began but huddles with friends to consider new action.

The action moves from the bright open court, a space whose vastness is even more impressive after it has emptied, to dimly lit confines rendered claustrophobic by the tight camera that presses the men toward the wall. The room, we will soon learn, is Hamlet's study (or "Apartment," as the screenplay labels it), entered through the mirrored door nearest the throne end at the right of the hall. The four-shot configuration from outside, with Horatio and Hamlet containing Marcellus and Barnardo, resumes as Horatio continues his narrative. It becomes the master shot of a highly unusual series of thirty-five two-shots that alternate quickly between Barnardo and Hamlet, on the one side, and Horatio and Marcellus, on the other. Again, as in the move from courtly interaction to soliloquy, the enormous shift of pacing, from the five-minute long take in the hall with its variety of bodily and camera movements to the staccato interchange of identical shots inside, breaks the long narrative into easily perceived units. The magnitude of change signaled by the combination of Shakespeare's dialogue and Branagh's energetic filmmaking is most evident when Barnardo begins to exit back into the hall. Hamlet emits an abrupt yelp to make him close the door and leads the men to a hidden doorway in a bookcase. The plot provides little practical motivation for this urgent caution. The openness of the men's arrival suggests that there is no need for a surreptitious exit. Branagh has imported the urgency from the end of act 1, scene 5, where the men swear not to reveal what they have seen and heard. Hamlet's surprising outburst indicates that everything has changed. After their exit, he pulls from his shelf an illustrated volume of demon lore and eagerly peruses it, anxiously anticipating the night but also revealing his early doubts about the ghost.[13]

One effect of Branagh's treatment of act 1, scene 2 is to provide an equivalent to the ending of the first movement in the typical feature film at a very typical time, twenty-seven minutes from the beginning. The full-text screenplay dictates that the end of act 1, scene 5 (where previous, streamlined *Hamlets* have ended their first movements) lies some fifteen minutes away, after a delaying excursion into the affairs of the Polonius family. With a keen sense of what a modern audience expects, Branagh makes viewers feel the storytelling gears shift now. He will similarly indicate a shift twenty-nine minutes into the postintermission film with the graveyard scene. For the rest of the film, he must deploy other methods of segmentation.

Act 1, Scene 3

The brief but intriguing interaction among Hamlet, Ophelia, and Laertes before the soliloquy stirred interest that will now intensify. Laertes and Ophelia are shown walking along the edge of the palace. Their behavior is affectionate and, at first, playful, but their unceasingly tight embrace realizes, with calibrated tentativeness, the screenplay's suggestion that "[a]s they walk with their arms around each other, they are very, some might say unnaturally, close."[14] The tedious obsessiveness that Shakespeare incorporates into Laertes' long speech on the dangers of Hamlet's professions of love is visually realized through the unvarying camera placement in relation to the siblings across the ninety-second tracking shot. The eye is focused on the shapely body of Kate Winslet's Ophelia and the incessant gestures of her brother's hand, which add an unappealing urgency to his message. Felt duration, and therefore added Laertean tedium, is extended by a dissolve midway through the interchange as the couple descend a stairway to Blenheim's beautiful water gardens. There nude statues form a suggestive background to Laertes' warning against opening her "chaste treasure" to Hamlet's "unmastered importunity" (1.3.30–31).

The arrival of Polonius moves the scene to the chapel, where Christian imagery replaces pagan nudes and soft organ music adds solemnity to Polonius's usually wearisome litany of platitudes. The counselor's surprising sensitivity and his son's visibly moved response create an impression of familial closeness that carries over as an essential background to the remainder. On

Laertes' departure, Polonius ominously closes a creaking iron gate, leads his daughter to the confessional, and pushes her onto its seat with unexpected brutality, demanding "Give me up the truth" (98). During and immediately following his subsequent lecture, a series of insets depicts Hamlet and Ophelia in sexual intercourse. David Sauer notes (correctly, I believe) that these insets are ambiguous, interpretable as either flashbacks or fantasies, either Ophelia's visualizations or "the father's imagining." Given the critical controversy over the insets, the precise nature of this ambiguity is worth reexamining.[15] In the most obvious sense, the insets all belong to Ophelia, for all are carefully framed by shots of her face, and visual evidence in film generally trumps other forms. Strengthening this attribution, the first and the two last occur while Ophelia is speaking. She speaks to her father in the first ("I do not know, my lord, what I should think" [103]), and in unmouthed aside in the fifth and sixth ("I shall obey, my lord" [135]). The second, third, and fourth, however, occur while Polonius is speaking. The third and fourth are especially suggestive because they occur when Polonius is recalling his own erotic experience:

> I do know
> When the blood burns, how prodigal the soul
> Lends the tongue vows. These blazes, daughter,
> Giving more light than heat, extinct in both
> Even in their promise . . .
>
> (114–18)

The third and fourth also depict Hamlet in bed positioned on top of Ophelia after the first and second depicted Ophelia on top. The net result is a cunningly deployed sequence that is identifiable as Ophelia's but also suggestively intersubjective, visualizations by the daughter that may also be taken as the worried father's imaginings—even as incestuous desire. For Ophelia, moreover, there is no way to determine whether these are memories or fantasies. Either form would explain her visible anguish.

Act 1, Scene 4

Branagh's orchestrating control of cinematic elements, consistently magisterial in the previous two scenes, again grows uneven in the second encounter with the ghost. The scene begins well, as two solemn walks by Hamlet and his companions toward the camera down dark hallways frame another creatively problematic inset, in which Claudius leads Gertrude and a band of celebrating courtiers toward the camera in a brightly lit hallway. In the "heavy-headed revel" (17) of the central panel, the royal couple drink repeatedly in a "custom" (15) that carries them into the queen's apartment, where Claudius lustily throws her onto the bed. The implication arises that the ghost returns during an act of royal sex. But do we assume this to be a true depiction, or one whose improbable excesses are the product of Hamlet's febrile imagination as he narrates it? We cannot know, and its presentation between shots of Hamlet looking off into the distance can imply either. The ambiguity of Ophelia's lovemaking insets in the previous scene makes the question yet more difficult, and the question will linger to color the interpretation of Hamlet's apparent visualization when the ghost narrates the murder.

Suddenly the three men are outside, and upon their reaching the familiar iron gate of the sentry post the ghost appears. The gate's prominence as a threshold between political Elsinore and the ghostly hinterland is made visible as each man delivers his initial responses to the ghost (58–68) while looking out through its bars. In one of his few textual transpositions, Branagh moves Hamlet's address to the ghost following "Angels and ministers of grace defend us" (39) to follow his argument with the men, extending the private encounter of father and son from act 1, scene 5 into act 1, scene 4. The dialogue thus can continue uncut while Branagh incorporates a movie "chase scene," although for the vertical chases of Olivier and Zeffirelli is substituted a horizontal quest more suitable for the wide screen. The speech is delivered in frantic voice-over to accompany a rapidly cut montage sequence—forty shots in under a minute, the film's most briskly edited long sequence—as Hamlet plunges through a disorienting forest landscape. First he and then his pursuing friends burst offscreen to the left, but Hamlet's trajectory is now traced through repeated shots of him running to screen right and forward toward the camera, a directional reversal that conveys ghostly disorder. No background is visible beyond the intertwined trees, which rise from a ground that splits open with flaming and steaming "blasts from hell" (41). We effectively participate through such means in Hamlet's confusion. Intercut with views of Hamlet's wild chase and subjective views of his passage through the woods are four shots that illustrate his spoken images of his father: two remembrances of "the sepulchre / Wherein we saw thee quietly enurn'd" (48–49) balanced by two of the returned ghost "again in complete steel" who "Revisits thus the glimpses of the moon" (52–53). The four insets are confusing but not creatively so, unless one is willing to appreciate the coming together of past (the corpse) and present (the ghost) as Hamlet rushes deeper into the dark woods.

Act 1, Scene 5

Hamlet scans the woods around him as the ghost begins his address. An armored hand thrusts him violently to a kneeling position, the position assumed voluntarily by Olivier's prince. This fraction of a second is the only time before the end that the ghost and Hamlet appear in the same frame, and all potential satisfaction at physical contact is eliminated through the violence of the hand gesture. This ghost scene is finding its innovative place in a tradition that has developed with surprising, intuitive attention to the most fundamental mirror-neuron mechanisms. Like Zeffirelli, whose quiet ghost scene is otherwise so different, Branagh employs the power of separation, constructing the interview across numerous close-ups of the ghost and Hamlet, as the ghost addresses Hamlet from on high.[16] We keenly await the registering of emotion on Branagh's expressive face, and convention dictates an expectation of reciprocal responses by the ghost. But the latter do not come, forcing us to share with Hamlet the disappointment of failed contact. Woven into the dominant framework of separation close-ups is a variety of matter, of varying effectiveness. On the one hand, images of bubbling mist, shifting earth, and gas flares blandly portray the purgatorial suffering that the ghost imports into the world. On the other, the "foul and most unnatural murder" (25) is introduced with a powerful visual equivalent of the "eternal blazon" that "must not be / To ears of flesh and blood" (21–22). Extreme close-ups of the ghost's whispering mouth and flashbacks to the ulcerating flesh and bleeding ear of the murder scene are images at the limits of what can comfortably be watched, especially in the epic definition of 70mm. Hamlet's response to this potentially overwhelming message is strong, his promise to sweep to his revenge intoned with calm determination. It is no wonder the ghost finds him "apt" (32).

Branagh combines Zeffirelli's poignant separation with Olivier's internalizing visualization. His visual recounting, however, is less linear. Old Hamlet in the orchard is seen first, but this story line gives way, to be finished last; perhaps such temporal breakdown, as in the earlier insets of past corpse and present ghost, is part of what Branagh's ghost is and means. Revelation of the murderer's identity stimulates recollection of a more recent event: Claudius in the State Room as he turns to Hamlet and prepares to call him "my son" (1.2.64). With painful irony, standing behind the king out of focus are Polonius and his children, the other family that Hamlet will destroy when he takes up the call to revenge. The seduction of Gertrude is next recounted.

In the hallway in which was recently depicted the "heavy-headed revel," a location that contaminates the objectivity of Hamlet's recollection, six shots portray the royal family entertaining themselves with an informal bout of curling. Apparent innocence gives way to more suggestive behavior by Gertrude, whom Claudius physically assists with a throw. The last two shots depict the two hugging and then a bodice being unlaced. With his typically cunning reticence, Branagh does not identify the parties involved. It is presumably Claudius unlacing Gertrude, as the logical outcome of his seduction, and after we have seen his hands on her back. But if so, one must also notice that Hamlet has imaginatively assumed his uncle's private recollection, restoring the oedipal context that critics often claim Branagh strives to eliminate.[17] As Samuel Crowl writes, "Branagh is certainly aware that his blond Hamlet bears an uncanny physical resemblance to Jacobi's Claudius."[18] Nowhere is the resemblance clearer than in these insets, where both men wear a green uniform. Because we have seen sex scenes with Hamlet and Ophelia, the bodice shot may depict them. If so, one must also notice that Hamlet's recollection of Ophelia is triggered by the image of his mother. If temporal breakdown earlier in the scene was merely confusing, it now expresses with marvelous economy the Freudian atemporality of the unconscious.

Enclosing both the seduction story and Hamlet's memory of Claudius within the murder visualization raises more issues of subjectivity. The ghost speaks vividly of the physical agony caused by the poison, and the visuals support his words, portraying a king writhing in pain. But whereas Olivier fleetingly revealed Claudius's face to confirm the murderer's identity, Branagh dwells on the reaction of Claudius. The smooth and seductive face of Claudius that is the focus of the other insets contrasts with his demeanor here, which reveals in two long close-ups a combination of fascinated interest and horror at what he has done. He is so affected by the sight that his mouth moves in an apparent attempt to speak, or perhaps in a more primal imitation of his brother's communicative face, after which a cut back to Hamlet reveals the younger man's mouth making similar motions. Hamlet's identification with his uncle appears to be elevating and inflecting Claudius's role in the inset, as it may have been doing in the "heavy-headed revel" inset. A cut back to the inset story focuses first on Claudius, who backs away from the scene in horror, suggesting a powerful internal conflict that Claudius does not show signs of elsewhere, although Hamlet does. Significantly, the ghost is then shown uttering "O horrible, O horrible, most horrible!" (80), the one line of the ghost that might be put into the others' mouths, and that Olivier puts in Hamlet's.[19]

The separation interchange reaches a peak of intensity when the ghost orders Hamlet not to taint his mind or contrive against his mother, speaking over six extreme close-ups of the two men's eyes. Here the discrepancy between the two is most pronounced, for the supernatural blue contact lenses worn by Brian Blessed assist the measured monotone of his husky whisper in removing the evidence of feeling that we cannot help but seek and that we read with abundance in the faces of kneeling Hamlet and the characters of the insets. No emotion is communicated visually, with the exception of a surprising blink. This normally small but now enormous gesture, astonishingly rare in film, interrupts our frustrated attempt to look into, so to speak, the soul of the ghost, to penetrate the heart of his mystery, which is the goal of looking into a person's eyes.[20] The ghost recedes with the crowing of the cock. The hands in Olivier's scene fail to meet; in Zeffirelli's, they meet ambiguously; now they appear to make contact, but as Hamlet's grip closes, the armored hand of the father fades away.

Branagh's format-encouraged horizontal approach compounds the difficulties of the remainder of the scene, resulting in one of the film's least successful sequences following one of its most brilliant. Hamlet's speech after the ghost's departure produces an impression of deep commitment to his new project of revenge. It ends with a sense of calm, strongly reinforced by Doyle's majestic music and a slow track-in to a close-up. Branagh now returns to the earlier style of supernatural effects and intense disorientation, which for the plunge into the forest usefully supported the suspense over what the ghost would do and say. When Horatio and Marcellus arrive, Hamlet whirls about, apparently looking for the ghost, but one does not know how to understand these frantic actions and the subjective pans of the forest that they produce. The pans suggest a genuinely hysterical reaction to the ghost's information, but this reaction conflicts with the calm of the first speech. Because the need to present the full text prevents Hamlet from seriously attempting to part from his friends, they move about aimlessly as they converse. The eruptions and shaking earth that accompany the ghost's command to swear recall the chaos of the voyage in, but to little purpose. Such violent effects, especially when accompanied by suspense-inducing music, are disproportionate to the men's action of swearing themselves to silence. The effect is a contrived climax, perhaps induced because the change in Hamlet's motivation would normally begin a new film movement.

Act 2, Scene 1

From Hamlet in the nocturnal woods the film cuts to a frontal view of Elsinore at night, implying continuous time more clearly than could a stage production. This continuity will later be exposed as untrue, when act 2, scene 1 is revealed to be continuous not with the ghost visit but rather with act 2, scene 2, containing such events as the ambassadors' return, but the felt sweep of events cannot be undone. The slowness of the first part of the scene is part of its point. While Hamlet confronts his momentous task of setting right the time out of joint, Polonius, comfortable in his privilege and power, mixes business with pleasure, spending the night "drabbing" (2.1.26), smoking, drinking, and wandering through overly elaborate instructions to Reynaldo for spying on his son in Paris. As we listen and marvel over this remarkable character's unique blend of slyness and absurdity, the eye is invited to notice small things that help define characters and relationships: the prostitute's furtive glance back at suave Gerard Depardieu's Reynaldo after he pushes her rudely away; the small portrait of a woman lit for our attention (the badly missed mother of Ophelia, one can only assume); the letter on the hidden door honored with an elaborate gold frame inset with a cameo of a man and woman. One senses the loss that complicates the personality of this Polonius. In addition to the implied family history, one cannot avoid pondering the timing of Reynaldo's visit, which leaves the poor woman ignored in the bed while Polonius lights a postcoital cigarillo.

Viewers who noticed ambiguity in the insets of Hamlet and Ophelia's lovemaking have new evidence to weigh. On the one hand, if the earlier claim by Polonius to know when the blood burns was taken to refer to his youthful past, this scene suggests otherwise. This Polonius could easily assume that Hamlet seeks merely to gratify his lust and could easily picture the younger man doing so with his daughter. On the other hand, the postcoital tenderness of the last inset shot of Hamlet and Ophelia would probably not emanate from the imagination of a man who conducts business while fastening his trousers and dismissing his drab with a click of his fingers.

Both the urgency of Hamlet's new mission and the questions surrounding his relationship with Ophelia return to our attention after Reynaldo exits and Ophelia runs in screaming through another hidden passage. Branagh places greater weight than his predecessors on Ophelia's claim, "I have been so affrighted" (72). She recounts Hamlet's visit to her closet in a tearful and excited state, moving almost uncontrollably across the room and back while describing his wild appearance. When her father asks what Hamlet said, Branagh avoids both Olivier's version of telling and showing and Zeffirelli's mere showing by allowing Ophelia to describe Hamlet's actions while vividly demonstrating them. Enacting Hamlet's pantomime in a second move from her father across the room to the door, she in effect repeats both her wild action on entering and Hamlet's at the same time, creating a visual link between their incipient madnesses. The insensitive and self-serving question, "What, have you given him any hard words of late?" (104), leads to renewed crying. When Ophelia seeks refuge on her father's bed, Polonius displays his characteristic self-absorption by delivering most of his last speech, despite its second-person address, to himself while across the room Ophelia weeps. Recovering the better, caring self that is never absent for too long in this film, he comforts his daughter. The sight, however, of him tenderly stroking and kissing her in the place still warm from the untenderly treated prostitute does not simplify one's view of the man.

Act 2, Scene 2

A virtuosic long take begins the business of the next day, following the royal couple from their bed to the throne, the two most important sites of their relationship. The shot's duration and trajectory link it to the first soliloquy, creating an ironic un-soliloquy that contrasts the situation of the king and the prince. That Claudius is dressing after sex with the queen, whom he threw onto the bed in our last sight of the couple, makes for an amusing parallel with postcoital Polonius. Claudius welcomes Rosencrantz and Guildenstern over coffee and a shoeshine, but his attempt at identifying them has to be corrected twice, belying his claim "that we much did long to see you" (2). Gertrude enters separately, allowing her appeal to the young men to be independent from Claudius's rather than an afterthought to it, and it clearly affects the visitors more powerfully. The impression made by the queen will be felt later; the two "friends" will erupt after the Mousetrap when Hamlet belittles her reaction.

More creative insets add welcome variety and more questions concerning subjectivity. Within the ambassadors' report, twelve inset shots visualize the threat and containment of Fortinbras. On horseback leading cavalry through a forest, the young Norwegian gazes into the distance; an eye-line match on Elsinore creates a highly abbreviated narrative of imagined conquest without implying that this action took place. His gaze on Elsinore is sandwiched between visually matched close-ups of old Norway's contemplative gaze into space and thus becomes Norway's mind's-eye viewing of his nephew's project when "better look'd into" (64). In other words, we see what Norway sees when, assisted by Claudius's missive, Norway understands what Fortinbras sees. This blurring of clear boundaries between subjectivities, by now familiar as Branagh's ambiguity-tolerant method, should prompt us to ponder the insets further in terms of the subjectivity of Claudius, who like Norway and Fortinbras is viewed in close-up during the report. The insets contain both an element of wish fulfillment for Claudius and an explanation for his wish to read the ambassador's message "at our more considered time" (81). Old Norway prevails instantly with a slap to the head, a surprising intrusion of violence, which after witnessing the poisoning we no longer dissociate from Claudius. This quick success of an uncle over a nephew contrasts with the situation at Elsinore, which will deteriorate until Claudius similarly slaps Hamlet in act 4, scene 3. Fortinbras's contrition and renunciation are questionable. He convinces his uncle, but we are allowed a final glimpse of ominously inscrutable eyes staring into the distance, eyes that no doubt still see Elsinore as he embraces the impotent old man and obtains concessions that will assist his conquest.

Polonius's report on Hamlet's madness to the king and queen follows in the more private "Ante State Room" behind the thrones. Consistent with his command, "Come, go we to the king" (2.1.114), he brings Ophelia with him. Less consistent with the care he showed in comforting her is that he makes her read Hamlet's love letter, until she breaks down at "her excellent white bosom" (2.2.112) and flees.[21] Her flight allows Branagh to create another extraordinary inset. As Polonius continues reading, the view moves to Hamlet and Ophelia after lovemaking in Ophelia's room. Polonius proceeds in voice-over until Hamlet takes over his own speech for the prose sequel to the poem, after which Polonius returns to voice-over. Appropriately for a group that knows Hamlet well, the sonic addition renders their shared subjectivity more intensely, without necessarily indicating that the depicted events happened, as in the Fortinbras inset, or implicating Ophelia's subjectivity, as in the previous lovemaking scene. "This in obedience hath my daughter shown me" (124), Polonius concludes, as the film shows more vividly what she has shown. The inset accompanies and cinematically represents the fact that the king, queen, and counselor come here to their point of closest agreement about Hamlet. The uniqueness of the technique reflects the uniqueness of the moment, which, as Jan Blits notes, is the only time Claudius asks the queen's opinion on anything.[22] To his "Do you think 'tis this?" she replies, "It may be; very like" (151–52, in Folio). Branagh here makes a rare choice of Quarto wording over Folio, opting for "like" over "likely." This choice encourages the audience to assess how "like" Hamlet's relationship with Ophelia might be to what was "shown." After Hamlet's voiced declaration of love at the center of an audiovisual ring composition, Polonius appropriately vows to find the truth, "though it were hid indeed / Within the centre" (158–59).

Polonius "boards" the prince on the upper level of the chapel. Hamlet's most sustained effort at antic disposition begins when he confronts Polonius wearing a skull mask, foreshadowing the counselor's fate in the area above where his body will soon lie in state, and reflecting Hamlet's growing hostility.[23] They exit to the State Hall gallery, where the large space allows Polonius to speak his asides to himself without being overheard. Hamlet is aggressively confrontational but does not exhibit Olivier's ridiculing exploitation of Polonius's confusion over theatrical role versus reality or Gibson's troubling violence. This powerful and intelligent Polonius holds his own with the madcap prince, dutifully observing him with almost clinical attention despite repeated insults. Polonius, visibly angry but self-controlled, follows Hamlet "out of the air" (205) with no apparent purpose but to demonstrate this self-control by bidding farewell.

After his confrontation with the man who for Hamlet is the worst example of "these tedious old fools" (219), he displays genuine relief on seeing Rosencrantz and Guildenstern arrive on Blenheim's narrow-gauge railroad, evoking the happier "young days" (2.2.11) of their friendship. This relief is tempered by a clear wariness. When the "friends" display little sympathy for his view of Denmark as a prison, he walks briskly away, forcing them to follow uncomfortably. This is a new variation of Hamlet's acquisition of a literal "following," which asks for comparison with Claudius's entourage. He then breaks into a trot after their arguments about ambition demonstrate either hopeless misunderstanding or an alliance with the king.

Following Zeffirelli's example, Branagh makes the reunion of childhood friends an outdoor tour to highlight the irony of imprisonment in "infinite space" (255). As he begins the great speech on losing his mirth, the trio enters the colonnade of the Great Court, allowing references to "this brave o'erhanging firmament, this majestical roof fretted with golden fire" (300–301) to embrace the daytime sky, rarely seen in the film, and Blenheim's baroque splendors. He imitates Zeffirelli as well in visually linking the players' arrival to the film's opening. As they discuss the players, the trio strolls, at first arm in arm, along the same colonnade past which Barnardo and Marcellus escorted Horatio, at first arm in arm, in the opening scene. As they pass the colonnade's distinctive black doors through which Horatio viewed the assembly of weapons in act 1, scene 1, precisely reversing the motion of the earlier trio, uncanny recognition forecasts a turning point in the plot. Many viewers by now are sufficiently familiar with Elsinore's geography to notice too that as Hamlet speaks of the new king's "picture in little" (362) he is looking out the Great Court toward his father's statue in the distance, from the same spot where the earlier trio confronted the ghost and charged it to speak.

The energy Hamlet derives from the arrival of the players, both as occasions to indulge his passion for theater and as emerging tools of revenge, is conveyed through a shift of camera styles as he returns to the State Hall gallery. His rush offscreen right is matched by a burst through the gallery door to view the players from above. He continues confiding in Rosencrantz and Guildenstern and then renews his ridicule of Polonius in a long take with nearly continuous tracking. In his descent to the players, an even longer take carries him across the hall and thrice around the players before bringing him onstage at the throne dais with the First Player. Again, the long take links itself to others, creating meaningful similarity and difference. His joyful spinning in company recalls the joyless motions of his first soliloquy, for example, in the opposite direction, and the motion both contrasts with the linearity of Claudius's procession in act 2, scene 1 and imitates its trajectory toward the throne, creating largely subliminal impressions of progress as we move toward the Mousetrap. The axis of the State Hall is being established as the film's most important line of action.

When the First Player takes over the Trojan story, camera movement largely ceases. It is replaced by editing that enacts and invokes the rhetorical principle of *enargeia*, "the poet's ability to make a situation vivid, as if before our eyes."[24] Branagh's creative insets now reflect the intentions of the poet, who according to Renaissance literary theory seeks to evoke sensory impressions with words. While Branagh is anchoring his practice in Renaissance theory, he is also playfully parading the devices of his modern medium. Noteworthy is the sheer number of devices set in the service of vividness, in imitation of such verbal devices as the passage's present-tense verbs, crowding into this drawn-out theatrical scene. Low camera placement for all shots of the Player applies the heroic aspect of the spoken to the speaker. In shots with the audience, the Player makes eye contact with both them and the camera, enlisting our presence among them. Long dissolves into the insets imply a gradual takeover of the mind's eye of the audience by the mind's eye of the speaker. For Priam's death, a dissolve simultaneously merges the speaker with Priam and assumes Pyrrhus's point of view, an emblem of the psychology of revenge based on identification with the aggressor. With a cut back to the Player from the lowest camera angle of all, the text shifts into its passionate apostrophe to "strumpet Fortune" (2.2.431) and the gods, a textual convention used for collapsing the distinction between the epic narrator and his represented world.

The segment ceases with a cut to Polonius complaining, "This is too long" (494), the abruptness of the remark amplified by a sudden halt of the nondiegetic music. The moment waxes marvelously metacinematic as the viewer notices how well Polonius's comment applies both to the local film scene and to the film as a whole and how heroically the filmmaker is attempting to counter an inevitable reality. Hamlet complains that Polonius requires "a jig or a tale of bawdry, or he sleeps" (496), in a film that adds visualized sex and was to include an extended dance sequence, which was filmed but not included in the final cut. As the Player continues, the music track recovers from its apparent offense and Branagh continues his blatant parade of devices. After previously using cuts back to the speaker, Branagh now dissolves back. Shakespeare provides "burning eyes of heaven / And passion in the gods" (513–14) as images corresponding to the visible signs of the actor's passion. Branagh adds the silent scream of Hecuba, visually merging the identities of speaker and spoken. The powerful image of Judi Dench's Hecuba overlaid on Charlton Heston's Player makes Polonius's surprise at the actor's passion even more surprising, although it cannot invalidate his comment on excessive length.

Hamlet directs Horatio, whom Branagh has imported into the scene, to follow Rosencrantz and Guildenstern, ensuring his privacy for the "rogue and peasant slave" soliloquy. He hastens into his apartment, seen earlier during the ghost report. During the long take of nearly four minutes, he continues the erratic motion of his introduction to the players, manifesting the continuous mental energy that leads from the idea of inserting lines into *The Murder of Gonzago* to its present refinement into the "most miraculous organ" (529), a reenactment of the murder with *enargeia* that will in effect strike "so to the soul" (526) with the impact of the Player's Priam and Hecuba. Following his movements around the room, we gain familiarity with the traits and interests reflected in his possessions: the mythological landscapes on his walls that recall his humanist fondness for classical and biblical exemplars;[25] the great globe that seems to represent kingship to him; and most of all, of course, the masks, puppets, and manikins that tell of Hamlet's love for theater, which in such scenes becomes inescapably an allegory for Branagh's love of cinema. His final declaration, "The play's the thing / Wherein I'll catch the conscience of the king" (539–40), is delivered while peering into his model theater from behind the scenes. As he sends the model king, dressed as Claudius will be only in the Mousetrap scene, into the hell beneath the stage, we see his deadly determination through that most cinematic of devices for communicating emotion, the close-up. Further calling attention to the apparatus of cinema, the focus racks out across the stage to the king and then back in to Hamlet's face, recalling in miniature the ostentatious focal changes of the film's opening scene.

Act 3, Scene 1

The sound of the model theater's trapdoor is matched by the sound of the doors opening into the State Hall. Far from tumbling into perdition, the king enters his seat of power through doors that appear almost to open magically, an effect enhanced by his holding his hands behind his back. As the group Claudius leads files into the room, Branagh deploys the device that earned him ridicule in *Mary Shelley's Frankenstein* (1994), though in *Hamlet* it has become a consistently effective device for redirecting viewer attention in long takes: the circling camera. Avoiding the dizzying excess of the earlier film, Branagh here uses it masterfully, catching small details that invite speculation and contribute to our understanding of the characters, each of whom has his own concerns and agenda. Hamlet's "friends" report to Claudius, but Gertrude and Polonius watch closely in the background. When Gertrude intervenes, the moving camera makes Claudius fall into the background. He exchanges a quick glance with Gertrude and then intervenes, despite the fact that Polonius is addressing not him but the queen. The king steps forward, giving a hearty endorsement to attending the play, to impress his wife with his love for her son, and we will soon learn why. Nervous perhaps because his account is misleading, Rosencrantz looks to Polonius for confirmation about Hamlet's joy on hearing about the players. Polonius, of course, nods, eager as always to claim knowledge he does not have. Silent and nervous Ophelia is seen glancing around the room, toward the corner where Hamlet resides and up to the gallery where he walks. Gertrude is holding her hand protectively. A small packet is briefly glimpsed in Ophelia's other hand then hidden as the camera continues its motion.

As Rosencrantz and Guildenstern depart, Claudius draws Gertrude from Ophelia to ask her to leave. The queen is taken aback, and Claudius adds to his hearty endorsement of attending the play the persuasion of a kiss and caress. He stares after her, with an expression we cannot see, as she walks back into the domestic quarters. The camera circles to reveal his face as he delivers his brief soliloquy on the "heavy burden" (55) of his crime. The burden is not only on his conscience, as Shakespeare's words inform us, but also, Branagh's camera tells us, on his relationship with his queen, to whom he must speak with "painted word" (54) because of what must remain forever hidden. Meanwhile, Polonius fidgets in the background at the mirror-doored room chosen for eavesdropping. He watches for the prince's arrival, indulging his lord as long as he can.

The most awaited sequence of any *Hamlet* begins as Polonius closes the door and Hamlet simultaneously opens another to enter. Having been "closely sent for" (29), he looks about warily and then stops to confront his image in the door through which his listeners have passed. His choice of doors is unexplained, but Branagh leaves no doubt about the coincidence, cutting immediately to the men watching through the two-way mirror.

Except for a single cut to Claudius within, "to be" is shot as a long take, like the other soliloquies. It is more subtly punctuated than the previous soliloquies, which organized themselves around changes of direction in Hamlet's motion. The glacially slow "push-in" track of the camera contrasts with its energetic motion in both the previous segment of act 3, scene 1 and the previous soliloquies. As Hamlet walks slowly toward his image, followed by the camera, all attention is directed toward his debate over the desirability of his own death. A cinematic punctuation mark is inserted after "there's the rub" (64), when otherworldly music, almost imperceptibly rising more in the manner of Morricone than Doyle, adds affect to the dilemma of the afterlife. At the thought of making quietus with a bare bodkin (75), Hamlet surprisingly draws a dagger from a position at his back, as did Olivier's prince at the prayer scene, provoking a reaction of terror from Claudius. From this midpoint, the soliloquy's double meditation on suicide and murder, including murder that involves self-destruction, comes to the fore, for the dagger moves toward the men on both sides of the mirror.

With "the dread of something after death" (78), the dagger's forward motion reverses. Throughout the soliloquy, the mirror image facing us in focus has held our attention rather than the out-of-focus right shoulder of the real man. After the camera's progress removes sight of the mirror's gold frame, a moment that is generally felt but not noticed, the camera ceases its tracking and the reflection becomes our only reality, deepening our immersion in meditation as Hamlet's deepens. The dagger's blade reenters at the last line, clicking against the glass, but the viewer remains absorbed within the more compellingly real mirror image. The entrance of Ophelia thus becomes a kind of return to reality. Along with Hamlet, the viewer is released from intense absorption when a footfall produces a cut to over his left shoulder and the music abruptly ceases. As he turns to see Ophelia, the camera pulls a quick refocus from the mirror image to the real man.

Branagh heightens the pathos of the "nunnery" section of act 3, scene 1 with repeated hints of hope. Unlike the suspicious and evasive Hamlets of Olivier and Zeffirelli, Branagh's is very glad to see Ophelia and at first openly affectionate. A shot of Claudius and Polonius hides an editing jump that moves Hamlet in an instant—such is the quickness of the eager lover—nearly across the vast room and allows his dagger to disappear. The lovers' interaction begins with normal over-the-shoulder conversational shots. These are mixed with medium two-shots in profile that place the familiar corridor dividing the apartments of the king and queen, now representing what Claudius's crime has denied them, between the two lovers. Hamlet breaches this gap with a passionate hug and kiss until Ophelia pushes him away. After the lovemaking insets, this is a serious rejection, but Hamlet remains for the moment conciliatory. His wrath breaks forth when, in addition to Shakespeare's making Ophelia return the remembrances and spout rhyming sententia in the manner of her father, Branagh has her cast a guilty glance to her left. Hamlet slaps the proffered packet away and becomes abusive. Despite his turn to rhetorical violence, however, the romantic musical "Hamlet theme" continues as a kind of counterpoint belying his words until a knocking sound confirms that others are present.

Ophelia's blatant lie about her father's presence produces a reaction of intense grief rather than fury, again sustaining hope. Hamlet covers his tearful face and bids Ophelia farewell. When she prays to "sweet heavens" (135) for help and tries to pull his hands from his face, his grief turns to uncontrollable fury. The combination of unwanted facial communication and conflicting hand gestures marks the scene's emotional climax. Hamlet drags her furiously almost as a hostage to open the mirrored doors along the wrong side of the hall. Attentive viewers who have located Hamlet's apartment at the corner of the hall behind the throne will notice that he leaves her with another "farewell" (142) to go to his room off-camera, suggesting an end to the confrontation. His return after she again prays for him is therefore a surprise to us as well as to her. Also surprising is his uncanny crossing of the hall with her to the very door of his soliloquy.

As he presses her face cruelly against the mirror, the musical Hamlet theme resumes, signifying an emotion countering his action. "I say we will have no more marriages" (146) is countered by his stroking her chin and kissing her. But Hamlet's look into the camera that looks out through the mirror indicates that he realizes, somehow, that the eavesdroppers wait within. Only now, after Claudius and Polonius have spied on an intimate moment of both cruelty and love, does Hamlet unmistakably reach a murderous point of no return, just as he will when Polonius spies on him from behind the arras. Such is, apparently, the fatal emotional combination for this Hamlet. Directing his threat that "all but one—shall live" (147) to his hidden witnesses, Hamlet flings open the door, only to find that the hidden observers have just managed to escape through a secret passage. Because Hamlet then runs out the door through which he entered the hall, in the opposite direction from that in which he believed the king escaped, we are left in the dark about his intentions.

Ophelia delivers her moving soliloquy on Hamlet's noble mind overthrown while on the floor in the doorway. As she speaks of Hamlet's madness, her posture ironically prefigures that of her mad scene before this same mirrored wall. A slow push-in track to close-up imitates the camera motion of Hamlet's soliloquy from the other side of the mirrored door, further pressing us to sense parallels between their situations. Her concluding line on the distinction between Hamlets past and present, "T'have seen what I have seen, see what I see" (160), is clarified in the film, for we too have now been eyewitness to two forms of physical interaction, the violent present and the loving past of the insets, whether real or fantasized. Claudius and Polonius reenter through a passage in the wall opposite to that where Hamlet sought them after bursting into the room. This entrance further confuses our understanding of what Hamlet knew and how he knew it, for they enter from the direction not of their departure but of Hamlet's. Claudius displays a new degree of angry coldness, ignoring Ophelia entirely. Polonius, in contrast, picks his daughter up from the floor and hugs her for the rest of the scene, even as he plans another round of eavesdropping. The distinction, unlike the two men's shared insensitivity in the two previous films, prepares us to view Hamlet's mistaken slaying of Ophelia's at least sometimes supportive father as a tragic error.

Act 3, Scene 2

A transitional shot reveals Horatio standing in the snowy dusk reading a newspaper bearing the headlines "Norwegian Army's Advance" and "Latest Dispatches from the Front." Fortinbras is seen against the background of artillery flashes, his eyes as ominous as when we last saw them gazing over his uncle's shoulder toward an imagined Elsinore. The headlines emphasize the rapid rush toward a climax on the international front as events move toward a climax within Elsinore. Horatio checks his pocket watch, enhancing the sense of urgency.

Like Polonius's earlier comment ("too long"), the headlines and pocket watch amusingly point to Branagh's challenge, as the hopelessly wordy instruction to the players encounters the need for brisk visual storytelling. As in the earlier parade of cinematic devices, the scene of instruction overloads conspicuously, now allowing the 70mm format to overload the screen with details that draw our eyes around the State Hall as it is prepared for the Mousetrap. While Hamlet unrolls his three long blocks of prose, the deeply focused camera tracks as he strolls around the gallery with the actor who will play Lucianus, bowed at repeatedly by elegantly uniformed men who take up their stations. Below, men light candles in a room already flooded with light. Hamlet checks the upper door to his room, greeting Horatio, who waits there. The enormous chandelier is raised. Upon the men's entering the area where the players have gathered, an abundance of paraphernalia teases with the possibilities of what will soon be put on stage. Will the tragic masks polished by the boy with such care be used? Or the ass's head that tops the torso of Hamlet reflected in the mirror, recalling his rebuke, "Why, what an ass am I" (2.2.517). These conspicuous props hint at the potential for Hamlet's plan to succeed tragically or founder comically.

Hamlet returns to his apartment. Touches of humor and suggestive details continue to enliven the preparations. Horatio, visibly tense from the press of events at home and abroad, makes a startled jump when Hamlet touches him on the shoulder upon entering. An elegantly uniformed messenger becomes the butt of Hamlet's canine joke about "candied tongue" licking "absurd pomp" (3.2.56), turning the remark into an insult against the king. The model theater dominates the foreground long enough to catch attention. Its stage backdrop, here seen for the first time, looks uncannily familiar: the circling camera of act 3, scene 1 swept three times past the actual Mousetrap backdrop, portraying a hilltop castle, which it closely resembles. The model king has returned onstage. He stands again precariously on the trapdoor as two figures approach him, perhaps the Player King and Queen, or Hamlet and Lucianus. Most surprisingly, as Hamlet's speech of flattery moves to "Give me that man / That is not passion's slave (67–68), the prince squats before seated Horatio (whose nervousness is turning into embarrassment), lovingly takes his hand, and speaks of wearing him in his heart's core while a startlingly baroque version of Doyle's

Hamlet theme plays, a theme that heretofore has been principally associated with Hamlet's relationship with Ophelia.[26] Hamlet's, and Branagh's, "Something too much of this" (74) resonates with polysemic humor. Branagh's visual wit has made short the ninety long lines that have swept through our consciousness since Horatio impatiently looked at his watch.

A cut to the Mousetrap scene finds Claudius kissing his queen in semidarkness as the chandelier rises toward the ceiling. We hear applause, and the camera tilts down in a delayed disclosure that the applause is rising from the courtiers, who have all turned backward to cheer their amorous sovereigns. Hamlet comes onstage as a master of ceremonies and delights the crowd with his exuberant banter. When seated with Ophelia, however, his remarks grow less well received. The dumb show is too oblique to offend. The courtiers appear confused, the king and queen more interested in food and drink. The awaited climax begins to appear anticlimactic.

The recited play, in conversational close shots of the Player King and Queen intermittently alternating with reactions of the audience, attracts greater interest. All appear to be pleasingly moved until the subject of remarriage after the king's death makes its potential offense obvious. Glances away from the action—some predictable, others more unsettling in their possible implications—signal the onset of crisis. Claudius glances at Hamlet and, more surprisingly, at Horatio watching with opera glasses, the watcher watched. Polonius, Rosencrantz, and Guildenstern look to the king. At "A second time I kill my husband dead, / When second husband kisses me in bed" (178–79), the courtiers take notice. Claudius and Polonius exchange looks at "The great man down, you mark his favourite flies" (198) and again at the reference to "a hollow friend" (202), encouraging speculation about how the line has applied or could apply to their relationship. If Claudius is suddenly nervous about the loyalty of Polonius, Hamlet's project is working better than one could have hoped.

The climax of the play within is also the climax of Hamlet's outrageous behavior. Gertrude and Claudius regain their composure as Hamlet descends to lead applause, then ascends toward the royal seat to announce the "knavish piece of work" (234). Music begins building in tempo and volume as Hamlet descends to the stage again, crying, "Begin, murderer" (245–46). The already briskly paced editing accelerates suddenly as Lucianus begins to speak: his and Hamlet's subsequent speech proceed at one shot per second as the alternation of attention to the stage, the royals, and the courtly audience continues. Horatio observes the king, and the king again watches him observing! After Hamlet takes the bottle of poison from the actor, a series of shots pushing in toward

Claudius is intercut eight times, bringing us ever closer to his face as Hamlet's provocation hits home, eliciting three flash cuts to Claudius's memory of the poisoning scene. The insets culminate in old Hamlet seen from the point of view of Claudius as poisoner. The accusation by old Hamlet pointing at him is visually repeated by young Hamlet holding forth the bottle of poison, a gesture that is accusing and threatening at the same time. At this point of crisis, with a Doyle "crash chord" not unlike Walton's in Olivier's film, the king rises.

This cinematically charged buildup predicts a violent outburst. So when the king pauses with all eyes upon him and then requests light in a calm tone, his self-control is all the more remarkable. The courtiers empty the bleachers efficiently, and the actors show an understandable eagerness to distance themselves from the offensive spectacle to which they have unwittingly contributed, but Branagh does not follow his predecessors in portraying utter pandemonium. The relatively brisk editing of the dramatic performances, moreover, is simply continued, in contrast to the frenetic increase in cutting rhythm at this point in the previous films. The exiting audience is silent, focusing attention on Hamlet, who sustains his loud-mouthed antic disposition.

Horatio reenters to confirm the king's appearance of guilt, but his reservations about Hamlet's behavior are evident in a restraining hand gesture. He does not succeed in calming Hamlet, but his presence markedly slows the editing rhythm. Hamlet's abuse of angry Rosencrantz and Guildenstern and then of Polonius stretches across a shot of nearly three and a half minutes. By the end of this sustained performance, Hamlet is breathing hard and out of control, and his quick exit without acknowledging the more skeptical Horatio, whom he insultingly lumps together with his other young "friends" (378), forecasts precipitous action.

Act 3, Scene 3

Several devices are used to direct expectations of this precipitous action toward the king rather than, as in the previous films, toward the queen. Like Hamlet, Claudius too confers with Rosencrantz and Guildenstern in a long take, creating parallel screen presences of the two disturbed antagonists who will soon collide. Hamlet's "witching time" (3.2.378) soliloquy is transposed to after the conference in Claudius's chambers, specifying whose hot blood it is that Hamlet might drink. The camera tracks in steadily toward the suddenly static prince during the soliloquy, but its closing lines are recited after a cut to the king in the chapel, and the music remains continuous over the cuts, overlapping the two men's scenes. A track-in to seated Claudius during his own soliloquy in the chapel creates a further parallel. Unlike other film *Hamlets*, this one provides no visual communication between Hamlet and his mother at the end of the Mousetrap scene. Instead, although he says, "now to my mother" (382), the structures of film declare that not a maternal but a paternal confrontation is imminent.

Unlike Olivier and Zeffirelli, who carefully represent Hamlet's encounter with praying Claudius as an accidental interruption of his journey to Gertrude's bedroom, Branagh does not visually report Hamlet's journey, allowing a nonaccidental reading. We conclude that Hamlet proceeds to murder the king at the witching time, acting in a sense as another return of the ghost. He returns in the form of another horror-film device, a hand that slides across the window of the confessional after Claudius kneels and makes his "assay" (3.3.69) at repentance. Another rapidly edited sequence, forty shots in just over two minutes, assumes the form of a climax after the long takes. The sequence, however, is both climactic and anticlimactic. It rushes into the predicted violent confrontation as Hamlet, triumphantly declaring "And so am I revenged" (75), drives his dagger into the king's ear. The extreme close-up of the king's ear spurting blood announces talion vengeance, for it recalls the first image of old Hamlet's murder, inset twice when the ghost labeled Claudius's crime. With this alteration to Shakespeare's plot, Branagh can bring his film to an end with a running time of just over two hours.

But, of course, this murder is imaginary and the film does not end. The violence is withdrawn from reality after a few seconds of suspense when a shot of Hamlet's eyes gives way to the view of Claudius unhurt, the dagger still merely poised at his ear. With a noninset that is unambiguously subjective and fantasized, the nature of the previous insets becomes even more problematic. Now, the filmmaker concludes, is the time to add more insets.

Hamlet's resolve to seek more horrid vengeance is supported viscerally by an inset of his father's death agony. From here, as Hamlet projects circumstances that would damn the king eternally, six insets of Claudius review moments from the film that prefigure future occasions for revenge. The entire sequence is framed by images of the earth opening and closing, and each inset is framed by extreme close-ups of Hamlet's darting eyes, windows to his churning mind:

> When he is drunk, asleep or in his rage,
> Or in th'incestuous pleasure of his bed,

At game a-swearing, or about some act
That has no relish of salvation in't.

(89–92)

The insets do not merely illustrate individual examples; their wildly unchronological ordering assists the viewer in experiencing the wildness of Hamlet's
unsystematic catalog.[27] Rearranged to follow the film's plot, they culminate in a
moment that was cut from the final film, a fortuitous opportunity to add more
interpretive mischief. Evoking Shakespearean bawdy language, "At game" as-
sociationally follows the incestuous bed, portraying the king and queen in
what Hamlet hopes is their last untroubled moment of passion as they kiss in
the royal box before the Mousetrap. This was a moment cheered by the audience but unseen by Hamlet, who was still backstage. The director appears to
enjoy mischief as much as his character.

Act 3, Scene 4

The rage motivating Hamlet to seek crueler revenge on Claudius carries over
into the closet scene. His triple address to "mother" (5) is exclaimed wildly before
he surprises both Gertrude and the viewer by entering her apartment through
a door hidden in the wall. He quickly escalates their encounter into a shouting
match and throws her down into a chair. On hearing a cry from behind the
curtain, he stabs Polonius repeatedly, the impulsive violence conveyed in a hectic
sequence of over three shots per second.[28] He drops his dagger on seeing that his
victim is Polonius, but the action appears to be motivated not by remorse but by
disgust at the "wretched, rash, intruding fool" (31). With a look of contempt at
her weakness, he orders his mother to leave off wringing her hands.

Branagh addresses the challenge of providing visual variety for a long,
uncut scene set within an enclosed room through careful segmentation, which
moves us to new locations while creating the feel of step-by-step progress
through the plot. After the quick release of violence, Hamlet's first extended
rant occupies a long take that carries him, gesturing vigorously, around the bed
onto which he has thrown his mother. The scene's longest speech is then divided precisely in half. For the first half, he joins Gertrude on the bed. Despite
the physical proximity, repeated close-ups of the two portraits provide a kind
of paternal presence that obviates oedipal associations. The photographs, inset
seven times, also direct attention to the two people who are more important
than Gertrude in this film as sources of Hamlet's rage. For the speech's second

half, Hamlet leaves the bed and moves back and forth around it, followed by the panning camera that sets him against the background of the room's walls, which are covered with trompe-l'oeil paintings filled with silent observers of Gertrude's shame. The paintings add a metacinematic overtone, evoking the film's repeated use of the abundance of background detail made available in its wide-screen format. As in the first court scene, where he entered from the background, Hamlet after entering through the painting is again airing his private anguish in public.

At Hamlet's most confrontational moment—when, after ignoring his mother's repeated pleas of "no more," he rants within inches of his mother's face—the ghost intervenes, appearing in the background between them and coming into focus as they exit the frame. Expressing none of the alarm or guilt of earlier Hamlets, he fixes his eyes longingly upon the cereclothed figure even as he obeys the command to speak to his mother. Branagh denotes the ghost's ability to select by whom he is seen with unproblematic shot combinations: views of the empty room framed by views of Gertrude, implying that she cannot see the ghost even though it is present; views of the ghost framed by views of Hamlet, implying that he can; views of Gertrude and Hamlet with the ghost in the background, with him obviously seeing it and her not. More interestingly, just as he adds ambiguity and subjectivity to the insets, so too does he problematize the ghost's presence by also including three shots from Hamlet's point of view that reveal a room devoid of the ghost. These include the first view from his point of view, validating Gertrude's conclusion, "Alas, he's mad" (102), before later shots make that conclusion not false but problematic. In effect, when Gertrude insists on Hamlet's hallucinatory madness (102, 112–20), the filmic language indicates that she is correct by not allowing us to see the ghost that Hamlet claims to see. When Hamlet pleads with the ghost, "O say" (106), and when he points at him (121–34) with tearful eyes and Doyle's desire-signifying Hamlet theme rising, the filmic language indicates that the ghost is present. Branagh again has it both ways.

Hamlet's rage returns after the ghost fades away. Branagh adds the Quarto response "Extasie?" (142) as indicating anger that Gertrude would deny the paternal presence that Hamlet desires so fervently. He violently transports his mother across the room to a third location, lecturing her on a sofa in another long take. When she confesses that her heart is cleft in twain, a conversational alternation of over-the-shoulder shots takes over, despite Hamlet's continuing largely in monologue. In this instance, the discrepancy between the monologue and the film device denoting dialogue suggests that Hamlet may perceive a genuine exchange of views occurring that his mother may not. The discrepancy combines with Gertrude's declining to communicate her sympathy for Hamlet to create suspense about her subsequent behavior.

Act 4, Scene 1

This suspense is maintained throughout the next scene. Gertrude's first action following Hamlet's departure with the body of Polonius is to cross the corridor toward the king's apartment, adding doubt about her change of heart, a change usually revealed in performance though not necessarily implied by Gertrude's meager lines. At the start of a continuous shot lasting nearly three minutes, Claudius, Rosencrantz, and Guildenstern rush toward the royals' end of the corridor with unnaturalistic speed, since they are too distant to hear her "profound heaves" (4.1.1). This may suggest the kind of prescience shown at this point by Zeffirelli's Claudius, who enters inquiring about Hamlet before learning of the murder. The camera follows the royal couple into the king's room, where the king's speech beginning "O heavy deed" starts as a direct address to his wife. It then appears to modulate into an address to himself as he hurries back across the corridor to examine the bloody crime scene, including the telltale portrait miniatures that remain on the bed. He drops the portrait of his brother back onto the bed, then after contemplating his own throws it down with considerable anger while declaring, "But so much was our love, / We would not understand what was most fit" (19–20). The gesture is difficult to interpret: perhaps an action that combines disgust over his indulgence with self-loathing. It grows even more difficult after a powerful delayed disclosure, in which the moving camera reveals that Gertrude has followed him and that the impression of self-address was illusory. The device is repeated when the couple separate and the camera follows Claudius into the hall to issue orders to Rosencrantz and Guildenstern, only to have Gertrude follow the camera back toward her husband. The camera tracks back down the corridor to where the virtuoso shot began, displaying the distressed couple in a mutually comforting embrace. Branagh's Claudius has succeeded as a crisis manager in the manner of both Olivier's and Zeffirelli's king but even more so, for he has not yet lost the allegiance of his queen.

Act 4, Scene 2

A cut transfers the visual momentum of the outward tracking to guards running in the camera's direction, another visual manifestation of Claudius's efficiency.

Revealing that Hamlet's love affair is known to the king, or at least suspected, they burst into the room of sleeping Ophelia, who screams as they seek the killer in her bed. Hamlet has barely managed to stow the body when Rosencrantz and Guildenstern, followed by more armed guards, burst forth from the two entrances to his room near the throne. He leads the ever-expanding party of pursuers the full length of the State Hall with a combination of antic wit and intimidation, then agrees to see the king and starts up the stairway following his two "friends." At this point, Ophelia runs down the stairway in her nightgown, crying "My lord," her most characteristic phrase but here a non-Shakespearean line in a non-Shakespearean entrance.[29] In confronting his prince with his jilted lover after he has lugged her father's corpse into the neighboring room, Branagh offers a better explanation than mere madness, real or feigned, for using the Folio's "Hide fox and all after" (28) and its implied wild flight.

Hamlet enters a mirrored door and sprints frantically toward his apartment through the hidden side doors that connect the mirrored rooms adjoining the State Hall, chased as frantically by the "friends." Tracked through the missing exterior wall, they pass through the six intervening rooms, interrupting a man working at his desk, three groups of men and women engaged in some indiscernible activity, and a man and woman making love: a provocative paradigm for what goes on behind the scenes at Elsinore. The pace is made even more frantic by adding independently shot passages through three of the rooms by Rosencrantz and Guildenstern, creating in effect a nine-room chase in a mere fifteen seconds. In the end, to use the screenplay's description, "as he closes the door to his apartment, apparently safe . . . a gun barrel trains itself on his head."[30] He has escaped poor, abandoned Ophelia, but he cannot escape the ruthlessly efficient Claudius.

Act 4, Scene 3

The king has retreated into the solitude offered by the Folio's lack of attendants, allowing his speech resolving upon "desperate appliance" (10) that would appear "all smooth and even" (7) to become his second soliloquy, delivered while seated at his desk. The contrast of his current, thoughtful efficiency with his anguish in the prayer scene is thus made clear. The single take of his soliloquy is followed by a long take covering Hamlet's interrogation and sending off to England, rhythmically supporting a sense of controlled power in contrast to Hamlet's mad escape attempt. When Hamlet is forcibly brought in front of the king, the camera circles their face-off one and one-half times, taking in repeatedly not only Rosencrantz and Guildenstern, the imperial guards, and the constabulary massed at the door but also the ancestral presences of the portrait paintings, whose power Claudius has appropriated. Claudius slaps the prince violently at asking the whereabouts of Polonius, but the explosive anger counters control over Hamlet with a crack in his self-control. Like previous Hamlets, Branagh's wins the game of one-upmanship, now with the farewell kiss to his "dear mother" (48), at which Claudius flinches and displays the nervous mouth-movements of the murder scene and the Mousetrap climax. The uselessness of this victory is revealed when Hamlet is hustled off. He whispers a non-Shakespearean "Stay" to Horatio, who promptly disobeys and follows his friend. The danger of this victory is evident when Claudius closes the doors and forecasts "The present death of Hamlet" (63) with explosive fury.

Act 4, Scene 4

Before bringing in Fortinbras, Branagh inserts a shot of the bloody corpse of Polonius being carried into the chapel and Ophelia rushing up to the chapel gates, through which she emits repeated screams. Sight of the familiar gates generates painful ironies; having enclosed her with her father in act 1, scene 3, they now keep her from him.[31] The sexual insets of act 1, scene 3, with the man who has just killed her father and rudely fled at her approach, took place in the bed from which she has just been rousted. With her trauma intensified both in its causes and in its representation beyond what is feasible in a stage production, Branagh has done what he can to make Ophelia's subsequent madness believable in a nineteenth-century setting and to a twentieth-century audience.

As her scream resonates over a distant shot of Elsinore behind the willowy brook, two dissolves to Fortinbras—at first a mere speck in the snowy distance, then a warrior on horseback—link the present scene visually to the insets of the ambassador report in act 2, scene 2, where Fortinbras and the goal of his conquest were also visualized and the "promised march" (4.4.3) now taking place across Denmark was originally requested. A close-up of him looking off into the distance is nearly identical to a close-up of him, in the same armor, from the inset. Because act 2, scene 2 presents Fortinbras at least visualizing Elsinore as the object of conquest, the visual echo will suggest to the alert viewer that the Captain's report is not what it seems. On learning of the Norwegian's new mission, Hamlet dismisses Rosencrantz and Guildenstern to begin his final soliloquy. In a much-discussed shot, the camera cranes outward during the entire speech, beginning imperceptibly and slowly accelerating to reveal the vast snowy landscape and the "army of such mass and charge" (4.4.46) in the valley below.[32] As Hamlet comes to identify with his Norwegian counterpart and resolve that his thoughts be equally bloody, his reduction to a tiny figure in the distance equates him with the scene's first shot of Fortinbras. Out of such emphatic likeness, however, difference emerges. Hamlet stands with hands outstretched in a sacrificial pose to be seen again at his death. Fortinbras proceeds forward, surely and methodically, toward the place where the two princes will finally meet.

Act 4, Scene 5

Branagh inserts his intermission 158 minutes into the film, much longer than his original suggested two-hour limit but only five minutes longer than Olivier's film. The division accords with Harley Granville-Barker's argument that what he calls the play's second movement cannot be interrupted until after the last soliloquy. It also accords with Emrys Jones's analysis of the play's "structural rhyming": the play's two parts end with Fortinbras, and the second part presents "an ironical reversal of the first. Laertes is now the injured son, whose father has been murdered; Hamlet is now, from this point of view, the murderer who must be put to death."[33]

Following the intermission, Branagh interposes Claudius's audit to Gertrude of sorrows that come "not single spies / But in battalions" (4.5.78–79), a military image that links the events inside Elsinore with the massed forces of Fortinbras in the previous scene. Claudius speaks his account for the audience, who needs it more than does its original auditor, over a montage sequence of eight silent shots, the first six of which efficiently illustrate the king's list. An interpretive challenge arises on the seventh, an outtake of Laertes looking very benign as he petitions to return to France in the first State Hall scene, in visual conflict with the king's report of his menacing return. Perhaps the unexpected leap back to a joyous earlier time, and what was probably Claudius's last sight of Laertes, underscores the calamities of the present, imprinting the image of a man who will soon face the royal couple again at the throne but wearing a very different expression. The next shot is challenging as well. Claudius, in his nightgown, is pacing the chapel in anguish. The dress and location recall the prayer scene, where he escaped another "murdering-piece" (95), but of course he is unaware of his narrow escape.

Ophelia is seen from above bouncing madly against the walls of her padded cell, conveniently set up in a mirror-doored room of the State Hall. Her madness in its first phase is betokened by wild movement, which she will eventually abandon in favor of stasis and death. When the camera tilts up to reveal Gertrude, Horatio, and a white-uniformed woman as the observers through an opening in the gallery floor, the violence below adds urgency to the appeals by the latter two to "let her come in" (16) from confinement to the openness of the empty hall. A surprising cut to Gertrude poised tensely above the straightjacketed woman lying prone, a seal-like form on the checkerboard floor, leaves open the question of how she escaped confinement. Did her wild motions break her free? When Gertrude approaches, her movement uncovers the uniformed attendant who had been eclipsed behind her. One infers from this comforting clinical presence, belatedly, that all is under control, but the suggestion has been made that the madwoman cannot be contained. We have been prepared for her escape, if not yet for her suicide.

Gertrude unfastens the straightjacket, and Claudius, entering mysteriously from a mirrored room adjoining the padded cell—carrying out independent observation of the madwoman?—raises Ophelia from the floor. His action recalls that of Polonius after the "to be" soliloquy, as Claudius attempts to expand his usual role of substitute parent beyond adopting Laertes. He does not succeed. At his "Conceit upon her father" (45), Ophelia runs twirling toward the throne end of the hall, where she dances out the Saint Valentine song. When she returns, the sexual dimension of her affliction is displayed in a hard pelvic thrust to Claudius, continued thrusting on the floor, and two insets with Hamlet in her bed. The film's set of sexual insets concludes, leaving unresolved the issue of whether these are fantasies or flashbacks. As others have noted, Hamlet is assigned no insets with Ophelia, keeping alive the former possibility. The wildness of her motions is measured by the precisely moving camera against the graph of the tiled floor, along which the camera moves from horizontal to vertical alignment (along the throne's axis) then back again for Claudius's attempt to restrain her and return her to her cell. Eluding him, she escapes into the corridor leading to the royal apartments, crying "good night" (73), followed by Horatio and the attendant. Because the royal bedrooms lie at the end of this corridor, she seems to have a delusive destination in mind.

Left with Gertrude in the empty hall, Claudius walks right then left and puts his hand to his head, imitating his motions in the chapel inset, suggesting a similar state of despair. Gertrude follows him supportively, as she did more tentatively in act 4, scene 1, delaying her shift in allegiance longer than in the previous films, as the full text encourages. The film gives them good reason for both despair and solidarity, because it presents the return of Laertes in visual terms of "impetuous haste" and "riotous head" (4.5.100–101, modified). The transposition of the king's speech to the postintermission montage leaves only his cry "O Gertrude, Gertrude" (77) to stand between Ophelia's madness and Laertes' rebellion, replacing the play's delay with a quicker launch into the action described. The rebellion begins in three insets, the first of which has already begun over the second "Gertrude." The messenger's report remains, but the action continues in two more insets as she speaks. In the third, the camera shifts from lateral and facing shots of the rebels, images of their threat, to track them from behind, in effect joining the mob. When the location of the mob's onset becomes identifiable, the sense of violation grows: the rebels are approaching the State Hall doors through the familiar corridor, entering through the royal's private space into the public State Hall, as Fortinbras will do eventually in a more successful takeover. From inside the hall, we see them break through the doors and surge within, Laertes emerging at their "head."

Gertrude's allegiance to the king is quickened by the crisis. She angrily condemns the "false Danish dogs" (110) before the doors open and moves boldly to intercept Laertes at the throne as he sprints toward the king with sword drawn. Claudius lives up to his wife's example, facing down the wild young man with impressive calm. But, of course, Ophelia must enter to complete the stand-down. A cut reveals her rushing, chased by the doctor, through the same set of side rooms through which Hamlet ran to escape her and through which we could hear her following him, suggesting continuing method to her madness. Her straightjacket has been replaced by a simple white gown, but she remains barefoot and unkempt, implying that she has been tended to but only until she could escape once again.

On entering the State Hall, Ophelia gazes at her brother in what seems half-recognition before proceeding to the mirrored room adjacent to her padded cell. His presence moves her madness from a manic phase to one that is more depressive. She sits on the floor joined by Laertes, beginning a remarkable "conversation" sequence, divided into three panels by shots of Claudius and Gertrude, who stand silently watching a farewell nondialogue between a sister fully divided from herself and a brother increasingly so. The mirror reflection converts twenty-five over-the-shoulder two-shots and single close-ups, the standard fare of conversations, into, respectively, surreal three-shots and two-shots. These are sutured together in a way that would normally present speeches, reactions, and the eye-line matches that accompany them. Only three of the shots (for lines 160–67), however, fit into normal alternations of speaker and listener. The others alternate conversationally as Laertes reflects to himself on his sister's madness and Ophelia recites her nonsense and weaves and hands out imaginary herbs. In the third shot, Laertes places his hand on Ophelia's face, and she reciprocates, but this is their only, and sadly final, physical contact. The two Ophelias cannot answer the question directly posed to her by the two Laertes: "is't possible a young maid's wits / Should be as mortal as an old man's life?" (158–59). Nor can doubled Laertes respond to doubled Ophelias' plea to "call him a down-a" (165–66). A stranger and sadder conversation would be difficult to imagine.

Ophelia ends the conversation with her first song to be actually sung, on bonny sweet Robin. She then turns away from her brother and sings, "And will he not come again" (183), in the first view of the two siblings without doubling reflections. As the camera moves to push Laertes off the screen and her lonely voice reverberates in the vast room, her final song becomes a moving soliloquy, delivered from a posture recalling her previous soliloquy. Reentering her padded cell voluntarily, she stands facing the back wall against which she earlier slammed in violent desperation. "Do you see this, O God?" (193), Laertes asks, leaning against the edge of the door and appearing about to fall into madness himself. Ever resourceful, Claudius takes advantage of the man's despair and enervation. He was glimpsed in reflection already moving forward to seize the moment as Laertes rose to follow his sister, and Claudius is now ready with a steadying embrace. Ineffective with Ophelia, his fatherly approach works better with the son who has been infected with "pestilent speeches of his father's death" (91). Redirecting the son's attention from his sister to the revenge that will respond to both of his losses at once, he leads Laertes off with a paternal arm around the shoulder.

Act 4, Scene 6

Having opted not to visualize *Hamlet's* most famous "unscene," as Marjorie Garber labels Ophelia's account of Hamlet's visit to her closet, Branagh opted to be consistent with the play's other prominent unscene, the escape with the pirates.[34] Oddly, while this scene starts well enough, it collapses into absurdity in the end. Horatio walks quickly with a messenger down an unfamiliar hallway, his visible urgency to obtain the sailor's letters explained by his voiced belief that they must be from Hamlet. He stops momentarily to observe Ophelia, who is being "treated" for her madness with a high-pressure hose. Ironically, the key she has hidden in her mouth will allow her to escape such inhumane psychiatry through drowning. A "dangling cause" awaiting an effect has been efficiently planted. In Horatio's reading of the letter aloud in the colonnade of the Great Court, he reasonably registers surprise about pirates, improbabilities in the late nineteenth century, and puzzlement over the request to join Hamlet "with as much haste as thou would'st fly death" (22–23, in Folio). The stage convention of reading aloud, however, strains awkwardly here within the conventions of film, especially when Horatio, disconcerted to notice that the sailors are listening, moves out of earshot rather than reading "silently" in voice-over.

Act 4, Scene 7

Shakespeare's act 4, scene 7 has never been accused of laconic efficiency. One feels viscerally in the 126 lines partitioned into Claudius's sixteen speeches the labor that prompts him to exclaim in the end, "How much I had to do to calm his rage!" (190). Olivier and Zeffirelli lessened the need for Claudius's labor, and therefore the need for many of his words, by transposing the coaxing of Laertes to after Ophelia's burial. Olivier further mitigated the scene's wordiness through creative camerawork, Zeffirelli through intercutting smaller scenes. Branagh responds audaciously with film structures that support rather than mitigate Shakespeare's challenging wordiness. Taking place behind closed doors in the king's apartment, the coaxing of Laertes is broken down into three distinct parts characterized by changing camera styles. The incongruity of form and content in the "conversation" before the mirror with Ophelia is replaced by a systematic, conspicuously belabored congruity that corresponds to the crafty king's systematic method of persuasion and to the structured order that traumatized Laertes needs.

In the first segment, with the camera tracking through what is by far the longest take after the intermission, Claudius explains the "two special reasons" (10) for not proceeding harshly against Hamlet. He swings through an arc around the furniture away from and then back to Laertes, allowing the perigee of his orbit to divide the two reasons neatly. When Laertes concludes that he is being left to seek revenge by himself, Claudius is in position at the end of his arc to place a fatherly hand on Laertes' shoulder and then crouch down to speak intimately of his plot for Hamlet's death in England. The echo of Hamlet's "proposal" to Horatio in act 3, scene 2 is unmistakable, reinforcing the sense of talion revenge. At this moment, the messenger arrives bearing Hamlet's letters, and the game plan changes.

The letter to the king initiates a second, clearly demarcated phase that is not about calming Laertes but about working him up again to a new goal. During a steadfastly repetitive series of nine shots/reverse-shots across the round table, Claudius toils to whet the interest of Laertes with a teasing account of Hamlet's envy, in which he carefully declines to name both the skill that Hamlet envies and the source of the praise that caused this envy. The shots are as laboriously systematic as the king's rhetoric, all in over-the-shoulder format, in contrast to the randomly alternating over-the-shoulder and close-up shots of the mad interchange with Ophelia. This, the camera implies with its almost oppressive repetition, is a real conversation controlled by a relentless king. Following this exchange, a long two-shot of the men displays the excited exchange of information that the crafty king's tactic has elicited.

Claudius draws up short with the teasing, "Now out of this—" (104), and begins another well-demarcated phase. Intensity is ratcheted up from the over-the-shoulder to the separation style. A long sequence of eleven shot/reverse-shot close-ups moves from the king's boldest provocation, "Laertes, was your father dear to you?" (106), to Laertes' angry wish "To cut his throat i'th'church" (124). The emotional tension produced by both the verbal content and the relentless visual form is relieved by a long two-shot during which Claudius, pleased with the young man's response, goes over some practical details for the murder by "sword unbated" (136). Laertes briefly imposes his own emotional control over the shot selection, initiating a new series of close-ups, three in number, with his plan to poison the sword, but the more convivial two-shots return as Claudius more calmly reasons out his "back or second" (151) plan: the poisoned wine.

Nine minutes of sustained conversation, long for any film audience but made, surprisingly but effectively, to feel longer by Branagh's craft of segmentation, are brought to an abrupt halt by Gertrude's interruption. Because it is spoken without the extensive visualization of the earlier films, and because Branagh's version of act 4, scene 7 is so highly structured, Gertrude's account of Ophelia's drowning and Laertes' reaction are more thoroughly integrated into the scene as a fourth segment. Its integration, in turn, highlights its host of differences from the previous segments. Laertes, who has been seated the entire time, now stands throughout the segment. Music, absent until now, heightens the emotional impact of the lyrical narrative that replaces manipulative persuasion. The slow track-in to Gertrude replaces conversational camera styles with one associated with soliloquy, suggesting that accompanying Gertrude's communication to Laertes is self-reflection. The suggestion will be confirmed when her allegiance subsequently shifts.

Claudius responds to Laertes' distress with his usual paternal gesture, but Laertes is no longer responsive. Because we have experienced the labor of Claudius through belabored shot selection, it is small wonder that he feels upset at the breakdown of the scene he has heretofore controlled so thoroughly. His complaint about the effort required to calm the young man is muttered angrily, and the truth of his claim to heroic effort is as clear to the viewer as is the only partial truth of his claiming to have calmed Laertes' rage. The full-text and Branagh's treatment make the anger of the king, who is focused on the effect of the report on Laertes rather than on the tragedy of Ophelia and its effect on Gertrude, entirely understandable. But because Gertrude does not share our experience, her failure to see the king's reaction as reasonable is also understandable. She responds coldly to her husband's command, "Therefore let's follow" (192), finally making the break of allegiance that other filmmakers located earlier. The only visualization of Ophelia's death, a brief shot of the drowned girl underwater, occurs after Claudius leaves the room alone. It becomes the conclusion of Gertrude's "soliloquy," an identification of one woman with another that Claudius cannot make.

Act 5, Scene 1

Branagh brackets off his graveyard scene from the rest of his film more thoroughly than other directors. Spatially, the scene occupies a tightly constricted space viewed in an establishing shot repeated several times for punctuation. Unlike the willowy brook where Ophelia drowns, which is shown twice with Elsinore in the background, her final resting place is, uniquely among the film's settings, not located in relation to any other site.[35] Temporally, Branagh unifies the scene by imposing a consistently brisk pace of editing despite the fact that its sections flow verbally according to quite different rhythms. Although carefully divided into discrete units characterized by distinct camera styles, it is by far the film's longest segment of uniform pacing, proceeding methodically at about four seconds per shot. Time slows down as a result, carrying us toward the duel eager for the excitement of tempo changes.

A sense of leisurely progression is established from the beginning. The camera tracks slowly, stopping to peer at the burial setting through an opening in a dilapidated iron fence. One gravedigger takes a break from his labor, occasioning the other, who has been lazily reading a newspaper and smoking, to speculate on Ophelia's burial. The discussion of suicide and the diggers' profession stretches its sixty lines across forty-two close shots of a single speaker or listener, punctuated by a mere four medium two-shots. The abstract and impersonal nature of the discussion allows this long separation sequence to create effects quite different from the emotional intensity of Hamlet's interaction with the ghost, the only other scene containing an extensive conversation in alternating high and low shots—and a scene placed in a similarly unmappable and nocturnal wood. The subliminal connections that might be made with the ghost encounter lend an aspect of parody to this scene, as from on high Billy Crystal instructs the lower-placed Simon Russell Beale in matters of less than pressing importance. Absorbed in the highly unequal clash of wits, we and the two men lose track of time, an effect that will explain the diggers' panicky haste to complete preparations when the funeral procession arrives.

The first gravedigger leaves his high perch to delve in the hole after sending his companion for a stoup of liquor. The second conversation links itself to the first by beginning with a repeat of the establishing shot through the gap in the fence after Hamlet and Horatio are seen walking along the earlier track of the camera, and by continuing at precisely the same editing pace while intercutting between Hamlet speaking with Horatio and the first digger's whistling and playing with bones at the grave. Crystal's singing digger reveals himself to be a connoisseur of relics. He adroitly cleans five skulls fetched from below and lines them up to form a growing audience, whose empty eyeholes return the stares of his as-yet-unseen observers. Branagh introduces a novel editing scheme to highlight the incongruity between Hamlet's reality and the gravedigger's. The gravedigger systematically assembles his skulls during a desultory set of shots randomly varied in angle and distance. In contrast, Hamlet converses desultorily with Horatio during a highly systematic set: nine middle shots of Hamlet and Horatio together, followed by five close-ups of Hamlet and Horatio separately, followed by nine middle shots of Hamlet and Horatio together. In the central close-up, Hamlet declares his response to the sight of so many bones: "Mine ache to think on't" (87–88). Hamlet's revulsion focused through elaborate symmetry meets Goodman Delver's complacent self-entertainment. Before Hamlet declares, "How absolute the knave is. We must speak by the card or equivocation will undo us" (133–34), the structural encounter has made an equivalent statement.

With Hamlet's verbal encounter, the shot/reaction-shot style of the two gravediggers' colloquy returns, introducing a comic variant with "over-the-knee" shots from crouching Hamlet's vantage. This return continues with Yorick's skull. Hamlet holds the skull before his face in a lengthy, lateral two-shot that might serve as a souvenir photo to hang in the long gallery of such depictions across the centuries. After this classic pose, almost as eagerly awaited as the words "to be or not to be," the segment turns ironically "conversational." Branagh adds to the irony of the skull's nonreply, a device also used by Zeffirelli, a more interesting interaction between Hamlet's words and the images presented in two of his signature insets. Hamlet's view of the skull dissolves first to an intimate flashback in which young Hamlet, after mock-strangling the jester, is hoisted up to his lap and kisses him twice on the painted cheek. After another view of the skull, Hamlet flashes back again. In a more precise match, the skull's eye sockets and mouth dissolve into Yorick's corresponding features. We next see Yorick setting the table on a roar, directing his flashes of merriment at young Hamlet, seated with his father and uncle, his back to us in an implied point of view.

Although Branagh has been both praised and castigated for his insets, the flashbacks to Yorick have received relatively little attention. Yet they are certainly no less provocative than the other insets. The film medium's abundance of information may facilitate overinterpretation, but to ignore evidence laid plainly before our eyes is to belittle the medium's potential for the creation of complex and powerful meanings, even if these meanings are not necessarily articulable in words. The first inset dissolves to Yorick over Hamlet's statement of "how abhorred in my imagination it is" (176–77). This collision of a happy, imagined visual against an opposed verbal evaluation may be viewed as simple contrast of the past and present images, but the vagueness of "it" combines with visual details to intimate more. The playful strangling follows "My gorge rises at it" (177), suggesting that Hamlet's throaty discomfort in the present is repeating something from the past in a displaced manner. Resistance to visualizing what his words plainly recall is implied when the child kisses Yorick twice, but on the cheek rather than on "those lips that I have kissed I know not how oft" (178–79). At the very least, one can say that the inset adds an ambivalent combination of aggression and affection to the already powerful combination of desire and repulsion in Shakespeare's words.

Both insets transport us to the king's apartments, on whose red walls hang the ancestral portraits that have been viewed repeatedly.[36] Both the painted female figure near the door to the corridor and the male figure with rifle next to her hover over the action in the first inset, but only the male is present in the second. Conspicuously absent in the family gathering of the second is another female. Gertrude has been displaced at the table by face-painted Yorick, who favors young Hamlet with his attention over Hamlet's two father figures. As Hamlet continues, to the skull, "Now get you to my lady's chamber and tell her, let her paint an inch thick, to this favour she must come" (182–84), the mind's eye might seek the absent parent across the familiar corridor in the queen's chamber, where Hamlet has struggled with his mother and attempted to kill his father. The inset reveals in Hamlet both a powerful desire to imagine his mother and an equally powerful need to avoid doing so. Hamlet's cross-gender comparison of the jester's and lady's favors has developed into a more complex scenario implying that his confrontation with death has heightened an already formidable ambivalence toward his mother. This heightened ambivalence will soon reemerge over the grave when he declares his passion for his "lady" in the guise of Ophelia but rejects her in the guise of his mother.

The screenplay's Hamlet follows stage tradition in throwing the skull down in disgust after gasping at its stench at line 190. The film uses the long meditation on Alexander and Caesar, eliminated by Olivier and Zeffirelli, to continue the visually implied conversation with Yorick's skull, linking the two parts with continuous music and adding for good measure a shot over Yorick's nonexistent shoulder. The change allows Hamlet at his concluding couplet (204–5) to look directly into the camera. The next shot reveals him looking into the eyes of the skull, confirming that we have been momentarily afforded the vantage of the dead. Through deceased Yorick's eye sockets, we contemplate a Hamlet whose conflicted Shakespearean psychology has been entered through images no less than words.

At this moment, Hamlet notices the funeral procession, not by hearing it, as in previous films, but by looking in the direction of a bird's cry. The second gravedigger, long departed in other productions, hurriedly returns to assist in the preparation of the grave. All present are clearly surprised that the procession would arrive in the deep of night. If Ophelia's nocturnal burial in a decrepit and obscure cemetery is technically Christian, it is no less "hugger-mugger" than her father's (4.5.84). In hushed tones befitting a secret ceremony, the priest defends the maimed rites to Laertes. Complaining that "great command o'ersways the order" (5.1.217), he glances at Claudius, who is looking at Gertrude. The king's look provides a reason for his overswaying command, for his obtuse response to Ophelia's death report grievously damaged the royal relationship. The return glance he seeks will not be granted during the entire scene, even though the couple is shown together fifteen times and never apart until the end.

Obeying the Folio stage direction, Laertes leaps into the grave and opens the rough-hewn casket. He breaks the hushed atmosphere with his shouted rant, prompting Hamlet to leave his hiding place and compete with his own shout, declaring his identity. Physical aggression comes entirely from Laertes, who throws Hamlet to the ground, but from this point Hamlet's verbal vehemence breaks forth, while the tender attention of Gertrude quickly converts Laertes' rage into enervating sorrow. After the explosion of frustrated desire, the other side of Hamlet's ambivalence toward his "lady" takes over. Calming down, he delivers his "I loved you ever" (279) lines of reconciliation to Laertes, glances toward Claudius at "Let Hercules himself do what he may" (280), but declines to look upon his mother, who stands between the two men addressed. Moved by her son's sudden tenderness, even if it is not for her, Gertrude walks toward him with tears on her cheeks. But Hamlet, suddenly and surprisingly, turns and walks out of the cemetery, leaving his mother standing with her back to us but with her emotions needing no additional revelation. Now with the king and queen on-screen separately for the first time in the graveyard, as if the need for a public show of harmony has passed, Claudius coldly orders her, "set some watch over your son" (285). Gertrude turns her head far enough to reveal her contempt but avoids returning his gaze. She departs in the direction of Hamlet, but the soldiers that Claudius gestures to follow her confirm that her "watch" will not mean loving reconciliation. The king promises Laertes immediate action ("present push" [284]) and then, on parting in the opposite direction, tosses the gravediggers a purse, all aspects of his hugger-mugger mission efficiently accomplished. In a poignant image, Laertes is left standing alone with his grief at the center of the screen, looking toward the camera. Is he gazing after Hamlet or at us?

Act 5, Scene 2

A double transition adding suspense over the upcoming violence moves the action from the graveyard to Hamlet's apartment. As Laertes turns to walk from the grave, his movement is precisely matched through a dissolve to Francisco pacing in sentry duty before Elsinore's main gate. Nervous, he glances about warily, as before the ghost's arrival. The visual match connects his unease with the violence we expect when Laertes' grief is converted back into aggression. From the grand exterior, we proceed to the interior. The sentry's uneasy watchfulness gives way to Horatio's, as he enters with Hamlet onto the balcony above the State Hall. While Hamlet eagerly and too loudly confides the salutary role played by his "rashness" and "indiscretion" (7–8) in his escape, Horatio nervously glances toward the hall interior and at one point covers his own mouth with his hand, as bold a gesture of restraint as the prince's deferential friend will dare.

The camera setup for the scene is unique in the film. A lens of very long focal length flattens the space of the corridor in a way unseen before. As the two men walk toward the camera, the visually shorter distance appears to take longer to traverse than it should, introducing a temporality that slows the pace of action as the story approaches its climax. The long lens also allows the men to walk forward through a space that becomes increasingly intimate, less public, as a slowly racked focus separates their clear images off from the increasingly unfocused background and Hamlet's awakening discretion lowers the volume of his talk.[37] At the most sensitive moment, as he declares "Ah, royal knavery" (19), the men have, fortunately, reached the end of the hallway and can enter the privacy of Hamlet's book-lined room.

Branagh builds on Zeffirelli's creation of a personal room to which Hamlet can return for privacy.[38] The three previous uses of Hamlet's apartment—for the ghost report, the "rogue and peasant slave" soliloquy, and the planning for the Mousetrap—have progressively revealed more characterizing details and have allowed the camera more freedom each time to construct a three-dimensional enclosure in the mind's eye. The room is now seen for the first time nearly in its entirety, including the living level and the library gallery and all four walls, allowing the fragmentary views of the earlier scenes to be fitted together. Such fitting is accomplished through the use of shots from a greater distance, including one downward from the gallery and one that takes in three walls as Hamlet circles around the toy theater and back, and more extensive views of backgrounds in the interchanges with Osric, whom Hamlet also circles, and the Young Lord.

The appointments of Hamlet's room reflect and complement his words. The theatrical interest underlying his ability to outplot his foes—"Or I could make a prologue to my brains, / They had begun the play" (30–31)—is made visible when he touches the theater turret while speaking the lines. His acquiring the clerkly hand that enabled his forgery is evoked as he hovers over handwriting practice sheets. The cleverness that impresses Horatio when Hamlet describes his imitated "earnest conjuration from the King" (38) is seen as well on a chessboard where more-numerous white pieces bear down on the black side's depleted ranks. As the plot moves toward the fatal public spectacle, we share over ten minutes with Hamlet in his private space, a space that is, of course, a purely cinematic invention. Connecting his past with his present, we grow more intimate with him before parting, much as does Horatio, who closes the scene by embracing his friend.

The film's long-delayed assembly of the room's details into a spatial gestalt and the connections made between Hamlet's past and present are satisfying accompaniments to Hamlet's acquisition of a new temporal perspective for which Jan Blits offers a concise description: "His sense of urgency seems gone, replaced by a new sense of providence or fate."[39] Horatio's most emphatic agreement is with "There's a divinity that shapes our end" (10). Rather than slings and arrows of outrageous fortune, which have required concerted efforts of resistance, Hamlet now envisions a providentially shaped end, a preordained trajectory for which "The readiness is all" (200). Reflecting this falling away from urgency is a new editing tempo. In Hamlet's room, the radically slowed temporality of the lengthy opening shot across the State Hall balcony seems to contaminate the continuing conversation between Hamlet and Horatio despite the return to normal lens setups, even in the shot/reverse-shot conversational sequences. The entries of Osric and the Lord pressing for Claudius's promised "present push" represent intrusions of the active upon the contemplative. The contrast is felt in the editing tempo, which cuts more than twice as quickly in the presence of Claudius's emissaries as in their absence.[40]

From an intimate embrace in close-up, the film cuts to an expansive high view of the public State Hall lined with courtiers awaiting the fencing match. Hamlet walks with Horatio along the fencing mat toward Laertes and the Young Lord, who will soon reveal his involvement in the plot to kill Hamlet. The two fencers focus exclusively on each other, Laertes motivated by intense hatred, Hamlet by his entry into what Branagh calls the "beatific zone" evinced in the previous scene.[41] Hamlet's beatific geniality, however, does not work to his benefit, for his mood leads him to indulge his theatrical tendencies. He apologizes to Laertes in a soft voice, with every appearance of sincerity. A cutaway during more than half of the apology to the forces of Fortinbras descending upon Elsinore and attacking Francisco at the gate presents a powerful contrast with Hamlet's attempt at reconciliation, further enhancing the impression of sincerity. But buoyed by the applause that greets his apology, Hamlet plays exuberantly to the crowd, causing Laertes to reply, "You mock me, sir" (254), with startling fury. The incompatible mind-sets of the two men only enhance Laertes' misunderstanding and antagonism.

In the first bout, fought in masks and body armor with rapier and dagger, Hamlet in a sudden onslaught drives his opponent to the end of the mat, knocks him down, and scores a palpable hit on the chest. His spirited celebration is echoed by the crowd. Horatio, we might note, stands out as the lone unsmiling presence, both before the first bout as he faces a grinning Young Lord (his opposite as Laertes' second) and after as he attends to the rejoicing queen. Ever the would-be moderating influence on his friend, only he seems attentive to the effect on Laertes of Hamlet's blithe exuberance.

Instead of preliminaries to the second bout, another cutaway to the advancing forces of Fortinbras precedes Osric's ceremonial splitting of swords to launch the contest. The effect is not only to connect the larger geopolitical story with the local revenge plot—one is reminded that both have private causes and public consequences—but also to reemphasize the connection between the psychologies of Hamlet, Laertes, and Fortinbras, who is replacing Claudius as a triangulating figure in the conflict. Laertes to this point resembles Fortinbras in ruthless violence and treachery yet differs from him in lacking the sangfroid that is increasingly visible in the Norwegian's appearances in the film. In the second bout, fought with masks removed and foils only, Laertes can be seen to recover his self-control, while Hamlet's demeanor grows more frenzied.

The contest soon threatens to veer from sport to genuine violence, and cutaways to the audience reveal expressions of alarm. Hamlet swings mightily at his opponent's head, a bloodthirsty move that negates the effect of bated sword-points in a contest fought without masks. It is soon Laertes' turn to be overly aggressive. His final sprinting attack drives Hamlet to the floor, but the prince manages to score a hit as Laertes sails wildly past him. Defeated again, Laertes approaches Claudius. His intention, we soon learn, is finally to execute the plan for the unbated and envenomed sword that Branagh has craftily held in abeyance, allowing its restoration to be viewed as the product, at least in part, of Hamlet's imprudent behavior.

While smiling Claudius coolly tells Laertes, "Our son shall win" (269), Gertrude takes advantage of his distraction to remove the cup from his hand. When she is about to drink, he shouts her name loudly enough to bring the room to a standstill. A track-in reveals his anguish. He pleads with her not to drink with as much appeal as he can muster, but it is not enough. We are not surprised, for the scene has signaled her alienation from him from the start. In relocating the royal couple to the side of the State Hall for the contest, the queen was also relocated to the king's left, the traditional subordinate position in royal protocol and Shakespearean productions. The privileged position she has held in Branagh's throne room from the start is replaced by the position she held in the cemetery scene, where her alienation was apparent. It is no less apparent now, as the camera places her before her accustomed throne, and her smiling son before her husband's. Despite their show of amity, as in the graveyard she and Claudius have not exchanged glances. Now, despite the king's altered tone and his shift of modifiers, his command not to drink is no more acceptable than his earlier instruction to "set some watch over your son." She turns around more fully than she did at the grave, finally looking him in the eye for her first and only act of disobedience.

Meanwhile, Laertes has huddled with the Young Lord. The latter appears to unbate the sword. He then, more clearly in close-up, applies poison to the point. The moment is one of revelation for the *Hamlet*-literate, who will delight to see Branagh's sly revision of a tradition, followed by Olivier, that assigned Osric complicity in the plot. The redundant character has found his vocation, without added lines, and with added possibility for moral commentary when the two characters' fates are compared. As the contestants cool down in their undershirts, Hamlet, again showing remarkable insensitivity, very loudly declares to Laertes, "I am afeard you make a wanton of me" (282), eliciting laughter from the crowd. Laertes replies with his "best violence" (281), as Hamlet requested, slashing him from behind on the shoulder. The third bout, which usually ends (Olivier) or at least pauses (Zeffirelli) before Laertes' fatal attack, thus becomes a duel to the death from the start.

The final contest, unfortunately, is the most uneven section of the entire film. It creates confusion that at times effectively immerses the audience in the excitement of a chaotic moment but at other times simply leaves it unsure how to interpret what it sees. Russell Jackson describes the moment as a shift into "an action mode, an Errol Flynn mode," but there is also an unmistakable overlay of comedy, now much less effective than in the pre-Mousetrap scenes.[42] A more frenetic version of the music that accompanied the second bout signals the start of madcap action. With his sword properly poised to start a bout but improperly standing outside the fencing mat, Laertes looks toward Osric, who is understandably baffled about how and whether to continue his role as master of ceremonies now that the rules have been abandoned. The more experienced courtiers offer no guidance, at one time chasing Hamlet as Laertes flees wildly, at another clearing a path as if to allow the game to continue. Nor does the king exert control. As the action starts, he places the wine cup down on a table. Seven seconds later, he is shown holding it. Another seven seconds later, he is putting it down again, looking as if he is trying to avoid implication in a poisoning plot. The result is confusion, and it would be difficult to argue that this is creative confusion.

In an effective action sequence, Hamlet trips his opponent, recovers Laertes' sword, examines a red stain on its unbated tip, and tosses him his own weapon. Is the substance the poison or Hamlet's blood? What does Hamlet conclude, given that he (unlike us) has not seen the poison applied? All that is certain is that he now knows the point is unbated. When the men take their fight to the upper balcony, comically diligent Osric follows them in time to issue his next judgment, "Nothing neither way" (284), after Laertes slams Hamlet into a glass door. Following this obviously intentional hilarity, Osric's urgent "Look to the Queen there, ho!" (288), directed from the stairway halfway across the enormous hall to those who are clustered about the queen's writhing form, poses a more difficult question about whether the comedy is intentional. Hamlet and Laertes move their combat to the central balcony bridge. In a surprisingly conspicuous continuity error, Laertes displays a wound on his right shoulder nearly identical to that on Hamlet's left shoulder—before we see Hamlet inflict it in close-up. Hamlet's having viewed the tainted sword supports the idea that he is inflicting a symmetrical punishment, but is this an act of restraint, mere harmless blood for blood with an unbaited sword, or deadly hate with a poisoned one? As Laertes, who has mysteriously lost his sword, lunges at Hamlet and tumbles over the railing, Hamlet's sword sweep toward his head suggests the latter. But after Laertes' confession, he registers surprise: "The point envenomed too!" (306). Branagh should either be credited for cinematic re-creation of Shakespearean ambiguity or criticized for inattention to detail. My inclination, after observing the effect of such challenges on the popular audience that Branagh seeks, is the latter.

Laertes' paralyzing tumble to the floor far below is accompanied by a "crash chord" that ends the music and the madcap violence. For the death of the queen and the confession of Laertes, the film momentarily recovers its pathos. Branagh transposes the cries of "Treason! Treason!" (328) backward one line to follow "the King's to blame" (326) rather than Hamlet's wounding the king, eliminating an ambiguity about who is being accused by the courtiers, in this case two intrepid women who have not joined the general exodus. Here begins another section of madcap action and music that, again, uneasily mixes meaningful and dubious details. In the former category are the contrasting fates of innocent Osric and the guilty Young Lord. Osric is the first to attend to fallen Laertes. He looks at the Young Lord with dawning awareness at the revelation of the "treacherous instrument" (301), at which the Lord quickly departs, presumably to begin a post-Claudian career of smiling villainy. Overwhelmed by the realization of his king's treason, Osric takes refuge in one of the side rooms but is promptly stabbed. He will return heroically to announce the arrival of Fortinbras. The antimoralistic contrast is consistent with Branagh's restoration of Fortinbras, for whom Laertes' principle of just punishment for one's own treachery clearly does not apply.

Claudius also flees, but Hamlet hurls the poisoned sword with gyroscopic precision and a loud whoosh across the hall, pinning him to the throne. The throw generally does not go over well with audiences, for the film's world, after four hours and numerous incursions of the non-naturalistic, has not included this kind of superhero improbability. Hamlet's forcing the poisoned wine on Claudius adds a grace note of poetic justice, as dying Laertes observes. But the enormous chandelier that he sends careening down onto the king satisfies less without a context to make it meaningful. The chandelier was conspicuously featured as the hall was being prepared for the Mousetrap and again as the Mousetrap scene opened. Is this Hamlet's final response to "Give me some light"? Would that it were so.

The shameless desertion of the courtiers allows Claudius's call for help from "friends" (329) to echo ironically through the nearly deserted hall. Like the unfair fate of Osric, it contributes to what Samuel Crowl calls the film's "devastating . . . critique of the play's politics."[43] It also alters Hamlet's dying address to "You that look pale and tremble at this chance" (318), preventing the kind of public honoring seen in Olivier's and Zeffirelli's films. Only Horatio remains to tremble. He does so literally, as he raises the poisoned cup toward his mouth. A final irony of Hamlet's life lies in his handing Horatio the cup, by which his "wounded name" (349) might lose all chance of remedy. He dies on the red carpet at the spot where the duel began, bringing the scene full circle.

The disorderly departure of the courtiers contrasts with the meticulously executed invasion by the troops of Fortinbras. The soldiers crash through the upstairs windows and pour in through every door of the State Hall, but they can train their guns only on corpses and a few forlorn stragglers. This overwhelming show of force is followed by the arrival of a prince whose every move bespeaks power. He enters through the familiar doorway from the royal quarters, implying that he has already usurped the private domain. His entrance into the public domain of the State Hall is shot with a lower, more heroic camera angle than those of Claudius and Laertes through the same doors. His series of point-of-view shots, including a tracking subjective shot that brings him into the room and a pan of the carnage, is unique in the film, communicating a kind of dominance unseen before. He seats himself on the king's chair, at which the disciplined troopers instantly put up their weapons. A crown is quickly placed on his head. Looking at the camera from the symmetrical composition he forms with his guards, he asserts "rights of memory in this kingdom, / Which now to claim my vantage doth invite me" (373–74).

His "vantage" becomes a new Shakespearean pun linking conquest to the cinematic means that express it.

The film moves toward its end with a series of religious images that cannot be interpreted without some irony. The gold cross atop the crown of Fortinbras is echoed in the outstretched arms of Hamlet as his body is borne out of the hall, which is perhaps an allusion to Olivier's film, and again in the inverted sword he holds in the open casket, perhaps an allusion to Zeffirelli's. As the camera cranes out to reveal a state funeral that fills the Great Court of Blenheim Palace, a chorus swells with a final variation of the film's most familiar theme, a Doyle composition to which are now added biblically inspired words by script adviser Russell Jackson:[44]

> Diligite justitiam
> O judices terrae,
> Illi autem sunt in pace.
> (Love righteousness
> O rulers of the earth.
> But they are at peace.)

We do not know whether old Hamlet loved righteousness, but his spirit is presumably now at peace. His statue is torn down, making way for an image of the next king, who no less than Claudius will need the lyric's admonishment.

However one assesses its merits, most will agree with Samuel Crowl that Branagh's *Hamlet* is "the most ambitious and audacious Shakespeare film ever made."[45] The full text is awesomely challenging, both on the local level of the scene and on the global level of the larger film. Branagh does not always rise to the challenge—most notably, in the ghost and duel scenes. But the number of times he does so rise is impressive indeed. Meeting challenges on the local level required a surprising variety of approaches: one thinks of such inspired invention as the sense of unease sustained in the first ghost scene, the cunningly ambiguous insets, the concentration of the slow track-in for the "to be" soliloquy, the comical metacinema of the pre-Mousetrap scenes, the surrealist doubling of Ophelia and Laertes in their mirrored "conversation," the relentlessness of Claudius's persuasiveness underlined by the relentless structuring of act 4, scene 7. Such individual triumphs, through their sheer variety, add up to a larger success in avoiding the slowing effect of excessive regularity and repetition, which would have been fatal in a four-hour film.

Also ambitious is Branagh's balancing of complication and clarification. A good example is the Fortinbras material, much complained about by critics, especially the non-Shakespearean invasion of Elsinore. Locally, as we have seen, his insets can both complicate and clarify: they serve the former function for Horatio in act 1, scene 2 and for Claudius in act 2, scene 2; the latter function for Claudius in act 1, scene 2. The same is true for Fortinbras on a global level. Because his repeated presence converts the play's verbal references into the film convention of a crosscut secondary plot, Branagh adds unity by satisfying classical film's demand for character-driven plots whose actions are clear, at least in the end. When in act 3, scene 2 the inset newspaper reports on "rapid and successful troop movements into Polish territory," an issue left open in the play is resolved in a way that can logically entail the invasion of Elsinore. Shakespeare's inconsistency in combining Horatio's report of "lawless resolutes" with the disciplined army of act 4, scene 4 (explained by Jenkins in his Arden note to 1.1.101 as a change of "design in course of composition") has not been removed but rather emphasized and transformed into complicating questions about Horatio's knowledge and therefore about larger issues of knowledge crucial to the play. At the same time, we can conclude that Fortinbras has manipulated both old Norway and Claudius from the start. His violent invasion of Elsinore is driven by the anger, resolution, and cleverness visible in the insets. The Fortinbras plot has been made classically coherent but without impoverishing our experience of Shakespearean polysemy. Perhaps only Kenneth Branagh, with his unparalleled mastery of both Shakespeare and the film medium, could attempt such an audacious synthesis.

MICHAEL ALMEREYDA'S
Hamlet
Uncanny Imagination

Within a year of the release of the full-text *Hamlet*, Almereyda was pondering an adaptation that would define itself against Branagh's lavishly produced historical film and dynamic, mature hero. In the preface to the published screenplay, Almereyda praises what Orson Welles called the "rough charcoal sketch" approach to his filmed *Macbeth*. Welles's undeniably rough and sketchy production provoked "a sharp suspicion that you don't need lavish production values to make a Shakespeare movie that's accessible and alive." While studying the existing films, Almereyda was also "struck by the fact that no film of *Hamlet* features a truly young man." Viewing Shakespeare's protagonist as "a radiantly promising young man who doesn't quite know who he is," he asked, "Why not entrust the role to an actor in his twenties?" Making a virtue of necessity because he could not afford a studio setting, he opted to locate "a new *Hamlet* in the immediate present" and to rely on found settings in Manhattan.[1]

Almereyda throughout his career has proven himself a master of delayed disclosure and retrospective interpretation. So it should not be surprising that the film's most significant "baring of the device" occurs near the end.[2] Just before receiving the challenge to duel with Laertes, Hamlet uses his hyperactive "mind's eye" to make a comparison:

> But I am very sorry, good Horatio,
> That to Laertes I forgot myself;
> For by the image of my cause I see
> The portraiture of his.
>
> (5.2.73–76)

Hamlet is standing beside a bookshelf in Horatio's seedy apartment. His eyeline points to a Russian name highlighted in pink foil letters on the spine of a book. Wiktor Woroszylski's *Life of Mayakovsky* rests within a horizontal stack of books that closer examination reveals to be translated works by the Russian Futurist/Dadaist poet. The effects of the allusion will, of course, vary across the multiple audiences according to their knowledge. For some, the image will simply indicate that Hamlet's fellow student is bookish. For others, it will clarify his literary tastes and political leanings. Others, admittedly fewer, will contemplate deeper connections among three parties: the book's plebeian but literate owner; his dear friend Hamlet, who displays portraits of Mayakovsky by celebrated photographer Aleksandr Rodchenko on his wall; and the doomed and damaged Russian who at age fifteen was traumatized by his father's death and eventually committed suicide with a pistol formerly used as a movie prop.

The lingering shot, the longest in the scene, presents for our leisurely perusal other titles indicating Horatio's intellectual interests, but I wish to pause for reflection on an anomaly in the horizontal stack. Sandwiched between Mayakovsky texts is a slim volume bearing the word *uncanny* on its spine. Again, response will vary among the varied audiences, but anyone who notices the title will likely find some kind of relevance. In an interview given while he was filming *Hamlet*, Almereyda explained that the "offbeat, almost surrealistic" style of his first feature, the dysfunctional-family comedy *Twister*, derived from "looking at ordinary things in a way that recognizes what's special and uncanny about them."[3] It is indeed uncanny in this commonplace sense of extraordinary and strange to be invited to find, and even more so to recognize, similarities between Shakespeare's characters and a Russian poet at the point where Hamlet is seeing similarities between his cause and Laertes'.

Does Hamlet also see dissimilarities between image and portraiture? In both commonplace usage and in Freud's fertile elaboration of the concept, uncanniness depends on an interplay of similarity and difference, of the familiar and the unfamiliar. The lines Hamlet speaks keep both sides of these dualities in play through his author's dazzling verbal dexterity. As a causal "cause," the image of Hamlet's slain father, the original object seen in his mind's eye earlier in the play, is equivalent to the portraiture of Laertes' slain father. The two causes as quests or goals, however, imply dissimilarity. As Harold Jenkins observes in the note to the passage in his Arden edition, "the image which shows Laertes as a revenger like Hamlet must also show Hamlet as revenge's object." When the polysemic complexity of Shakespeare's language here is recognized, it might be said that Almereyda's allusion is continuing the bard's method. While we are weighing similarities and differences between avenging sons, what Hamlet could view as respectively familiar and unfamiliar, we are being invited as well to compare a poet who commits suicide and a suicidal character who does not (Or does he? That is the question) and even between a laconic owner of Mayakovsky's writings, whose bookshelves are neatly organized, and a voluble collector of Mayakovsky "portraitures," whose collection of images, books, and objects is wondrously chaotic.

The conspicuous presence of a volume entitled *The Uncanny*, a museum catalog for an exhibition of figurative sculpture, "bares the device" in pointing to this particular scene's procedures for making meaning. It also provides a useful name for the film's Formalist "dominant," the prevailing principle that organizes devices into a whole. As we will see, the uncanny interplay of familiar and unfamiliar permeates this *Hamlet*, beginning with the insertion of an Elizabethan fiction into a modern New York setting, both familiar in themselves to varying degrees among the audience but not in their juxtaposition. Visual details within scenes are often calibrated to promote a combination of recognition and nonrecognition, as in the readable and unreadable, and relevant and irrelevant, titles on Horatio's bookshelf and in the remarkable collage wall behind Hamlet's desk, which ranges from the most reproduced image in the history of photography (Alberto Korda's photo of Che Guevara) to an abundance of meaningful images that delight when recognition dawns and even to the stubbornly unidentifiable.[4] In a diachronic version of this uncanny interplay, delayed disclosure will often promote one reading of a scene, only to reverse or qualify it, making the apparently unfamiliar familiar or vice versa. Across the film as a whole, scenes will provoke us into recalling previous scenes to suggest likeness and difference, usually both at the same time, and often as subtle visual complements to the Shakespearean text and markers of a character's progress or relation to another character.

The uncanny in the film extends beyond this commonplace variety to include as well the concept's full Freudian development. For Freud in his famous essay on the subject, "the uncanny [*unheimliche*]" is "something which is secretly familiar [*heimlich-heimisch*] which has undergone repression and then returned from it," most commonly infantile fears and desires. Thus in Freud's analysis of E. T. A. Hoffmann's "Sandman," the image of eyelessness elicits the repressed fear of castration associated with the Oedipus complex. In addition to the infantile fear of castration, which is often evoked through the upwardly displaced threat to vision, Freud specifies the "double" as a phenomenon underlying all of "those themes of uncanniness which are most prominent." The double disturbs and fascinates because it harkens back to "an early mental stage, long since surmounted" in which "the ego had not yet marked itself off from the external world." A third important phenomenon that Freud links to the uncanny is repetition. At psychological depths below the commonplace uncanny, perceiving unexpected similarity can evoke the surmounted infantile mental stage in which coincidental repetition conveys meaning, especially the meaning that events are "fateful and inescapable." Freud also links uncanniness to repetition by noting "the dominance in the unconscious mind of a 'compulsion to repeat.'" "Whatever reminds us of this inner 'compulsion to repeat,'" he concludes, "is perceived as uncanny."[5] Almereyda's *Hamlet* is no less Freudian than Olivier's or Zeffirelli's, but its inspiration comes as much from Freud's Sandman as from his Oedipus.

The First Movement

Rather than entering the plot directly, Almereyda carefully introduces his audience to the situation and, most important, to his main character. Forty seconds of film precede the appearance of Hamlet in close-up poised to deliver his first lines. The first shot is a view through the skylight of a vehicle traversing the skyscraper canyons of Manhattan. A sequence of titles reveals the date, location, and background situation. The mixed discourse of "The King and C.E.O. of Denmark Corporation is dead" announces the kind of Shakespearean adaptation we are entering: "King" and "Denmark" represent the Shakespearean language that the characters will speak, while "C.E.O." and "Corporation" proclaim the modern American referents, which the film will convey visually, to Shakespeare's words and story.[6] "The King's widow has hastily remarried his younger brother," we are then told, and the title sequence ends with "The King's son, Hamlet, returns from school, suspecting foul play . . ." Olivier's film announced that it was "the tragedy of a man who could not make up his mind," encapsulating the filmmaker's interpretation and offering a handle for the uninitiated. Almereyda's preamble not only gives us essential facts but also brings us within Hamlet's point of view. It contains nothing that he does not know, agrees with Gertrude's admission of an "o'er-hasty marriage" (2.2.57), prepares us to observe the prince overcoming the tentativeness of "suspecting" and the vagueness of "foul play," and, in the ellipsis, piques our interest in how he will respond when this tentativeness and vagueness are eliminated.

In less than half a minute, the opening shot has also presented much food for thought visually in the form of "found objects," an Almereydan signature device that derives in part from his interest in surrealism and that the urban setting will proliferate.[7] As a framing device, the skylight calls attention on its left and right edges to advertisements for theatrical productions and to a skyline display of financial data. The arts and high finance, the two flagship activities of Manhattan, find their first of many juxtapositions in the film. Soon we arrive at one of America's most recognizable and culturally resonant locations. Emerging on the right edge of the frame is the postcard site of Two Times Square, the twenty-five-story tower faced with vertically stacked supersigns, one of the square's two iconic promotional venues for multinational capitalism. The Rock of Prudential signifying stability sits atop Samsung's ellipse symbolizing the earth turning in space, which sits atop Suntory Whisky's evidence that the desire for chemical quietus transcends international borders.[8] While we contemplate this compressed form of signification and are being primed to interpret the film's important made-up logo, a soundtrack suggests the noise of jet aircraft. The long opening shot implies that as Hamlet "returns from school" he is journeying from afar to what one recent book on Times Square calls "the central spot not only of New York but of the country, and even, not so fancifully, of the world."[9]

In the second shot, law-abiding pedestrians are dutifully using the crosswalk at One Times Square, the familiar setting of the New Year ball-dropping.

Hamlet jaywalks diagonally across the intersection beneath the Denmark Corporation logo, which through one of the film's few digital special effects is placed on the most expensive advertising site in the world, the 1,400-square-foot NBC "Astrovision" screen that dominates the Times Building. Surrounded by the NBC peacock, a TDK Electronics logo, and two enormous billboards announcing big-budget movie premieres, the logo suggests that old Hamlet the CEO headed an international multimedia company. The Denmark logo's central circular device, resembling a camera diaphragm, is set against a revolving grid of latitudinal and longitudinal lines, conveying an impression of global power and surveillance. Also surveilling Hamlet's jaywalk from his billboard is one of the world's most recognizable faces, a found object with fortuitous relevance to the story: grim Clint Eastwood, an iconic figure associated with action films and various kinds of "foul play," especially with violence in which the lines of vengeance and justice blur.[10] A low-angle power shot of the Hotel Elsinore's impressive metal and glass entry, its absolutist symmetry reinforced by a centrally placed doorman, is followed by a closer shot of one of its revolving doors. The spinning door both informs us that Hamlet has entered and, in its visual echo of the Denmark Corporation logo, presents one more sign of the power he will confront.

The opening minute has abundantly characterized the world to which Hamlet is returning. A revision of Shakespeare's plot now introduces us to the remarkable complexities of the young man himself. The shooting script began with the ghost upon the "battlements," but an early test screening revealed that the language of the play's opening scene confused the audience. In addition, Almereyda notes, "it was troublingly clear that Hamlet's first appearance in the film came too late and felt flat."[11] Almereyda's inspired solution was to transform an abbreviated and slightly modified version of the "most poetic prose speech in the play,"[12] the famous encomium on man originally delivered to Rosencrantz and Guildenstern, into an opening soliloquy: "I have of late, wherefore I know not, lost all my mirth. What a piece of work is a man, how noble in reason, how infinite in faculties, in form and moving how express and admirable, in action how like an angel, in apprehension how like a god. The beauty of the world, the paragon of animals. And yet to me, what is this quintessence of dust?" (2.2.261–74, modified). Hamlet speaks directly to us in the intimacy of grainy PixelVision, his sincerity and passion visible in the tight close-up of his face. We watch this pensive face for nearly ten seconds before he speaks. The pause and a series of shifts—from public exterior to private interior, from urban commotion to stillness, from cinematography of depth and vibrant color to flat monochrome, from the repetitive guitar riffs of the "trip-hop" band Morcheeba to the plaintive orchestration of Neils Gade's "Echoes from Ossian"—encourage the audience to listen carefully. "The idea," Almereyda explains, "was to frame and foreground Shakespeare's words, trusting them to bring the audience closer."[13]

Framed and foregrounded as an opening soliloquy, Shakespeare's words simplify the issue of the speaker's sincerity but complicate his psychology. In the play, Hamlet's plea of ignorance about the cause of his melancholy is an attempt to deceive his untrustworthy "friends": unlike them, we know that the ghost has brought sufficient "wherefore" for loss of mirth. In the film, this loss is more likely to be viewed as a cause than as an effect of the suspicion of foul play. Alessandro Abbate finds that Hamlet "looks as though he lost his mirth well before his father's death."[14] The images that accompany "the beauty of the world, the paragon of animals"—a stealth bomber taking off, a bomb-sighted target destroyed, a voracious cartoon dragon, a barrage of antiaircraft artillery—may tell us something about Hamlet's thoughts on recent family events, but they do so indirectly, by expressing his bleak view of the world. When, in a brilliantly delayed disclosure, we learn at the end of this sequence that we and Hamlet have been viewing a video diary containing Hamlet's past rather than his present thoughts, or perhaps we should say his present thoughts as they can be expressed by his past thoughts, we are encouraged to probe more deeply into this mysterious character's history. We will seek, for example, in his clothing, behavior, and art evidence of an alienation reaching far back beyond his father's death. This is a young man deeply disaffected with his parents' corporate world, with its combination of violence and appetite and its slick media "product" that caters to this combination. Because this is also a young man who responds to crisis through a technological art that allows him to repeat the recorded past endlessly, to call forth his electronic double effortlessly, we might also begin here to see something at work susceptible to psychoanalytic explanation.

As with so much in this film, the diary appears simple but reveals remarkable complexity upon closer examination. The opening soliloquy reveals Hamlet to be an artist who can creatively assimilate recognizable influences within the history of experimental film and manipulate form to explore his interests. These features are best illustrated through a shot list:

1. Hamlet addressing camera
2. Hamlet waving a glass

3. Hamlet addressing camera

4. Hamlet performing a magic trick

5. Hamlet addressing camera

6. wall image: skeletons of man and dinosaur

7. wall image: philosopher and saint

8. bomber taking off

9. bombsight and explosion

10. cartoon dragon

11. aerial explosions

12. Hamlet looking down

13. screen with Hamlet's hands

14. blank screen with static

Although Almereyda has made Hamlet's implied knowledge of film wide and deep—through, for example, the photo of Jean Vigo behind his desk, stills from experimental filmmakers on his walls, and a Hitchcockian playbill for the Mousetrap—the inescapable influences on Hamlet's filmmaking practice are, as often noted, Sadie Benning and, less often noted, Bruce Conner.[15] In shots 1 through 7, the soliloquy most resembles Benning's early PixelVision film *If Every Girl Had a Diary* (1990), which combines shots of Benning's face with close-ups of objects around her room. Following his direct address, Hamlet too shows objects from his room—images from the collage wall behind his desk—but the viewer does not understand what these are until later in the film, when uncanny recognition identifies them retroactively. The next segment, shots 8–11, while retaining Benning's signature PixelVision, is Conneresque in its splicing together of found footage from disparate media to construct a continuous but nonconventional narrative.

Hamlet synthesizes his borrowed images and techniques into an original vision. His principal concern is one of the play's central themes: the rich perplexities of temporal experience, most particularly the never-straightforward relation of past to present. The opening movement demonstrates that the present impacts our view of the past. Shot 1 ends with Hamlet pausing and sniffing after "I know not." Shot 2 suggests an interruption of the speech, a quite understandable break for a drink. Shot 3 tells of the loss of mirth, while shot 4 complicates matters by appearing to illustrate this mirth. Shot 4, in other words, appears to reach back into the mirthful past rather than remaining in the mirthless present as shot 2 appeared to do. But shot 4 also includes details, including the position of Hamlet's forelock and some meager background, that link it to shot 2, relocating the drink in the mirthful past of the magic trick. What we first read as an edited sequence communicating action in one time plane is reread as alternating between past and present.

Almereyda as director continues Hamlet's manipulation of temporality at the end. In the final movement, Hamlet appears in a new present, attired in black as in Times Square rather than white as in the diary, in color and on the full screen once again. Watching him manipulate his video equipment forces us to repeat the earlier act of rereading, placing the speaking Hamlet in the past. But by now, present and past have become even more thoroughly interfused. From where and when do the words emanate in the voice-over of shots 8–11, which continues the speech of the talking heads? The voice-over is quieter, almost whispering, a shift that might suggest a change of speaker, and no viewer would be surprised to see the mouth of the present Hamlet move at the end. But it does not, and we turn to the clamshell screen at the end expecting to see the monochrome Hamlet ask, "What is this quintessence of dust?" There he continues to confound. His hand gesture both recalls the silent conjuror of shot 4 and embodies his imagining of the dust of which he speaks, or does not speak; his hand prevents us from seeing his mouth and thus locating him within the two time planes of shots 1–5. In the scene's final labor to tease us into thought, the image on screen twists sideways, revealing the space outside its immediate frame. We have been seeing Hamlet not directly in front of a camera but in a video of a video, an image of a past Hamlet relayed into the diegetic present by a later past Hamlet.

As if this mise en abyme were not challenging enough, the wall imagery comes into play, asking for both temporal distinctions and interpretation. The combination of photos—one fully toned and the other in photogram-like silhouette—and an obviously painted head portrait translates Conneresque diachronic montage of disparate media into synchronic collage. At the very least, the viewer will notice the collision of the prehistoric and the historic and will perhaps register on some level of consciousness the parallel collision of cartoon dragon and stealth bomber. Viewers who are more alert might note the Flintstonian anachronism of the human and dinosaur skeleton inhabiting the same photo and distinguish the time of the haloed saint from that of the suited man. Finally, there is the fully informed viewer, who could conceivably identify Nietzsche's best-known portrait and the cutout from one of Giotto's most famous paintings.[16] In *The Deposition of Christ*, the beloved apostle John stands in anguish viewing the divine body. Now his cutout head looks askance upon the mad philosopher who proclaimed a different kind of death of God.

The viewer who would make this connection at this point, and find in it another explanation for Hamlet's loss of mirth, may be a hypothetical construct, a film version of the narratological ideal reader, but we will see the images again, more clearly and with greater leisure for pondering their identity and meaning—and for becoming more ideal viewers. Belated and retroactive understanding, I suggest, is precisely the point.

The repeated challenges of the experimental diary sequence end abruptly with a cut to the title "HAMLET," a transition designed to produce the most emphatic punctuation possible. Graphic clarity of block letters on a glowing red background counters the blue screen of visual static that terminates Hamlet's soliloquy. The powerful opening of the Brahms First Symphony replaces electronic noise, functioning, we soon see, as a kind of royal overture. The real movie begins now, the audiovisual language declares, and all that is past is mere prologue. Our knowledge about Hamlet and the world he is reentering is already considerable.

After the title's four long seconds, Hamlet enters videotaping and moving from left to right, the screen direction of his crossing of Times Square. At a press conference well attended by both the corporate "court" and the press, Claudius is announcing his marriage and accession to the corporate "throne" into a bank of microphones. Although the location is a modern auditorium, Almereyda deploys a traditional geometry of power from the royal court to structure the action. Gertrude sits in her wonted place at the CEO's left side, reverting to her pre-Branagh location. All movement and perception in the scene are aligned along two perpendicular axes. The king controls the vertical axis (from auditorium front to rear, though in most shots a horizontal screen axis), drawing attention from all eyes, ears, and their technological extensions toward the throne. Within this Cartesian system of coordinates, Hamlet's motions take on meaning. Only Hamlet changes position, as he traverses the hall horizontally, turning his back to videotape the photographers (thus momentarily assuming the orientation of the king), before resuming the prescribed orientation toward the throne. His mobility, though limited, contrasts with the fixity of the other photographers lined up along the back of the hall, who can only stand and shower the royal couple with flashes from afar. Except for Hamlet's entrance, horizontal action is limited to the exchange of gazes and smiles and eventually a kiss between the king and queen. Hamlet stops his progress toward the throne at precisely the point where he can subvert the power dynamics of the hall. He stands beneath a frowning portrait of his father, a location that also happens to place him beside the row where Polonius and his family are seated.

A dance of glances now begins, with what remains unseen as important as what is seen. Ophelia, contained between father and brother, exchanges glances with Hamlet. When this attracts the scolding glance of Laertes, Ophelia quickly returns her gaze to the king's vertical axis, as does Hamlet. Gertrude notices Hamlet and turns her loving gaze from husband to son. Hamlet returns her look and then looks down. Hamlet's downward look suggests that he breaks off the visual contact with his mother, but a cut back to the throne reveals Gertrude gazing once more at her husband, who has reclaimed her attention with the announcement of their marriage. The limits of Hamlet's power over the gaze are thus revealed through interaction with the two women in his life. Claudius and Gertrude kiss. Looking disgusted, Hamlet removes the tape from his recorder. A cut to Ophelia reveals her to be looking at Hamlet. She now turns toward the throne without the prompting of an admonishing look. The action demands an explanation that is not provided, further focusing our attention on the nonverbal communication that is telling us more than the continuing flow of Claudius's speech. Was Ophelia staring at Hamlet during the royal kiss so that she now must look to the throne to explain his evident disgust? Perhaps. Or is she following the example of Gertrude in initiating the breaking of the gaze, beginning the kind of adulatory relationship between Ophelia and the queen that is evident in Zeffirelli's version? The visual choreography makes connections and poses questions but does not answer them all.

The kiss, which prompts sustained applause, proves to be the first of the king's artful manipulations of the crowd. With a glance and hand gesture, he directs Gertrude's completion of his line "for all—our thanks" (1.2.16), a demonstration of royal like-mindedness that prompts a second round of applause despite the obviousness of its pretended spontaneity. Warming to the game, the Machiavellian king flashes a copy of *USA Today* with a picture of Fortinbras featured above the fold. The camera now joins in on the king's assertion of power, shooting Claudius for the rest of the scene from the heroic low position. Another power play occurs as Ophelia attempts to pass to Hamlet a packet arranging a rendezvous, but Laertes thwarts her, wordlessly redirecting her gaze forward, while Polonius with a quick sidelong glance sizes up the situation and returns to his role as cheerleader when Claudius tears the image in two and tosses it into the air. Claudius's domination, however, is revealed to be incomplete, for the final shot shows Hamlet and Ophelia taking advantage of the crowd's rapt attention to hold each other in their first undeterred gaze.

The fully public event becomes more private as the two families file into an adjoining room following the press conference. The power struggles continue, but they find new means of cinematic expression. In rhythmic contrast to the briskly cut previous scene, this scene consists of three shots arranged in perfect symmetry: a brief two-shot of Hamlet and Ophelia sandwiched between two twenty-three-second group shots in a structure that signifies containment no less than did the seating arrangement of Polonius and family. In the two lengthy shots, the struggles that were earlier conducted through the gazes of fixed parties are now fully kinetic. In the first, as the king deals with Laertes even while dancing and snuggling with the aroused queen, Polonius draws Ophelia away from Hamlet. In the third shot, as the king deals with Polonius while continuing to carouse, Laertes pulls Ophelia away from Hamlet. Despite the efforts of father and brother, whose relative power over Ophelia is indicated by having only Laertes need to move his sister physically, Ophelia manages to pass her packet to Hamlet. He signals his agreement to the rendezvous with a nod. Claudius offers Laertes a friendly pat on the chest but then gives us a first glimpse of his violent side with a less gentle twisting of Hamlet by the arm, a gesture that Hamlet turns to his advantage by kissing Ophelia, paralleling the way Hamlet made Claudius's domination backfire in the press conference.

The film continues its modernizing transfer of public to private when act 1, scene 2 continues in an exterior scene, shot almost entirely from a low angle to allow the skyscrapers of Park Avenue to loom overhead. The king's voice booms out, "My cousin Hamlet, and my son" (1.2.64), as the camera follows Hamlet from behind. In an interesting moment of indirection, an arm enters from the left, and we assume that it belongs to Claudius, the source of the speech, who may be resuming his barely contained physical aggression. But only momentarily can we make this assumption, for the arm belongs to Gertrude, who will make her appeal more privately still, outside the king's hearing.

Hamlet's resistance to familial pressure is conveyed visually. To Gertrude's question, "Why seems it so particular with thee?" (75), Hamlet takes off his sunglasses and looks her directly in the eye—or, rather, looks into her sunglasses, which she defensively keeps in place, just as she keeps her gloves on when she caresses his face. Hamlet has been moving from right to left, a sign of the compulsion underlying the scene after we have twice watched him walk left to right autonomously. Now he asserts himself by stopping. The low camera angle has served to imprison Hamlet with the weight of the towers above him. Now, as he turns toward his mother and the camera views him frontally, the angle momentarily signifies power, but this implication is emphatically countered in two cutaway shots to glowering Claudius, who is in effect competing for the implication of the camera angle. Even the king's pinstripes are put to work, linking him to the corporate power manifest in the skyscraper verticals. Behind Hamlet is another fortuitous found object, a window cleaner's platform seen hanging high on the glass side of a skyscraper as Hamlet removes his glasses and claims he knows, "not seems" (76).

At a signal from Gertrude, Claudius takes over the scolding, first putting on a forced grin to cover his anger. He speaks in reasonable tones, but the underlying anger breaks loose with the accusation of "unmanly grief" (94), which is accompanied by a rough pull on Hamlet's arm, Claudius' second act of near-violence. The result is another eye-to-eye confrontation, with Claudius forcefully imposing his will as he asks Hamlet not to return to Wittenberg. Gertrude returns to the struggle. From inside the limo, she rolls the window halfway down. The allusion points generically to gangster film—and more specifically, to Baz Luhrmann's use of the convention in *William Shakespeare's Romeo + Juliet*, where few who would attend this *Hamlet* would not have seen it at a similar position in the film. Ironically, through the window peers not the mobster father of Romeo but Diane Venora, the actress who played Juliet's mother. She removes her glasses and makes her plea in a soft voice, finalizing the "good cop, bad cop" persuasion by imitating her son's gesture of sincerity.

The film opened with a long continuum of music, three minutes and forty seconds that intensified the emotional dimension of Hamlet's return to his home and the new familial situation. The music abruptly ended when the royal kiss provoked loud applause, after which four minutes without music signaled exhaustion in Hamlet's psyche. Now begins a sequence of two and a half minutes overlaid with music composed for the film by Carter Burwell.[17] Alone in his room, Hamlet recovers his emotional intensity.

Burwell's continuous orchestral score unifies the "solid flesh" (1.2.129) soliloquy with two brief insets depicting Ophelia waiting for Hamlet's arrival at the waterfall that she had sketched on the packet during the press conference. Because Hamlet clearly nodded his agreement to Ophelia after receiving the packet, both Ophelia and we are expecting him to show up. In the first inset, she looks from side to side expectantly in close-up. A cut moves the camera back for a long shot with Ophelia looking off to the left, but instead of Hamlet entering in his established autonomous direction, a man in a dark suit walks across most of the frame. Almereyda is building a series of movements to create unease subliminally: two entrances by Hamlet left to right, which is the more comfortable direction for the eyes to move, are followed by an entrance screen left by a character unexpectedly not Hamlet.[18] As our eyes move to watch this figure exit to the right, the film cuts to a dark screen. A full second of mysterious darkness ends when the camera, tracking right at the same speed as the man's traversal, allows Hamlet to come into view seated at his desk. In a haunting transition, the camera has assumed the viewer's eye movement. It is as if we have been made to turn our eyes away from Ophelia to focus on Hamlet, thereby participating in what we gradually understand to be happening: Hamlet is too preoccupied with his own sorrows to remember, or perhaps even desire, to keep his appointment.

The soliloquy proceeds in voice-over as Hamlet manipulates the play-back of video images. With compulsive repetition, affording us repeated views of the same footage in distant and close shots of the monitor, Hamlet plays images of his father in his father's room and his father and mother happily skating at an ice rink. The former is especially intriguing, because we see old Hamlet, after lighting a cigarette, covering the lens with his hand, obviously displeased with his son's activity. This disapproved activity might be labeled experimental videography if we choose to see a corporate father concerned about his son's wayward career plans, or it might be given the more psychologically inflected label of voyeurism. Freudians cannot miss the phallic cigarette, which condenses with the film cliché of the postcoital smoke, the castrating gesture of denied vision, and the suggestion of a primal scene. The deep psychic connections in Hamlet between parental figures and the love-object of adulthood become evident when he summons up the image of Ophelia, alternating her consoling presence with painful parental memories. Ophelia is seen reading a book and then holding it in front of the camera, in a variation of old Hamlet's blocking gesture that substitutes the sexually ambiguous elderly face on the book's cover (most viewers will not know until later whose face this is) for her own. The soliloquy concludes with a freeze-frame on her face in a pose strangely familiar. Into the mind's eye of many (perhaps even most) viewers will enter Vermeer's *Girl with a Pearl Earring*, an image never more pervasive in American popular culture than at the time the film was made.[19] Only when he arrives at this virginal portrait is Hamlet able to stop, and only for a moment, his compulsive repetitions.

Unfortunately for Ophelia, Hamlet's obsession with reliving scenes with his parents, combined with a preference for her manipulated image over her real presence, prevents him from keeping his appointment. The freeze-frame opens the possibility that Hamlet will break off his meditation and go to meet her. At this point, the cut back to Ophelia at the waterfall might instill new hope. But the second insert runs painfully to exactly twice the length of the first. By repeating in the second the dual camera placements of the first—close-up then long shot—the scene insists on comparison, and now we see the suited man's purposive stride across the screen replaced by the frustrated Ophelia's back-and-forth motion as she balances on the edge of the pool. A series of echoing images linking Ophelia ominously to water has begun.[20]

The scene that follows the passionately obsessive soliloquy begins devoid of all emotion except for a vague sense of dread. With a ringing doorbell, Burwell's music ceases and Hamlet turns off his video equipment. Rising with a palpable air of exhaustion, as the camera offers us a comprehensive view of his collage wall, he shuffles into the front room of his hotel suite. The tracking camera follows his entrance at midtorso from behind, delaying disclosure as Hamlet's black-clad body blocks our sight of who awaits him. The first disclosed figure is a large black man in uniform who eyes Hamlet carefully, suggesting a cop sizing up a suspect for interrogation. The blond female Marcella, who has replaced Shakespeare's Marcellus, smiles wanly at Hamlet's greeting, but grave and initially silent Horatio quickly retreats to a sofa and lights a cigarette. Hawke removes from "I am very glad to see you" (1.2.167) the warmth his character traditionally exudes upon seeing his beloved comrade. Textual cuts remove all of the badinage with which they profess their friendship (for example, lines 161–62 and 170–73) and leave Hamlet beginning the conversation with three rather impatient-sounding questions on the theme of "Why are you here?" The three visitors have let themselves into Hamlet's hotel suite—a change from the script, where Hamlet goes to the door—but rather than implying amicable familiarity, that fact adds to the uneasy feeling of intrusion. Marcella's sex change, generally lamented by critics, serves a useful function here, drawing Horatio farther away from his fellow student. The tie of Horatio and Marcella is the primary bond visible in the scene as they sit closely together and smoke, a nervous couple on an uncomfortable mission.

The ice is broken when Horatio confesses to seeing the ghost. Two chairs that served to separate Hamlet and Bernardo from the couple on the sofa now bring the two old friends together; they sit a few feet apart while Horatio tells his story, dramatized in two inset scenes. In these insets, Hamlet's three visitors see the ghost in a surveillance monitor and pursue it through a janitorial basement until, following Horatio's attempt to communicate with it, it disappears into a Pepsi vending machine. By moving this material from the opening and presenting it as a flashback, Almereyda creates a complex analogy with the previous scene. The earlier representation of old Hamlet on video, where he remained silent and looked "frowningly" (1.2.230), while

Hamlet's emotional response was conveyed through reaction shots, parallels the representation of the silent and frowning ghost through flashbacks in this scene, where the emotional impact is registered through the reaction shots of the intercut conversation in Hamlet's hotel room.

The paternal image communicated by Horatio is powerful enough to affect Hamlet's body language. After hearing about the ghost, Hamlet conducts his friends to the door with physical cordiality, nearly hugging Horatio, patting Marcella on the arm, and initiating a handshake with Bernardo, in contrast to his earlier wary response to the guard's proffered hand. On entering the room, his movements were languid, and his hands quickly retreated into his pockets. Now he gesticulates excitedly as he anticipates exchanging the sight of the father in the "mind's eye" (1.2.184) with one "upon the platform 'twixt eleven and twelve" (250). In the shooting script, Hamlet "bounds into the front room" to admit his visitors.[21] With a sure directorial hand, Almereyda changed the original conception into a scene that conveys with cinematic efficiency the transformation from depressed torpor to excitement. Hamlet closes with the eager declaration, "Would the night were come. / Till then sit still my soul" (254–55). But Hamlet has already missed a 3:30 appointment that he seemed eager to keep. Will he appear as promised at midnight? The ghost and Ophelia have entered a competition for Hamlet's attention.

The film now turns to Ophelia where the play first introduced her. The scene unfolds accompanied by a series of delayed disclosures. It opens with an extreme close-up of a handheld snapshot, another of Almereyda's signature devices.[22] A younger Hamlet, 35mm camera in hand, lurks in a closet. The metallic thumbnail of the hand holding the photo is identifiable as Ophelia's: we saw it earlier in the closest shot of the news conference, when she wrote the message on her package. The pleasure inherent in solving this relatively simple puzzle encourages the viewer to tease out further implications of this opening shot, held for five seconds while Laertes drones on about the dangers of Hamlet's love. We do not know who took the picture, but we suspect that it was Ophelia (who else?). Support for this suspicion increases when she begins photographing her father. Curiosity about her relationship with Hamlet deepens when both its long duration and the couple's shared interests are revealed. The photograph documents both Hamlet and Ophelia indulging in the reflexive play of recording the recorder, as we saw Hamlet doing in the press conference. Her contemplation of an old image in response to the missed appointment recalls Hamlet's use of video footage in the soliloquy, with complex irony arising from the fact that Hamlet's voiced-over thoughts have been replaced by Laertes' anti-Hamlet monologue, which no doubt in some ways reflects, though in other ways it contradicts, disappointed Ophelia's ambivalent feelings.

The sensuous soundscape contributes to another artfully contrived disclosure. A cut from the handheld photo of Hamlet to a two-shot of Laertes and Ophelia places the two siblings in strangely suggestive proximity. With only their upper torsos on screen, the sister appears to be sitting on her brother's lap; the impression is even stronger for those familiar with the play's recourse to such "country matters" elsewhere (3.2.110). Students of Shakespearean film will recognize a new twist on a phenomenon that reaches back to the wanton but somehow innocent flirtatiousness of Olivier's Ophelia.[23] Now, however, incestuous overtones are to be found not in Ophelia, who is impatient with Laertes and decidedly unforward, but in the implications that the apparent seating arrangement brings out in Laertes' pressing concern with his sister's sexuality. When his warning turns most explicitly sexual, with "or your chaste treasure open / To his unmastered importunity" (1.3.30–31), Ophelia breaks eye contact and visibly gulps. The next line, "Fear it, Ophelia, fear it, my dear sister" is nearly whispered. In this context, Ophelia's admonition against the "puffed and reckless libertine" who "Himself the primrose path of dalliance treads" (48–49) acquires a more fully sexual suggestiveness. The intimate exchange ends when Laertes hears his father arrive upstairs and, as at least two other critics notice (though without the explanation I am offering), "stands stiffly, looking vaguely guilty as Polonius approaches."[24] Laertes quickly sneaks a kiss on Ophelia's cheek and stands up like a teenage lover caught in the act. Only now, as his hasty rise continues to signify guilt, is there clear evidence of his innocence, because this rise also reveals that Ophelia was not seated on his lap. Even if the facts contradict it, an uncanny linkage has begun between Laertes and Hamlet.

Much is learned in the scene about Polonius, who at this point does not match Hamlet's characterization of him as a "rash, intruding fool" (3.4.31). Intrude he does, perhaps, but this owner of a modernist house filled with books and abstract art is at this point neither as rash as the Polonius of Branagh and Zeffirelli nor as foolish as Olivier's counselor. In the play, Polonius reserves his longest speech for the moment when its length is least appropriate, forgetting that he has just scolded his son for being late to depart for France. Almereyda deletes only four lines from the famous speech but removes Polonius's foolish inconsistency by having him deliver it while helping Laertes hurriedly pack; the CEO's trusted lieutenant takes timely advantage of his son's failure to prepare.

No hypocrite, the well-dressed counselor preaches "costly thy habit as thy purse can buy" (1.3.69) while enabling his son to follow his advice by slipping a wad of money into Laertes' jacket. Even his intruding shows limits: he stands aside to allow his children a private farewell. The last third of this highly symmetrical three-part scene, Polonius's advice to Ophelia, is postponed until after Hamlet's encounter with the ghost. As a result, the usually downplayed poignancy of the moment—his father will not see Laertes again, nor will his sister see him while she remains sane—is not compromised. Father and daughter share a moment of sadness, looking offscreen following Laertes' departure.

Jan Blits rightly observes that act 1, scene 3 is "the most domestic scene in *Hamlet*. It is the only one that contains only members of a single family."[25] This is not true in the film, which reshapes the Shakespearean narrative in accord with modern expectations about the primacy of private life. Act 1, scene 3 is sandwiched between the scolding of Hamlet for excessive grief, where only the bodyguard intrudes on the family's private intervention, and an even more private subsequent scene. The limousine last seen on Park Avenue turns up Broadway conveying Claudius and Gertrude. Claudius's new *USA Today* proclaims, "Denmark Thwarts Fortinbras," vindicating the cockiness of his paper-tearing gesture and explaining the erotic excitement of the royal couple, for whom power is clearly an aphrodisiac. This is a very private recapitulation of the public press conference, accompanied once again by the triumphal strains of the Brahms First Symphony. So we are surprised when, precisely halfway into the scene, a cut reveals that Hamlet is also inside the car, again sullenly observing his mother kissing Claudius and again turning away in disgust. The king and queen are sharing a moment so privately engrossing that they pay no attention to the passenger opposite them. Delayed disclosure of Hamlet's presence has been put to new use.

They arrive at an event called in the screenplay "a major movie premiere" but left unspecified in the film.[26] This change allows us to add to the association of a premiere, which would in any event be cause for celebration for moguls of a multimedia corporation, the idea that the cheering reporters and photographers, who combine the roles of the standing press and the seated "court" of the press conference, are celebrating the corporate victory over Fortinbras. The elated couple are no less oblivious to Hamlet in the publicity of the crowd than they were in the privacy of the car. Doubly alienated, from both the success of the premiere and the success of resisting the hostile takeover, Hamlet turns away. The wordless scene primes him to hear the words of his father's spirit.

The ghost's visit begins with Horatio, Marcella, and Bernardo clustered around the surveillance monitors. Marcella checks her watch, suggesting that Hamlet is about to miss another appointment. When Bernardo phones Hamlet's room, there is a cut to him asleep on the couch, with light from the television flickering. Whisky bottles and beer cans help explain why he has missed this appointment, though the ghost's appearance on a balcony outside Hamlet's room suggests that this "accident" is fortuitous, perhaps even interpretable as providential. Changing his pattern of visitation, the ghost can now encounter his son in a more intimate manner than the play allows, continuing the film's series of family-only encounters.

The film has made much use of proxemics: the enforced closeness of arm grabbing and Hamlet huddling with Ophelia after the press conference, Gertrude drawing Hamlet off to herself on Park Avenue, the deceptively intimate Laertes-Ophelia interview. The plot's most intense interchange, not surprisingly, is carefully punctuated by moments of physical proximity. In contrast to Branagh's violent apparition, this ghost is at first reluctant to impose himself: he waits for Hamlet to approach the door before he moves toward it. When Hamlet opens the door, the ghost does not enter until he receives an affirmative answer to an interrogatively inflected, "Mark me" (1.5.2). He walks into the middle of the room, while Hamlet backs up against the closed door, glad to maintain the distance between them. The ghost then approaches and makes physical contact with his son in a way that conveys both menace and affection, a visual equivalent of the way his words about purgatorial terrors frighten even as they assure Hamlet that he will not actually disclose the "eternal blazon" (21) of purgatorial torment to mortal ears.

This uneasy tension between menace and affection pervades the scene. Sam Shepard's craggy and intense ghost backs a visibly terrified Hamlet into a corner. Hamlet's knees buckle and he sits down on the window ledge. The ghost's hands on Hamlet first enact the image of hairs standing on end "like quills upon the fearful porpentine" (20), then lovingly caress his cheeks, then envelop his neck with sufficient menace to make Hamlet's exclamation "O God!" (24) more a response to the horror movie scenario he finds himself within than a profession of love for his father. When the ghost places his left hand on Hamlet's chest, Hamlet glances down at it, as confused as we are about whether his visitor wishes him good or ill. We and perhaps Hamlet notice the wedding ring, and the ghost pats his son gently and calls him by name. "Now, Hamlet, hear" (34) marks the end of this studiously ambiguous first encounter.

The ghost walks away while exposing the falsity of Claudius's story about the stinging serpent. Less frightened now, Hamlet follows him, but his approach turns quickly into a retreat followed by the panning and tracking camera until he is backed up against the window on the opposite wall, with the ghost angrily venting about the "wretch" (51) Claudius mere inches from his son's face. As at the end of the first segment, so now at the end of the second, we hear Hamlet's gasping breath. The ghost moves away a second time while uttering, "But soft, methinks I scent the morning air" (58); chastened, Hamlet declines to follow him, slipping instead into the security of his desk chair, which has become his favored place from which to view visitors from the past. A third time the ghost approaches, bearing down on Hamlet with horrific words, but with the description of the poisoning, Hamlet's pity appears to prevail over his terror. We are not surprised that Hamlet rises and follows when the ghost next turns away. Hamlet stands his ground through the advice to leave his mother to heaven's punishment, and when the ghost quickly turns back from what appears to be his final departure, Hamlet accepts his strong embrace willingly. His audible gasp at the ghost's departure, expressing his astonishment at the visit and message, serves as a final punctuation mark for a rigorously structured encounter.

In accordance with the film's emphasis on the private family, most of the postvisitation part of the scene—Hamlet's declaring the ghost "honest" (137), the swearing to secrecy, the announcement of his "antic disposition" (170)—is deleted. Horatio's query, "What news, my lord?" (116), is no longer the play's urgent request to relate the ghost's message but a matter-of-fact question to someone who has missed an appointment and not answered the phone. Hamlet simply shows his friends the ghost, who remains briefly visible on a balcony, and declares that "there are more things in heaven and earth . . . Than are dreamt of in our philosophy" (165–66). The impact of the visitation is made apparent not through Hamlet's "wild and whirling words" (132) to his friends but through two lines, "The time is out of joint. O cursed spite, / That ever I was born to set it right" (186–87), delivered as the voice-over for an abstract montage. In the montage, two appearances of the Denmark Corporation logo, accompanied by the sound of connecting to the Internet via modem, enclose two telephoto "news shots" of the bustling city.[27] From within this highly mediatized Hamlet's subjectivity, we view his lonely quest for revenge set against the vast power he must confront to complete it.

Polonius's interview with Ophelia, the third panel of act 1, scene 3 in the play, is now inserted after the ghost's visit. The reordering, as usual in this film, generates meaningful parallels: a one-on-one interview of parent and child succeeds another, and in both, the parent strongly charges the child to take difficult and unpleasant action. Polonius's entry from the place on the screen (center left) where we have last seen the ghost and then looked for him again after he vanished, visually underscores his parallel role. Ophelia will obey her parental charge, but Hamlet will find himself torn between obedience to his father and resistance to Ophelia's. A significant contrast also arises. Almereyda makes extensive textual cuts in the ghost scene, including most of Hamlet's initial address to the ghost, his entire speech following its departure, and all but a few lines of interchange with his friends. As a result, the film's ghost is even more dominant verbally than the play's. The cuts in the following scene have the opposite effect. Of the twenty-two lines cut (out of forty-nine), only two are Ophelia's. Relatively less dominant in terms of dialogue lines than in the play and other films, Polonius is also less foolish, domineering, and self-interested. He is a more modern parent suited to the film's modern setting. While issuing fatherly advice, he ties her shoe, a gesture that has been interpreted as part of the film's infantilization of Ophelia but is better read as a sign of paternal care, like the slipping of cash into Laertes' coat. Robert Wood rightly notes that a modern single parent differs from a Shakespearean one and that Polonius's "gestures, however misplaced, are those of someone who has been a caregiver rather than just an authority figure."[28] Only Almereyda's version develops Ophelia's character enough before act 1, scene 3 to make her father's intervention sympathetic. He is responding to his daughter's sadness, which he does not understand but we do, and which does not afflict her in other versions at this point. He has observed her seeking escape from her troubles first by calling Moviefone and then by gazing into a diorama "featuring a view of a gravel road disappearing into a dim forest glade," a recurring Almereyda prop signifying both the fantasy of escape from oppression and the danger inherent in this fantasy.[29] In both cases, Polonius stops her, understandably preferring to get at the root of the problem. Importantly for the plot, however, he does announce in "plain terms" that Ophelia must not see Hamlet: "Look to't, I charge you" (1.3.131, 134).

The Second Movement

One would expect the second movement to start right after the ghost's visit, as the change in knowledge and situation leads to new action. Placing Polonius's interview with Ophelia after the ghost's visit might be considered a move away from Hollywood structure, but in fact the change emphatically makes Polonius's stricture against a relationship with Hamlet a defining part of the new situation. The screenplay places Hamlet's two plots in parallel, as Bernardo brings Hamlet a gun while he is composing his love poem. The better wisdom of the finished film enhances their competition, continuing the already established rivalry between Ophelia and the ghost. Hamlet's courtship becomes an evasion of filial responsibility but, at the same time, a return to his better nature, which now acquires a more spiritual dimension consistent with his address of Ophelia as "the celestial and my soul's idol" (2.2.108).

When next seen, Hamlet is in his room; without the intervening scene, we might expect him to be responding to the trauma of the ghostly visit. And perhaps he is responding to the ghost, though if so his response is the surprising one of turning his full attention to Ophelia, who has been charged not to see him. In a contrast to the purgatorial flames on the television screen during the ghost's visit, the television is playing the film's most extensive modern addition to the script, as the Vietnamese Buddhist monk Thich Nhat Hanh proposes to replace the phrase "to be" with "to inter-be." Almereyda described the addition as "a perfect ramp leading up to Hamlet's most famous soliloquy," and indeed it is, in interesting ways.[30] Viewers may know that Hanh was a nominee for the Nobel Peace Prize, an advocate of nonviolence who may be affecting or reflecting Hamlet's choice of action. Those who simply listen to Hanh's message will hear (although, one hopes with some irony) this choice articulated: "You need other people in order to be. Not only do you need mother, father, but also uncle, sister, society." Hamlet's response to the ghost involves a choice between family and nonfamilial society. In the earlier soliloquy scene, he had chosen family, the mother and father to whose video images he returned instead of keeping his appointment with Ophelia. Now he makes a different choice. The image on which he gazes throughout the scene is Ophelia's, a continuation of the video segment that he earlier replaced with familial images that were more compelling. The clamshell video also functions as a "ramp" toward "To be or not to be." As Hamlet compulsively repeats the diary segment, it reveals the identity of the book Ophelia was reading and the author whose face on its cover displaced hers: Jiddu Krishnamurti's *On Living and Dying,* a title that might define Hamlet's choice or pose an alternative to viewing it as a choice: "and" rather than "or."

Soon Hamlet has decided to prefer the real presence to the manipulated image. Rather than simply having Polonius report Hamlet's love letter to the king and queen, a situation that in most productions comically undercuts any potential for taking his love poem seriously, we see Hamlet furthering the love plot by struggling to write in two quick coffee-shop scenes. His struggle continues as he composes in voice-over while walking in front of a grocery store whose displayed wares begin a series of Halloween references. He looks up across the street and turns back, then halts again and looks up: his back-and-forth motion echoes Ophelia's at the waterfall after he failed to meet her. A Halloween skull appears in the store window behind him, eerily shadowing the outcome of this visit.

A low shot from behind of Hamlet crossing the street left-to-right echoes the film's first image of him; he is also carrying the same bag and wearing the same clothes. He is not crossing Times Square into the center of multinational capitalism, however, but is traversing a forlorn street toward Ophelia's dingy tenement. Inside, she is hanging pictures to dry in her darkroom. Though the script specified that Ophelia's photos were of her father, the film shows her hanging a picture of herself, a change that implies a more Lacanian response to her plight, a return to the mirror stage in response to the threat of dissolution. The embrace of the lovers in the erotic red light of the darkroom marks the end of the romantic plot's upward arc and their only real moment of intimacy. Polonius arrives with birthday balloons, which suggestively float away when he picks up the letter, dropped by Hamlet in his hasty escape. The erotically escapist electronic music (which will be heard again) fades upon Polonius's arrival, to be replaced by another Burwell composition carrying a greater sense of dramatic plot movement. This music will continue through the next two sequences, pulling them together to show the momentous consequence of the romance plot's failure.

Back in his room after this disastrous outing, Hamlet delivers the first half-line of his famous soliloquy in a scenario of considerable resonance. Some of this resonance derives from cultural and cinematic history. Mayakovsky's doom manifested itself in a famous suicide, as did the doom of grunge rocker Kurt Cobain, a model for Hawke's modernizing portrayal of Shakespeare's hero.[31] Many in the original audience would recall not only Cobain but also the suicidal character played by Mel Gibson in the enormously popular *Lethal Weapon* series of films, even if they did not know that the scene that this Hamlet's actions closely imitate inspired Zeffirelli to cast Gibson as his own (ironically, nonsuicidal) Hamlet. Some of this resonance is psychological, layering additional complexities onto Hamlet's mental life. Like Ophelia, who turned in crisis to her own image in the darkroom, Hamlet watches himself in close-up on the video monitor. More precisely, he watches two of his selves: one who intones "To be, or not to be" from the past with a pistol pressed to his temple and throat, concluding with an enigmatic smile after looking off-camera (at what? a mirror, like Branagh's hero?); and one in the present reflected in the monitor's glass, who can indulge in the magical undoing of rewinding, the compulsive repetition of replaying, and the contemplative luxury of freeze-frame. Adding to the blurring of self-boundaries is the black apparel of the live and video Hamlets, which distinguishes them from the diary character who elsewhere wears a white T-shirt.

The sequence of replay and rewind occurs three times, like so many other things in the play and the film. The first instance ends in a metacinematic glance into the camera. The past Hamlet directs his smile to us and to his future self, who exists only because of the answer he delivered to this great existential question at the time the video was made, and who the present Hamlet may be accessing to find encouragement in this precedent. The final repetition is incomplete. The camera joltingly cuts away to the next scene after the third "to be," leaving a conundrum: does Hamlet end with affirmation, or does the rest of the film form the second part of the truncated question?

The scene shifts to the Denmark Corporation's skyscraper headquarters, its aura of power enhanced by a nearly vertical camera. Despite the scene change, the continuing Burwell theme unites Hamlet's action with the previous two scenes, implying a causal chain that begins with the surprise arrival of Polonius in Ophelia's apartment and ends only when Hamlet bursts into Claudius's office. In a hallway high above the urban landscape, Hamlet is replaying his video diary again, technologically updating Shakespeare's portrayal of the prince who enters "reading on a book" (2.2.167). He is seeking in the white-clad Hamlet's speech on the "vicious mole of nature" (1.4.23–36) motivation to do—what, we do not yet know, though one might fill in the missing "not to be" as an answer that produces more questions, the same questions that Hamlet's spectacularly ambiguous soliloquy has provoked for centuries. Does Hamlet contemplate self-destruction or murderous revenge, or does "not to be" indicate his recognition that the latter will entail the former, fortunately or unfortunately?

Polonius interrupts to begin a highly abbreviated version of the fishmonger scene, during which Hamlet reveals to us his gun but not his intentions. The mystery continues, with Hamlet's reference to his grave (2.2.204) and to his willing parting with his life continuing the suicidal implications. In a composition that brilliantly visualizes Hamlet's internal divisions—and echoes the photo of a two-headed man glimpsed on Hamlet's wall while Hanh spoke of inter-being—he delivers his parting words to Polonius, "except my life" (212). He is peering around a mirrored corner that splits the screen in half, producing not merely two Hamlets facing us but also a third reflected from behind. The fact that this is an echo of the triple Hamlet of the first "to be" scene recalls his suicidal desire. Seeing Hamlet armed and striding with determination through the office while slightly slowed motion builds anticipation of violence would ordinarily resolve any doubt that his intention is murder, but holding back the second and third instances of "except my life" for voice-over insertion here complicates matters. So does the fact that Hamlet makes no effort to conceal his weapon from the office workers or the surveillance camera system to which Polonius has just confided his "still harping on my daughter" (187) speech. A shot through the screen of an office divider disturbingly presents the workers' point of view, revealing how easily they might observe Hamlet's homicidal behavior. His entry into Claudius's office attracts the attention of a secretary outside. Even after he has burst in and aimed at the empty chairs, we see the head of a passerby in the hall, as though Hamlet remains unconcerned about potential witnesses to his bloody deed.

After three intense minutes united by Burwell's composition and culminating in the reckless attempted murder, Polonius's report to the king and queen at the penthouse poolside, nearly four and one-half minutes in one location, offers a change of pace and tone. A low-volume music track of piano jazz underscores the improvisational verbal "art" that Polonius denies using. Coming so soon after Hamlet's brazen gun wielding, Polonius's presentation of Hamlet's love letter in a plastic evidence bag (echoed when the gun is later seen in a similar bag) creates an effect of subjective disproportion: the exposure of something so personal is understandably mortifying to Ophelia yet utterly trivial from any other perspective, despite her father's protestations. The ironic nature of the scene is further brought out by a device borrowed from Branagh. At the height of his vengeful emotion, we see Branagh's Hamlet plunge his dagger into Claudius's skull, only to see the act retroactively nullified with a surprise cut to the unwounded king. Ophelia similarly cancels her father's intolerable recitation by jumping suicidally into the pool, followed by a cut that redefines the action as imaginary. Despite the comic disproportion it implies, Ophelia's action generates pathos through its uncanny linkages. She first walks with a balancing motion along the pool's edge, as she had done in the first soliloquy inset. When she is later found drowned in the waterfall pool, the penthouse and waterfall pools condense into one, in effect converting this imaginary jump into a flash-forward. Under water during this imaginary escape from her father, she covers both eyes with her hands. This is a crucial gesture that the film meaningfully repeats.

Almereyda observes that the second "to be or not to be" scene, located in a Blockbuster video store, was cited "by more than a few critics as if it were the adaptation's defining conceit, the most audacious thing in the movie."[32] How much more audacious would the scene have been had circumstances not thwarted the filmmaker's original plan! Almereyda had envisioned shooting part of the soliloquy at the Whitney Museum, within a complicated installation of mirrors and video projections by video artist Bill Viola.[33] Even without Viola's installation, the scene is richer in implication than has been acknowledged in the critical commentary, which for the most part is satisfied with noting the irony of the indecisive hero's presence in the store's action film section.

As in previous films, Hamlet's movements are carefully choreographed to complement Shakespeare's highly anticipated words. Hamlet first ambles slowly down a central aisle, glancing left and right at the shelves of videotapes, with the low camera placement affording sight of no details in the other aisles. Reaching the end, he looks up to watch the monitors. A cut away from the monitors then reveals him walking toward the camera from another aisle until he stands once more beneath the monitors. He proceeds up the central aisle, back to the point of indecision where he began. His movements imply that he has traversed the entire store without finding what he needs to "Go Home Happy," as the Blockbuster motto exhorts. A higher camera position at the end reveals that the next aisle contains "Action" films as well. Hamlet is trapped in a world without generic alternatives, a situation that helps to explain why, more than any film predecessor, he has so utterly lost his mirth.

Much as Pyrrhus's slaughter of Priam, avenging his father's death, defines the quintessential tragic deed against which Hamlet's actions are judged in the play, the film's quintessential action film deed is defined by shots from Tim Pope's *The Crow II: City of Angels* (1996).[34] The allusion becomes recognizable in a distant monitor behind Hamlet, then in the triple monitor when a longer version of the film's climactic scene is repeated. A motorcycle explodes. Its rider flies spectacularly through the air. The hero, Ashe Corven, who has returned from the dead to avenge his death and the death of his son, stands with rifle in hand. The large segment of Almereyda's original audience that knew the film would have recalled that this is the moment when Corven kills his most despised enemy, played with memorable repulsiveness by punk-rocker Iggy Pop. Later parts of the scene play as Hamlet walks back up the central aisle. Another shot, presented out of sequence, reveals Corven passing through a wall of flames toward his victim in a second point-of-view shot of the triple monitor at the very end of the soliloquy, a powerful image of the action hero who will stop at nothing to obtain his revenge.

As if projecting his repetition compulsion outward, this repeated violent imagery adds subjectivity to Hamlet's Blockbuster visit. Ashe Corven becomes an ego ideal replayed much as Hamlet replayed his own videos and will soon replay snippets of old film as he conceives the Mousetrap. The soliloquy is itself a repetition, a return to the question "To be or not to be" following his earlier multiple returns to a still earlier version of the question on video, with a gun to his head. Olivier pioneered the mixed soliloquy—part voice-over and part mouthed speech—to dramatize outbursts of emotion that could not be contained within silent thought. Almereyda's variation works to blur the distinction between inside and outside. The shift from voice-over to speech occurs as Hamlet returns to the central aisle, allowing the speech to pivot on "ay, there's the rub" (3.1.64), as the thought of eternal oblivion, or worse, transforms the video store into a more fully subjective space where Hamlet speaks without the possibility of being overheard. The store, sparsely populated during the voice-over by a barely glimpsed female clerk and a single male customer, after the shift is unpopulated except for the imaged participants in Hamlet's psychodrama.

At the same time that Ashe Corven is defining the kind of action heroics to which Hamlet feels called, additional film allusions complicate the reduction to one generic possibility. Titles of some of the videocassettes become recognizable as Hamlet returns up the central aisle. Near the monitors, one notices *Aeon Flux, Akira,* and *The Guyver,* ultraviolent films that belong in a category with *City of Angels;* indeed, all four of these films derive from teen-oriented graphic media. But as Hamlet concludes his meditation, we see such titles as *The African Queen, A Man for All Seasons, The Man Who Knew Too Much,* and finally, in a lingering shot of Hamlet observing how "enterprises of great pitch and moment . . . lose the name of action" (86–88), *The Third Man.* Such classics, which would not be placed in a normal video store's action section, present complex and conflicted characters who inhabit worlds filled with confusion and moral ambiguity. Almereyda's Hamlet returns to such a world after his brief Blockbuster foray, a world whose resistance to generic simplification Polonius ironically proclaims with his reference to "tragical-comical-historical-pastoral" (2.2.394–95).

In the play, Hamlet's encounter with Rosencrantz and Guildenstern immediately follows the "fishmonger" encounter with Polonius. The film separates the two encounters with the attempt to murder Claudius, the pool scene, and the soliloquy at Blockbuster. A cut from Ashe Corven walking through flames to Hamlet sitting at a dark bar can thus highlight the severe enervation that replaces his earlier impulsive action. He is staring offscreen, no doubt seeing the unattainable action ideal in his mind's eye, a suggestion supported by the orange glow on his face. As he turns away from the vision, the vacancy behind his stare is reflected in a Primal Scream song that has been called "an acid soaked rocker."[35] At this moment, Ethan Hawke comes closest to realizing his conception of Hamlet as Kurt Cobain, tragically drug dependent and suicidal.

Despite the film's brevity, Almereyda makes room for Rosencrantz and Guildenstern, unlike Olivier, to give Hamlet suitable victims when he begins his action phase. They enter the plot without the play's royal requests to assist in diagnosing and relieving Hamlet's melancholy. Cutting these requests allows some viewers to share Hamlet's belief that these truly are his "excellent good friends" (2.2.219), as the warmth of his greeting also suggests, especially in comparison with his earlier cold greeting of Horatio. Numerous beers later, disagreement arises about whether Denmark is a prison. In the play, this difference of outlook leads to Hamlet's discovery that they were "sent for" (274). Hawke's Hamlet, in contrast, displays no suspicion, and the three drunken "friends" end with an amiable clink of the glasses.

Hamlet's lack of suspicion amplifies the outrage inherent in the subterfuge of Rosencrantz and Guildenstern. Their collusion is revealed in the following scene, as the film jumps to act 3, deleting the introduction of the players in the rest of act 2, scene 2. With his usual masterful use of delayed disclosure, Almereyda cuts to a close-up of Gertrude's face and bare shoulder against a background of bed linens. The shot suggests that she is naked and that Claudius's voice-over query, "And can you by no drift of conference / Get from him why he puts on this confusion" (3.1.1–2), is addressed to her. What exactly is Claudius proposing to his wife, we must ask, and under what circumstances? Tinny phone voices and then a longer shot soon clarify: Claudius and Gertrude are hearing the report of Hamlet's "friends" over a speakerphone, and although she is not naked, she does proceed to undress Claudius as they listen. The queen's ardor is not cooled by discussing Hamlet, for as the scene ends she is drawing Claudius down upon her in the bed.

At the moment when the king is rolling into a prone position on the queen's receptive body, a cut to Hamlet lying prone on his bed introduces one of the film's most innovative and complex scenes with appropriate sexual innuendo. As the "rogue and peasant slave" (2.2.485) soliloquy begins, Hamlet is watching two segments of a James Dean television production.[36] In the first segment, Dean is driving, a reluctant action hero escaping from a firing gun; in the second, he interacts with a father figure. The identifications in this oedipal scenario grow more complicated as we make connections between this soliloquy and the first, an activity encouraged by the reuse of Burwell's earlier music. Only the father figure speaks, while Dean signals his acceptance of paternal domination by covering his mouth: one might recall Hamlet's "but break, my heart, for I must hold my tongue" (1.2.159). At the same time, Dean's conspicuous cigarette recalls old Hamlet's combination of phallic instrument and postcoital convention. In the play, Hamlet compares himself unfavorably with an actor who can enter with total conviction into a fictive character. The film layers onto this comparison another with the well-established persona of James Dean. "What would he do" (2.2.554) becomes a question about how Hamlet might emulate another action hero and rebel without a cause, while the play's reference to the old actor playing father Priam doting on mother Hecuba is translated into the young actor playing the son who is in competition with the father. Hamlet is making progress from earlier silence and inaction to a kind of action, if yet only the video artist's representational action that will make murder, though it have no tongue, speak "With most miraculous organ" (529).

The most important visual difference between the two soliloquies is the use of the second large monitor. As in the first soliloquy, a rightward track moves the camera behind Hamlet, now sitting again at his cluttered desk. The eye is first drawn to a close-up on the larger screen on the right showing John Gielgud addressing Yorick's skull, "Shakespeare's most famous prop" in Shakespeare's most visibly remembered scene.[37] With its middle-aged actor dressed in Renaissance costume, recorded by a fixed camera in sharp focus, this is truly "classic" Shakespeare, the straightforward recording of a theatrical performance. The impression is strengthened if one recognizes the iconic footage, much reprinted in both still and motion form, from the legendary 1944 production that prompted James Agate, the influential critic from the London *Sunday Times*, famously to declare that "this is, and is likely to remain, the best Hamlet of our time."[38]

In Freudian terms, the Gielgud footage represents the play's conscious manifest content, the result of the dream-work's efforts to convert the disturbing material of the unconscious latent content into something more acceptable and comprehensible. The latent content now comes into view on the other monitor as Hamlet seeks the deeper "cunning of the scene" that will strike "guilty creatures sitting at a play" "to the soul" (2.2.525–27). A "narrative" of monochrome images, punctuated by an opening and closing yellow rose, is run through three times:

1. the profiled faces of a man and woman kissing
2. an extreme close-up of a woman's eyes
3. a close-up of a man's face
4. a human effigy being held in a candle flame
5. a woman covering/uncovering her empty eye sockets with her hands.

The images run in this order in a medium shot that includes Hamlet and Gielgud, then more quickly in reverse order and again in the original order in a close-up of the screen as Hamlet indulges his compulsion to repeat. For most viewers, the images will indicate Hamlet's interest in horror and pornographic film, "lower" genres representing the psychic territory that Hamlet is tapping. Hamlet is being defined as what film scholar Joan Hawkins calls a "cutting edge" cineaste such as Jean-Luc Godard, one of Almereyda's favorites, who uses "paracinematic" imagery to blur the line between high and trash culture.[39] Cutting-edge Hamlet parallels Hamlet's Yorick speech with an implied narrative that includes a struggle for sexual dominance through the gaze, resulting in the woman's grotesque mutilation. Perhaps the imagery contains an explanation for the excision of Gertrude from Branagh's Yorick flashback, her replacement by a man whose eye sockets now too are empty.

The Freudian viewer will find here the film's clearest evocation of the depth-psychological uncanny, a return of repressed castrational anxiety associated with eyelessness and countered with a wish-fulfilling narrative of oedipal dominance. The student of film genres will notice Hamlet's use of conventions: the eyelessness common in zombie/voodoo films, the mesmeric control of the female victim in vampire films. The viewer familiar with the film from which the images are taken, the 1963 Mexican horror film *La Maldición de la Llorona* (*The Curse of the Crying Woman*), will further appreciate the complexity of Almereyda's allusiveness. The popular Latin American mythic tale of La Llorona, the abandoned woman who drowns her children and fades into a spectral weeping presence, resonates provocatively with the film's representation of Ophelia, who assumes the tale's roles of both mother and children.[40] As Pascale Aebischer observes, in the play "Hamlet's own reflections over Yorick's skull never explicitly evoke the possibility of his own death but displace his own mortality onto 'my lady' . . . in an uncanny flashback (or is it a flashforward?) to the death of Ophelia."[41] In the film, as Hamlet prepares to provoke his mother and stepfather, he explores the psychic pressures that produce this displacement.

A slow fade to black is followed by a close-up of a playbill for "The Mouse Trap: a film/video by Hamlet." The close-up is held a full three seconds, a long time for such a static and speechless shot, during which we hear mysterious sounds, very familiar but not immediately identifiable. We also contemplate the playbill's spiral design, a motif associated with delirium in film history— most famously in Alfred Hitchcock's *Vertigo*, which, like Hamlet's film/video, advertised itself with a white spiral on a red background. (Hamlet even seems to know the background of this renowned image, for stills from graphic filmmaker John Whitney, whose "spiral of time" animations inspired Saul Bass's design for the film's publicity and title sequence, are posted on Hamlet's walls.)[42] We have time, too, to speculate on which character might be holding the playbill, engaged in similar contemplation. No identifying thumbnail aids us as it did in the earlier shot of Hamlet in the closet. A cut reveals it to be held by Gertrude, who is sitting on the king's lap in his corporate office: another echo of the scene at the Polonius residence. Her serious demeanor indicates that she is clearly provoked by Hamlet's title and graphic, but her concerns do not stop her from fondling her new husband in a way that links the scene to the royal bedroom scene, forming an eroticized parental frame around Hamlet's soliloquy. The framing effect is enhanced by the continuation of Rosencrantz and Guildenstern's report over the phone.

With the next cut, this erotic charge turns more troublesome. Polonius is attaching a listening device to Ophelia, revealing that Velcro fasteners were the source of the mysterious-but-familiar sound. At one point, the screen is divided between the lascivious couple on the left and the father insensitively exploiting his daughter on the right, a visual innuendo that ties mischievously into the film's dichotomy of latent and manifest content. Polonius's abuse here reads not as erotically motivated but as heedlessly outrageous, as Almereyda sacrifices his previous kind paternalism to build sympathy for abused Ophelia and to make more plausible her approaching madness and suicide. As he typically does in the tragedies, Shakespeare uses the moment to establish, if here only momentarily, a reassuring community of women. In the play, the scene contains the only communication between Gertrude and Ophelia before the latter goes insane. The film handles the moment with brilliantly grim irony. Polonius's behavior reaches a climax of outrageousness when, groping under his daughter's blouse to attach a microphone near her breast, he turns to

Gertrude (!) with a grin and a wink. Under the circumstances, it is difficult not to hear cynically obscene overtones in Gertrude's reference to Ophelia's "beauties" as the cause of Hamlet's madness and her "virtues" as a means to "bring him back to his wonted way again" (3.2.38–39). Nor is it surprising that Ophelia does not answer, "Madam, I wish it may" (42). Instead, this abused avatar of La Llorona wipes away her tears, distraught with being forced into a sleazy spy operation inspired by the infamous entrapment of Monica Lewinski by Linda Tripp.[43]

Rather than encountering Ophelia in the course of his "to be" soliloquy, Hamlet now encounters her in a situation that makes her blame more evident. A symbolic transition begins with a sculpted woman with arm raised in front of the head of an ominously predatory horse. Some will decipher the laurel garland and palm frond as iconography of Victory, perhaps even recognize one of the most famous works of American sculpture, Augustus Saint-Gaudens's winged Victory leading General Sherman southward from Central Park; such viewers will find irony in the contrast with Ophelia's sordid and unpromising mission. Others will experience an uncanny but elusive familiarity: the image by "the American Michelangelo" has influenced many other works of art and was remodeled for use on American coins.[44] At the very least, its puzzling nature may lock it in the memory for anticipated future use. Another baleful waterfall follows, its familiar melancholy associations reinforced by the totally empty outdoor café seating for which it serves as a background.

Ophelia arrives at Hamlet's apartment bearing a box stuffed with letters, which requires four handfuls to unload onto the table, evidence of a long and loving relationship. Because we have watched Hamlet struggle mightily to compose a single love letter, his response to their mass return convincingly produces hurt feelings. She then pushes even the box toward him at "There, my lord" (101), as if the container itself is too contaminated to remain in her possession. The box's design is an added visual provocation, its red-and-white spiral design recalling Hamlet's deliberately provocative playbill. Despite this strong rejection, Hamlet remains surprisingly tender even as he denies loving her. His tone, caresses, and kisses, accompanied by Burwell's sentimental Ophelia theme, belie his declaration—until, that is, he discovers the intimately located microphone. This discovery that he is being spied on, in the most blatant and unambiguous surveillance in the tradition of filmed *Hamlet*s, is thus also the most ironic, because it is produced not by the eavesdroppers' carelessness as in Zeffirelli's film (a glimpsed shadow) or Branagh's (a telltale noise) but by Hamlet's very ardor.

After her embarrassing exposure, she hurries home to burn photographs in her decrepit bathroom while suffering more abuse from Hamlet on the answering machine. In another cleverly delayed disclosure, reversing the previous pattern, we see who is holding the contemplated image but do not see immediately what is depicted. Is it Hamlet, whose image she wishes to erase from her heart, or is it Ophelia herself, whose darkroom is filled with self-imaging attempts to shore up the ruins of her besieged self? On the one hand, the revelation that it is Hamlet's image burning is encouraging, given the alternative. On the other hand, as Abbate argues, her behavior manifests "an ontological shift from reality to simulacrum" implying that "Hamlet will only disappear when the pictures of him are destroyed."[45] Ophelia's encroaching madness could be thought of as succumbing to the postmodern condition.

Hamlet's response to this crisis is to revisit the video store, to gather images rather than destroy them. Beeps emanating from the checkout machinery echo those of Ophelia's answering machine, underlining difference through resemblance to show him sublimating his anger into art. On the monitor overhead, *The Crow II: City of Angels* continues, but now Hamlet pays it no heed. The clerk looks at him askance and raises her eyebrows, prompting us to wonder what is on the nine tapes, which we assume to be raw materials for the Mousetrap.

Replacing the play-within-a-play with a film-within-a-film eliminates all of the business with the players in acts 2 and 3 as well as, of course, the staged Mousetrap itself. Almereyda supplies visual details to compensate for the deleted passages, which Shakespeare used to create an abundance of implicit comparisons and contrasts among the inner and outer frames of representation. Seated in the row behind Hamlet and Ophelia and framing them visually are two couples, Horatio and Marcella on the right and a younger man with an older woman on the left. The "normal" same-age relationship and the oedipal relationship that is the psychic substratum of the normal repeat the pattern of manifest and latent content displayed respectively on the right and left monitors during the soliloquy and echoed in the scene of wiring Ophelia. The vertical axis also develops a sexual dynamic. Hamlet and Ophelia in the foreground are placed in positions that visually match Claudius and Gertrude in the background, allowing Hamlet's bawdy antics to comment on the royal couple's relationship. The distress produced in Ophelia by Hamlet's inappropriate "country matters" (3.2.110) contrasts with the obvious pleasure of his mother, who, as Hamlet does not really need to tell us, looks cheerful while cavorting with her husband. As a visual echo of the opening press conference, the screening measures Hamlet's progress: he now takes charge, provides the applause (before the film begins!), and climbs over the seats from the right aisle to Ophelia, who is no longer physically and morally enclosed by her family. He has, in a sense, also displaced Polonius, complicating the oedipal tangle.

Of all of the film's sequences, the Mousetrap has most polarized critics, whose responses range from intense admiration to vitriolic contempt.[46] The contempt, I propose, derives from a lamentable inability to appreciate even the kind of experimental filmmaking for which there are recognizable and respected precedents. The Mousetrap cleverly transforms Shakespeare's dumb show into a nondialogue, dreamlike montage narrative set to classical music, very much in the manner of Bruce Conner, arguably the foremost filmmaker of the American avant-garde. The principal model is Conner's 1978 *Valse Triste*, which included the spinning earth, a dream sequence from a pajama-clad little boy in bed, time-lapse imagery of a blooming plant, and outdoor exercises by girls in a physical education class, all edited to follow a Sibelius score much as the Mousetrap is edited to Tchaikovsky. The film/video begins with playful paratextual framing, another Conner hallmark. In the title sequence in white block letters on a red background announcing "THE MOUSETRAP / A TRAGEDY BY / HAMLET / PRINCE OF DENMARK," the third title is identical to the title used to introduce Almereyda's film more than fifty minutes earlier. Both are accompanied by a High Romantic orchestral score, with Tchaikovsky's symphonic poem *Hamlet* now replacing Brahms's First Symphony. The current title differs visually only in aspect and size, as befits the difference between Hamlet's short experimental work and Almereyda's Miramax feature. Shakespeare's players present no material actually written by Hamlet, with the possible exception of the mysterious "dozen lines, or sixteen lines" (2.2.477) that Hamlet requests to have inserted into the Gonzago play. Hamlet's film/video is similarly unoriginal, an assembly of found footage. To understand the film's variety of sources and continuity of action, a shot list is helpful:

1. [fade in to] a red rose opens (time-lapse color)
2. [dissolve to] a young boy standing before his seated parents (color live-action)
3. [cut to] the young boy is lifted up to sit on the couch between his parents (color live-action)
4. [cut to] a young boy is dandled on his father's lap (b&w live-action)
5. [cut to] the father leads the young boy off (b&w live-action)
6. [cut to] the father watches the boy get into bed (b&w live-action)

7. [dissolve to] the earth turns in space (crude model animation)

8. [fade out, fade in to] a hand holds a poison bottle (b&w animation)

9. [dissolve to] swarming microscopic cells (b&w animation)

10. [dissolve to] the hand holds the poison bottle (b&w animation)

11. [cut to] a hatted man enters (color cut-out animation)

12. [unseen] a man is lounging in a chair (color cut-out animation)

13. [cut to] a hand pours a drop of liquid from a test tube (color cut-out animation)

14. [cut to] the drop descends (color cut-out animation)

15. [cut to] the drop enters an ear, a circle of sound expands (color cut-out animation)

16. [unseen] a man in a room staggers and falls (b&w silent film)

17. [cut to] a queen with Roman soldiers and prisoner (b&w silent film)

18. [unseen] an elephant falls to the ground (b&w live-action)

19. [cut to] a line of men fall in sequence (b&w live-action)

20. [cut to] a second sequence of falling men (b&w live-action)

21. [unseen] a bright vortex spins (b&w and color animation)

22. [dissolve] the rose ripens and decays (time-lapse color film)

23. [cut to] the boy from 3–5 comes downstairs, peeks into the living room (b&w live-action)

24. [cut to] a soldier kisses the hand of the queen from 17 (b&w silent film)

25. [cut to] a woman and a man French kiss (color live-action)

26. [cut to] the woman is having sexual intercourse *a tergo* (color live-action)

27. [unseen] a well-dressed audience in a hall applauds (color live-action)

28. [unseen] a man before a mirror places a crown on his head (b&w silent film)

29. [cut to] the man, now crowned, nods in approval (b&w silent film)

A sequence like this is not designed to be reduced to complete rational coherence. Its variety of film forms, its shifting of signifying mode between narrative and symbolism, and the multiplicity of narratives all conspire against logical paraphrase. The challenge is compounded by the interaction of these factors, which produces multiple competing structural patterns. For example, the poisoning sequence of 8–16 is composed of three different film forms, the last of which (black and white silent film) is taken up in shot 17, inviting us to ask whether the poisoning narrative continues into the queen-soldiers sequence (17 and 24). The dissolve transitions connecting 8–10 further divide this part from the later, color poison sequence (11–15). The dissolve and symbolic rose of 22 punctuate the boy's predream and postdream experience and add a somewhat mystifying division between 2–21 and 23–29. Or are there three stories here: 2–6, 8–21, and 23–29? To cite but one more example, the shift from color to black and white suggests discontinuity between 2–3 and 4–6, while the subject matter and period style suggest continuity, although the mother figure of 5 is elderly, shifting the parallel from "manifest" Horatio-Marcella to the "latent" couple on the other side of the screening room. The very fact that the two family sequences display an interpretable difference reflected in the audience encourages attempts at discerning and interpreting the relations between other sequences.

The best explanation for the film's willful obscurity is that Hamlet is not trying to be understood but to understand, through provoking without making his provocations too dangerously clear. Because the poisoning contains the most hazardous material, it is conveyed in the less illusionistic film forms of animation (the masterful collage work of Lewis Klahr) and highly stylized silent film. It is also framed with great care. Shot 8 can be considered the start of the boy's dream, a nightmare that will bring him back downstairs in 23. The ambiguous endpoint of the sequence prevents the viewer from definitively connecting the poisoning to the soldier-queen story and, in turn, to the self-crowning king. It prompts guilty Claudius to make these connections while not allowing him to be certain that the filmmaker did.

Some devices intensify the impact on the audience and, at the same time, hide Hamlet's motives behind conventions. The boy's dream is preceded by what the screenplay describes with the statements, "The earth spins calmly on its axis. All is well in the world."[47] But the turning globe is also a generic marker, the famous logo of Universal Studios associated with the first great generation of horror films in the 1930s, and the fade-in to the next shot reads as a second beginning for the film, producing a film within the film within the film. The Universal logo is rendered less recognizable by being a model of childish crudeness and a mirror-image reversal of the spinning earth and thus, as well, a poor imitation of the Denmark Corporation logo. The spiral vortex at the (possible) end of the dream is, as the cinephiles Hamlet and Almereyda well know and Gertrude may have been reminded by the playbill, another image associated with the horror and thriller genres. As Hamlet is provoking Claudius by implicitly labeling him a "Universal Horror" monster, the generic references also disguise the poison plot as but one more convention included with apparently unintended "mischief" (3.2.130).

Intercut reaction shots reveal the success of this mischief with utmost economy. The early family scenes are watched with rapt attention by the full audience: four carefully arrayed couples in the audience are drawn into the universal, "Universal" oedipal story. Claudius and Gertrude are isolated as a couple distressed by the image of poison, suggesting murderous complicity. This suggestion is undercut when only Claudius in close-up responds with alarm to the more specific image of poisoning by ear. Gertrude is not viewed alone in close-up until following shot 26, which is footage from the pornographic film *Deep Throat* (1972). Because *Deep Throat* is strongly associated with the Times Square neighborhood, having premiered there to tremendous controversy and legal challenge at the, yes, World Theatre, might one not conclude that Hamlet is exposing the sordid latent content of the Denmark Corporation's manifest product, even perhaps of the very film Gertrude has just watched with Claudius at the celebratory "premiere?"[48] The clip, which features not the star, Linda Lovelace, but an obscure actress resembling Diane Venora, flusters her severely. One now might conclude that her guilt involves infidelity rather than violence. Her outrage at Hamlet's implicit charge of lust and promiscuity is visible, but this can also be read as disgust at her son's brazenly displayed primal scene fantasy. Claudius next responds to the self-crowning of shots 28–29, during which Tchaikovsky's symphonic poem is replaced by triumphal music from the ending of the horror film *La Maldición de la Llorona*, in which the evil characters are destroyed. He rises in alarm as Hamlet, having displayed the method of fratricide, now displays the motive.

The Third Movement

Shakespeare's Hamlet is in no hurry to exploit the Mousetrap's confirmation of his uncle's guilt. He banters with Horatio, orders music, teaches Rosencrantz and Guildenstern that they cannot pluck out the heart of his mystery, schools Polonius on the shapes of clouds, and finally promises to visit his afflicted mother "by and by" (3.2.376). In contrast, Almereyda's Hamlet instantly displays action film urgency, very effectively marking progress into the third movement. He tucks his pistol into his trousers and hurries into the street in a murderous frenzy well labeled by the neon "Mania" market sign in front of which he hails a cab. But his attempted change of generic role is immediately frustrated. Following quickly, Rosencrantz and Guildenstern squeeze him into the middle of the taxi, revealing to Hamlet for the first time their treachery. Adding insult to injury, Eartha Kitt comically intrudes with a recorded seatbelt reminder that long annoyed New York cab passengers. All will understand that the aspiring action hero does not wish to be told that cats have nine lives while he has but one. Others will appreciate the allusion to Kitt's role as Catwoman on the 1960s *Batman* television series. Eager to defeat evil on the streets of Gotham City, the would-be hero has first to listen to Batman's seductive adversary preach and growl.

Despite such comic resistance, we next see Hamlet, having somehow escaped his "friends," planning his violence in front of Hotel Elsinore. His mania now finds external reflection in steam rising from the street and Nick Cave's goth-rock song "Hamlet (Pow-Pow-Pow)." Taking the place of the limousine driver, Hamlet overhears the king planning to send him to England and meditating in anguish upon the rank offense of his fratricide. Claudius speaks aloud through the point of his recalling "those effects for which I did the murder, / My crown, mine own ambition, and my queen" (3.3.54–55), at which Hamlet raises his gun. But now the resistance to Hamlet's becoming Ashe Corven is internal. For reasons left unspecified, he cannot bring himself to shoot. Claudius's apparent repentance is eliminated as a factor, for his line "Try what repentance can—what can it not?" (65) occurs in voice-over. Almereyda cuts Hamlet's entire "Now might I do it pat" (73) speech, eliminating Hamlet's preference, abhorrent to so many through the centuries, to slay the king in a moment with "no relish of salvation in't" (92). What we are left with is consistent with Ethan Hawke's description: "Hamlet is decisive, he just also happens to be a thoughtful and decent human being who doesn't take lightly the thought of killing another human being."[49] He is not an instinctive action hero.

The film adds complexity to the scene through point of view. The play presents first Claudius's private moment alone on stage, then Hamlet's response while he theatrically "eavesdrops" on the silently praying king. In the film, Hamlet similarly eavesdrops within the car, but he is allowed to hear all of the king's lines except for the single voice-over expressing faith in the power of repentance. While we watch and listen to Claudius, we also watch Hamlet's reactions, affording us two points of view simultaneously rather than sequentially. Thus, as in the Mousetrap, responses can be tied to particular moments. The screenplay, for example, specifies that Hamlet swerves to avoid a car, tossing Claudius about, but the film also implies that the swerve is Hamlet's reaction to Claudius's phrase "primal eldest curse" (37). Hamlet's two aggressive actions in the driver's seat are in this way linked to his father's murder and his mother's marriage. Claudius's mental state is also imaged in the television screen visible to Claudius but not to Hamlet. The king channel surfs from an advertisement reading "Stop living paycheck to paycheck!" to an animation of a skeleton sipping coffee over the morning newspaper to Bill Clinton's state of the union address delivered in the midst of the impeachment process to, finally (with the royal hand across the screen), a documentary image of a mountain accompanied by cryptic captions.[50] What these images convey will vary across the audience gamut, but most filmgoers would surely perceive their common theme of precariousness: of poverty, death, removal from power, isolation. We share these bleak images with Claudius. Our resulting empathy may then be applied to interpret Hamlet's otherwise mysterious retreat from vengeance.

Hamlet exits the car, tucking his gun in his pants as he did in exiting the screening room, bringing his attempt at action to a close. Having entered the taxicab at the Mania market to the growls of Catwoman, he leaves the limousine at a theatrical marquee announcing the "best musical of the year" and the "1998 Tony Award." An illuminated image of Mickey Mouse adjoins this display. Almereyda is marking Hamlet's return from the action world with an allusion to *The Lion King*, the title his camera carefully declines to bring into view. Hamlet's failure of nerve occurs in front of the famous New Amsterdam Theatre, where Julie Taymor is bringing Disney's version of the *Hamlet* story to Broadway, transforming a Shakespeare-derived animated film into musical drama.[51] Perhaps Hamlet senses the uncanny presence of his own story in the musical despite its translation to the African savanna.

For those acquainted with the history of the Disney Corporation, the emergence of the new "king and CEO" from his spiritual crisis at the venue of *The Lion King* will uncannily bring to mind Michael Eisner, the Disney chairman and CEO who was much in the news for his ruthless consolidation of power following the death of the previous CEO. Eisner is credited with turning Disney into a vast multimedia conglomerate, for expanding its hotel holdings, for personally guiding Disney's entry into Times Square with the renovation of the New Amsterdam, and for maneuvering to avoid a late 1990s hostile takeover by rising Internet-based companies.[52] Claudius reenters the Manhattan night pulling on his overcoat and looking bewildered. But the low camera angle, reminiscent of the Park Avenue power shots, expresses his rapid recovery. As if he is reminded of Eisner's lifting of Disney's fortunes, a glance upward at the vast half-acre display of financial information streaming across the three levels of the Morgan Stanley sign, a sign that we might recall from the film's opening shot, literally reorients him: he turns ninety degrees to align himself with the sign's dramatic diagonal and walks determinedly off in the direction from which the glowing data flows. One can predict that there will be no more self-doubt for the king and CEO of Denmark Corporation.[53]

The screenplay deletes Gertrude's request, delivered by both Rosencrantz and Polonius, that Hamlet visit her in her closet. As a result, Hamlet's visit must be seen as, in some way, a result of his failure to shoot Claudius, which is his immediate goal after the Mousetrap. Also deleted is the first half of 3.4.1, "A will come straight," which suggests that Polonius in advising the queen to "lay home to him" is not preparing her for an imminent interview but rather offering general counsel to a mother afflicted by her child's "pranks" (2). These deletions enhance the violence of the prince's arrival, at which startled Polonius must look around for a place to hide; Almereyda has revised Zeffirelli's revisionary removal of Polonius's plan to eavesdrop. Hamlet knocks violently, rings the doorbell a dozen times (Is it midnight?), shouts "mother" with unrepressed anger, and knocks anew with sufficient force to shake the door. We can only expect another attempt to execute an action plot after his previous failure.

After recalling Zeffirelli's scene by having Gertrude violently slap her son, Almereyda has Hamlet cruelly press Gertrude's face onto the mirrored closet door in an unmistakable allusion to his treatment of Ophelia in Branagh's nunnery scene. This remarkable allusion transports those who have seen Branagh's film into Hamlet's mind. When we recall to the mind's eye the unforgettable image of a terrified Claudius facing Hamlet's dagger behind Branagh's two-way mirror, we are seeing what the present Hamlet consciously imagines when he finally brings himself to fire his gun. Moreover, when we overlay Branagh's image of Ophelia pressed against the mirror onto Almereyda's Gertrude, we experience Hamlet's unconscious fusion of the two women. Does this not help to explain why Hamlet can finally pull the trigger after his recent failures? The film's first attempted murder failed only because Claudius was not in his office. It culminated a sequence, unified by continuous music, that began with Polonius disrupting Hamlet's passionate meeting with Ophelia in her apartment. Unable to shoot Claudius to avenge his father or to indulge a simple oedipal antagonism, Hamlet can work himself up to murder only when Ophelia is added to the oedipal scenario. Ophelia's uncanny presence here is consistent with Almereyda's use of her scenes to end his film's first and third movements.

The motif of the mirror, resonant throughout the film and much commented on in the criticism, develops in this scene an astonishing range of meanings. Hamlet first succeeds as an action hero when his bullet shatters the mirror and penetrates the right eye of Polonius. The shattered mirror, of course, is a well-known Shakespearean trope, most famously in *Richard II*, where the mirror's shattering indicates the king's recognition of his fall. Almereyda develops this idea with a complexity answerable to Hamlet's knottier psychology, in which murder and suicide are never far apart. In the first attempted-murder sequence, Hamlet rushed from Ophelia's apartment to replay his suicidal "To be or not to be" line on his self-mirroring video before directing his violence outward in the mirrored headquarters of Denmark Corporation. A set of related actions occurs in the closet scene, but in reverse order. After the shooting, Hamlet points his pistol, the same pistol he pointed at himself in the recording, at his own image in the fractured mirror. When he asks, "Is it the king?" the film layers new meaning onto the play-text, for if Hamlet has murdered Claudius, then the mirror toward which he points his gun reflects the new king. Hamlet cannot escape the psychodynamics of revenge, which requires identification with the aggressor for its repetitious, magical undoing of an offense.

Polonius tumbles out, his hand over his bloody eye socket. This image, too, links with others in the film, continuing a theme of upwardly displaced castration: Old Hamlet covered his intrusive son's lens; Ophelia covered her eyes in her fantasy of drowning to escape her father's phallocentric oppression; Hamlet's "rogue and peasant slave" soliloquy was haunted by the image of the eyeless woman covering her disfigurement. Hamlet momentarily experiences closure of this sequence through eye-for-an-eye revenge and oedipal supremacy, until he learns that "it" was not and therefore is not the king on either side of the mirror.

When Hamlet offers to wring his mother's heart, she asks simply, "What have I done?" (3.4.37). The dialogue leaps over twenty-eight missing Shakespearean lines to make Hamlet's answer the question, "Have you eyes?" (65), which is notably not occasioned here by a comparison of the image of her two husbands. To use the visual terms of Hamlet's latent content archive, his unconscious desire is to transform his mother from the lovely-eyed woman exchanging glances with the mesmerist into the eyeless woman, La Llorona. This desire issues in his wild struggle with Gertrude on the bed. The struggle ends, of course, with the return of the ghost. But unique to this version is the extent to which erotic conflict has become a contest for phallic dominance displaced upward to the eye. "Do not look upon me," Shakespeare's Hamlet pleads with the ghost, "Lest with this piteous action you convert / My stern effects" (123–25). Disturbed by the visual dominance of his father's gaze rather than by its softening effect, this film's Hamlet for the only time raises his voice to his father, shouting an angry "Do not look upon me" as the oedipal contest continues. The contrast with Branagh's teary-eyed Hamlet, overwhelmed at this moment with tenderness and grief, could not be starker.

The extensive textual cuts make Hamlet's quarrel with his mother briefer than usual and reconciliation quicker. Renewed intimacy and understanding between mother and son are marked by the return of Burwell's longing theme. The music links the part of the scene where Hamlet is with his mother to its final two minutes, when they are apart. Hamlet is next seen dragging the body in a locker-lined basement. When he bumps into a pay phone, he pauses to call his mother, reinforcing a parallel between her and the only other woman he phones. Against this similarity stand out contrasts in both content and form. To Ophelia he rants madly and repeatedly from the past via an answering machine. With his mother, he converses calmly, with intercutting between locations. Cut from the text are Shakespeare's mocking insults and implicit threat following "One word more, good lady" (178). As a result, Gertrude's reply, "I have no life to breathe / What thou has said to me" (196–97), delivered through her tears, is less an effort of self-defense than a declaration of maternal love. Even after he hangs up, Hamlet holds her present in his mind, addressing his final "Goodnight, mother" (215) to the empty hallway.

A cut to an extreme close-up of Hamlet's left eye begins yet another delayed disclosure. We do not see where he is or what he is doing. What we do see is a shot that echoes the end of the "rogue and peasant slave" soliloquy, which faded out upon Hamlet's right eye. Together, the complementary shots punctuate Hamlet's bold foray into dangerous provocation and attempted revenge. This foray has achieved success in the competition for his mother's affection and loyalty, but it has otherwise been disastrous. The next cut reveals a surprising context. The royal prince sits alone in a forlorn Laundromat, staring blankly into the dryer containing the shirt that had been soaked with Polonius's blood. If the previous scene's allusion to Branagh's Hamlet underlined his attempt to match that version's swashbuckling heroism, a new allusion underlines his failure. The glass dryer doors form a row of mirrors on each side of the Laundromat, the floor of which is tiled in checkerboard black and white. If the setting seems strangely familiar, indeed it should, for it recalls Branagh's magnificent tile-floored, mirror-lined State Hall. The contrast between the settings measures how poorly Hamlet has fared.

So too does the behavior of Hamlet's former friends, once they have located him. Rosencrantz and Guildenstern, shedding all pretense of amity, reveal themselves to be eager agents of the king. The king in turn reveals the depth of his antipathy. Attempting to escape, Hamlet is thrown violently up against the row of dryers by the king's henchmen. Now Hamlet becomes the victim rather than the perpetrator of cruelty against the mirrored surface. When his mad discourse waxes too insulting, he is struck ferociously by Claudius, who has assumed the role of a ruthless film gangster. The king's brutality is magnified through a trick of (almost) invisible editing. The blow that doubles Hamlet over is repeated after a small fraction of second from a slightly closer camera placement, lengthening his painful response and bringing it nearer to our pained perspective. That Claudius can quickly reassume an air of benevolence as Hamlet's "loving father" (4.3.48) after such violence makes him even more sinister. Nevertheless, Hamlet kisses him on the lips while calling him "my mother" (50), adding another parallel to Branagh's version.

Hamlet's embrace of his drunken mother at the airport while Claudius hopes out loud for "The present death of Hamlet" (63) is followed by the close-up of a handheld postcard of an airplane flying into the sunset. When the still-unidentified holder leafs through additional postcards, one is reminded of the delayed disclosures of Ophelia's snapshot of young Hamlet and Gertrude's handling of the playbill. Now in question is not only the holder's identity but also the meaning of the images. The second and third postcards, reproducing an oil painting of a nude woman and an ancient sculpted head of a man, suggest a family romance scenario and the possibility of (re)interpreting the first postcard as a sexual metaphor, a Freudian flying dream that aeronautically updates the speeding train as a "stock symbol of sexuality in the Hollywood cinema."[54] The familiar music adds further complications. It is the sensual track (Damian O'Neill's "Moon Tide") from Hamlet's visit to Ophelia's apartment. With a cut to Hamlet looking down and another to Rosencrantz and Guildenstern in airline seats, some of the mystery subsides. The music fades slightly to allow some ambient sound (notably, Rosencrantz's mindless munching on his free peanuts) and disappears when Hamlet removes his headphones, revealing its diegetic nature in a way that is reminiscent of the Laertes-Ophelia interview. We have been within Hamlet's subjectivity, remembering with him a rare and brief moment of happiness while sharing his private world of sexually charged imagery.

As usual in this adaptation, echoes from within the film and recognition of specific allusions produce additional meaning. While sharing Hamlet's gaze upon Watteau's eighteenth-century reclining nude, it is hard not to think of two women: Ophelia, evoked by the music and matched by the woman's youth and the "love-sickness" theme of the painting; and Gertrude, whose face was the camera's focus a mere second earlier, after she rejoined Claudius in the limo at the airport, and whom Hamlet recently threw down in a similar diagonal position on the "enseamed bed" (3.4.90). Looking at Senusret III, perhaps the most individualized face in ancient Egyptian art, does Hamlet, in addition to completing the familial pairing, find significance in the missing nose?[55] He would surely see in the pharaoh's famously heavy lids and deep-set quartzite eyes a resemblance to the eyeless woman compulsively imaged on his monitor.

This depth-psychological turbulence will soon lead to Hamlet's final soliloquy, when he exclaims, "How all occasions do inform against me, / And spur my dull revenge" (4.4.31–32). The airliner sequence offers a surprising series of provocative "occasions." Upon the oedipal reverie so symptomatic of Hamlet's brooding inaction intrudes the contrasting image of Fortinbras, first on the cover of the *Wired* magazine read by Guildenstern, to which Hamlet turns after gazing at Senusret. Despite his defeat in the attempted corporate takeover, Hamlet's rival for the succession is the featured interviewee in this trendy publication, which declares him to be "moving into the new millennium." Fortinbras is enigmatic, as suggestive as he is elusive. On the magazine cover, he holds his left hand over his eye, recalling but mirror-reversing Polonius's response to the gunshot, and through the reversal prominently displaying a ring, coupling his media success with implied erotic satisfaction.[56] Hamlet cannot help but be provoked by the image.

When Hamlet turns away, the inescapable Fortinbras again appears, now on the in-flight television tuned to a news network. He speaks and gestures with confident authority about something we cannot identify, conspicuously fondling his ring. Between his silent talking-head performances, which are powerful public contrasts to Hamlet's private video diary, we see an enigmatic act of violence: Fortinbras shoots an approaching metallic android with a powerful handgun in a neon-lit setting that suggests Times Square. My students have regularly interpreted this image as an attack on C3PO from the *Star Wars* films. This could represent either Fortinbras's success within the action world of Lucasfilms or, more likely, a more successful attack on it than Hamlet's Conneresque experimentalism. It could also be an allusion to the model for the *Star Wars* android, the counterfeit Maria of Fritz Lang's *Metropolis*. She appears in the collection of figures in *The Uncanny* on Horatio's bookshelf.[57] She is a villain in one of Lang's "big budget spectacles," the type of movie that Almereyda while filming *Hamlet* recalled that he had "mad dreams" of directing when he entered filmmaking.[58] In the violent destruction of either a good male or an evil female robot (figures from blockbusters of the 1920s or late twentieth century), strong-armed Fortinbras is being true to his name.

In the play, Hamlet's soliloquy is spurred explicitly by the idea of thousands dying in a military quest for honor over worthless land, if implicitly as well by frustrations plaguing other parts of the character's complicated psyche. Shedding the military context helps the film concentrate on the latter. Using language with vagueness and plurality appropriate to the images, from which one concludes that Fortinbras has everything Hamlet lacks, he asks a uniformed man, "Good sir, whose powers are these?" (4.4.9). Rising and beginning his soliloquy, Hamlet walks slowly down the aisle, his imprisoned state heightened by closed windows throughout the cabin and a camera that tracks his motion through the narrow space between the overhead luggage bins. His movement launches from the example of Fortinbras, the aspired-to future implied in the "large discourse, / Looking before and after" (35–36); increasingly encounters reflections of his own powerlessness in the passengers dozing in "bestial oblivion" (39); and finally halts at the ultimate past (looking "after" temporally but "before" spatially), an infant sporting a version of Hamlet's knit cap. As all others in the rear of the cabin sleep and dream, Hamlet has an oneiric, regressive encounter with his infantile double. They hold extended eye contact, as if they recognize each other.

A remarkable web of similarity and difference reaches back to the three major earlier soliloquies. The "too solid flesh" and the "rogue and peasant slave" speeches were linked by identical music, the latter scene using this sameness to help mark Hamlet's small progress through his more complex and active manipulation of video images. The final soliloquy employs music that is very close to the previous composition but discernibly different, suggesting both continuity and something new. "How all occasions" recalls the Blockbuster portion of the "to be" soliloquy through Hamlet's strolling down an aisle looking at evidence on either side and through his use of Olivier's mixed speech, which again progresses from voice-over to mouthed speech. But unlike the video store sequence, this stroll does not return him to where he began. By aborting the screenplay's plan to have Hamlet "slowly retracing his steps down the aisle," the film allows Hamlet's linear trajectory to contrast with his earlier fruitless circle.[59]

The mixed speech also develops into something new. Following the encounter with his infantile double, we next see him confronting his own image in the restroom mirror, one eye-to-eye interchange replaced by another. In the first, brief installment of "to be" at his desk, it was a past self from the video diary that spoke, even as the present self was also visible through reflection on the screen. Now, after a ritualistic washing of his face, Hamlet continues his mouthed speech to his present image, confronting himself directly in this way for the first and only time in the film. Or, one could say, since camera placement allows the reflection instead of the original to be seen speaking, Hamlet finds in his present self the authority he previously assigned to the diary's past speaker who addressed him and who, appropriately, from this point no longer appears in the film. The final soliloquy, which concludes with Hamlet resolving, "from this time forth / My thoughts be bloody or be nothing worth" (64–65), expresses the most important transition in Hamlet's psychology for the plot of both play and film, from irresolution to resolution, inaction to action, self-division to integration. Almereyda has found impressive audiovisual means for conveying this transition.

While Hamlet is developing resolution and a more unified self in the film's most confined private space, Ophelia is losing the last remnant of her sanity in a vast public space. Over Burwell's resounding percussive crescendo, a cut from the airplane restroom to the film's most spectacular setting reveals Ophelia twirling along the handrail as she spirals up the ramp of the Guggenheim Museum. The spiral shape has portended psychic breakdown in the film, but the museum setting seems at first to resist this implication. The king and queen are at the height of recovered glory, presiding over a high-society event from the gallery's upper levels. On the levels below cluster the well-dressed guests, conversing softly over barely heard chamber music. Shakespeare presents the two intrusions of act 4, scene 5 as political threats: Ophelia's generating "Dangerous conjectures in ill-breeding minds" (15) and Laertes' leading the rabble in open revolt. Because the film's corporate setting is not logically compatible with such perils, Almereyda transforms political danger into the threat of public embarrassment.

As in the Zeffirelli version, Ophelia's madness is used to distinguish between the disintegration of Gertrude and the resilient mastery of Claudius. The low sound level is first broken by Gertrude's raucous laughter, which resonates uncomfortably against the sight of Ophelia's anguish. As Gertrude delivers her "sick soul" soliloquy in voice-over, an attendant's whispered news of Ophelia's arrival interrupts her smiling social face only momentarily. When Ophelia confronts her, Gertrude pays her as little heed as possible, glancing around instead to determine the guests' reactions. This disregard turns Ophelia's "Pray you mark" (4.5.35) into a shrieking cry for attention. In contrast, Claudius at the bodyguard's whispered news immediately descends the ramp and inquires, "How do you, pretty lady?" (41). Granted, his more sensitive intervention is ultimately ineffective, because Ophelia answers with a bloodcurdling scream directed into the museum's echoing rotunda, which rivets the crowd's attention and terminates the music. But masterful Claudius responds by covering Ophelia's mouth and handing her off efficiently to the bodyguard, who carries her to privacy, while Gertrude looks ridiculous trying to reassure the crowd with a forced smile.

The play's leisurely pace allows Claudius to reflect on his vicissitudes, observing, "When sorrows come they come not single spies / But in battalions" (78–79). The film translates this verbal reflection on onrushing events into abrupt pacing. As soon as Ophelia is silenced, Laertes bursts onto the scene. He has taken the elevator to the top, knowing where to find the object of his wrath, rather than winding tortuously upward; one notes that he also follows the normal traffic plan of the Guggenheim, which assumes a descending walk through the gallery. He drops his luggage at the elevator doors and is immediately "charging straight at them."[60] Despite the difference in movement patterns, like his sister Laertes shows uncontrolled passion and poses the threat of public scandal. The angry words that accompany his manhandling of the king draw inquiring glances from the partygoers below.

Shakespeare's Claudius halts Laertes' impetuous advance by invoking Elizabethan royalist ideology and "treason" (124), its most fearsomely punished violation. To calm Gertrude, Claudius the CEO states, "There's such divinity doth hedge a king" (123), but without real ideological support he must confront Laertes' rage with shrewdness and courage. When Laertes grabs Claudius and tosses him away from the rotunda handrail, the king turns his motion to advantage. The next shot finds him briskly leading Laertes into a private room, removing the threat of public shaming. Laertes seizes Claudius by the throat, at which the king's near-smile and sustained eye contact, while asking "Who shall stay you?" (135), effectively stays him. Claudius converts Laertes' violence into a more ambiguous physical exchange by placing his own hands affectionately on the young man's neck and speaking like a proud father to a "good child and a true gentleman" (147). When he claims that his innocence will appear to Laertes' judgment "As day doth to your eye" (151, modified), he turns his head to his left, as if presenting the sight that will persuade. On cue, there stands Ophelia, weeping and tossing snapshots to the ground.

In the play, the ambiguity of Ophelia's mad verses balances the loss of her father and of her beloved as the twin causes of insanity, belying the self-serving claim of Claudius that "It springs / All from her father's death" (75–76). The film's spoken "songs" retain both causes, but Hamlet's "death" to Ophelia is given more weight through filmic resources. Her loudest scream, which in effect replaces the first half of her Saint Valentine song, is shot to echo her imaginary drowning scene, the low angle and horizontal railing recalling the view from the underwater camera. She imagined jumping when Polonius reported his forbidding her relationship with Hamlet: "This must not be" (2.2.139). Her scream now opposes the pointedly silent non-expression of her earlier outrage. The snapshots that Ophelia distributes recall the one she contemplated after Hamlet's missed appointment and those she burned in the nunnery scene after her brutal rejection. She passes them out accompanied by an achingly mournful acoustic guitar version of Burwell's Ophelia theme, first heard when Hamlet failed to show up at the waterfall—the same waterfall where we will soon see her drowned.

Act 4, scene 5 ends with Claudius proclaiming, "where th'offence is, let the great axe fall" (210). In the play, this is overtly the king's promise to sacrifice himself to Laertes' revenge should he be found guilty "by direct or by collateral hand" (198). Buried within this primary meaning is the dramatic irony of Claudius's resolve to have Hamlet executed, known to the audience from his "Do it, England" (4.3.63) soliloquy but unknown to the other characters. The film Claudius introduces the next scene by speaking the "great axe" line to himself while standing before the cracked mirror through which Polonius was killed. The line now applies only to Hamlet, and we quickly deduce that in viewing himself in Polonius's place (and Hamlet's place, enacting the identification with the aggressor that enables revenge), Claudius is steeling himself to begin plotting with Laertes. When Laertes arrives with the bodyguard and the three men move into a room where they cannot be overheard by a visibly suspicious Gertrude, Claudius immediately hands Laertes Hamlet's pistol, hoping to facilitate the young man's vow that his "revenge will come" (4.7.30). Although the play posits that Claudius is expecting to hear of Hamlet's death in England, the film's modern setting makes the viewer assume that Claudius already knows that the Rosencrantz and Guildenstern plot has failed. The fax that arrives from Hamlet does not surprise Claudius with the fact of Hamlet's being alive, as it does in the play. Assigned either a question mark or an exclamation point in modern editions, "From Hamlet?" (38) already in the screenplay is assigned a period.

Once the men have agreed to their deadly plan, Gertrude arrives to announce Ophelia's death, just missing a glimpse of the weapon. Laertes responds with the simple question, "Drowned?" (163), but he does not ask, "O, where?" even though for the film this question, of dubious interest in the play, is crucial. Gertrude's postnarration line "Drowned, drowned" (182) is split between the present of speech and the past of the drowning, with the comma accompanied by brilliantly effective cinematic punctuation. After the screen goes black, a tracking camera creates the film's second false wipe, revealing Ophelia far below, face down in the pool at the waterfall. The high camera and curving concrete repeat a graphic composition from the Guggenheim Museum, contrasting the pathetic movements of Ophelia in the gallery with equally pathetic stasis. Both the location and the false wipe, along with the fullest orchestral version of Burwell's Ophelia theme, recall her earlier frustration at the waterfall. When the spiral-decorated box and Hamlet's floating love letters dissolve into view, her entire relationship with Hamlet is visually evoked as the cause of her madness and death with remarkable poignancy and economy. The screen goes black again to complete the funereal frame. Perhaps we will recall that it first went black after we first saw her at the waterfall.

The Fourth Movement

Following the report of Ophelia's death, Shakespeare begins the fifth act with a radical shift in tone. The comic verbosity of the two long stretches of pseudo-scholastic quibbling has long offended neoclassical purists, including most notoriously Voltaire, who eliminated this material entirely. Almereyda's film, though not his original screenplay, similarly cuts these interchanges. His explanation suggests both typical woes of low-budget production and a shrewd filmmaker's intuition that film, or at least this type of film adaptation, is better served by Voltairian strictures of tonal consistency: "The scene seemed to fly. But in the editing room it became clear that I'd failed to get it right. The tone and timing were off, and the whole episode seemed to sidetrack Hamlet's response to Ophelia's death. The movie worked better with the prized scene cut out."[61] Because Shakespeare's Hamlet assumes Ophelia is alive, his badinage is acceptable, if painful. It is not acceptable when modern communications imply that Hamlet knows, since Horatio has arranged to meet him at the airport and transport him to the cemetery. Implied knowledge of his lover's death combines with the example of Fortinbras to reinforce the sense of a new filmic movement beginning. Again, Ophelia must be added to the equation to move Hamlet to violence.

Almereyda replaces Shakespeare's tonal shift into comic relief with a shift in generic signals, to a world that combines impending tragedy and action film's freedom of movement. The numbed expression on Hamlet's face as he exits the airport, Horatio's sad demeanor, and the dirgelike drone music ("Greentone" by Acceleradeck), which will be used again over the film credits following the multiple deaths, orient the audience for a different approach to the graveyard scene. Hamlet's narrative moves from talking to himself in the restroom to the film's final and visually most complex use of the mirror image. The passage through sliding reflective glass doors at the airport momentarily confuses inside and outside, entering and exiting, as Hamlet returns to freedom in the prison of Denmark. Passage through the mirror, effortless and wordless as befits an action hero, is followed by a vertiginous sequence featuring a landing aircraft and a transit vehicle that speeds out of the plane's trajectory. In the bright autumn sunshine, both the camera and its objects indulge a new freedom and fluidity after the claustrophobia of the airliner and the rigid curves of the Guggenheim. As Alexander Leggatt observes, "As they leave the airport we see wide open space for the first time."[62] Appropriately, Horatio and Hamlet take to the open road on a motorcycle, the preferred vehicle of Ashe Corven and his generic kindred.

The graveyard scene is brief and perfunctory, reduced from almost three hundred lines of dialogue to twenty-six, plus a few verses of Bob Dylan's "All Along the Watchtower" sung by the gravedigger. Reversing tradition, Hamlet is more aggressive than Laertes, who fights only after much verbal and physical provocation. That may be the point, helping to show that Hamlet's resolve that his "thoughts be bloody" has supplanted his earlier physical timidity and preparing us for the later recounted and enacted violence. Neither man, however, displays much stomach for a sustained fight. Laertes, after all, is not Hamlet's enemy, and Laertes' function as a double of Hamlet is growing, soon to acquire a more interesting complexity. After tumbling down a hill with Hamlet, Laertes soon releases his grip on Hamlet's neck and rolls sobbing onto the leaf-strewn ground. Horatio's motorcycle revs in the background before Laertes arises.

A ride across the bridge into Manhattan brings the two young men to Horatio's apartment. Our first glimpse of its interior reveals the semitransparent ghost of Hamlet's father seated at the bedside of sleeping Marcella, "grave and sympathetic, as if sharing her troubled dream."[63] The ghost's prescience in knowing where his son will be, coupled with his evident sadness, sustains the atmosphere of impending tragedy. Its presence also occasions a brief instance of indirection. The ghost looks up toward the door upon hearing the men enter. A cut to his eye-line shows Horatio turning to look into the bedroom and then interrupting Hamlet with a hand gesture. Convention implies that the cut back to the bedroom, from Horatio's eye level, will reveal the ghost, but the ghost is no longer there: Horatio, it turns out, was calling attention not to the ghost but to his sleeping girlfriend, indicating that Hamlet should keep his voice down. Because the lesson Hamlet draws from his story of evading death in England is "There's a divinity that shapes our ends, / Rough-hew them how we will" (5.2.10–11), the suggestion is unavoidable that this ghost partakes somehow in this providential shaping behind the scenes, and part of his program now is to delay revealing himself until Hamlet can articulate this lesson and declare "Let be" (201–2). In contrast to their last hostile exchange of glances in the closet scene, the exchange between father and son that closes this scene bespeaks mutual understanding.

After recounting his in-flight altering of the death orders on a laptop computer, Hamlet heatedly proclaims the righteousness of his cause in response to the shocked Horatio's near-interrogative, "So Guildenstern and Rosencrantz go to't" (56). As Hamlet's justification turns into a defense of murdering the king, his raised voice—the change underlined by the music's disappearance—awakens Marcella, who enters the kitchen looking dismayed at the rapidly gathering tragic storm. Hamlet's threat to the king is quickly replaced by the king's threat to Hamlet in the form of the duel, news of which arrives by fax, creating a symmetry with the veiled threat in Hamlet's fax appropriate to the dynamics of revenge. Modern communications accelerate the plot's movement toward doom.

The transition to the duel involves changes of scene. Sandwiched between brief shots of Claudius in his apartment poisoning the wine (in a more realistic way than the usual onstage business) and a quick establishing shot of the Hotel Elsinore skyscraper, we watch a wordless Hamlet for forty-five seconds in his room. The sequence is pulled together as a unified transition through the music, which begins just before Hamlet declares "Let be" and proceeds until a cut reveals Hamlet apologizing to Laertes on the rooftop. The music is again from the memorable first movement of Brahms's First Symphony. It begins precisely where the first two uses of the symphony ended, developing a theme that terminated the music accompanying both the press conference and the movie premiere. Imitating the "A-A-B" pattern of Burwell's music in three soliloquies, which traced Hamlet's progress, the musical cue links the film's ending to its beginning through a kind of harmonic inevitability. As the press conference finds a visual echo in the duel scene, so too do Hamlet's early anguish and alienation proceed toward death, as Hamlet has come to understand would happen with tragic inevitability.

The longest scene of the transition conveys this understanding visually as well. The camera tracks in slowly toward Hamlet standing before his collage wall, removing pictures as if he were packing for a journey to the undiscovered country. Into view come two previously unseen photos, of Che Guevara and Malcolm X, widely familiar images that remind us of the film's countercultural subtext and support the sense of impending doom. A cut to Hamlet's point of view very briefly reveals the wall's second photo of Mayakovsky, carrying much the same message, though to a more restricted audience. Indeed, the same message issues as well from the large photo adjoining Mayakovksy's. The portrait of Jean Vigo and his wife, Lydou, which remains on-screen after Mayakovsky's is removed, has enjoyed a privileged status on the collage wall through its size and central location between Hamlet's monitors. An image for the full audience of the marital happiness denied to Hamlet and Ophelia, it is also for the cinephile an image of doom, for the young filmmaker was dead within a year of the photograph, taken at the start of filming *L'Atalante* (1934), his only feature film.[64] Blurring the boundaries of life and art, the couple stands in the village street through which the film's newlyweds pass in the opening sequence, with Lydou holding the comically enormous bouquet of wildflowers gathered for the bride. A trick of editing continues the blurring of boundaries begun by the photo. A cut to a reaction shot implies that Hamlet is gazing at the picture intently. Another cut to his point of view reveals him taking down two photographs of Ophelia, which a final reaction shot shows him gazing at intently as well. A complex act of identification is occurring that may be beyond pinning down. Hamlet contemplates his beloved Ophelia. Hamlet contemplates Vigo, or identifies with Vigo and contrasts the present Lydou with the absent Ophelia. Almereyda's representative within the film contemplates the son of the man after whom he named himself. The sequence is provocative, moving, entangled in the confusions of love and identification. Perhaps its very strangeness is its point, and we should recall Hamlet's outrage at the attempt to pluck out the heart of his mystery.

We are not allowed to ponder this mystery for long, for Hamlet's gaze upon his dead beloved is soon interrupted by the appearance of Horatio at the doorway. A dramatic rack focus, a device used minimally and unobtrusively until now, draws us and Hamlet together out of our deepest reverie toward the solemn young man who will lead us back into the plot. The friends exit toward the impending tragic conclusion. On the threshold, Hamlet glances backward and then turns out the light.

As a result of disruptions in filming atop a midtown skyscraper and the inability to reshoot because financing and actors were not available, as in

Branagh's film the duel is the most disappointing scene in the film.[65] That said, there is much to admire in the finished product. As in previous *Hamlet* films, the duel scene is the longest in duration and contains the largest number of shots. This remains true even though the screenplay reduced Shakespeare's lines from 198 to 98 and subsequent parings removed 45 more. As we have seen in previous chapters, film's inherent ability to portray the physical action implied between Shakespeare's words, which are relatively sparse here to begin with, has tempted directors to draw out the scene with lengthy swordplay. That is not Almereyda's approach. The editing pace is relatively rapid (exactly twice the pace of the scene in Horatio's apartment, for example) but concentrates less on action than on reaction and on the evolving relationship between the two young men entwined by fate. The fight is a public event held, like the press conference, in front of a seated court and standing photographers, but it is also, strangely, a "personal and familial" conflict occurring atop the familial hotel and filmed mostly through much closer shots than are used for the duel in previous films.[66]

In the play, Hamlet's apology to Laertes, prompted by the king's joining of hands, is not much of an apology at all, since he untruthfully blames not himself but his madness for the death of Polonius. The film eliminates this specious denial. The sincerity evident in Hawke's face and voice are supported by camera placement, which sets him farther below his "brother" (5.2.221) Laertes than the difference in height between the actors would indicate, a submissive or supplicational configuration reflecting Hamlet's subjectivity. When Laertes stoically responds by stealing Hamlet's line "Give us the foils" (231), Hawke's facial expression bespeaks his disappointment as eloquently as Laertes' terse command bespeaks his determination. Laertes' rejection is accompanied by the camera's drawing back, which replaces the vertical corroboration of Hamlet's supplication with a horizontal relationship that will become formalized by the electronic fencing apparatus.

By now, the film has cut away twice to focus on the spectators' close observation of the fencers. The first shows Gertrude watching her son while Claudius slips away from the chair next to her. Her eyes follow her husband without a corresponding head movement, speaking volumes about her growing mistrust. She looks back to Hamlet to avoid Claudius's seeing her seeing him. Claudius turns to Laertes and grins conspiratorially, but when Laertes picks another sword and walks toward him Claudius is confused, as are we, and a little frightened. Has Laertes reinserted the poisoned sword backup plan that the screenplay removed? Is there some kind of identification between the two young men that is a danger to Claudius? Further cutaways from the fencers occur when Claudius asks about the wager and orders the wine, which is eyed warily by Gertrude. A camera glance at Horatio too, accompanied by Marcella and Bernardo, adds to the background of rising wariness. Additional cutaways show Claudius smoking nervously, then sitting down beside Gertrude, a close-up of Horatio, a close-up of Gertrude . . . and finally the fight begins.

As the pattern continues during the two fencing passes, the duelists' masks add to the deflection of interest onto the observers' emotions. When the masks come off after the second hit, and the distinction between performers and observers falls away, an effective balance is maintained between clarity of motivation and intriguing mystery. Gertrude's suspicions, which were visible in the scene of Laertes' visit, are solidified when Claudius is overly careful in placing the poisoned wine away from the rest. She knowingly saves Hamlet by killing herself, in the tradition of Olivier, but her drinking the wine also reminds us of the escapism evident in her drunken farewell at the airport, a scene echoed as well by Hamlet's initial coldness followed by his embrace. Is he suspicious about her eagerness for wine? Laertes is even more enigmatic. The screenplay's substitution of the gun for the poisoned sword facilitates the generic shift to action-hero associations and allows the duel to connect meaningfully with several earlier scenes, including both "to be" speeches, James Dean on Hamlet's television, and Fortinbras on the airline monitor, and to such external references as Mayakovsky and Kurt Cobain. It also allows the weapon that Hamlet aimed simultaneously at an imagined Claudius and his reflected self finally to realize both murderous and suicidal intentions. But it also eliminates Claudius's plan for an apparent "accident," making Laertes potentially as self-destructive as Hamlet. What is his motivation for shooting Hamlet, and for shooting him now, before the row of photographers who raise their cameras as he proceeds?

The straightforward answer that ignores complications is that he desperately responds to the failure of the poisoning scheme. But the substitution of the gun for the bated sword as a backup has made the issue problematic from the beginning. Laertes, played with a disturbing edge and inscrutability by Liev Schreiber, has been oddly complex: in his erotically charged scene with Ophelia, in ceding aggression to Hamlet at the cemetery but stealing his aggressive line before the duel, in frightening Claudius. Can another answer be seen in the exchange of glances between the opponents as Hamlet embraces his mother, a reminder that Laertes has no family left or that Claudius is the shared oedipal rival? Laertes more fully becomes Hamlet's double if his act too is both murderous and suicidal, and details suggest that the latter combines with the former. His grappling with Hamlet, gun drawn, before shooting is what causes his own death, while Hamlet shoots Claudius from a safe distance. In the film but not in the screenplay, after being shot Laertes emerges from the dancelike clench holding the gun, and he then gives it to Hamlet to kill Claudius. We do not actually see who shot whom and who shot first.

Before declaring that "the rest is silence" (342), Hamlet undertakes a final filmmaking project in his mind's eye, a silent recollection of all of the characters except Polonius for whose death he is in some way responsible. Converted into his private PixelVision medium, the outtakes from *Hamlet* form a series that is for the most part unchronological:

1. Ophelia with Hamlet
2. the ghost on Hamlet's balcony (end of visit)
3. Gertrude in her closet raising hands to her ears
4. Laertes attacked by Hamlet at the graveyard
5. Ophelia with Hamlet
6. the ghost in Hamlet's room (beginning of visit)
7. the Laundromat struggle, Claudius punching Hamlet
8. Ophelia with Hamlet, kissing

Hamlet's found footage includes both an examination of conscience and an act of repression. Gertrude appears at the point of Hamlet's greatest cruelty to her, silently mouthing "speak no more, Hamlet." He does not seek a moment of lost happiness, as in the video diary, but endures a moment that must prompt guilt and remorse. Laertes arrives in a similar moment, followed by the object of their quarrel, who is also a source of the two men's mutual identification. The ghost asserts his power over Hamlet's memory with a second appearance, renewing a competition with Ophelia for Hamlet's attention. Reversing polarity, Claudius enters as the bad father at his most vicious; he was last seen falling, imprinting his blood on the rooftop railing with his right hand, the hand now seen in violent motion. The memory adds a final satisfaction of talion symmetry and perhaps confirms the justice of Hamlet's action. Only the three appearances of Ophelia from the nunnery scene form a plot, the successful love story that life denied.[67] Seeking a final moment of happiness, Hamlet rewinds his memory to the point just before he discovered Ophelia's betrayal—and just before the cruelty that must produce his greatest remorse.

Ophelia's triple appearance in Hamlet's memory is followed by an appropriate symbolic image. Horatio's prayer that "flights of angels sing thee to thy rest" (344) becomes a vapor trail glowing in the evening sky as a jet descends the screen toward the equestrian statue of Victory leading Sherman. The image condenses two visual metaphors from the nunnery scene, punctuating the film in a way that strangely parallels Hamlet's final remembrance. Ophelia's unfortunate role in the scene was heralded ironically by gilt Victory glowing in sunlight. Hamlet's denial of his love ushered in the metaphoric vapor trail as a jet ascended the screen. Together, the two images from the nunnery scene and the full sculpture delineate a trajectory, not heroic but tragic, and Shermanesque in its destructiveness. But like Hamlet in his mental video, we can, if we prefer, suppress the irony and see in the sculpture two lovers together in the end.

Borrowing a device from Baz Luhrmann's *Romeo + Juliet*, the film ends with Robert MacNeil's newscast reporting and commenting on the bloody outcome. His speech borrows words from the new king Fortinbras, the Ambassador, and the Player King, but when the speech reappears scrolling up the teleprompter, it offers for our redoubled contemplation only the Player King's lines: "Our wills and fates do so contrary run / That our devices still are overthrown. / Our thoughts are ours, their ends none of our own" (3.2.205–7). The message is appropriate for a Hamlet whose expiring "video" is both realistic and escapist, both regretting unintended "ends" and desperately replacing ends with thoughts that Hamlet can keep his own. The message is no less appropriate for a *Hamlet* that uncannily finds new ends for the images it borrows and the images it creates.

Notes

Introduction

1. I am especially indebted to the many students who have studied with me over the years in a freshman dean's seminar devoted to *Hamlet* on film at The George Washington University. As later notes will suggest, the seminars were at times an invaluable laboratory for testing what is perceived by audiences on conscious and unconscious levels.

2. Alan Dent, "Text-Editing Shakespeare with Particular Reference to *Hamlet*," in *Hamlet: The Film and the Play*, ed. Alan Dent (London: World Film Publishers, 1948), 25.

3. Michael Almereyda, *William Shakespeare's* Hamlet: *A Screenplay Adaptation* (London: Faber and Faber, 2000), vii.

4. Thomas M. Leitch, "Twice-Told Tales: Disavowal and the Rhetoric of the Remake," in *Dead Ringers: The Remake in Theory and Practice*, ed. Jennifer Forrest and Leonard R. Koos (Albany: State University of New York Press, 1990), 45. Leitch uses the examples of Olivier, Richardson, and Zeffirelli *Hamlets* to describe not his highest classification, "true remakes," but his lowest: "[T]he remake ignores or treats as inconsequential" earlier cinematic adaptations. He is right enough about Richardson but not, as shown later in this volume, about Zeffirelli.

5. John A. Mills, *Hamlet on Stage: The Great Tradition* (Westport, CT: Greenwood Press, 1985), 198.

6. Olivier recalls the visit in his *On Acting* (London: Weidenfeld and Nicolson, 1986), 79.

7. Peter S. Donaldson, *Shakespearean Films/Shakespearean Directors* (Boston: Unwin Hyman, 1990), 35.

8. Terry Coleman, *Olivier* (New York: Henry Holt, 2005), 58.

9. Ibid., 80.

10. In his 1982 Arden edition note to the line, Harold Jenkins reviews the history of the emendation, which was popularized by John Dover Wilson. Mills, in *Hamlet on Stage*, 233–37, collects the available information on the Guthrie stage production. Because the latest Arden edition (2006, edited by Ann Thompson and Neil Taylor) is likely to prove the standard for scholars, quotations from *Hamlet* throughout this book cite this edition.

11. Coleman, *Olivier*, 84.

12. Jan Herman, *A Talent for Trouble: The Life of Hollywood's Most Acclaimed Director, William Wyler* (New York: G. P. Putnam, 1995), 197.

13. Coleman, *Olivier*, 147.

14. Olivier's film won four Academy Awards, including best picture. For the most comprehensive treatment of *Hamlet*'s film lineage, see Bernice Kliman, *Hamlet: Film, Television, and Audio Performance* (Rutherford, NJ: Fairleigh Dickinson University Press, 1988). Mention must be made of Grigory Kozintsev's *Gamlet* (1964), which is an inspired work of cinema. A self-conscious response to Olivier's psychological *Hamlet*, it restores the play's political dimension, but as a Russian-language work it is beyond the scope of this book and plays only a minor role in the evolving tradition that it traces, although both Almereyda and Branagh have commented on it admiringly. Oddly, Zeffirelli fails to mention Kozintsev in any of his writings and interviews.

15. Franco Zeffirelli, *Zeffirelli: The Autobiography* (New York: Weidenfeld and Nicolson, 1986), 15.

16. Franco Zeffirelli, *Zeffirelli: Autobiografia* (Milan: Mondadori, 2006), 89.

17. Zeffirelli, *Autobiography*, 201.

18. Ibid., 69.

19. Ibid., 200.

20. John C. Tibbetts, "Breaking the Classical Barrier: Franco Zeffirelli Interviewed by John Tibbetts," *Literature/Film Quarterly* 22 (1994): 139.

21. Zeffirelli, *Autobiografia*, 378, 387.

22. Kenneth Branagh, *Beginning* (New York: St. Martin's Press, 1989), 16–17.

23. Mark White, *Kenneth Branagh* (London: Faber and Faber, 2005), 137.

24. Kenneth Branagh, Hamlet *by William Shakespeare: Screenplay, Introduction and Film Diary* (London: Chatto and Windus, 1996), v.

25. White, *Kenneth Branagh*, 58–59.

26. Samuel Crowl, *The Films of Kenneth Branagh* (Westport, CT: Praeger, 2006), 129.

27. Mario Falsetto, *Personal Visions: Conversations with Contemporary Film Directors* (Los Angeles: Silman-James Press, 2000), 3–6.

28. Almereyda, *William Shakespeare's* Hamlet, viii.

29. Agee lost his father at age seven. Schiele and Mayakovsky lost theirs at fifteen. Biographers note the shaping trauma of these deaths. Dean lost his mother and was callously abandoned by his father at age nine. The fullest discussion of the "Almereyda affair" is in the opening chapter of P. E. Salles Gomes, *Jean Vigo* (London: Faber and Faber, 1998). Vigo's father invented the name as a scatological anagram, from "y a (de) la merde." Michael Almereyda's sister is the actress Spencer Kayden, whose surname is probably of Irish origin. If Almereyda's family background is Irish, the repressed returns very insistently in his films: in the Kansas comedy *Twister*, the family has lost its Irish mother; in the vampire film *Nadja*, the character Renfield is from Ireland, a lost paradise referred to nostalgically as "land of music" and "no snakes"; the family of *The Eternal* returns to the mother's ancestral home in Ireland and confronts a resurrected druid priestess drawn from Irish mythology; a large map of Ireland hangs in Hamlet's bedroom. Mark Thornton Burnett, in *Filming Shakespeare in the Global Marketplace* (Houndmills, UK: Palgrave Macmillan, 2007), 54–62, makes interesting observations about the uses of Ireland in Almereyda's *Hamlet*.

30. David Thomson, *The New Biographical Dictionary of Film* (New York: Alfred A. Knopf, 2002), 898.

31. Salles Gomes, *Jean Vigo*.

32. Falsetto, *Personal Visions*, 8.

33. Ibid., 27.

34. Ethan Hawke, introduction to Almereyda, *William Shakespeare's* Hamlet, xiii–xiv.

35. Teun A. Van Dijk and Walter Kintsch, *Strategies of Discourse Comprehension* (New York: Academic Press, 1983), 348.

36. Edward Branigan, *Narrative Comprehension and Film* (London: Routledge, 1992), 15.

37. Colin McGinn, *The Power of Movies: How Screen and Mind Interact* (New York: Vintage, 2005), 39.

38. Stefan Sharff, *The Elements of Cinema: Toward a Theory of Cinesthetic Impact* (New York: Columbia University Press, 1982), 1.

39. George Barbarow, "*Hamlet* through a Telescope," *Hudson Review* 2 (1949): 103.

40. David Bordwell, Janet Staiger, and Kristin Thompson, *The Classical Hollywood Cinema: Film Style and Mode of Production to 1960* (New York: Columbia University Press, 1985), 157.

41. Noël Carroll, *Theorizing the Moving Image* (Cambridge: Cambridge University Press, 1996), 78–80.

42. Jean Mitry, *The Aesthetics and Psychology of the Cinema*, trans. Christopher King (Bloomington: Indiana University Press, 1997), 89–168.

43. Pavlov's notion of an orienting reflex reacting to novelty was extensively developed by the Russian "psychophysiologist" Evgeny Sokolov in the 1980s. The series of articles by Lang and her colleagues report for the most part on experiments testing responses to television segments, relying largely on measuring heart rate. The concept was popularized through articles on "television addiction" and by Al Gore's best-selling *The Assault on Reason* (New York: Penguin, 2007).

44. Sharff, *Elements of Cinema*, 157–66.

45. Annie Lang, "The Limited Capacity Model of Mediated Message Processing," *Journal of Communication* 50, no. 1 (2000): 46–70.

46. Lang's conclusions and those produced by researchers of cinematic transitions relying on other empirical methods are not entirely congruent. Lang's early research concluded that "memory was better for information presented after related cuts than it was for information presented after unrelated cuts" (i.e., within-scene vs. between-scene cuts); see Annie Lang, Seth Geiger, Melody Strickwerda, and Janine Sumner, "The Effects of Related and Unrelated Cuts on Television Viewers' Attention, Processing Capacity, and Memory," *Communication Research* 20 (1993): 4–29. In "Temporal Accent Structure and the Remembering of Filmed Narratives," *Journal of Experimental Psychology* 18 (1992): 37–55, M. Boltz found that postviewing memory was better for items at "event boundaries" (scene changes) than for those between event boundaries. Also relevant are Christopher Kurby and Jeffrey Zacks, "Segmentation in the Perception and Memory of Events," *Trends in Cognitive Sciences* 12, no. 2 (2007): 72–79; and Joseph P. Magliano, J. Miller, and R. Zwaan, "Indexing Space and Time in Film Understanding," *Applied Cognitive Psychology* 15 (2001): 533–45. The inescapable constant within the research conclusions is that between-scene transitions affect memory differently from within-scene transitions.

47. For a popular account of mirror neurons, see Marco Iacobini, *Mirroring People: The New Science of How We Connect with Others* (New York: Farrar, Straus and Giroux, 2008). For a more technical account, see Giacomo Rizzolatti and Corrado Sinigaglia, *Mirrors in the Brain: How Our Minds Share Actions and Emotions*, trans. Frances Anderson (Oxford: Oxford University Press, 2006). An important consideration of faces in films, without reference to mirror neurons, is Carl Plantinga, "The Scene of Empathy and the Human Face on Film," in *Passionate Views: Film, Cognition, and Emotion*, ed. Carl Plantinga and Greg M. Smith (Baltimore, MD: Johns Hopkins University Press, 1999), 239–56.

48. Iacobini, *Mirroring People*, 61.

49. Johannes Riis, "Film Acting and the Communication of Emotion," in *Film Style and Story: A Tribute to Torben Grodal*, ed. Lennard Højbjerg and Peter Schepelern (Copenhagen: Museum Tusculanum Press, 2003), 143.

50. Sharff, *Elements of Cinema*, 25. Sharff prefers the term *slow disclosure*, though he uses *delayed disclosure* as well. The latter term is more precise, because it refers to the order rather than the speed of disclosure. Many delayed disclosures are not slow but occur with the rapidity of an editing cut.

51. Ibid., 59.

52. Ibid., 64.

53. Ibid., 21.

54. My count ignores the conventional division of the fourth scene into 1.4–1.5 introduced in the eighteenth century. To compare the organizational schemes of the play and films more thoroughly, one might also consider the forty or so smaller "segments" into which Mark Rose divides the play in *Shakespearean Design* (Cambridge, MA: Belknap Press, 1972).

55. Olivier's film contains one-half as many shots as the typical film of its length from the period. Its average shot length is 21 seconds, while Barry Salt reports a Hollywood average of 10.5 for the period 1946–50, in *Film Style and Technology: History and Analysis*, 2nd ed. (London: Starword, 1992), 231.

56. Kristin Thompson, *Storytelling in the New Hollywood: Understanding Classical Narrative Technique* (Cambridge, MA: Harvard University Press, 1999), 27 (emphasis in original).

57. In the 2006 Arden edition, the four movements of the Second Quarto text, delineated by motivational turning points, consist of 844, 1130, 1053, and 675 lines. Because most of the Folio-only passages occur within the central segments, Branagh's compound text is even less balanced. I find Thompson's descriptions of the four movements as setup, complicating action, development, and climax less useful for my analysis than her arguments about balance and shifts in motivation. Timings for the four movements, rounded to the nearest minute, are as follows: Olivier, 45, 36, 35, 33; Zeffirelli, 34, 38, 31, 27; Almereyda, 27, 30, 30, 16. Zeffirelli, who shared screenwriting duties with the experienced Christopher DeVore, most closely follows the model. Almereyda's short final movement can be explained by the problems encountered in filming the late scenes. The equivalent breakdown for Branagh is 51, 69, 67, 43.

58. David Bordwell, *The Way Hollywood Tells It: Story and Style in Modern Movies* (Berkeley: University of California Press, 2006), 58.

59. Although his version was apparently not influenced by the Russian filmmaker, Zeffirelli's restoration of the social matrix resembles Kozintsev's but without the

international context and the inescapable reference to an actual regime. For Zeffirelli's medievalism, see Patrick J. Cook, "Medieval *Hamlet* in Performance," in *Shakespeare and the Middle Ages*, ed. Martha W. Driver and Sid Ray (Jefferson, NC: MacFarland, 2009), 105–15.

60. Bordwell, *Way Hollywood Tells It*, 60.

61. Bernice Kliman, "The Unkindest Cuts: Flashcut Excess in Kenneth Branagh's *Hamlet*," in *Talking Shakespeare: Shakespeare into the Millennium*, ed. Deborah Cartmell and Michael Scott (Houndsmills, UK: Palgrave, 2001), 165.

Laurence Olivier's Hamlet

1. Laurence Olivier, "An Essay in *Hamlet*," in *The Film* Hamlet: *A Record of Its Production*, ed. Brenda Cross (London: Saturn Press, 1948), 11.

2. Barbarow, "*Hamlet* through a Telescope," 98.

3. Sheryl W. Gross, "Poetic Realism in Olivier's *Hamlet*," *Hamlet Studies* 2, no. 2 (1980): 63.

4. Kliman, *Hamlet*, 23–24, 27.

5. Olivier, *On Acting*, 196, 203.

6. Jack Jorgens, *Shakespeare on Film* (Bloomington: Indiana University Press, 1977), 211.

7. Sharff, *Elements of Cinema*, 6.

8. Kliman, *Hamlet*, 24.

9. For a discussion of silent film masking techniques, see David Bordwell and Kristin Thompson, *Film Art: An Introduction*, 3rd ed. (New York: McGraw-Hill, 1990), 172–73.

10. Peter Donaldson provides a psychoanalytic explanation for Olivier's use of staircases for violence and escape, linking such imagery to "Olivier's account of being raped, or nearly raped, on a staircase at All Saints School at age nine" (*Shakespearean Films*, 35). On the heritage of Elsinore's Norman arches, which derive from the Victorian production of Charles Kean, see Cook, "Medieval *Hamlet* in Performance."

11. Olivier, *On Acting*, 185.

12. Gielgud's renowned 1934 production attempted such a discovery of Hamlet in act 1, scene 2, a detail that caught the attention of the London *Sunday Times* critic James Agate, as noted in Mills, *Hamlet on Stage*, 214.

13. The mouthed soliloquies of Paul Czinner's lamentable *As You Like It* (1936) and George Cukor's only somewhat more successful *Romeo and Juliet* (1936) are delivered as stagy and static set pieces. In *Henry V* (1944), Olivier's Henry delivers the soliloquy "Upon the king!" (starting at 4.1.236) in voice-over. The technique is simple, but the result is dazzlingly effective. The camera pushes in slowly toward Olivier's face in the flickering firelight, then moves out to reveal a sleeping soldier in the foreground and the glimmering dawn in the distance. The proximity of the soldier naturalizes the use of Shakespearean cinema's first voice-over soliloquy, while Olivier's eye and head movements carefully punctuate the evolving meditation.

14. Kliman, *Hamlet*, 33.

15. Fixing, or at least modernizing, Shakespeare's anticlimactic sequence, Olivier addresses the ghost as "Hamlet, / King, father" (1.4.44–45), then cuts to our first sight of the

ghost before the fourth term, "royal Dane," which is thus visually attached to "O answer me" (45). In his Arden note to the passage, Jenkins observes, "Some eds. call for a pause after *father*, seeing this rather than *royal dane* as the natural climax." Olivier's cinematic punctuation is an impressive solution to this small problem.

16. In his Freudian interpretation of the film, Donaldson links this image of the royal couch to other images expressing "the film's emphasis on emptiness" (*Shakespearean Films*, 55). He observes, "As the queen's infidelity is revealed the ghost fades out and, in the ambient mist, the royal couch fades in briefly, so that Hamlet's gesture (hand outstretched to the apparition) becomes ambiguous, as his longing for his father becomes confused with the question of his relation to the incestuous bed his father's discourse evokes" (41).

17. Ernest Jones, *Hamlet and Oedipus* (Garden City, NY: Doubleday, 1949), 102.

18. Donaldson, *Shakespearean Films*, 42.

19. For an excellent discussion of the film's "spatial articulation, see Anthony Davies, *Filming Shakespeare's Plays: The Adaptations of Laurence Olivier, Orson Welles, Peter Brook, Akira Kurosawa* (Cambridge: Cambridge University Press, 1988), 40–64.

20. In *What Happens in* Hamlet, 3rd ed. (Cambridge: Cambridge University Press, 1956) 101–14, John Dover Wilson argues strenuously that Hamlet enters at act 2, scene 2, line 159, contrary to the stage directions in the First and Second Quartos and the First Folio.

21. The proximity in screen time obscures the longer duration implied when Ophelia asks Hamlet, "How does your honour for this many a day?" (3.1.90). In addition, the film implies that Ophelia may not have reported Hamlet's visit to her father. The intrusion of Polonius's hand recalls a similar use of offscreen space in William Wyler's *Jezebel* (1938), a film that Olivier undoubtedly knew. On this moment in the Wyler film, see Bordwell and Thompson, *Film Art*, 174.

22. Jan H. Blits, *Deadly Thought: "Hamlet" and the Human Soul* (Lanham, MD: Lexington Books, 2001), 178.

23. Barbarow, "*Hamlet* through a Telescope," 101.

24. Kliman, *Hamlet*, 34; Jones, *Hamlet and Oedipus*, 96.

25. Donaldson, *Shakespearean Films*, 46.

26. Olivier's suggestive special effects have led to a variety of objects being perceived at the opening of the soliloquy. For Anthony Davies, "the eyes of the ghost appear briefly in the waves below Hamlet" (*Filming Shakespeare's Plays*, 57). N. L. Alkire finds that "the player's tragedy and comedy masks appear then vanish in the waves" in "Subliminal Masks in Olivier's *Hamlet*," *Shakespeare on Film Newsletter* 16, no. 1 (1991): 5. Neither I nor my students have been able to see the eyes or the masks.

27. Jones, *Hamlet and Oedipus*, 100–101.

28. David Bordwell, "Who Blinked First: How Film Style Streamlines Nonverbal Interaction," in *Film Style and Story: A Tribute to Torben Grodal*, ed. Lennard Højbjerg and Peter Schepelern (Copenhagen: Museum Tusculanum Press, 2003), 46.

29. John Huntley, "The Music of *Hamlet* and *Oliver Twist*," in *The Penguin Film Review*, ed. Roger Manvell (London: Scolar Press, 1977), 113. As so often happens, Huntley mistakes the play's details for the film's. He claims that the crash chord accompanies Claudius's cry. In fact, Claudius's cry occurs during a halt in the music, which is

followed by several seconds of suspenseful music accompanying Hamlet's introduction of the torch.

30. Mills, *Hamlet on Stage*, 166.

31. Blits, *Deadly Thought*, 220.

32. Dale Silviria, *Laurence Olivier and the Art of Filmmaking* (East Rutherford, NJ: Fairleigh Dickinson University Press, 1985), 187. I have shown Olivier's scene with muted sound to students not familiar enough with the play to recall Hamlet's viciousness. Without Hamlet's words, they without exception interpret his mental activity as remorse and forgiveness inspired by the sight of Jesus. "More dark intent" is the screenplay's modernizing replacement for "more horrid hent" (3.3.88). For a contrary view that the statue is used "to persuade the audience that Hamlet is right to wait for a more propitious moment to kill Claudius," see Bernice Kliman, "A Palimpsest for Olivier's *Hamlet*," *Comparative Drama* 17, no. 3 (1983): 251.

33. The apparent beheading motion has not been commented on in the criticism, suggesting to me that it is a subliminal effect, although I cannot judge whether it is intended or accidental. Mills (*Hamlet on Stage*, 246) seems to offer an alternative explanation for the motion of the dagger: "He wipes the dagger on the arras after pronouncing Polonius' epitaph." When students are shown the scene in slowed motion and asked what they see, they often mention beheading or throat-slitting. Beheading is not a negligible image in the play. It is associated with both Polonius ("Take this from this if this be otherwise" [2.2.156]) and Hamlet ("My head should be struck off" [5.2.24]). In the fatal round of the duel, Hamlet makes a beheading sweep with his rapier that Laertes must duck to avoid; screams are heard from the crowd. As Ernest Jones would have known, Freud repeatedly comments on decapitation as an image of castration, the ultimate oedipal threat.

34. Donaldson (*Shakespearean Films*, 49) notices "a romantic, circling movement of the camera in keeping with a cinematic convention reserved for lovers." The movement is made only long enough to be discernible, then aborted, in what might be called an image of repression. On the camera's convention of circling around an embracing couple, see Bordwell, *Way Hollywood Tells It*, 135.

35. Mills, *Hamlet on Stage*, 246.

36. Silviria, *Laurence Olivier*, 186–87.

37. Davies (*Filming Shakespeare's Plays*, 63) writes, "The shortness and scarcity of outdoor shots, too, makes it difficult to fix the time of day at any point." The nocturnal time signals are thus more salient. Olivier adds the opening midnight toll and the three time sequences to the text's midnight hour for ghostly visits and the corresponding "witching time." He uses the standard Westminster Quarters derived from Handel's *Messiah*. The half-hour sequence is audible at 1.5.131, the first-quarter sequence at 3.4.138 and 4.3.53. An anomalous partial sequence sounds when mad Ophelia prepares to place rosemary "for remembrance" on Hamlet's chair, perhaps as a link to the ghost's visit.

38. Donaldson, *Shakespearean Films*, 61. Donaldson notes several instances of the motif: Hamlet's reaching for the ghost and the royal couch in act 1, scene 5 (41); Ophelia on the stairway (45); Hamlet reaching for the ghost in act 3, scene 4 (49); dying Hamlet and Laertes reaching for each other (61); and Claudius reaching for his crown (61). Ophelia's drowning gesture surely belongs with these. These gestures invite explanation through

the mirror-neuron system. Along with facial gestures, hand gestures, especially reaching and grasping, appear to be favored specializations of the system. One can explain this favoring phylogenetically, because human hand gesturing forms the evolutionary basis of language, and ontogenetically, because development of infantile hand-eye coordination follows hard upon developing facial communication. See, for example, Erhan Oztop, Michael Arbib, and Nina Bradley, "The Development of Grasping and the Mirror System," in *Action to Language via the Mirror Neuron System*, ed. Michael A. Arbib (Cambridge: Cambridge University Press, 2006), 397–423. Because "broadly congruent" mirror neurons, which can respond to complementary actions, outnumber their "strictly congruent" counterparts, which respond to identical actions, the system is more strongly activated during complementary actions. See, for example, Roger D. Newland-Norlund, Hein T. van Schie, Alexander M. J. van Zuijlen, and Harold Bekkering, "The Mirror Neuron System Is More Active during Complementary Compared with Imitative Action," *Nature Neuroscience* 10, no. 7 (2007): 817–18. In all of Olivier's examples except when Claudius reaches for the crown, an action that is both identical and complementary is being sought. The same is true for the gestures of Zeffirelli's ghost scene, and the idea has relevance as well to Branagh's and Almereyda's ghost scenes. Even in Olivier's otherwise flat ghost-report scene, the eager shaking of hands satisfies a desire stimulated by Hamlet's small hand gesture marking his wish to reach across the distance to Ophelia.

39. Donaldson, *Shakespearean Films*, 58.

40. Blits, *Deadly Thought*, 312.

41. Not surprisingly, Olivier's sophisticated treatment of the psychology of revenge fits with the psychoanalytic model. For the orthodox Freudian Otto Fenichel, the symmetries of the *lex talionis* arise because aggression-revenge is a "diphasic," or two-part, action: "Revenge is a special type of old magical 'undoing' of a humiliation, based on an identification with the aggressor" (*The Psychoanalytic Theory of Neurosis* [New York: Norton, 1945], 511–12).

42. Davies, *Filming Shakespeare's Plays*, 51. Laurence Guntner notices the use of "the same high angle shot" in the two scenes, suggesting that in the latter scene "this creates the impression that Hamlet overhears Claudius and Polonius, even though this may not necessarily be the case" ("A Microcosm of Art: Olivier's Expressionist *Hamlet* [1948]," in *Hamlet on Screen*, ed. Holger Klein and Dimiter Daphinoff, Shakespeare Yearbook 8 [Lewiston, NY: Edwin Mellen Press, 1997], 142). Assuming that Guntner means Laertes when he names Polonius, I agree with the idea of creating an impression, although the scene retroactively removes the possibility of overhearing.

43. Davies, *Filming Shakespeare's Plays*, 53.

44. Mysteriously to me, Donaldson (*Shakespearean Films*, 60) finds "mockery" in Olivier's version of the apology to Laertes, asserting that it masks "contempt." Silviria (*Laurence Olivier*, 204) appears to me to describe the film more accurately: "A cynical eye sees Hamlet as insincere, and perhaps in the play such a reading is possible. But in Olivier's reading, there is no irony. The actor employs the same lyrical naturalism that marks all the portraits of Hamlet at his zenith."

45. The description by Raymond Mander and Joe Mitchenson, authors of *Hamlet through the Ages: A Pictorial Record from 1799* (London: Salisbury Square, 1952), fits the

play's details: "Laertes, a better fencer than Hamlet, has been playing with him for some time, without allowing the Prince to notice it; he now assaults in earnest and succeeds in wounding him, as foreseen, with the poisoned foil" (136). As Jenkins admits in his Arden note to 5.2.266, for the king's proposal to celebrate if Hamlet "quit in answer of the third exchange," the paraphrase "equalize in a later bout a score made by Laertes in the third bout" "more strictly" interprets "in answer of." In a play rife with triplets, the third bout should be decisive—and probably is. Claudius, at least, seems to expect such an outcome.

46. Donaldson (*Shakespearean Films*, 60–61) offers an intriguing psychoanalytic explanation for the placement of Laertes between Osric and Claudius at his fatal moment of choice: "[I]t is only when trapped between the scornful disappointment in his manhood of Osric on one side and Claudius on the other that he strikes out in violation of the rules during a time out."

47. Thompson (*Storytelling*, 12) finds the "dangling cause" an important device of Hollywood storytelling: "One of the main sources of clarity and forward impetus in a plot is the 'dangling cause,' information or action which leads to no effect or resolution until later in the film."

48. Silviria, *Laurence Olivier*, 153.

49. Davies (*Filming Shakespeare's Plays*, 60) quotes Sandra Sugarman Singer's description of "'the eye through which we see the last moments of the film' as belonging to 'a solemn spectator,' who is not necessarily identified with us. There remains the invitation for us to participate in this 'solemn' point of view from which the final upward journey is visualized." I am arguing that our participation is, more specifically, with Hamlet's point of view.

50. Roger Furse, "Designing the Film *Hamlet*," in *Hamlet: The Film and the Play*, ed. Alan Dent (London: World Film, 1948), 28.

51. Sharff, *Elements of Cinema*, 167.

Franco Zeffirelli's Hamlet

1. James M. Welsh and Richard Vela, "Hamlet," in *Shakespeare into Film*, ed. James M. Welsh, Richard Vela, and John C. Tibbetts (New York: Checkmark Books, 2002), 23–24.

2. All citations of the script are from the draft screenplay by Christopher De-Vore and Franco Zeffirelli, freely adapted from William Shakespeare's tragedy, Marquis Films Limited, dated April 3, 1990. DeVore previously coauthored *The Elephant Man* (1980) with David Lynch and *Frances* (1982) with Graeme Clifford; for his work on the former, he received an Academy Award nomination for a screenplay based on material from another medium.

3. Kozintsev plays self-consciously with Olivier's impressive delayed disclosure. He tracks down the table of courtiers before mentioning Fortinbras to reveal Hamlet seated apart. When the camera makes a similar move as Claudius addresses Hamlet, his chair is seen to be empty. As I mention in the introduction, Zeffirelli has shown no awareness of Kozintsev's film, although critics have occasionally assumed its influence.

4. Welsh and Vela, "Hamlet," 23.

5. David Impastato discusses the importance of sunlight in the film, although he does not note its association with Gertrude, in "Zeffirelli's *Hamlet*: Sunlight Makes Meaning," *Shakespeare on Film Newsletter* 16, no. 1 (1991): 1–2. Samuel Crowl, in *Shakespeare at the Cineplex: The Kenneth Branagh Era* (Athens: Ohio University Press, 2003), 54, finds Gertrude to act as "a light-and-life-bringer."

6. William Van Watson, "Shakespeare, Zeffirelli, and the Homosexual Gaze," *Literature / Film Quarterly* 20 (1992): 320–21. Van Watson continues with a very different reading of the Hamlet-Horatio relationship: "Zeffirelli represses any potentially homoerotic tensions in the relationship of Hamlet and Horatio by undermining its intimacy. The two share none of the tight close-ups that characterized Zeffirelli's treatment of Romeo's relationship with Mercutio. Zeffirelli's Hamlet and Horatio hardly ever touch, and often do not even look at one another while conversing. Gibson's relatively more advanced age also serves to distance him from the noticeably younger actor playing Horatio." Van Watson's description certainly does not apply to the ghost-report scene. Mel Gibson and Stephen Dillane, who plays Horatio, were both born in 1956. A photo inside the DVD suggests that in filming, Zeffirelli enhanced the homoerotic dimension before reducing it in editing: mad Ophelia is paying back Hamlet's sexual abuse during the Mousetrap scene by repeating his words on "country matters" to an obviously nonresponsive Marcellus, who has replaced the "young page" of the shooting script (DeVore, screenplay, 131).

7. DeVore, screenplay, 3–4.

8. Van Watson, "Shakespeare, Zeffirelli," 315.

9. DeVore, screenplay, 28, 26.

10. Van Watson, "Shakespeare, Zeffirelli," 319, finds ideological significance in the unusual two-shot: "At one point, in a variation of the classic Hollywood over-the-shoulder shot, Zeffirelli's camera shoots the elder Hamlet's ghost from beside Hamlet's thigh from what could only be called his crotch's point of view. Such camerawork indicates the phallocentric bias of the patriarchal order Hamlet intends to champion." Without ruling out such significance, I would add that the point of view is closer to that of the hand, which is highlighted and seeking the contact it will be denied.

11. Sharff, *Elements of Cinema*, 62. As Sharff explains, "Such 'penetrations,' a way of physically connecting the two images, can be used to achieve amazing dramatic effects." I know of no precedent for Zeffirelli's ambiguous penetration. Sharff explains as well that "at the close of a series of pure separation shots comes a resolution, a required overview shot, which acts to stabilize the separation experience." The ghost remains a destabilizing influence.

12. The repeated battlement shot originally displayed the left side of the turret, while in looking at the ghost Hamlet is facing the right side. Most evident in the lighting, this error is not likely to be noticed, especially since the turret is symmetrical.

13. The return of Halley's comet in 1986 became a major international media event as Zeffirelli was contemplating his future projects after the success of his opera film, *Otello*. One must wonder whether he was also inspired to include the tapestry panel by Horatio's report of "stars with trains of fire" (1.1.120) before Julius Caesar's death. The comet appropriated by Augustus to underscore the divinity of the Julian dynasty occurred after

Caesar's death and was considered a sign of his apotheosis. On the use of the Bayeux Tapestry in other films set in the Middle Ages, see Richard Burt, *Medieval and Early Modern Film and Media* (New York: Palgrave Macmillan, 2008).

14. In his Italian-language *Autobiografia*, 387–95, the director describes Gibson's attempts to commandeer the film and his advice for making the murder of Polonius more realistic. Gibson's recommendation, rejected by Zeffirelli, was based on his observations of the eye movements of calves that he habitually strangled "for relaxation" ("per relassarmi," 394)!

15. Kathy M. Howlett, *Framing Shakespeare on Film* (Athens: Ohio University Press, 2000), 21, 31.

16. Impastato observes that "Hamlet walks but generates virtually no sense of forward progress since neither he nor his background change size. Hamlet seems, in effect, to be walking in place" ("Zeffirelli's *Hamlet*," 2). Howlett develops this idea, finding that "the visual effect is of a man floating in one place" and that "Hamlet feels he is static when in fact he is caught up in the relentless process of time and the world" (*Framing Shakespeare on Film*, 33). I do not believe that the shot creates such effects. Either through panning readjustments while tracking or using a handheld camera (the result is the same), both the background and Gibson's head shift horizontally back and forth as he moves, sustaining the impression of motion for both Gibson and the point-of-view gaze. Smaller tilting camera motions also occur in the shot. The effect of motion is magnified by the fact that each of two moving segments—the first down stairsteps, the second on even ground—is followed by a nonmoving segment. The ultimate effect, I propose, is the intimacy of shared motion rather than futile walking in place.

17. Crowl, *Shakespeare at the Cineplex*, 58.

18. Welsh and Vela, "*Hamlet*," 23.

19. Blits, *Deadly Thought*, 216.

20. Crowl, *Shakespeare at the Cineplex*, 59.

21. Ibid., 59.

22. A surprising number of students watching this segment have independently heard "bitch" in this odd utterance of Hamlet mounted over Gertrude.

23. On the art, see Bernard Meehan, *The Book of Durrow: A Medieval Masterpiece at Trinity College Dublin* (Dublin: Town House, 1996). A reproduction of Matthew's symbol, the man, stands behind Gertrude's bed. The interlace patterns of the stage in the Mousetrap scene are also taken from the *Book of Durrow*. The book uses the correlation of symbols to evangelists used by Irenaeus rather than the more common system favored by Jerome. The symbolism may relate to the inclusion of John the apostle in the chapel's crucifixion painting.

24. The screenplay (DeVore, 125) reads, "A small white face peers down at the sea," following a point-of-view shot of departing Hamlet looking up from the shore. The film has replaced this visual linkage of the lovers with one connecting Gertrude and Ophelia. Zeffirelli is seeking to enhance the effect of Ophelia's madness on the play's only other woman.

25. Welsh and Vela, "*Hamlet*," 23.

26. Plantinga, "Scene of Empathy," 239.

27. Anthony R. Guneratine, *Shakespeare, Film Studies, and the Visual Culture of Modernity* (New York: Palgrave Macmillan, 2008), 118.

28. Riane Eisler, *The Chalice and the Blade: Our History, Our Future* (San Francisco: Harper, 1988). Eisler's vastly popular work offers a vision of a feminist utopia based on equality, nonviolence, and harmony with nature, a return to the values of prehistoric, goddess-worshipping societies. The chalice "V" would have been widely recognized by the film's original audience, though students in the twenty-first century do not catch the allusion. Guneratine (*Shakespeare, Film Studies*, 50) suggests that Zeffirelli inverted the Millais iconography by turning Ophelia's face downward (toward the earth goddess, Eisler would observe), but it is not clear from the distant shot that she is turned downward. I am mystified by his describing her as "a pregnant, drowned girl." Despite her title, Gulsen Sayin Teker, in "Empowered by Madness: Ophelia in the Films of Kozintsev, Zeffirelli, and Branagh, *Literature/Film Quarterly* 34 (2006): 118, sees frustration where I see release: "Ophelia's dead body fails to reach the ocean/freedom/mother's womb and is stuck in the lagoon that is her confinement, her banishment from this male-centered world continues even after death."

29. Pascale Aebischer, "Yorick's Skull: Hamlet's Improper Property," *EnterText* 1, no. 2 (2001): 209.

30. Impastato interprets the discontinuity between the two shots that represent Hamlet's view of the sun over the ocean: "The second cut startles because of a radical discontinuity in the position of sun and clouds. This negates chronology, and evokes a sense of unearthly time in which moments are not strung in sequence but exist as a pattern in thought. Thus the only direct experience of the sun in Zeffirelli's *Hamlet* occurs under the species of the eternal" (*Zeffirelli's Hamlet*, 2). Interestingly, students viewing the film very rarely notice the discontinuity until asked to look for it. Their explanations are usually a version of "I was too engrossed in the beauty of the words and the music." Impastato's reading implies that the visuals are appropriate support for the temporality of Hamlet's speech, but the visual message seems to arrive subliminally. The woodwind music ends at the first view of the sun, giving way first to crashing waves and then to a violin melody, creating a musical continuity between the two shots that helps to suppress perception of the discontinuity. A less interpretable discontinuity occurs across the film, as the view from Hamlet's window changes from the main courtyard at the first soliloquy to the battlements where mad Ophelia is first seen by Gertrude to these seascapes. The error probably results from the plan to include a separate overlook room for Gertrude in the shooting script.

31. Howlett, *Framing Shakespeare on Film*, 50.

32. In "The Critic, the Poor Player, Prince Hamlet, and the Lady in the Dark," in *Shakespeare Reread: The Text in New Context*, ed. Russ MacDonald (Ithaca, NY: Cornell University Press, 1994), 292, Barbara Hodgdon notes her desire to "replace that last image with one from *Lethal Weapon 2*," in which Mel Gibson's character, wounded and similarly comforted by his police partner, is allowed to live. In addition to preserving the character's life, the earlier film also "glances at a same-sex relationship" between the partners more openly than Zeffirelli's film does. An interesting detail is that the rising crane shot of *Hamlet* imitates part of the other film's closing shot with precision, to the point of similarly

positioning the partners' bodies. Perhaps Zeffirelli thought of the homoerotically tinged Marcellus standing with his shadow on Hamlet as a visual counterpart to LW2's much discussed verbal innuendo.

33. In his English-language *Autobiography*, Zeffirelli observed, "There is a curious spice to our relationship; to me [Olivier] is the hero of my youth, yet I flatter myself that he is somewhat intrigued by me, the Italian who had the nerve to film Shakespeare, an activity once considered his personal preserve" (257–58).

Kenneth Branagh's Hamlet

1. Branagh, *Beginning*, 9–10.

2. Ramona Wray and Mark Thornton Burnett, "From the Horse's Mouth: Branagh on the Bard," in *Shakespeare, Film, Fin de Siècle*, ed. Mark Thornton Burnett and Ramona Wray (New York: St. Martin's Press, 2000), 172.

3. Crowl, *Films of Kenneth Branagh*, 137.

4. Charles Barr, "CinemaScope: Before and After," *Film Quarterly* 16, no. 4 (1963): 11, 18. I will summarize technical matters that are sometimes misstated. Films in Panavision Super 70 are projected with an aspect ratio of 2.20:1 in theaters so equipped, and in reduction prints in other (most) theaters using the CinemaScope ratio of 2.35:1. The aspect ratio (of frame width to height) of Olivier's *Hamlet* is 1.33:1, the standard established in the early 1930s. Zeffirelli's and Almereyda's are 1.85:1, the later American standard. The resolution of 70mm is approximately four times that of 35mm. On the aesthetics of the widescreen format, see also Bordwell, Staiger, and Thompson, *Classical Hollywood*, 358–64.; and Salt, *Film Style and Technology*, 246–50.

5. Sidney Lumet, *Making Movies* (New York: Vintage Press, 1995), 161.

6. Blenheim's splendors are well illustrated in the site's official guidebook: David Green, *Blenheim Palace* (Woodstock, UK: Blenheim Estate Office, 1976). For the historically minded, the location evokes associations of the War of the Spanish Succession and Winston Churchill. Its baroque horizontality is also splendidly suited to the wide screen.

7. Branagh uses the terms in his DVD commentary track to describe what is communicated by the sunrise shot that visualizes Horatio's description of "the morn in russet mantle clad" (1.1.165). For an opposing view of the film's technique of disorientation, see Kliman, "Unkindest Cuts," 154. Kliman finds, for example, that with the ghost "Branagh offers confusion," in contrast to "the richly ambiguous figure that Shakespeare's text limns." The armored ghost is admittedly a weak point of the film, but I find Branagh attempting repeatedly to create filmic correspondences to Shakespeare's rich ambiguity and often succeeding.

8. Anny Crunelle-Vanrigh notices the change and suggests that it acknowledges "the nature and the requirements of the film format" ("All the World's a Screen: Transcoding in Branagh's *Hamlet*," in Klein and Daphinoff, *Hamlet on Screen*, 354).

9. Branagh, *Hamlet by William Shakespeare*, 7.

10. Ibid., 9.

11. On the DVD commentary track, Branagh cites the influence of *Mayerling*, a 1968 remake, directed and written by Terence Young, of the 1936 classic starring Charles Boyer.

Set in 1888, the film depicts Crown Prince Rudolph's rebellion against his father the emperor and his love affair with a commoner. The late-nineteenth-century setting can be interpreted as pre-Freud, but Lisa Starks sees the film "correlating its period with that of Freud" ("The Displaced Body of Desire: Sexuality in Kenneth Branagh's *Hamlet*," in *Shakespeare and Appropriation*, ed. Christy Desmet and Robert Sawyer [New York: Routledge, 1999], 172).

12. Crowl, *Shakespeare at the Cineplex*, 135.

13. Hamlet's treatise on demonology is a finely crafted assemblage by the production designers. What the screenplay calls "a grotesque illustration of skeletons" (23) is a woodcut depicting the Orchestra of the Dead, from Hartmann Schedel's *Liber Chronicarum* (Nuremberg, 1493). Mixing early modern and nineteenth-century illustrations, the book also displays the demon Belphegor by Louis Breton, from Collin de Plancy's *Dictionnaire infernal* (Paris, 1863); the Tree of Death, from John Mandeville's *Travels* (London, 1499); and the Round-Head Devil, from John Taylor's *Devil Turn'd Round-Head* (London, 1642). We do not learn the content of any of the other books in Hamlet's massive collection.

14. Branagh, Hamlet *by William Shakespeare*, 23.

15. David Kennedy Sauer, "Suiting the Word to the Action: Kenneth Branagh's Interpolations in *Hamlet*," in Klein and Daphinoff, Hamlet *on Screen*, 371. Sauer's article is groundbreaking, but I find its description of the sexual insets misleading at points. Because he relies on the screenplay, he ignores the second depiction of Hamlet on top and the second inset into "I shall obey, my lord." Reliance on the screenplay may also explain Sauer's statement that the insets while Polonius is speaking may be "Ophelia's recollections, spurred by his words, with no visual clue to the audience" (331), despite Branagh's care to supply the visual clue of Ophelia's face framing all of the chapel scene insets. On the unreliability of Branagh's published screenplay, see Peter Holland, "Film Editing," in *Shakespeare Performed: Essays in Honor of R. A. Foakes*, ed. Grace Ioppolo (Newark: University of Delaware Press, 2000), 272–98. Branagh's comments on the DVD are worth quoting. Answering textual adviser Russell Jackson's question about to whom the flashbacks belong, he speaks of Polonius's "zealous interrogation of her, the detail and nature of the language he uses, which might be described as pretty hot, suggesting . . . [what] others might argue a sort of unnatural closeness or concern for Ophelia. I think . . . it could be either way." On the sexual insets, see also Kliman, "Unkindest Cuts," 159–62; Crowl, *Films of Kenneth Branagh*, 144–45; and Iska Alter, "'To See or Not to See': Interpolations, Extended Scenes, and Musical Accompaniment in Kenneth Branagh's *Hamlet*," in *Stage Directions in* Hamlet, ed. Hardin L. Aasand (Madison, NJ: Fairleigh Dickinson University Press, 2003), 163–65.

16. Kliman ("Unkindest Cuts," 156) observes that in act 1, scene 4, "the two Hamlets are disconnected, except for a very few moments when parts of the two appear together in the same frame." She appears to find the disconnection a fault, while I find it one of the scene's more effective elements.

17. More confident in an unambiguous identification, Lisa Starks ("Displaced Body of Desire," 174) writes, "In a brief clip designed to connote the queen's sexuality, the camera, shot from Claudius's perspective, shows Christie's back as he lustfully unlaces her corset from behind." Starks seems not to believe that the film locates the shot within Hamlet's mind. Working from a Lacanian perspective and considering the history of flashbacks in

film, Mark Pizzato views the insets more flexibly, implying that their unclassifiable nature does not undermine the film; see Pizzato, *Ghosts of Theatre and Cinema in the Brain* (New York: Macmillan, 2006), 139–42. On the oedipal dimension of the film, see Courtney Lehmann and Lisa S. Starks, "Making Mothers Matter: Repression, Revision, and the Stakes of 'Reading Psychoanalysis Into' Kenneth Branagh's *Hamlet*," *Early Modern Literary Studies* 6, no. 1 (2000).

18. Crowl, *Films of Kenneth Branagh*, 147.

19. In assigning 1.5.80 to Hamlet, Olivier is following a tradition traceable back to Samuel Johnson. For an extensive review of early supporters of this tradition, see the note by Horace Howard Furness in the New Variorum edition (Philadelphia: J. B. Lippincott, 1877). More-recent commentary on the line is available through www.hamletworks.org.

20. On the rarity of blinking in film, see the remarkable essay by Bordwell, "Who Blinked First." Branagh's most frequent blinks accompany his speech following the ghost's disappearance, until the end, when his steadfast eyes signify recovery of control. Several blinks of Jacobi's Claudius are also presented on-screen, further linking uncle and nephew. McGinn writes interestingly of eyes, which he calls "*the* great subject of cinema": "The screened eye commits us to an act of *double* looking into: first into the screen itself and then into the eye on the screen. . . . This use of the depicted eye is one of the most powerful tools of film in evoking the ancient reflex of looking into, upon which the effectiveness of cinema depends. It is the eye on the screen that most powerfully annihilates the screen for the viewer, to put it dramatically" (*Power of Movies*, 30–31; emphasis in original).

21. Ophelia flees into a door that will later be identified as leading into Hamlet's apartment. I suspect that we are not intended to notice this (retroactively), but who knows? The report in the Ante State Room was filmed two weeks before the aftermath of Polonius's killing, which affords a view through the doorway revealing recognizable details as Rosencrantz and Guildenstern emerge from it searching for Hamlet (see Russell Jackson's film diary in Branagh, *Hamlet by William Shakespeare*, 202, 206).

22. Blits, *Deadly Thought*, 140.

23. Like so many details of the film, the skull mask has produced both praise and condemnation. Crunelle-Vanrigh ("All the World," 365) finds it, as a reminiscence of "the medieval Dance of Death," an appropriate component of Branagh's "attempt to span the whole development of the performing arts from the origins to the present day and examine their compatibility." In addition, of course, to Hamlet's fascination with Yorick's skull, Hamlet's fascination with the danse macabre, evidenced in his poring over the demonology treatise, supports Crunelle-Vanrigh's idea. Coursen ("Critical Reception," 37), in contrast, finds it "just a localized effect, with neither motive, opportunity, nor resonance."

24. Baxter Hathaway, *Marvels and Commonplaces: Renaissance Literary Criticism* (Ithaca, NY: Cornell University Press, 1968), 49. Crunelle-Vanrigh ("All the World," 361) uses the related concept of hypotyposis to explain the inset: "The point is not to provide a helpful visual comment on complex action, but to respond to the text's hypotyposis, its vivid description of Pyrrhus, 'total gules, horridly tricked / With blood of fathers, mothers, daughters, sons,' 'With eyes like carbuncles . . .'"

25. For a discussion of Renaissance exemplarity that applies well to Hamlet, see Timothy Hampton, *Writing from History: The Rhetoric of Renaissance Exemplarity* (Ithaca, NY:

Cornell University Press, 1990). In the humanist manner, Hamlet compares himself with Hercules (1.2.153), Nero (3.2.384), Alexander (5.1.187), and Caesar (5.1.202) and implicitly to Pyrrhus in asking for the Player's recitation.

26. On the notes to the compact disc of the film's soundtrack, Doyle identifies the three principal themes as belonging to Hamlet, Ophelia, and Claudius. The film's enriched version of Claudius's character is evident not only in his association with a principal theme but also in the theme's musical style, which Doyle notes "takes the score much further into the realm of 20th-century harmonies." Before act 3, scene 2, Hamlet has brought his theme into the sexual insets of act 1, scene 3 and act 2, scene 1 and his interaction with Ophelia in act 3, scene 1. It is also used to express Hamlet's emotions after his meeting with the ghost in act 1, scene 5 and during the "lost all my mirth" speech of act 2, scene 2. For negative assessments of Doyle's music, see Samuel Crowl, "Hamlet," *Shakespeare Bulletin* 15, no. 1 (1997): 34; and Alter, "To See," 167–68.

A recurring perception from surprised students as Hamlet holds Horatio's hand is that this looks like a marriage proposal. The film is quite attentive to hand holding. In addition to the contact between Hamlet and the ghost, in the inset old Hamlet takes Gertrude's hand at "it went hand in hand even with the vow" (1.5.49). Watching the Player King caress his queen's hands, and after hearing "Hymen did our hands / Unite commutual" (3.2.153–54), Gertrude takes Claudius's hand, and soon after this we see that Claudius has taken Gertrude's hand. Ophelia's grasping of Hamlet's hands in the nunnery scene provokes him to violence. The final action of the sexual insets of act 1, scene 3 is a hand clasp.

27. The sequence of insets proceeds in the following order, according to the text originally corresponding to the film image: 1.4.9, 3.1.162, 1.4.17, (deleted scene), 3.1.1, 3.1.54. On use of the term *game* to mean sexuality (more particularly, prostitution), see Eric Partridge, *Shakespeare's Bawdy* (New York: E. P. Dutton, 1960), 119. Russell Jackson, in *Shakespeare Films in the Making: Vision, Production and Reception* (Cambridge: Cambridge University Press, 2007), 7–10, discusses parts of the shooting script that were not included in the film.

28. Sarah Hatchuel astutely comments that the killing "lasts for only ten seconds but consists of more than fifteen alternating shots on Hamlet, Polonius, and Gertrude. That succession of images and reactions, those rapid cuts, drive us directly into Hamlet's overheated mind" (*A Companion to the Shakespearean Films of Kenneth Branagh* [Winnipeg: Blizzard Publishing, 2000], 138).

29. Holland, "Film Editing," 279. Holland observes that as Hamlet runs through the mirrored rooms, "we hear Ophelia's voice echoing after him, 'My lord. My good lord Hamlet. My honoured Hamlet,' followed by a series of indecipherable words whose rhythms suggest to my ears further variations of such phrases and then a series of despairing cries of 'Oh.'"

30. Branagh, Hamlet *by William Shakespeare*, 116.

31. The gates through which Ophelia screams are sometimes misread, by students and critics, as the palace gates, probably because of the subsequent dissolve to an exterior shot. Crucial ironies, however, depend on recognizing the chapel. Prior to act 4, scene 4, the chapel gates are visible in act 1, scenes 3 and 5 (inset); act 2, scene 2; and act 3, scene 3.

32. For approving commentary on the final soliloquy, see Crowl, *Shakespeare at the Cineplex*, 138–40, and Crunelle-Vanrigh, "All the World," 364. For disapproving commentary, see Michael Anderegg, *Cinematic Shakespeare* (Lanham, MD: Rowman and Littlefield, 2004), 134.

33. Harley Granville-Barker, *Prefaces to Shakespeare*, vol. 1 (Princeton: Princeton University Press, 1946), 116; Emrys Jones, *Scenic Form in Shakespeare* (Oxford, UK: Clarendon Press, 1971), 74.

34. Marjorie Garber, *Shakespeare after All* (New York: Anchor Books, 2004), 497.

35. The graveyard and second ghost scenes occur in unmappable nocturnal woods, but in the latter the action begins at the familiar Great Court and proceeds outward toward the monument and into the woods. In the former, no orienting initial point is established for either of the groups, who enter and exit at opposite ends, with both exit directions leading eventually to Elsinore. Crunelle-Vanrigh ("All the World," 363) comments on the film's overall "bleak sense of claustrophobia" that rises higher in "the so-called Platform and Graveyard scenes." The average shot lengths of the segments are 4.0 seconds (two gravediggers), 4.0 (Hamlet and Horatio), 3.0 (Hamlet and first gravedigger), 4.4 (Hamlet and Yorick's skull), and 3.4 (the funeral group).

36. The king's apartment appears to be the only room at Elsinore inspired by a Blenheim interior. Like the Red Drawing Room, it contains multigenerational portraits and equestrian bronzes. All of the paintings in the nonbilliard wing of the apartment come into view repeatedly in the scene of Hamlet's banishment to England. One might have to follow antic Hamlet in identifying Claudius as his mother (which occurs in this room) to accept the comparison, but I am also reminded of the famous red interiors of Ingmar Bergman's *Cries and Whispers*. Bergman explicitly identified the color as a "Freudian" touch, signifying regression to the womb. See Frank Gado, *The Passion of Ingmar Bergman* (Durham, NC: Duke University Press, 1986), 408. Hatchuel discusses the influence of Bergman on the 1993 RSC production of *Hamlet* starring Branagh, including the green color of Ophelia's room, inspired by *Fanny and Alexander*; Hatchuel, *Companion to the Shakespearean Films*, 73–74.

37. The spatio-temporal distortion is enhanced by the rhythmic positioning of candle stands along the length of the corridor; their successive blurring helps the viewer to experience the increasing isolation of the two men within the very public space they are crossing. For the sake of added clarity, I will enlist the help of Bordwell and Thompson on cinematography: "A telephoto lens also affects subject movement. Movement toward or away from the camera seems to be prolonged, since the flattening effect of the telephoto makes the figure take more time to cover what looks like a small distance" (*Film Art*, 162).

38. As Branagh probably knows, he is also building on the nineteenth-century practice of hanging a front-cloth to create a separate room for the pre-duel action of act 5, scene 2 while the cumbersome sets for the graveyard and duel could be exchanged. For examples, see Mander and Mitchenson, *Hamlet through the Ages*, 139.

39. Blits, *Deadly Thought*, 352.

40. The average shot length with Claudius's emissaries is 4.3. With only Hamlet and Horatio present, it is 10.5.

41. Branagh makes this characterization on the DVD commentary track.

42. On the DVD commentary track, Branagh comments, "I do think that *Hamlet*, and indeed many Shakespearean tragedies where there's a fight at the end, does require I think for the audience a kind of physical release, a kind of physical orgasm, a sort of action crescendo that is part of what . . . Shakespeare is orchestrating."

43. Crowl, *Shakespeare at the Cineplex*, 150.

44. Placido Domingo sings the full aria over the credits. Jackson borrows ten of his lines, with minor alterations, from the apocryphal Wisdom of Solomon 1:1, 3:1–3, and 3:17. The remaining five lines, all invented, are in the spirit of that hortatory book. Lyrics and translation are included with the soundtrack compact disc.

45. Crowl, *Films of Kenneth Branagh*, 129.

Michael Almereyda's Hamlet

1. Almereyda, *William Shakespeare's* Hamlet, 7–8.

2. On "baring the device," see Kristin Thompson, *Breaking the Glass Armor: Neoformalist Film Analysis* (Princeton: Princeton University Press, 1998), 20. Drawing ultimately upon Roman Jakobson's model, Thompson defines the dominant as "the main formal principle [that] a work or group of works uses to organize devices into a whole. The dominant determines which devices and functions will come forward as important defamiliarizing traits, and which will be less important. The dominant will pervade the work, governing and linking small-scale devices to large-scale ones; through the dominant, the stylistic, narrative, and thematic levels will relate to each other" (43). I believe that most films do not possess such a singular "main formal principle," although (alone among the four *Hamlets*) Almereyda's certainly does.

3. Falsetto, *Personal Visions*, 9; Mike Kelly, *The Uncanny* (Arnhem, The Netherlands: Sonsbeek 93, 1993).

4. This claim about Korda's photograph was made in display materials by the curators of an exhibition entitled "Che! Revolution and Commerce" held at the International Center of Photography in Manhattan in 2006. Widely recognizable images on Hamlet's wall worth pondering, and of which the scope of this chapter precludes extensive discussion, include photos of Malcolm X, Baudelaire, and Poe. The most esoteric that I can identify is the evangelical calf of St. Mark from the seventh-century *Book of Durrow*, which I can only interpret as a sly allusion to Zeffirelli's *Hamlet*, which uses imagery from the book. Less elaborately decorated, Horatio's apartment prominently displays a photo of Amelia Earhart (a recurring Almereyda obsession about whom he has written an unfilmed screenplay); Vermeer's *View of Delft*; and Piero della Francesca's famous profile portrait of Federico da Montefeltro, whose disfigured nose recalls Hamlet's postcard of Senusret III. In both rooms, others will recognize figures that I do not, and some of the images are obviously meant to be personal mementos not identifiable by any audience. Much effort has gone into creating such wide allusiveness and such a wide and finely graded gamut of recognizability.

5. Sigmund Freud, "The Uncanny," in *The Standard Edition of the Complete Psychological Works*, trans. James Strachey, vol. 17 (London: Hogarth Press, 1953), 245, 236–38.

6. Almereyda's method of adaptation is most often compared to Baz Luhrmann's *William Shakespeare's Romeo + Juliet* (1996), set in a modern Verona that borrows from Mexico City and Miami. But while Luhrmann's film revels in amusing anachronism, as in assigning a gun the brand of "Sword," Almereyda's film downplays anachronism in favor of eliminating discrepancies between the 1600 reality of the language and the 2000 reality of the images. Almereyda acknowledges as precedents Akiru Kurosawa's *The Bad Sleep Well* (1960) and Aki Kaurismaki's satirical *Hamlet Goes Business* (1987), both of which import aspects of the *Hamlet* story into the world of the modern corporation. But with the exception of the oft-noted rubber duck that Ophelia tries to return to Hamlet, a reference to the Kaurismaki film, there is no meaningful direct influence to be seen.

7. Almereyda's interest in surrealism is evident in his 1994 film *Nadja*, which yokes the vampire film subgenre to Andre Breton's novel of that title. He notes, "I hope it shares a bit of a blood line. I think surrealism and horror movies are closely aligned. Cocteau is the obvious intersection. . . . There was a sense of just finding things, the idea of the found object" (Falsetto, *Personal Visions*, 18). Breton's novel, his theory and practice of the found object, and surrealism's relation to the Freudian uncanny are ably discussed in chapter 2 of Hal Foster's *Compulsive Beauty* (Cambridge, MA: MIT Press, 2000). In 2003, Almereyda made a short PixelVision film entitled *A Brief History of Surrealism*.

8. It is probably not accidental that Hamlet models his Mousetrap playbill on a design by Saul Bass, who in addition to his film work was a prominent designer of corporate logos.

9. James Traub, *The Devil's Playground: A Century of Pleasure and Profit in Times Square* (New York: Random House, 2004), xvii.

10. The Eastwood film advertised is *True Crime* (1999), costarring Diane Venora, Almereyda's Gertrude, as the Eastwood character's wife. The larger movie ad to the left of the Panasonic screen is for Luis Mandoki's *Message in a Bottle* (1999). Although the film can only be identified through minute scrutiny of the credits, Carolyn Jess suggests that it too is a meaningful allusion ("The Promethean Apparatus: Michael Almereyda's *Hamlet* as Cinematic Allegory," *Literature/Film Quarterly* 32 [2004]: 95). This may be overreading, but Almereyda's technique of uncanny reference makes the possibilities of interpreting his film nearly inexhaustible.

11. Almereyda, *William Shakespeare's* Hamlet, 135.

12. Blits, *Deadly Thought*, 152.

13. Almereyda, *William Shakespeare's* Hamlet, 135.

14. Alessandro Abbate, "'To Be or Inter-Be': Almereyda's End-of-Millennium *Hamlet*," *Literature/Film Quarterly* 32 (2004): 83.

15. The best introductions to Hamlet's two principal influences in experimental film are, for Benning, Mia Carter, "The Politics of Pleasure: Cross-Cultural Autobiographical Performance in the Video Works of Sadie Benning," *Signs: Journal of Women in Culture and Society* 23 (1998): 745–69; and, for Conner, Bruce Jenkins, "Explosion in a Film Factory," in *2000 BC: The Bruce Conner Story, Part II*, ed. Joan Rothfuss (Minneapolis: Walker Center, 2000), 210–24. Hamlet's wall postings include stills from 1960s experimental works by Jordan Belson, John Whitney, and Nam June Paik, in the form of plates taken from Gene Youngblood, *Expanded Cinema* (New York: Dutton, 1970). Youngblood's volume was enormously influential on the later American film and video avant-garde. More information

on Hamlet's favorites (though not including Benning) is found in the standard work by P. Adams Sitney, *Visionary Film: The American Avant-Garde, 1943–2000,* 3rd ed. (Oxford: Oxford University Press, 2002). Peter Donaldson ably situates Almereyda's various Pixel-Vision projects within the experimental tradition initiated by Benning; see Donaldson, "Remediation: Hamlet among the Pixelvisionaries; Video Art, Authenticity, and 'Wisdom' in Almereyda's *Hamlet,*" in *A Concise Companion to Shakespeare on Screen,* ed. Diana E. Henderson (Malden, MA: Blackwell, 2006), 216–37.

16. The portrait of Nietzsche, by an unknown photographer, appears on many book covers. The insane philosopher is being placed in a heroic pose by his sister in the interest of promoting anti-Semitic aspects of his work.

17. Carter Burwell is a very prolific composer best known for his scores for the films of Ethan and Joel Coen.

18. In *Cinematic Storytelling* (Studio City, CA: Michael Wiese Productions, 2005), Jennifer Van Sijll summarizes this directional device in the context of practical advice to screenwriters: "If you rented fifty studio-made movies, there's a good chance that the 'good guy' will enter screen left every time. When the 'good guy' moves left to right our eyes move comfortably. Subconciously, we begin to make positive inferences" (4). See also Sharff, *Elements of Cinema,* 168, on "directional thrust."

19. Tracy Chevalier's historical novel, *Girl with a Pearl Earring* (New York: Dutton, 1999), featuring Vermeer's most famous painting on its cover, was a *New York Times* best seller. The National Gallery of Art in Washington, DC, put on an immensely popular Vermeer exhibition in 1996, using the image in its publicity. Students in my freshman seminar on *Hamlet* on film rarely fail to connect Ophelia's freeze-frame with the painting.

20. The waterfall may have been inspired by a 1910 *Hamlet,* in which Hamlet stands before a waterfall during the first soliloquy. Almereyda writes, "I cut in a few seconds worth of an Italian version, circa 1910, during the film within the film, before learning that the BFI's price for the footage was unaffordable" (*William Shakespeare's* Hamlet, 131). For discussion of the silent film, see Kliman, *Hamlet,* 227–36.

21. Almereyda, *William Shakespeare's* Hamlet, 19.

22. In addition to other examples and variants later in *Hamlet,* handheld snapshots (of dead Irish mothers!) in close-up figure prominently in *Twister* and *The Eternal.* Worth noting also is Almereyda's abiding interest in the art of still photography, which is evident in several interviews (see, for example, Falsetto, *Personal Visions,* 15) and in his 2005 documentary, *William Eggleston in the Real World.*

23. The Ophelias of the films of Olivier and Branagh, but not Zeffirelli, have been viewed as incestuously inclined. Ophelia's incestuous urges receive their most blatant portrayal in Tony Richardson's 1969 version.

24. Kim Fedderson and J. Michael Richardson, "Hamlet 9/11: Sound, Noise, and Fury in Almereyda's *Hamlet,*" *College Literature* 31, no. 4 (2004): 154.

25. Blits, *Deadly Thought,* 71.

26. Almereyda, *William Shakespeare's* Hamlet, 28.

27. Within the enclosing Denmark Corporation logos, a shot of a street filled with cars is followed by what David Bordwell describes as "that cliché of television news—the telephoto shot of citizens on the street, jammed together and stalking to and from the camera" (*On the*

History of Film Style [Cambridge, MA: Harvard University Press, 1997], 246–47). Douglas Lanier interprets the connecting modem as signifying "the global reach of Denmark's corrupt techno-corporate apparatus" ("Shakescorp Noir," *Shakespeare Quarterly* 53, no. 2 [2002]: 172).

28. Robert E. Wood, "Medium Cruel: *Hamlet* in 2000," *Studies in the Humanities* 31 (2004): 64–65.

29. The diorama hangs on the wall of the sickroom of Dracula's son in *Nadja* and at the end of a hallway in the labyrinthine Irish mansion of *The Eternal*.

30. Almereyda, *William Shakespeare's* Hamlet, ix. The best discussion of Almereyda's use of Thich Nhat Hanh is Donaldson, "Remediation," 225–28.

31. Ethan Hawke, introduction to Almereyda, *William Shakespeare's* Hamlet, xiv.

32. Almereyda, *William Shakespeare's* Hamlet, 137.

33. Donaldson, "Remediation," 228–35, is illuminating on what might have been made of the Viola exhibition as a setting for "to be." It is interesting that stills from a color cathode experiment by one of Viola's mentors, Nam June Paik, are posted on Hamlet's collage wall. Perhaps Hamlet knows the background of Viola's work, just as his display of John Whitney stills indicates knowledge of the background of Saul Bass's designs.

34. Mark Thornton Burnett deserves credit for seeing that "the store contains only films of the 'action' genre," but he does not mention that this is true only if we accept the store's generic labeling and ignore the multigeneric films themselves; Burnett, "'To Hear and See the Matter': Communicating Technology in Michael Almereyda's *Hamlet* (2000)," *Cinema Journal* 42, no. 3 (2003): 57. Most discussions of the inclusion of *The Crow II* that go beyond its action film status refer to the postmodern condition. See, for example, Courtney Lehmann, *Shakespeare Remains: Theater to Film, Early Modern to Postmodern* (Ithaca, NY: Cornell University Press, 2002), where Hamlet is seen confronting "the infinitely recyclable products of postmodernity" and his own "status as a 'sequel' to his father" (97).

35. Aidin Vasiri, "Primal Scream," in *MusicHound Rock: The Essential Album Guide* (New York: Schirmer Trade Books, 1999), 896.

36. Critics routinely misidentify the James Dean clip. Some follow the screenplay, which reveals that Almereyda had planned to portray Dean in *East of Eden*. Others prefer *Rebel without a Cause* (1955), presumably from familiarity or for its more descriptive title. The footage is from a 1955 CBS television production, "The Unlighted Road," in the series *Schlitz Playhouse of Stars*. Ironically, Dean's character is conversing with the benevolent owner of a coffee shop who hires and provides a room for the needy young hitchhiker recently discharged from the army, although this kindly father figure is compromised in the end by covering up a murder. Dean's image as the prototypical son in conflict with an oppressive father trumps any specific reference.

37. Martin Walsh, "'This Same Skull, Sir . . .': Layers of Meaning and Tradition in Shakespeare's Most Famous Prop," *Hamlet Studies* 9 (1987): 74.

38. Quoted in John Gielgud, with John Miller, *Acting Shakespeare* (New York: Scribner, 1992), 122.

39. Joan Hawkins, *Cutting Edge: Art-Horror and the Horrific Avant-Garde* (Minneapolis: University of Minnesota Press, 2000), 16.

40. The Mexican film directed by Rafael Baledón omits significant details from the traditional story, including even the central trope of death by drowning, that Almereyda

can nevertheless assume allusion to La Llorona will introduce to a portion of his audience gamut. The clip has only been misidentified in the criticism, and with good reason. Wily cinephile Almereyda has chosen images that uncannily resemble images from other films. On first viewing, for example, I was certain that the man was Christopher Lee in one of the Dracula films from Hammer Film Productions, which invariably include a scene that cuts back and forth from close-ups of Lee asserting mesmeric domination to close-ups of his female victim. In these carefully chosen shots, Mexican actor Abel Salazar bears a remarkable resemblance to Lee's Dracula. Almereyda noted that his allusions in *Nadja* include "Hammer horror movies" among many others: "and Cocteau, and Breton and Peter Fonda's Corman movies" (Falsetto, *Personal Visions*, 20).

41. Aebischer, "Yorick's Skull," 209.

42. The John Whitney images on Hamlet's wall are color plates bound between pages 256 and 257 of Youngblood, *Expanded Cinema*.

43. Almereyda, *William Shakespeare's* Hamlet, xi.

44. The sculpture by "the American Michelangelo," Saint-Gaudens, was installed in Grand Army Plaza, at Fifth Avenue and 60th Street, in 1903. The sculptor subsequently adapted the face of this Victory for the face of Liberty on gold coins that are among the most renowned and expensive on today's numismatic market.

45. Abbate, "To Be or Inter-Be," 85.

46. Katherine Rowe observes that "the film/video vividly evokes Bruce Conner's cinematic formalism" ("'Remember Me': Technologies of Memory in Michael Almereyda's *Hamlet*," in *Shakespeare the Movie II: Popularizing the Plays on Film, TV, Video, and DVD*, ed. Richard Burt and Lynda E. Boose [London: Routledge, 2003], 52). The elephant hunt (shot 18) was probably inspired by a similar shot in Conner's first film, *A Movie* (1958). The opening rose may be an allusion to the title sequence of Martin Scorsese's 1993 film *The Age of Innocence*, designed by *Vertigo* title artist Saul Bass. In "'The Mousetrap' and Remembrance in Michael Almereyda's *Hamlet*," *Shakespeare Bulletin* 23, no. 4 (2005): 19–32, Yu Jin Ko judiciously assesses the range of response to the Mousetrap. The most negative assessment comes from H. R. Coursen: "'Gonzago,' a work of staggering imbecility, is the only thing that could make the film surrounding it look relatively professional" (*Shakespeare in Space: Recent Shakespeare Productions on Screen* [New York: Peter Lang, 2002], 154). Other discussions are much more approving. Lanier, for example, brilliantly explores the way the Mousetrap "rejects the corporate media system in which film and video elsewhere in the movie seem so inextricably implicated" ("Shakescorp Noir," 175).

47. Almereyda, *William Shakespeare's* Hamlet, 69.

48. Freud most fully discusses the primal scene, including the tendency for the observed or fantasized sex to occur *a tergo*, in his analysis of the Wolf Man; see *Standard Edition*, vol. 17, 1–123. Because the Mousetrap was assembled before the rest of *Hamlet* was shot, one assumes that Diane Venora's look was designed to recall the actress in *Deep Throat* (Dolly Sharp) playing Lovelace's friend, Helen, who prefers multiple partners and positions. The World Theater was originally the Punch and Judy Theatre, with a lobby that resembled an English pub served by staff in Elizabethan costume.

49. Hawke, introduction to Almereyda, *William Shakespeare's* Hamlet, xiv.

50. The skeletal cartoon clip is from the 1991 short *Grim*, by animator John Schnall, whose work may be viewed at www.squarefootagefilms.com. The desert mountain is drawn from German filmmaker Ulrike Koch's 1998 documentary, *Saltmen of Tibet*.

51. On the relationship of *The Lion King* to *Hamlet* the play, see Stephen M. Buhler, "Shakespeare and Company: *The Lion King* and the Disneyfication of *Hamlet*," in *The Emperor's Old Groove: Decolonizing Disney's Magic Kingdom*, ed. Brenda Ayres (New York: Peter Lang, 2003), 117–29.

52. James B. Stewart *DisneyWar* (New York: Simon and Schuster, 2005).

53. Lynn Sagalyn describes the Morgan Stanley sign, a half-acre expanse of glowing LEDs, in fascinating detail, quoting the designer: "The idea is that for the information to appear integral to Morgan Stanley, it had to emerge smoothly as if from the heart of the building, travel, and reenter the building smoothly, as if for reprocessing" (*Times Square Roulette: Remaking the City Icon* [Cambridge, MA: MIT Press, 2003], 330).

54. Jenkins, "Explosion," 216. Jenkins is discussing Conner's use of the sexual train symbol in *Valse Triste*. The most famous example is the closing scene of Hitchcock's *North by Northwest*, to add another uncanny Hamlet association.

55. Among critics of the film, only Alexander Leggatt seems to have found the statue's damaged state worth mentioning. Interestingly, he sees Hamlet as "surveying the fragments that survive of an older, low-tech culture." "Urban Poetry in the Almereyda *Hamlet*," in *Shakespearean International Yearbook*, vol. 4, ed. Graham Bradshaw and Tom Bishop (Aldershot, UK: Ashgate, 2004), 176. For the oblique and fascinating relationship of Watteau's painting to the love-sickness theme, see Donald Posner, "Watteau's *Reclining Nude* and the 'Remedy' Theme," *Art Bulletin* 54 (1972): 383–89.

56. Mark Thornton Burnett comments perceptively on the "grim joke" of the journal's title "in a culture in which the majority of players are at some point or another wired." He asserts that Polonius's posture is "identically replicated" by Fortinbras's, but the left-right reversal is an important change. See Burnett, "'I See My Father' in 'My Mind's Eye': Surveillance and the Filmic *Hamlet*," in *Screening Shakespeare in the Twenty-first Century*, ed. Mark Thornton Burnett and Ramona Wray (Edinburgh: Edinburgh University Press, 2006), 40.

57. Kelly, *Uncanny*, 65.

58. Falsetto, *Personal Visions*, 5.

59. Almereyda, *William Shakespeare's* Hamlet, 97.

60. Ibid.

61. Ibid., 140.

62. Leggatt, "Urban Poetry," 170.

63. Almereyda, *William Shakespeare's* Hamlet, 113.

64. Salles Gomes, *Jean Vigo*, 218–19.

65. For a description of the multiple difficulties of shooting the duel scene, see Almereyda, *William Shakespeare's* Hamlet, 142–43. One result is continuity errors: (1) after Hamlet fires his first shot at Claudius, he turns to his right to fire the second and third, even though Claudius has not moved in that direction; (2) while Laertes is telling Hamlet that the king is to blame, Horatio's hand reaches in from screen right to help Hamlet grasp the gun, but then Horatio approaches Hamlet after the subsequent cut and reaches

his hand in to help after Hamlet is holding the gun. To me, these appear to be the film's only significant errors. The portrait of old Hamlet on the bedside table in Gertrude's "closet" vanishes while the ghost is in the room, but that may be an intended effect. A case for intended effect may also be made for the surprising return of Gertrude's sunglasses to her face at the end of the Park Avenue scene.

66. Wood, "Medium Cruel," 66. Like Wood, most critics who locate the duel place it atop the hotel, as do students reliably. Almereyda accomplishes this localization with sleight of hand. The opening sequence implied that the press conference was held in the hotel auditorium as part of the film's innovative refiguring of private and public. The copper pyramidal roof and tower of the Helmsley Building at Park Avenue and 47th Street looms behind Claudius in the subsequent outdoor stroll, suggesting a more (French) Renaissance-inflected domicile that contrasts with the International Style of the corporate headquarters where Hamlet first tries to kill Claudius. The roof of the Crown Building (on Park Avenue a block south of Grand Army Plaza) shot at night to locate the duel echoes the Helmsley convincingly enough. Viewers reliably intuit that the Mousetrap is screened in the corporate headquarters, since Hamlet follows Claudius from there to the familiar hotel entrance. The playbill shot playfully cuts off part of the word "Denmark" (presumably from "Denmark Corporation Screening Room") at bottom screen.

67. The use of silent outtakes recalls the postintermission montage of Branagh's *Hamlet*. The contrast between Branagh's chronological recounting for audience comprehension and Almereyda's subjective evocation of uncanny connections largely defines the difference between the films. Burnett asserts that the sequence "unfolds in a continuous temporal sequence and not according to stop-and-start logistics. Incarcerating circularity has ceased" ("I See My Father," 40). I would say that via replay logistics Hamlet has overcome the incarcerating nature of circularity, though this is most obviously read as wish fulfillment repeatedly repressing the moment of Ophelia's betrayal.

Bibliography

Abbate, Alessandro. "'To Be or Inter-Be': Almereyda's End-of-Millennium *Hamlet*." *Literature/Film Quarterly* 32 (2004): 82–89.

Aebischer, Pascale. "Yorick's Skull: Hamlet's Improper Property." *EnterText* 1, no. 2 (2001): 206–25. http://www.brunel.ac.uk/faculty/arts/EnterText/hamlet/hamlet.htm.

Alkire, N. L. "Subliminal Masks in Olivier's *Hamlet*." *Shakespeare on Film Newsletter* 16, no. 1 (1991): 5.

Almereyda, Michael. *William Shakespeare's* Hamlet: *A Screenplay Adaptation*. London: Faber and Faber, 2000.

Alter, Iska. "'To See or Not To See': Interpolations, Extended Scenes, and Musical Accompaniment in Kenneth Branagh's *Hamlet*." In *Stage Directions in* Hamlet, edited by Hardin L. Aasand, 161–69. Madison, NJ: Fairleigh Dickinson University Press, 2003.

Anderegg, Michael. *Cinematic Shakespeare*. Lanham, MD: Rowman and Littlefield, 2004.

Arbib, Michael, ed. *Action to Language via the Mirror Neuron System*. Cambridge: Cambridge University Press, 2006.

Ashworth, John. "Olivier, Freud, and *Hamlet*." *Atlantic Monthly* 183, no. 3 (1949): 30–33.

Babcock, George. "George Lyman Kittredge, Olivier, and the Historical *Hamlet*." *College English* 11 (1949–50): 256–65.

Barbarow, George. "*Hamlet* through a Telescope." *Hudson Review* 2 (1949): 98–104.

Barr, Charles. "CinemaScope: Before and After." *Film Quarterly* 16, no. 4 (1963): 4–24.

Bellour, Raymond. *The Analysis of Film*. Edited by Constance Penley. Bloomington: Indiana University Press, 2000.

Biggs, Murray. "'He's Going to His Mother's Closet': Hamlet and Gertrude on Screen." *Shakespeare Survey* 45 (1992): 53–62.

Billigheimer, Rachel V. "Psychological and Political Trends in 'To Be, or Not To Be': Stage and Film *Hamlets* of the Twentieth Century." *Literature in Performance* 7, no. 1 (1986): 27–35.

Blits, Jan H. *Deadly Thought: "Hamlet" and the Human Soul*. Lanham, MD: Lexington Books, 2001.

Boltz, M. "Temporal Accent Structure and the Remembering of Filmed Narratives." *Journal of Experimental Psychology* 18 (1992): 37–55.

Bordwell, David. *Narration in the Fiction Film*. Madison: University of Wisconsin Press, 1985.

———. *On the History of Film Style*. Cambridge, MA: Harvard University Press, 1997.

———. *The Way Hollywood Tells It: Story and Style in Modern Movies.* Berkeley: University of California Press, 2006.

———. "Who Blinked First: How Film Style Streamlines Nonverbal Interaction." In *Film Style and Story: A Tribute to Torben Grodal,* edited by Lennard Højbjerg and Peter Schepelern, 45–58. Copenhagen: Museum Tusculanum Press, 2003.

Bordwell, David, Janet Staiger, and Kristin Thompson. *The Classical Hollywood Cinema: Film Style and Mode of Production to 1960.* New York: Columbia University Press, 1985.

Bordwell, David, and Kristin Thompson. *Film Art: An Introduction.* 3rd ed. New York: McGraw-Hill, 1990.

Bourus, Terri. "The First Quarto of *Hamlet* in Film: The Revenge Tragedies of Tony Richardson and Franco Zeffirelli." *EnterText* 1, no. 2 (2001): 180–91. http://www.brunel.ac.uk/faculty/arts/EnterText/hamlet/hamlet.htm.

Bowser, Eileen. "The Brighton Project: An Introduction." *Quarterly Review of Film Studies* 4, no. 4 (1979): 509–38.

Branagh, Kenneth. *Beginning.* New York: St. Martin's Press, 1989.

———. Hamlet *by William Shakespeare: Screenplay, Introduction and Film Diary.* London: Chatto and Windus, 1996.

Branigan, Edward. *Narrative Comprehension and Film.* London: Routledge, 1992.

Buchman, Lorne M. *Shakespeare in the Cinema: Ocular Proof.* Albany: State University of New York Press, 2002.

———. *Still in Movement: Shakespeare on Screen.* Oxford: Oxford University Press, 1991.

Buhler, Stephen M. "Double Takes: Branagh Gets to *Hamlet.*" *PostScript* 17, no. 1 (1997): 43–52.

———. "Shakespeare and Company: *The Lion King* and the Disneyfication of *Hamlet.*" In *The Emperor's Old Groove: Decolonizing Disney's Magic Kingdom,* edited by Brenda Ayres, 117–29. New York: Peter Lang, 2003.

Burnett, Mark Thornton. *Filming Shakespeare in the Global Marketplace.* Houndsmills, UK: Palgrave Macmillan, 2007.

———. "'To Hear and See the Matter': Communicating Technology in Michael Almereyda's *Hamlet* (2000)." *Cinema Journal* 42, no. 3 (2003): 48–69.

———. "'I See My Father' in 'My Mind's Eye': Surveillance and the Filmic *Hamlet.*" In *Screening Shakespeare in the Twenty-first Century,* edited by Mark Thornton Burnett and Ramona Wray, 31–52. Edinburgh: Edinburgh University Press, 2006.

———. "The 'Very Cunning of the Scene': Kenneth Branagh's *Hamlet.*" *Literature/Film Quarterly* 25 (1997): 78–82.

Burt, Richard. *Medieval and Early Modern Film and Media.* New York: Palgrave Macmillan, 2008.

Campbell, Kathleen. "Zeffirelli's *Hamlet*—Q1 in Performance." *Shakespeare on Film Newsletter* 16, no. 1 (1991): 7–8.

Carroll, Noël. *Theorizing the Moving Image.* Cambridge: Cambridge University Press, 1996.

Cartelli, Thomas, and Katherine Rowe. *New Wave Shakespeare on Screen.* Cambridge, UK: Polity Press, 2007.

Carter, Mia. "The Politics of Pleasure: Cross-Cultural Autobiographical Performance in the Video Works of Sadie Benning." *Signs: Journal of Women in Culture and Society* 23 (1998): 745–69.

Bibliography

Cartmell, Deborah. "Franco Zeffirelli and Shakespeare." In *The Cambridge Companion to Shakespeare on Film*, edited by Russell Jackson, 212–21. Cambridge: Cambridge University Press, 2000.

———. "*Hamlet* in 2000: Michael Almereyda's City Comedy." In *Plotting Early Modern London: New Essays on Jacobean City Comedy*, edited by Dieter Mehl and Angela Stock, 209–15. Aldershot, UK: Ashgate, 2004.

———. "Reading and Screening Ophelia: 1948–1996." In Klein and Daphinoff, Hamlet *on Screen*, 28–41.

Chang, Chris. "The Pleasures and Terrors of Michael Almereyda." *Film Comment* 36, no. 3 (2000): 56–60.

Charnes, Linda. "Dismember Me: Shakespeare, Paranoia, and the Logic of Mass Culture." *Shakespeare Quarterly* 48 (1997): 1–16.

Chevalier, Tracy. *Girl with a Pearl Earring*. New York: Dutton, 1999.

Coleman, Terry. *Olivier*. New York: Henry Holt, 2005.

Collick, John. *Shakespeare, Cinema and Society*. Manchester: Manchester University Press, 1989.

Cook, Patrick J. "Medieval *Hamlet* in Performance." In *Shakespeare and the Middle Ages*, edited by Martha W. Driver and Sid Ray, 105–15. Jefferson, NC: MacFarland, 2009.

Costa, J. R. "The Film's the Thing: Film Translation and Its Effect on a Silent, Edited and Full Text *Hamlet*." *Ilha do Desterro* 36 (1999): 371–88.

Coursen, H. R. "The Critical Reception of Branagh's Complete *Hamlet* in the U.S. Popular Press." *Shakespeare in the Classroom* 5, no. 2 (1997): 29–39.

———. *Shakespeare in Production: Whose History?* Athens: Ohio University Press, 1996.

———. *Shakespeare in Space: Recent Shakespeare Productions on Screen*. New York: Peter Lang, 2002.

———. *Watching Shakespeare on Television*. Rutherford, NJ: Fairleigh Dickinson University Press, 1993.

Cross, Brenda, ed. *The Film* Hamlet: *A Record of Its Production*. London: Saturn, 1948.

Croteau, Melissa. "Celluloid Revelations: Millennial Culture and Dialogic 'Pastiche' in Michael Almereyda's *Hamlet*." In *Apocalyptic Shakespeare: Essays on the Visions of Chaos and Revelation in Recent Film Adaptations*, edited by Melissa Crouteau and Carolyn Jess-Cook, 110–31. Jefferson, NC: Macmillan, 2000.

Crowl, Samuel. *The Films of Kenneth Branagh*. Westport, CT: Praeger, 2006.

———. "Flamboyant Realist: Kenneth Branagh." In *The Cambridge Companion to Shakespeare on Film*, edited by Russell Jackson, 222–40. Cambridge: Cambridge University Press, 2000.

———. "*Hamlet*." *Shakespeare Bulletin* 15, no. 1 (1997): 34–35.

———. *Shakespeare at the Cineplex: The Kenneth Branagh Era*. Athens: Ohio University Press, 2003.

Crunelle-Vanrigh, Anny. "All the World's a Screen: Transcoding in Branagh's *Hamlet*." In Klein and Daphinoff, Hamlet *on Screen*, 349–69.

Davies, Anthony. *Filming Shakespeare's Plays: The Adaptations of Laurence Olivier, Orson Welles, Peter Brook, Akira Kurosawa*. Cambridge: Cambridge University Press, 1988.

———. "The Shakespeare Films of Laurence Olivier." In *The Cambridge Companion to Shakespeare on Film*, edited by Russell Jackson, 163–82. Cambridge: Cambridge University Press, 2000.

Davison, Peter. *Hamlet*. Text and Performance Series. Manchester: Manchester University Press, 1995.

Dent, Alan. "Text-Editing Shakespeare with Particular Reference to *Hamlet*." In *Hamlet: The Film and the Play*, edited by Alan Dent, 7–30. London: World Film Publishers, 1948.

DeVore, Christopher, and Franco Zeffirelli. *Hamlet*. Marquis Films Limited. Draft screenplay dated April 3, 1990.

Donaldson, Peter S. "Remediation: Hamlet among the Pixelvisionaries; Video Art, Authenticity, and 'Wisdom' in Almereyda's *Hamlet*." In *A Concise Companion to Shakespeare on Screen*, edited by Diana E. Henderson, 216–37. Malden, MA: Blackwell, 2006.

———. *Shakespearean Films/Shakespearean Directors*. Boston: Unwin Hyman, 1990.

Duffy, Robert A. "Gade, Olivier, Richardson: Visual Strategies in *Hamlet* Adaptations." *Literature/Film Quarterly* 4 (1976): 141–52.

Eisler, Riane. 1988. *The Chalice and the Blade: Our History, Our Future*. San Francisco: Harper, 1988.

Fabiszak, Jacek. "Almereyda's *Hamlet*, or the Art of Visual Silence." *Kwartalnik Neofilologiczny* 51 (2004): 353–60.

———. "Elizabethan Stage vs. Cinema in Kenneth Branagh's *Hamlet*." *Studia Anglica Posnaniensia* 34 (1999): 333–40.

Falsetto, Mario. *Personal Visions: Conversations with Contemporary Film Directors*. Los Angeles: Silman-James Press, 2000.

Fedderson, Kim, and J. Michael Richardson. "Hamlet 9/11: Sound, Noise, and Fury in Almereyda's *Hamlet*." *College Literature* 31, no. 4 (2004): 150–70.

Fenichel, Otto. *The Psychoanalytic Theory of Neurosis*. New York: Norton, 1945.

Forsyth, Neil. "Ghosts and Courts: The Openings of *Hamlets*." In Klein and Daphinoff, Hamlet on Screen, 1–17.

Foster, Hal. *Compulsive Beauty*. Cambridge, MA: MIT Press, 2000.

Freud, Sigmund. *From the History of an Infantile Neurosis*. In *The Standard Edition of the Complete Psychological Works*, translated by James Strachey, vol. 17, 1-122. London: Hogarth Press, 1953.

———. "The 'Uncanny.'" In *The Standard Edition of the Complete Psychological Works*, translated by James Strachey, vol. 17, 219–56. London: Hogarth Press, 1953.

Furse, Roger. "Designing the Film *Hamlet*." In *Hamlet: The Film and the Play*, edited by Alan Dent, 26–32. London: World Film, 1948.

Gado, Frank. *The Passion of Ingmar Bergman*. Durham, NC: Duke University Press, 1986.

Garber, Marjorie. *Shakespeare after All*. New York: Anchor Books, 2004.

———. *Shakespeare's Ghost Writers: Literature and Uncanny Causality*. New York: Routledge, 1987.

Gielgud, John, with John Miller. *Acting Shakespeare*. New York: Scribner, 1992.

Gore, Al. *The Assault on Reason*. New York: Penguin, 2007.

Granville-Barker, Harley. *Prefaces to Shakespeare*, vol. 1. Princeton: Princeton University Press, 1946.

Green, David. *Blenheim Palace*. Woodstock, UK: Blenheim Estate Office, 1976.

Grodal, Torben. *Embodied Visions: Evolution, Emotion, Culture, and Film*. Oxford: Oxford University Press, 2009.

Gross, Sheryl W. "Poetic Realism in Olivier's *Hamlet.*" *Hamlet Studies* 2, no. 2 (1980): 62–68.

Guneratine, Anthony R. *Shakespeare, Film Studies, and the Visual Culture of Modernity.* New York: Palgrave Macmillan, 2008.

Guntner, Lawrence. "*Hamlet, Macbeth,* and *King Lear* on Film." In *The Cambridge Companion to Shakespeare on Film,* edited by Russell Jackson, 117–34. Cambridge: Cambridge University Press, 2000.

———. "A Microcosm of Art: Olivier's Expressionist *Hamlet* (1948)." In Klein and Daphinoff, Hamlet *on Screen,* 133–52.

Hale, David G. "'Didst Perceive?': Five Versions of the Mousetrap in *Hamlet.*" In Klein and Daphinoff, Hamlet *on Screen,* 74–84.

Halio, J. L. "Three Filmed *Hamlets.*" *Literature/Film Quarterly* 1 (1973): 316–20.

Hampton, Timothy. *Writing from History: The Rhetoric of Renaissance Exemplarity.* Ithaca, NY: Cornell University Press.

Hapgood, Robert. "Popularizing Shakespeare: The Artistry of Franco Zeffirelli." In *Shakespeare, the Movie: Popularizing the Plays on Film, TV, and Video,* edited by Lynda E. Boose and Richard Burt, 80–94. New York: Routledge, 1997.

Hatchuel, Sarah. *A Companion to the Shakespearean Films of Kenneth Branagh.* Winnipeg: Blizzard Publishing, 2000.

———. "Leading the Gaze: From Showing to Telling in Kenneth Branagh's *Henry V* and *Hamlet.*" *Early Modern Literary Studies* 6, no. 1 (2000). http://www.shu.ac.uk/emls/06-1/lenmhaml.htm.

———. *Shakespeare, from Stage to Screen.* Cambridge: Cambridge University Press, 2004.

Hathaway, Baxter. *Marvels and Commonplaces: Renaissance Literary Criticism.* Ithaca, NY: Cornell University Press, 1968.

Hawke, Ethan. Introduction to *William Shakespeare's* Hamlet: *A Screenplay Adaptation,* by Michael Almereyda, xiii–xv. London: Faber and Faber, 2000.

Hawkins, Joan. *Cutting Edge: Art-Horror and the Horrific Avant-Garde.* Minneapolis: University of Minnesota Press, 2000.

Herman, Jan. *A Talent for Trouble: The Life of Hollywood's Most Acclaimed Director, William Wyler.* New York: G. P. Putnam, 1995.

Hirsch, Foster. *Laurence Olivier on Screen.* Boston: Twayne, 1979.

Hirsch, James. "To Take Arms against a Sea of Anomalies: Laurence Olivier's Film Adaptation of Act Three, Scene One of *Hamlet.*" *EnterText* 1, no. 2 (2001): 192–203. http://www.brunel.ac.uk/faculty/arts/EnterText/hamlet/hamlet.htm.

Hodgdon, Barbara. "The Critic, the Poor Player, Prince Hamlet, and the Lady in the Dark." In *Shakespeare Reread: The Text in New Context,* edited by Russ MacDonald, 259–93. Ithaca, NY: Cornell University Press, 1994.

Holderness, Graham. "Shakespeare Rewound." *Shakespeare Survey* 45 (1992): 63–74.

Holland, Peter. "Film Editing." In *Shakespeare Performed: Essays in Honor of R. A. Foakes,* edited by Grace Ioppolo, 272–98. Newark: University of Delaware Press, 2000.

Hopkins, Lisa. "'Denmark's a Prison': Branagh's *Hamlet* and the Paradoxes of Intimacy." *EnterText* 1, no. 2 (2001): 226–46. http://www.brunel.ac.uk/faculty/arts/EnterText/hamlet/hamlet.htm.

Howlett, Kathy M. *Framing Shakespeare on Film.* Athens: Ohio University Press, 2000.

Hunter, Patrick. "Hamlet's Ghost on the Screen." In Klein and Daphinoff, Hamlet *on Screen*, 18–27.

Huntley, John. "The Music of *Hamlet* and *Oliver Twist*." In *The Penguin Film Review*, edited by Roger Manvell, 110–16. London: Scolar Press, 1977.

Iacobini, Marco. *Mirroring People: The New Science of How We Connect with Others*. New York: Farrar, Straus and Giroux, 2008.

Impastato, David. "Zeffirelli's *Hamlet* and the Baroque." *Shakespeare on Film Newsletter* 16, no. 2 (1991): 1–2.

———. "Zeffirelli's *Hamlet*: Sunlight Makes Meaning." *Shakespeare on Film Newsletter* 16, no. 1 (1991): 1–2.

Jackson, Russell. "Kenneth Branagh's Film of *Hamlet*: The Textual Choices." *Shakespeare Bulletin* 15, no. 2 (1997): 37–38.

———. *Shakespeare Films in the Making: Vision, Production and Reception*. Cambridge: Cambridge University Press, 2007.

Jenkins, Bruce. "Explosion in a Film Factory." In *2000 BC: The Bruce Conner Story, Part II*, edited by Joan Rothfuss, 210–24. Minneapolis: Walker Art Center, 2000.

Jensen, Michael P. "Mel Gibson on *Hamlet*." *Shakespeare on Film Newsletter* 15, no. 2 (1991): 1–2, 6.

Jess, Carolyn. "The Promethean Apparatus: Michael Almereyda's *Hamlet* as Cinematic Allegory." *Literature/Film Quarterly* 32 (2004): 90–96.

Jones, Emrys. *Scenic Form in Shakespeare*. Oxford, UK: Clarendon Press, 1971.

Jones, Ernest. *Hamlet and Oedipus*. Garden City, NY: Doubleday, 1949.

Jorgens, Jack. *Shakespeare on Film*. Bloomington: Indiana University Press, 1977.

Kelly, Mike. *The Uncanny*. Arnhem, The Netherlands: Sonsbeek 93, 1993.

Khoury, Yvette K. 2006. "'To Be or Not to Be' in 'The Belly of the Whale': A Reading of Joseph Campbell's 'Modern Hero' Hypothesis in *Hamlet* on Film." *Literature/Film Quarterly* 34 (2006): 120–29.

Klein, Holger, and Dimiter Daphinoff, eds. Hamlet *on Screen*. Shakespeare Yearbook 8. Lewiston, NY: Edwin Mellen Press, 1997.

Kliman, Bernice. *Hamlet: Film, Television, and Audio Performance*. Rutherford, NJ: Fairleigh Dickinson University Press, 1988.

———. "A Palimpsest for Olivier's *Hamlet*." *Comparative Drama* 17, no. 3 (1983): 243–53.

———. "The Unkindest Cuts: Flashcut Excess in Kenneth Branagh's *Hamlet*." In *Talking Shakespeare: Shakespeare into the Millennium*, edited by Deborah Cartmell and Michael Scott, 151–67. Houndsmills, UK: Palgrave, 2001.

Ko, Yu Jin. "'The Mousetrap' and Remembrance in Michael Almereyda's *Hamlet*." *Shakespeare Bulletin* 23, no. 4 (2005): 19–32.

Konigsberg, Ira. "Film Theory and the New Science." *Projections: The Journal for Movies and Mind* 1 (2007): 1–24.

Krishnamurti, Jiddu. *On Living and Dying*. New York: Harper Collins, 1992.

Kurby, Christopher A., and Jeffrey M. Zacks. "Segmentation in the Perception and Memory of Events." *Trends in Cognitive Sciences* 12, no. 2 (2007): 72–79.

Lang, Annie. "Involuntary Attention and Physiological Arousal Evoked by Structural Features and Emotional Content in TV Commercials." *Communication Research* 17, no. 3 (1990): 275–99.

———. "The Limited Capacity Model of Mediated Message Processing." *Journal of Communication* 50, no. 1 (2000): 46–70.

Lang, Annie, Seth Geiger, Melody Strickwerda, and Janine Sumner. "The Effects of Related and Unrelated Cuts on Television Viewers' Attention, Processing Capacity, and Memory." *Communication Research* 20 (1993): 4–29.

Lanier, Douglas. "'Art Thou Base, Common, and Popular?': The Cultural Politics of Kenneth Branagh's Hamlet." In *Spectacular Shakespeare: Critical Theory and Popular Cinema*, edited by Courtney Lehmann and Lisa S. Starks, 149–71. Madison, NJ: Fairleigh Dickinson University Press, 2002.

———. "Shakescorp Noir." *Shakespeare Quarterly* 53, no. 2 (2002): 157–80.

Lawson, Chris. "'A Palpable Hit': Franco Zeffirelli's *Hamlet* (USA, 1990)." In Klein and Daphinoff, Hamlet *on Screen*, 230–49.

Leggatt, Alexander. "Urban Poetry in the Almereyda *Hamlet*." In *Shakespearean International Yearbook*, vol. 4, edited by Graham Bradshaw and Tom Bishop, 169–81. Aldershot, UK: Ashgate, 2004.

Lehmann, Courtney. *Shakespeare Remains: Theater to Film, Early Modern to Postmodern*. Ithaca, NY: Cornell University Press, 2002.

Lehmann, Courtney, and Lisa S. Starks. "Making Mothers Matter: Repression, Revision, and the Stakes of 'Reading Psychoanalysis Into' Kenneth Branagh's *Hamlet*." *Early Modern Literary Studies* 6, no. 1 (2000). http://www.shu.ac.uk/emls/06-1/lenmhaml.htm.

Leitch, Thomas M. "Twice-Told Tales: Disavowal and the Rhetoric of the Remake." In *Dead Ringers: The Remake in Theory and Practice*, edited by Jennifer Forrest and Leonard R. Koos, 37–62. Albany: State University of New York Press, 1990.

Lesser, Simon O. "Freud and *Hamlet* Again." *American Imago* 12 (1955): 207–20.

Lumet, Sidney. *Making Movies*. New York: Vintage Press, 1995.

MacDonald, Andrew, and Gina MacDonald. "(Re)Writing Shakespeare for Film: Devore/Zeffirelli's *Hamlet* vs. Branagh's *Hamlet*." *Creative Screenwriting* 5, no. 2 (1998): 42–53.

Magliano, Joseph P., J. Miller, and R. Zwaan. "Indexing Space and Time in Film Understanding." *Applied Cognitive Psychology* 15 (2001): 533–45.

Maher, Mary Z. "'Neither a Borrower, Nor a Lender Be': Zeffirelli's *Hamlet*." In Klein and Daphinoff, Hamlet *on Screen*, 250–61.

Mander, Raymond, and Joe Mitchenson. *Hamlet through the Ages: A Pictorial Record from 1799*. London: Salisbury Square, 1952.

McComb, John P. "Toward an Objective Correlative: The Problem of Desire in Franco Zeffirelli's *Hamlet*." *Literature/Film Quarterly* 25 (1997): 125–31.

McDonald, Neil. "The Relationship between Shakespeare's Stagecraft and Modern Film Techniques (with Special Reference to the Films of Laurence Olivier)." *Australian Journal of Screen Theory* 7 (1980): 18–33.

McGinn, Colin. *The Power of Movies: How Screen and Mind Interact*. New York: Vintage, 2005.

McManaway, James G. "The Laurence Olivier *Hamlet*." *Shakespeare Association Bulletin* 24 (1949): 3–11.

Meehan, Bernard. *The Book of Durrow: A Medieval Masterpiece at Trinity College Dublin*. Dublin: Town House, 1996.

Meier, Paul. "Kenneth Branagh with Utter Clarity: An Interview." *TDR: The Drama Review* 41, no. 2 (1997): 82–89.

Metz, Christian. *Film Language: A Semiotics of the Cinema.* Translated by Michael Taylor. New York: Oxford University Press, 1974.

Mills, John A. *Hamlet on Stage: The Great Tradition.* Westport, CT: Greenwood Press, 1985.

Mitry, Jean. *The Aesthetics and Psychology of the Cinema.* Translated by Christopher King. Bloomington: Indiana University Press, 1997.

Newland-Norlund, Roger D., Hein T. van Schie, Alexander M. J. van Zuijlen, and Harold Bekkering. "The Mirror Neuron System Is More Active during Complementary Compared with Imitative Action." *Nature Neuroscience* 10, no. 7 (2007): 817–18.

Olivier, Laurence. "An Essay in *Hamlet.*" In *The Film* Hamlet: *A Record of Its Production*, edited by Brenda Cross, 11–15. London: Saturn Press, 1948.

———. *On Acting.* London: Weidenfeld and Nicolson, 1986.

Ottenhoff, John. "Hamlet and the Kiss." In Klein and Daphinoff, Hamlet *on Screen*, 98–109.

Oztop, Erhan, Michael A. Arbib, and Nina Bradley. "The Development of Grasping and the Mirror System." In *Action to Language via the Mirror Neuron System*, edited by Michael A. Arbib, 397–423. Cambridge: Cambridge University Press, 2006.

Partridge, Eric. *Shakespeare's Bawdy.* New York: E. P. Dutton, 1960.

Pilkington, Ace. 1994. "Zeffirelli's Shakespeare." In *Shakespeare and the Moving Image*, edited by Anthony Davies and Stanley Wells, 163–79. Cambridge: Cambridge University Press, 1994.

Pizzato, Mark. *Ghosts of Theatre and Cinema in the Brain.* New York: Macmillan, 2006.

Plantinga, Carl. "The Scene of Empathy and the Human Face on Film." In *Passionate Views: Film, Cognition, and Emotion*, edited by Carl Plantinga and Greg M. Smith, 239–56. Baltimore, MD: Johns Hopkins University Press, 1999.

Posner, Donald. "Watteau's *Reclining Nude* and the 'Remedy' Theme." *Art Bulletin* 54 (1972): 383–89.

Quigley, Daniel. "'Double Exposure': The Semiotic Ramifications of Mel Gibson in Zeffirelli's *Hamlet.*" *Shakespeare Bulletin* 11, no. 1 (1993): 38–39.

Quinn, Edward. "Zeffirelli's *Hamlet.*" *Shakespeare on Film Newsletter* 15, no. 2 (1991): 1–2, 12.

Rigney, James. "Hamlet and the Jester's Skull: The Graveyard Scene on Film." In Klein and Daphinoff, Hamlet *on Screen*, 85–97.

Riis, Johannes. "Film Acting and the Communication of Emotion." In *Film Style and Story: A Tribute to Torben Grodal*, edited by Lennard Højbjerg and Peter Schepelern, 139–52. Copenhagen: Museum Tusculanum Press, 2003.

Rizzolatti, Giacomo, and Corrado Sinigaglia. *Mirrors in the Brain: How Our Minds Share Actions and Emotions.* Translated by Frances Anderson. Oxford: Oxford University Press, 2006.

Rose, Mark. *Shakespearean Design.* Cambridge, MA: Belknap Press, 1972.

Rosenberg, Marvin. *The Masks of Hamlet.* Newark: University of Delaware Press, 1992.

Rothwell, Kenneth S. *A History of Shakespeare on Screen: A Century of Film and Television.* Cambridge: Cambridge University Press, 1999.

Rowe, Katherine. "'Remember Me': Technologies of Memory in Michael Almereyda's *Hamlet.*" In *Shakespeare the Movie II: Popularizing the Plays on Film, TV, Video, and DVD*, edited by Richard Burt and Lynda E. Boose, 37–55. London: Routledge, 2003.

Rutter, Carol Chillington. "Snatched Bodies: Ophelia in the Grave." *Shakespeare Quarterly* 49 (1998): 299–319.

Sagalyn, Lynne B. *Times Square Roulette: Remaking the City Icon.* Cambridge, MA: MIT Press, 2003.

Salles Gomes, P. E. *Jean Vigo.* London: Faber and Faber, 1998.

Salt, Barry. *Film Style and Technology: History and Analysis.* 2nd ed. London: Starword, 1992.

Sanders, Julie. "The End of History and the Last Man: Kenneth Branagh's *Hamlet.*" In *Shakespeare, Film, Fin de Siècle*, edited by Mark Thornton Burnett and Ramona Wray, 147–64. New York: St. Martin's Press, 2000.

Sauer, David Kennedy. "Suiting the Word to the Action: Kenneth Branagh's Interpolations in *Hamlet.*" In Klein and Daphinoff, Hamlet *on Screen*, 325–48.

Sharff, Stefan. *The Elements of Cinema: Toward a Theory of Cinesthetic Impact.* New York: Columbia University Press, 1982.

Shakespeare, William. *Hamlet.* Edited by Horace Howard Furness. The New Variorum edition. Philadelphia: J. B. Lippincott, 1877.

———. *Hamlet.* Edited by Harold Jenkins. Arden edition, 2nd series. London: Methuen, 1982.

———. *Hamlet.* Edited by Ann Thompson and Neil Taylor. Arden edition, 3rd series. London: Thomson Learning, 2006.

Shaltz, Justin. "Three *Hamlets* on Film." *Shakespeare Bulletin* 11, no. 1 (1993): 36–37.

Silviria, Dale. *Laurence Olivier and the Art of Filmmaking.* East Rutherford, NJ: Fairleigh Dickinson University Press, 1985.

Simmons, James R., Jr. "'In the Rank Sweat of an Enseamed Bed': Sexual Aberration and the Paradigmatic Screen Hamlets." *Literature/Film Quarterly* 25 (1997): 111–18.

Sitney, P. Adams. *Visionary Film: The American Avant-Garde, 1943–2000.* 3rd ed. Oxford: Oxford University Press, 2002.

Skovmand, Michael. "Mel's Melodramatic Melancholy: Zeffirelli's *Hamlet.*" In *Screen Shakespeare*, special issue of *The Dolphin* (no. 24), edited by Michael Skovmand, 113–31. Aarhus: Aarhus University Press, 1994.

———. "Melodrama at Elsinore: Zeffirelli's *Hamlet.*" In Klein and Daphinoff, Hamlet *on Screen*, 262–79.

Sloboda, Noel. "Visions and Revisions of Laurence Olivier in the *Hamlet* Films of Franco Zeffirelli and Kenneth Branagh." *Studies in the Humanities* 27 (2000): 140–57.

Stamerov, Maxim I., and Vittorio Gallese, eds. *Mirror Neurons and the Evolution of Brain and Language.* Amsterdam: John Benjamins Publications, 2002.

Starks, Lisa S. 1999. "The Displaced Body of Desire: Sexuality in Kenneth Branagh's *Hamlet.*" In *Shakespeare and Appropriation*, edited by Christy Desmet and Robert Sawyer, 160–78. New York: Routledge, 1999.

Stewart, James B. *DisneyWar.* New York: Simon and Schuster, 2005.

Stivers, Cyndi. "*Hamlet* Re-Visited." *Premiere* 4, no. 6 (1991): 50–56.

Swan, Jim. "*Hamlet* and the Technology of the Mind's Eye." In *Seventh International Conference on Literature and Psychology*, 87–102. Lisbon: Instituto Superior de Psicologia Aplicada, 1991.

Taylor, Neil. "The Films of *Hamlet.*" In *Shakespeare and the Moving Image*, edited by Anthony Davies and Stanley Wells, 180–95. Cambridge: Cambridge University Press, 1994.

Teker, Gulsen Sayin. "Empowered by Madness: Ophelia in the Films of Kozintsev, Zeffirelli, and Branagh." *Literature/Film Quarterly* 34 (2006): 113–19.

Thompson, Kristin. *Breaking the Glass Armor: Neoformalist Film Analysis*. Princeton: Princeton University Press, 1998.

———. *Storytelling in the New Hollywood: Understanding Classical Narrative Technique*. Cambridge, MA: Harvard University Press, 1999.

Thomson, David. *The New Biographical Dictionary of Film*. New York: Alfred A. Knopf, 2002.

Tibbetts, John C. "Breaking the Classical Barrier: Franco Zeffirelli Interviewed by John Tibbetts." *Literature/Film Quarterly* 22 (1994): 136–40.

Traub, James. *The Devil's Playground: A Century of Pleasure and Profit in Times Square*. New York: Random House, 2004.

Tyler, Parker. "*Hamlet* and Documentary." *Kenyon Review* 11 (1949): 527–32.

Van der Gaag, Christiaan, Ruud B. Minderaa, and Christian Keysers. "Facial Expressions: What the Mirror Neuron System Can and Cannot Tell Us." *Social Neuroscience* 2, nos. 3–4 (2007): 179–222.

Van Dijk, Teun A., and Walter Kintsch. *Strategies of Discourse Comprehension*. New York: Academic Press, 1983.

Van Sijll, Jennifer. *Cinematic Storytelling*. Studio City, CA: Michael Wiese Productions, 2005.

Van Watson, William. "Shakespeare, Zeffirelli, and the Homosexual Gaze." *Literature/Film Quarterly* 20 (1992): 308–24.

Vasiri, Aidin. "Primal Scream." In *MusicHound Rock: The Essential Album Guide*, 896. New York: Schirmer Trade Books, 1999.

Walker, Elsie. "A 'Harsh World' of Soundbite Shakespeare: Michael Almereyda's *Hamlet* (2000)." *EnterText* 1, no. 2 (2001): 317–41. http://www.brunel.ac.uk/faculty/arts/EnterText/hamlet/hamlet.htm.

Walsh, Martin W. "'This Same Skull, Sir . . . ': Layers of Meaning and Tradition in Shakespeare's Most Famous Prop." *Hamlet Studies* 9 (1987): 65–77.

Weiss, Tanja. *Shakespeare on the Screen: Kenneth Branagh's Adaptations of* Henry V, Much Ado About Nothing *and* Hamlet. Frankfurt am Main: Peter Lang, 1999.

Weller, Philip. "Freud's Footprints in Films of *Hamlet*." *Literature/Film Quarterly* 25 (2005): 119–24.

Welsh, James M. and Richard Vela. "*Hamlet*." In *Shakespeare into Film*, edited by James M. Welsh, Richard Vela, and John C. Tibbetts, 17–26. New York: Checkmark Books, 2002.

White, Mark. *Kenneth Branagh*. London: Faber and Faber, 2005.

Wilmeth, Thomas L. "Fortinbras on Film: Safe Passage for the Prince." In Klein and Daphinoff, Hamlet *on Screen*, 43–55.

Willson, Robert F., Jr. "Kenneth Branagh's *Hamlet*: The Revenge of Fortinbras." *Shakespeare Newsletter* 47, no. 1 (1997): 7, 9.

———. "Olivier's *Hamlet*: Film Realism versus Poetic Ambiguity in II.i and IV.vii." *Hamlet Studies* 1 (1979): 137–39.

Wilson, David M. *The Bayeux Tapestry*. London: Thames and Hudson, 1985.

Wilson, John Dover. *What Happens in* Hamlet. 3rd ed. Cambridge: Cambridge University Press, 1956.

Wood, Robert E. "Medium Cruel: *Hamlet* in 2000." *Studies in the Humanities* 31 (2004): 60–68.

Woods, Leigh. " 'Abstract and Brief Chronicles' on Film: The Players' Scenes in *Hamlet*." In Klein and Daphinoff, Hamlet *on Screen*, 56–73.

Woroszylski, Wiktor. *The Life of Mayakovsky*. Translated by Boleslaw Taborski. New York: Orion Press, 1970.

Wray, Ramona, and Mark Thornton Burnett. "From the Horse's Mouth: Branagh on the Bard." In *Shakespeare, Film, Fin de Siècle*, edited by Mark Thornton Burnett and Ramona Wray, 165–78. New York: St. Martin's Press, 2000.

Youngblood, Gene. *Expanded Cinema*. New York: Dutton, 1970.

Zeffirelli, Franco. *Zeffirelli: The Autobiography*. New York: Weidenfeld and Nicolson, 1986.

———. *Zeffirelli: Autobiografia*. Milan: Mondadori, 2006.

Filmography

1910. *Hamlet.* Directed by Mario Caserini. Italy.
1913. *Hamlet.* Directed by Cecil Hepworth. UK.
1926. *Metropolis.* Directed by Fritz Lang. Germany.
1934. *L'Atalante.* Directed by Jean Vigo. France.
1936. *As You Like It.* Directed by Paul Czinner. UK.
1938. *Jezebel.* Directed by William Wyler. USA.
1939. *Wuthering Heights.* Directed by William Wyler. USA.
1940. *Rebecca.* Directed by Alfred Hitchcock. USA.
1944. *Henry V.* Directed by Laurence Olivier. UK.
1948. *Hamlet.* Directed by Laurence Olivier. UK.
1949. *The Third Man.* Directed by Carol Reed. UK.
1951. *The African Queen.* Directed by John Huston. UK.
1955. *East of Eden.* Directed by Elia Kazan. USA.
1955. *Rebel without a Cause.* Directed by Nicholas Ray. USA.
1956. *The Man Who Knew Too Much.* Directed by Alfred Hitchcock. USA.
1958. *A Movie.* Directed by Bruce Conner. USA.
1958. *Vertigo.* Directed by Alfred Hitchcock. USA.
1959. *North by Northwest.* Directed by Alfred Hitchcock. USA.
1960. *The Bad Sleep Well.* Directed by Akira Kurosawa. Japan.
1963. *La Maldición de la Llorona.* Directed by Rafael Baledón. Mexico.
1964. *Hamlet.* Directed by Grigori Kozintsev. Russia.
1966. *A Man for All Seasons.* Directed by Fred Zinnemann. UK.
1968. *Mayerling.* Directed by Terence Young. UK.
1972. *Deep Throat.* Directed by Gerard Damiano. USA.
1972 *Cries and Whispers.* Directed by Ingmar Bergman. Sweden.
1973. *Brother Sun, Sister Moon.* Directed by Franco Zeffirelli. Italy.
1977. *Star Wars.* Directed by George Lucas. USA.
1978. *Valse Triste.* Directed by Bruce Conner. USA.
1980. *The Elephant Man.* Directed by David Lynch. USA.
1982. *Frances.* Directed by Graeme Clifford. USA.
1982. *Blade Runner.* Directed by Ridley Scott. USA.
1983. *Fanny and Alexander.* Directed by Ingmar Bergman. Sweden.

1987. *Lethal Weapon*. Directed by Richard Donner. USA.

1987. *Hamlet Goes Business*. Directed by Aki Kaurismaki. Finland.

1988. *Akira*. Directed by Katsuhiro Ôtomo. Japan.

1989. *Twister*. Directed by Michael Almereyda. USA

1989. *Henry V*. Directed by Kenneth Branagh. UK.

1990. *Hamlet*. Directed by Franco Zeffirelli. USA.

1990. *If Every Girl Had a Diary*. Directed by Sadie Benning. USA.

1991. *Grim*. Animated by John Schnall. USA.

1991. *The Guyver*. Directed by Steve Wang. USA.

1992. *Peter's Friends*. Directed by Kenneth Branagh. UK.

1993. *The Age of Innocence*. Directed by Martin Scorsese. USA.

1993. *Much Ado About Nothing*. Directed by Kenneth Branagh. UK.

1994. *Nadja*. Directed by Michael Almereyda. USA.

1994. *Mary Shelley's Frankenstein*. Directed by Kenneth Branagh. USA.

1995. *Aeon Flux*. Directed by Peter Chung. Hong Kong.

1996. *The Crow II: City of Angels*. Directed by Tim Pope. USA.

1996. *William Shakespeare's Romeo + Juliet*. Directed by Baz Luhrmann. USA.

1997. *Saltmen of Tibet*. Directed by Ulrike Koch. Germany.

1998. *The Eternal*. Directed by Michael Almereyda. USA.

1999. *True Crime*. Directed by Clint Eastwood. USA.

1999. *Message in a Bottle*. Directed by Luis Mandoki. USA.

2000. *Hamlet*. Directed by Michael Almereyda. USA.

2003. *A Brief History of Surrealism*. Directed by Michael Almereyda. USA.

2005. *William Eggleston in the Real World*. Directed by Michael Almereyda. USA.

Index